Cybercrime

CW00839923

Cybercrime is a growing problem in the modern world. Despite the many advantages of computers, they have spawned a number of crimes, such as hacking and virus writing, and made other crimes more prevalent and easier to commit, including music piracy, identity theft and child sex offences. Understanding the psychology behind these crimes helps to determine what motivates and characterises offenders and how such crimes can be prevented. This textbook on the psychology of the cybercriminal is the first written for undergraduate and postgraduate students of psychology, criminology, law, forensic science and computer science. It requires no specific background knowledge and covers legal issues, offenders, effects on victims, punishment and preventative measures for a wide range of cybercrimes. Introductory chapters on forensic psychology and the legal issues of cybercrime ease students into the subject, and many pedagogical features in the book and online provide support for the student.

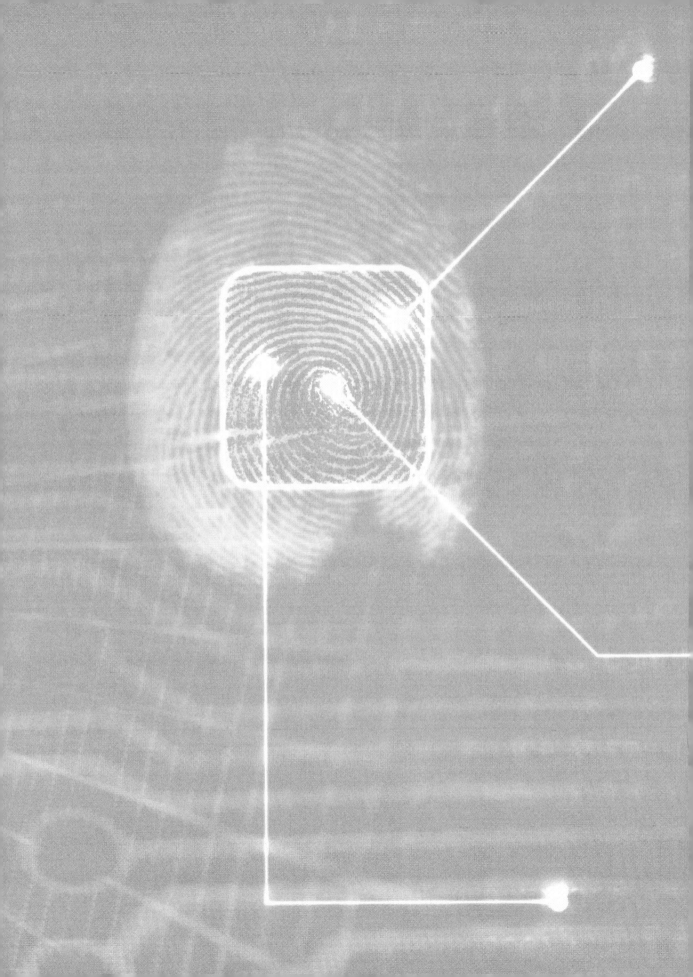

Cybercrime

The Psychology of Online Offenders

GRÁINNE KIRWAN AND ANDREW POWER

CAMBRIDGE
UNIVERSITY PRESS

CAMBRIDGE
UNIVERSITY PRESS

University Printing House, Cambridge CB2 8BS, United Kingdom

Cambridge University Press is part of the University of Cambridge.

It furthers the University's mission by disseminating knowledge in the pursuit of education, learning and research at the highest international levels of excellence.

www.cambridge.org
Information on this title: www.cambridge.org/9780521180214

© Gráinne Kirwan and Andrew Power 2013

This publication is in copyright. Subject to statutory exception and to the provisions of relevant collective licensing agreements, no reproduction of any part may take place without the written permission of Cambridge University Press.

First published 2013

A catalogue record for this publication is available from the British Library

Library of Congress Cataloguing in Publication data

Kirwan, Grainne, 1978–
     Cybercrime : the psychology of online offenders / Gráinne Kirwan and Andrew Power.
     pages   cm
     Includes bibliographical references.
     ISBN 978-1-107-00444-3 (Hardback) – ISBN 978-0-521-18021-4 (Paperback)
     1. Computer crimes–Psychological aspects.   2. Criminal psychology.   I. Power, Andrew, 1965–.
II. Title.
     HV6773.K567 2013
     364.16′8–dc23
                                                                                  2012049448

ISBN 978-1-107-00444-3 Hardback
ISBN 978-0-521-18021-4 Paperback

Additional resources for this publication at www.cambridge.org/kirwan-power

Cambridge University Press has no responsibility for the persistence or accuracy of URLs for external or third-party internet websites referred to in this publication, and does not guarantee that any content on such websites is, or will remain, accurate or appropriate.

CONTENTS

DETAILED CONTENTS

ILLUSTRATIONS

TABLES

PREFACE

This textbook examines the psychology of cybercrime. It aims to be useful to both undergraduate and postgraduate students from a wide variety of disciplines, including criminology, psychology and information technology. Because of the diversity of backgrounds of potential readers, this book presumes no prior knowledge of either the psychological or technological aspects of cybercrime – key concepts in both areas are defined as they arise in the chapters that follow. The chapters consider research that has been conducted in each area, but also apply psychological theories and models to each type of cybercrime. The chapters also consider many aspects of each cybercrime – they do not simply consider the offender, but also effects on the victims, suitable punishments, potential preventative measures and comparisons to similar offline offences. Most chapters stand alone, so it is possible for the reader to dip in to any point in the book. However, most readers may wish to start with Chapters 1 and 2, which provide an overview of forensic psychological theory and of cybercrime. We hope that you enjoy reading this book as much as we enjoy researching this evolving and cutting-edge topic.

Overview of the book

This book is divided into four sections. The first two chapters introduce the reader to the key concepts involved – specifically forensic psychology and cybercrimes. Following this, the book considers offences that could not exist without the use of computers; hacking and malware. The third section (Chapters 5 to 9) considers crimes that can occur without computers but that have become more prevalent or easier because of technology – such as copyright infringement, fraud, identity theft, terrorism, bullying, stalking, child pornography and sexual predation of children. The final chapter considers crime in virtual worlds. A little more detail on the contents of each chapter is included below.

- Chapter 1 provides a brief overview of cybercrime, before describing the discipline of forensic psychology and exploring various theories of crime that were originally proposed to explain offline criminal events.
- Chapter 2 examines how cybercrimes can be considered from a legal perspective. In particular, it investigates how governance and soft law might be useful when contemplating suitable approaches to cybercrime.
- Chapter 3 considers the psychology of hackers, describing their methods and motives, and exploring the profile and personality characteristics of hackers.

There has been a considerable amount of research completed on hacking, compared to many other cybercrimes, and this research is evaluated.

- Chapter 4 explores malware – computer viruses, worms, spyware and other malicious software. A history of malware is provided, along with a description of the motives, profile and personality of offenders.
- Chapter 5 investigates identity theft and online fraud. Comparisons are made to similar offline offences, and the chapter explores why potential victims may be particularly vulnerable to these offences.
- Chapter 6 considers child-related online offences. The diagnosis and characteristics of paedophiles are described, before examining how this research informs our understanding of online child predators and users of online child pornography.
- Chapter 7 investigates both cyberbullying and cyberstalking. For each, it examines how the behaviour is similar to, or different from, its offline equivalent. The methods by which each is carried out, as well as the traits of perpetrators and victims, are identified.
- Chapter 8 considers digital piracy and copyright infringement. The psychology of offenders is examined, with particular focus on how psychological phenomena (such as neutralisations and social learning) and psychological theories (such as the theory of planned behaviour) can contribute to our understanding of these offences.
- Chapter 9 examines cyberterrorism. It identifies how terrorists use the internet, while exploring the literature examining the psychology of terrorists. Conflicting definitions of cyberterrorism are assessed.
- Chapter 10 explores the rather unusual case of disruptive behaviour in virtual worlds. While the term 'crime' is used to describe these in this book, they are not necessarily recognised by offline authorities as criminal events. Nevertheless, if the same event took place offline, it would most certainly be considered a crime, and so they are considered in depth here.

Pedagogical features

Each chapter in the book includes a number of pedagogical features that are designed to aid student learning as well as providing lecturers with ideas and resources for classroom activities. Some additional resources are also available on the companion website for the book.

Chapter resources

Some case studies are provided in each chapter, giving examples of how the cybercrimes considered in the chapter might affect internet users. In most cases these are fictional, but Chapters 3 and 4 (on hackers and malware respectively) include examples of real life cases.

The case studies are directly followed by sections providing an overview of the chapter and definitions of key concepts.

Throughout the chapters, summary boxes are provided. These summary boxes reiterate the key points in the preceding section(s), and are useful in reinforcing student learning. Students can also use these sections to check that they thoroughly understand key concepts in the area before moving on to the next section.

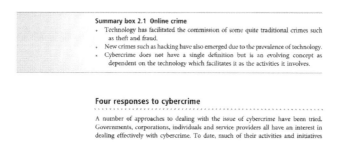

Each chapter includes a number of potential activities that students can complete either alone or in class. These are distributed at key points throughout the chapters, and often require little additional resources except an internet-enabled computer.

> **Activity 2.1 Types of crime**
> An example of online activity resulting in crime in the real world was the murder of Zhu Caoyuan, a Chinese man who sold a virtual sword won by fellow gamer Qiu Chengwei in the online game Legend of Mir 3. Review this case and consider the reaction of the police to the initial report by Qiu of the theft of his 'property', and how the reaction might be different with a greater awareness of online activity.
>
> Crimes which exist entirely online also have serious negative impacts on their victims. In August 2005 a Japanese man was arrested for using software 'bots' (web robots, or 'bots' are software applications that run automated tasks over the internet) to 'virtually' assault online characters in the computer game Lineage II and steal their virtual possessions. He was then able to sell these items through a Japanese auction website for real money (Knight, 2005). Consider if the crime committed is limited to theft or if there was also a crime committed in the assault. Further examples of such crimes are given at the end of this chapter.

Towards the end of each chapter, some sample essay questions are included. Lecturers may wish to set assignments using these questions, or students may wish to test their knowledge of the topic by preparing answers.

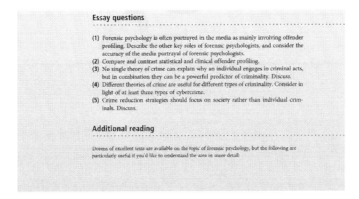

At the end of each chapter, a list of suggested additional reading is included. These vary from chapter to chapter, but generally include both websites and books/journal articles. These readings allow students who have interest in specific topics to read about them in more depth.

Online resources

The companion website for this textbook includes additional resources for students and lecturers. Specific resources are provided for each chapter.

Summaries of the key points in each chapter are included. Also available are a collection of links – some to useful external websites with relevant content, and some to journals that specialise in publishing papers on the specific topic. Students can follow these links to search for relevant literature in the area.

One or more online activities are provided for each chapter. In some cases these involve testing student learning, especially of typologies or multi-faceted concepts, although there are other types of activities included.

A short multiple-choice quiz is provided for each chapter, to allow students to test their own learning.

Finally, discussion boards are provided so that students can collaboratively examine key debates relating to the subject area.

About the authors

Gráinne Kirwan and Andrew Power work in the Institute of Art, Design and Technology (IADT) in Dun Laoghaire, Dublin (www.iadt.ie).

Gráinne Kirwan is a lecturer in psychology, teaching on both a BSc (Hons) in Applied Psychology and an MSc in Cyberpsychology. She lectures in topics including forensic psychology, cyberpsychology, computer-mediated communication and the psychology of virtual reality and artificial intelligence. Her doctorate research examined the ethics, motives and interpersonal relationships of hackers. She also holds an MSc in Applied Forensic Psychology, a Postgraduate Certificate in Third Level Learning and Teaching and an MLitt in Psychology by Research.

Andrew Power is Head of the Faculty of Film, Art and Creative Technologies at the Institute of Art, Design and Technology; prior to this Andrew spent 18 years in the ICT industry. Originally trained as an engineer, Andrew holds an MA from the University of Dublin, an MBA from the University of Strathclyde and his doctoral research in Queens University Belfast examined the links between social networking and active citizenship. Andrew has taught and supervised student research at both undergraduate and postgraduate level.

Acknowledgements

We would like to thank all those in Cambridge University Press who worked with us during the development of this book. Particular thanks go to Hetty Marx, who reviewed the original proposal and who has been the source of great advice and support. We would also like to thank Ed Robinson, Josephine Lane and Carrie Parkinson who clarified several of our queries during the writing process.

We are fortunate to work in an environment where our students and colleagues perpetually encourage us to examine cutting-edge topics in fascinating disciplines. We would like to thank all the staff and students in IADT who have provided their support during lectures, in meetings and in the canteen over more cups of coffee than we can count.

The photographs in Illustrations 2.1, 4.1 and 9.1 were designed and taken by Claire Burke, whose creativity and flair have helped to illustrate key topics. All other illustrations in the book (with the exception of Illustration 4.2) were prepared and photographed by Liam Kirwan, who sadly passed away during the writing of this book. We're thankful for his talent, enthusiasm and support when preparing these images for us.

While a very enjoyable process, writing a book is also very time-consuming. We're especially grateful to our long-suffering families and friends who have excused our absences while we tap away at keyboards. Particular thanks to Glen and Eleanor, and to Shannon and Rachel, for their good-humoured encouragement and patience during the writing of this book.

1 Psychology of cybercrime

Case studies

Jack's computer has been running very slowly for a few days, and eventually he asks his friend to take a look at it for him. His friend downloads the latest version of an antivirus software program, which finds a virus on Jack's computer. Jack remembers downloading an email attachment received from his sister just before the computer began to slow down. When he searches through his sent messages, he discovers that the file has sent itself on to all of his contacts. Jack feels embarrassed having to tell all his contacts that he was the victim of a virus, and that they should all check their computers. He wonders why anyone would create such a malicious file, and what they have to gain from infecting his computer.

Michael has just been arrested. Police officers have found over 10,000 images and videos of child pornography on his computer, which Michael has downloaded from the internet. Michael claims that he hasn't really done any harm as he has never abused a child himself, nor has he ever uploaded any images to the internet.

Chapter overview

This chapter is designed to introduce the reader to forensic psychology. It may be that you are studying cybercrime as part of a wider forensic psychology module or course, in which case you may have already come across many of the concepts in this chapter, and you may prefer to move directly on to the rest of the chapters in this book. However, if you have never studied forensic psychology before, this chapter will provide you with some of the fundamental concepts of the field, especially those that relate to the study of the psychology of cybercrime.

Firstly, a brief description will be provided of forensic psychology, followed by a cursory overview of the different types of cybercrime and their categorisation. Following this the key areas that forensic psychologists specialise in are described, including offender profiling, offender assessment, punishment and rehabilitation, risk assessment, juries, helping victims, crime prevention and police psychology. Finally, an overview will be provided of some of the key theories of crime – the possible reasons why crime exists and why certain individuals are more likely to become criminals than others. These theories are offered at various levels, from societal to individual, and many of the theories can be applied to cybercriminal acts.

Forensic psychology

Forensic psychology has enjoyed considerable popularity in the media for some time, with films such as *The Silence of the Lambs* and television programmes such as *Cracker* and *Criminal Minds* attracting large audience numbers and introducing many viewers to forensic psychological concepts. However, most of these programmes and films focus on one specific area of forensic psychology – offender profiling. While this is undoubtedly a very interesting topic within the field, and understandably popular among screenwriters and producers, relatively few forensic psychologists engage in offender profiling, and the majority of forensic psychologists actually work in prison settings (British Psychological Society, 2011). Torres *et al.* (2006) indicate that only about 10 per cent of forensic psychologists and psychiatrists have ever worked in offender profiling. Forensic psychology is made up of considerably more areas than offender profiling, and an overview of some of the definitions of forensic psychology provides insight into how diverse this field is.

Brown and Campbell (2010) indicate that even the 'term forensic psychologist is unhelpful and potentially misleading as no one individual can hope to have the breadth and depth of knowledge … Rather we think that there are a family of settings within which forensic psychology is applied and that context is critical to limiting claims of expertise' (p. 1). They argue that there is a lack of consensus as to the definition of forensic psychology. This is evident among the many definitions of forensic psychology that have been offered.

Some definitions, such as that of Blackburn (1996), are quite narrow in focus, suggesting that forensic psychology is 'the provision of psychological information for the purpose of facilitating a legal decision' (p. 7). Others are much broader, such as Wrightsman's (2001) definition of forensic psychology as 'any application of psychological knowledge or methods to a task faced by the legal system' (p. 2). Davies *et al.* (2008) also favour a broad definition, indicating that forensic psychology is a combination of both '*legal psychology* covering the application of psychological knowledge and methods to the process of law and *criminological psychology* dealing with the application of psychological theory and method to the understanding (and reduction) of criminal behaviour' (p. xiii). Nevertheless, Davies *et al.* (2008) do recognise that the use of the term 'forensic psychology' to encompass both legal and criminological psychology has been contentious.

Both Howitt (2009) and Brown and Campbell (2010) favour the broader definitions of forensic psychology, to allow for the inclusion of the work of psychologists who work in a wide variety of forensic-related settings, such as those described below. In this book, a similar stance will be taken, and a broad definition of forensic psychology will be subscribed to, encompassing any way in which psychology can aid in any stage of the criminal justice process.

Summary box 1.1 Forensic psychology definitions

- Many different definitions for 'forensic psychology' have been suggested, varying widely in the scope involved.
- While many of the general public associate forensic psychology with offender profiling, in fact only a small minority of forensic psychologists engage in this activity.
- For the purposes of this book, a broad definition of forensic psychology will be used, to encompass any way in which psychology can aid in the criminal justice process.

Cybercrime: a brief introduction

There are many different types of cybercrime, some of which will be explored in this book. As with crime in general, most types of cybercrime can be divided into 'property crimes' (such as identity theft, fraud and copyright infringement) and 'crimes against the person' (such as cybercrimes involving the sexual abuse of children).

Similarly, cybercrimes can be divided into internet-enabled crimes and internet-specific crimes. Internet-enabled crimes are those types of crimes that can also exist offline (for example, copyright infringement and the distribution of child pornography), but the presence of internet-enabled devices allows for easier and/or faster execution of such offences. Internet-specific crimes are those cybercrimes that do not exist without an online or computer-enabled environment (such as malware distribution and hacking offences such as denial of service attacks on websites). A third type of cybercrime is also possible – specifically 'crimes in virtual worlds' (Power, 2010; Power and Kirwan, 2011). These are events which occur between avatars (or characters) within online virtual worlds, which in offline settings would be considered to be criminal events (such as murder, theft, sexual assault or violence).

As with many other types of crime, cybercrimes vary in severity, method and motive. They also vary in how they are perceived by criminal justice systems around the world – what is considered illegal in one jurisdiction may not break any specific laws in another. In particular, crimes in virtual worlds can be difficult to define from legal perspectives, due to the varying acceptability of different behaviours in various virtual worlds.

Summary box 1.2 Cybercrime

- Cybercrimes can be defined in two main ways.
- They can be 'property crimes' or 'crimes against the person'.
- They can also be 'internet-specific', 'internet-enabled' or a 'crime in a virtual world' (Power, 2010; Power and Kirwan, 2011).
- Laws regarding cybercrimes vary across jurisdictions.

Components of forensic psychology

As mentioned above, forensic psychology involves many different activities and responsibilities, and most forensic psychologists choose to specialise in one or more of these areas. Two of the most common specialisms include offender rehabilitation and offender assessment, where a psychologist will try to determine if the offender is suffering from a psychological abnormality, if they are likely to reoffend and if they can be rehabilitated to reduce the likelihood of reoffending. Other psychologists examine how witnesses and victims can be helped when trying to recall details of an offence, while others attempt to find strategies that will encourage offenders to confess to their crimes, without increasing the risk of 'false confessions'. The detection of deception is another key area of forensic psychology, where specialists try to determine what the most reliable methods are for determining the truthfulness of responses. Some forensic psychologists work with police forces, attempting to reduce stress levels and devise the best methods of police recruitment and training. Others examine the behaviour of juries, trying to determine who makes up the most reliable juries and how members of the jury make decisions about guilt or innocence. The psychology of victims is also considered, and psychologists attempt to determine how victims can be helped within the criminal justice system and how they can reduce their likelihood of being revictimised. Similarly, psychologists can also work within communities in order to help in the development of educational strategies and other interventions that may reduce levels of crime. In this section, an outline will be provided of some of these activities, along with a brief overview of how they have been applied to cybercriminal events.

Offender profiling

Douglas *et al.* (1986) define offender profiling as 'a technique for identifying the major personality and behavioural characteristics of an individual based upon an analysis of the crimes he or she has committed' (p. 405). However, there are many approaches that can be employed during profile development (Ainsworth, 2001). These include:

- *crime scene analysis*. This is used as the basis for the United States Federal Bureau of Investigation's technique.
- *diagnostic evaluation*. This technique relies on clinical judgements of a profiler.
- *investigative psychology*. This technique utilises a statistical approach to profiling (although it should be noted that investigative psychology is generally considered to have a broader remit than profiling alone (Canter and Youngs, 2009).

Due, at least in part, to the popularity of offender profiling among the general population, a significant number of profilers have published descriptions of the cases that they have worked on and the profiles that they have developed (see, for example, Britton, 1997, 2000; Canter, 1995, 2003; Douglas and Olshaker, 1995, 1999, 2000).

Underlying most profiling methods are two key assumptions, as outlined by Alison and Kebbell (2006). These are the 'consistency assumption' and the 'homology assumption'.

- The 'consistency assumption' states that offenders will exhibit similar behaviours throughout all their crimes. So, for example, if someone engages in online fraud using an auction website, the consistency assumption dictates that they would use auction websites for most of their offences. However, there are problems with this assumption – the offender may have to change their method if they are banned from specific auction sites, or if they find that they are not making sufficient money from such a technique.

- The 'homology assumption' suggests that 'similar offence styles have to be associated with similar offender background characteristics' (Alison and Kebbell, 2006, p. 153). So for example, if the offender is generally a conscientious person, then that conscientiousness will be evident in how they complete their crimes. For example, perhaps the same fraudster described above will display a high degree of conscientiousness in managing their fraud, taking care to manage details of their crimes in such a way as to avoid apprehension. The homology assumption predicts that the same offender will also be conscientious in their day-to-day lives, perhaps ensuring a high quality of work in their employment or a carefully maintained filing system for personal documents. Again, there are problems with this assumption – individuals do not always display the same characteristics in different settings. For example, it is likely that you behave quite differently when you are among your classmates than when you are speaking to one of your lecturers. In relation to this, Canter (1995) describes the 'interpersonal coherence' aspect of the interaction between victim and offender, referring to how variations in criminal activity may reflect variations in how the offender deals with people in non-criminal circumstances.

Illustration 1.1 Offender profiling and suspect characteristics. Offender profilers examine evidence from current and previous crime scenes, comparing what is known about the current offences to the behaviours of previously apprehended offenders. This information is used to predict the characteristics of the current offender.

While it should be remembered that it is difficult to verify the effectiveness and utility of offender profiling (Alison and Kebbell, 2006; Alison *et al.*, 2003), there are several studies which have examined how offender profiling might be useful in cybercrime cases. Gudaitis (1998) outlines a need for a multi-dimensional profiling method for assessing cybercriminals, while Nykodym *et al.* (2005) also indicate that offender profiling could be of use when investigating cybercrimes, especially where it is suspected that the offender is an insider in an affected company. Rogers (2003) indicates that offender profiling could be useful in a variety of ways for cybercriminal investigation, including helping the investigators to search hard drives more effectively, narrowing the pool of potential suspects, identifying a motive and determining the characteristics of victims which make them more appealing to offenders.

There is conflicting evidence regarding the consistency assumption in cybercrime cases. Jahankhani and Al-Nemrat (2010) suggest that due to the rapid changes in technology over time, it is possible that cybercriminal behaviour may also undergo rapid changes. Nevertheless, Preuß *et al.* (2007) report the analysis of twelve hacking incidents in Germany, and found that the methods used years ago were still the preferred methods of more contemporary hackers.

One of the key large-scale studies involving offender profiling and cybercrime was the Hackers Profiling Project (Chiesa *et al.*, 2009), which produced a large quantity of information such as demographics, socioeconomic background, social relationships, psychological traits and hacking activities. The results of this study are considered in more detail in Chapter 3. However, it should be noted that this project aimed to create a profile of hackers based on completion of a self-report questionnaire, rather than any attempts to develop a profile of a hacker from their activities and offences alone. Nevertheless, the scale and scope of the Hackers Profiling Project is an important initial step in developing the database of information required to make accurate profiles of offenders in the future.

Summary box 1.3 Offender profiling

- There are three main approaches to offender profiling: crime scene analysis, diagnostic evaluation and investigative psychology (Alison and Kebbell, 2006).
- Most approaches to offender profiling are based on two main assumptions – the 'consistency assumption' and the 'homology assumption'. However, there are flaws with both of these assumptions.
- While the potential benefits of offender profiling for cybercriminal cases have been noted by several authors, limited empirical research has been produced to date.

Psychological disorders and offender assessment

One of the most common activities carried out by practising forensic psychologists involves assessment of offenders. When serious crimes are reported in the news, people often feel that the perpetrator must have some psychological disorder, otherwise they would not have been able to carry out such horrendous acts. It is often the role of the forensic psychologist to assess whether or not the offender meets the diagnosis for a psychological disorder and to provide a report or expert testimony in court (Gudjonsson and Haward, 1998). However, this role is sometimes complicated by a lack of agreement between psychology and legal systems as to what constitutes a psychological disorder.

While defining abnormal behaviour seems on the surface to be simple, when analysed in depth it is quite difficult to achieve. For example, in most cases if a person cries easily and frequently, we would consider their behaviour to be abnormal. However, if the person has just lost a close friend or family member but they do *not* show signs of psychological distress, then we would also consider their behaviour to be abnormal. As such, one of the key methods of determining abnormality relates to *discomfort* – is the person experiencing distress that continues over a long period of time or is unrelated to their current circumstances?

A second consideration of abnormality involves *dysfunction* – can the person manage their daily life effectively? Are they able to study, work and socialise, and can they maintain interpersonal relationships? It is important to consider the person's potential when doing this – if a student is generally weak at a subject like maths, and gets a poor grade, he or she may still be reaching their potential. However, if a normally strong student who usually gets A or B grades suddenly starts to fail their courses, it may be indicative of a problem.

A third method of defining abnormality involves *deviance*. In this sense, deviance refers to unusual (rather than specifically criminal or antisocial) behaviour. So, if a person experiences a symptom that most members of the population do not (such as violent mood swings or hallucinations), it may indicate a psychological disorder. Nevertheless, deviance alone is insufficient to define abnormality – it is unusual for a student to receive straight As in their exams, but it certainly would not be considered to be abnormal.

Psychological disorders are quite carefully defined, and lists of them (and their corresponding symptoms) can be found in the American Psychiatric Association's *Diagnostic and Statistical Manual* (*DSM*, 2000, 2011). Any offender may be suffering from a psychological disorder, and forensic psychologists will assess the suspect for symptoms of these disorders using a combination of clinical interviews, psychometric tests, clinical history and observations. Most abnormal psychology textbooks base their content on the DSM, but it is important to remember that the concept of *insanity* is a legal one, rather than a psychological term (Huss, 2009). There are many types of psychological disorders, and not all would lead to a diagnosis of insanity from a legal perspective. Indeed, the definitions of insanity have varied over time and jurisdiction, but most relate to understanding of right and wrong, or the control of impulses (see Foucault, 1965; Huss, 2009).

Activity 1.1 Psychological disorders

Using a current textbook on abnormal psychology, or a reputable website on the internet, identify the main signs and symptoms of the following psychological disorders: depression; bipolar disorder; schizophrenia; dissociative disorder; and antisocial personality disorder. How do the concepts of deviance, dysfunction and discomfort help to define these disorders?

There has been very little research to date investigating the link between psychological disorders and cybercriminals. However, it has been suggested that there is a link between Asperger's Syndrome (AS) and hacking behaviours (Hunter, 2009). AS is a disorder on the autistic spectrum, which is characterised by a significant impairment in social interaction skills, a lack of emotional reciprocity and repetitive and strong interests in a limited number of activities (Sue *et al.*, 2005), although there is intact cognitive ability and no delays in early language milestones (Toth and King, 2008). Several hackers have been diagnosed with this disorder, including Gary McKinnon and Owen Walker (Gleeson, 2008). Hunter (2009) indicates that these characteristics could lead AS individuals to spend more time with computers, indicating that 'For a person with Asperger's Syndrome, computers can provide a perfect solitary pastime as well as a refuge from the unpredictability of people' (p. 46). Certainly the focus that individuals with AS have on certain activities would benefit them if they wished to become accomplished hackers. However, care should be taken to remember that not all individuals with AS are hackers. Similarly, not all hackers have AS. As such, while there is substantial anecdotal evidence to suggest a link between hacking and AS, until an empirical study is completed in this area, a strong correlation between the two cannot be assumed.

Summary box 1.4 Psychological disorders and offender assessment

- Forensic psychologists are sometimes required to assess offenders or suspects in order to determine if they have any underlying psychological disorders, or if they meet the definition of insanity in their jurisdiction.
- Insanity is primarily a legal term, rather than a psychological one.
- Abnormal psychological states are often defined in terms of dysfunction, discomfort and deviance.

Punishment, rehabilitation and risk assessment

While it is common for serious offenders to be assessed when they are apprehended and before trial, a forensic psychologist may also be involved in later stages of their experience within the criminal justice system. Forensic psychologists often help to devise appropriate rehabilitation strategies and interventions and may be asked to assess the offender's risk of further offending behaviours, should the perpetrator be released. Such risk assessments can play an important part in the determination of early release suitability.

Legal systems often have a variety of punishments available, of which certain subsets are deemed to be suitable for various offences. If the offence is minor, the perpetrator may face a relatively light punishment (such as a fine for a parking offence). More serious crimes are associated with more severe punishments, such as imprisonment, community service, probation and in some jurisdictions corporal and capital punishment. Similarly, different punishments may have different aims, including deterrence, rehabilitation, restitution or incapacitation (preventing the offender from committing further acts by 'incapacitating' them – perhaps by imprisonment or preventing them from accessing certain equipment or people).

Deterrence can be 'general' or 'specific'. Specific deterrence is aimed at the individual offender, in the hope that they will not reoffend, while general deterrence is aimed at society as a whole, in the hope that by punishing the individual, other members of society will be deterred from criminal acts. Both types of deterrence have been used in cybercrime cases. Smith (2004) discussed the case of Simon Vallor, who spent eight months in prison for writing computer viruses. Vallor stated that he '... would never try to create a virus again ... Going to prison was terrible. It was the worst time of my life' (Smith, 2004, p. 6). In this instance, specific deterrence seems to have been achieved, although Smith also suggests that general deterrence is less effective in hacking cases, as many hackers feel that convictions can be difficult to obtain, and punishments only occur in rare cases. General deterrence has also been utilised in copyright infringement cases, where a relatively small number of individuals have received severe punishments for the illegal distribution of material such as songs, videos and software, although it again appears that this tactic has limited effectiveness in deterring most users from these activities.

It could be suggested that in an ideal world, all offenders should be fully rehabilitated so that they are no longer a danger to society and will not reoffend. In practice, unfortunately, this is unlikely to occur, although forensic psychologists attempt to determine the best strategies for working with offenders to reduce their risk. Rehabilitation programmes vary greatly – some of the most common ones involve substance abuse rehabilitation programmes that attempt to discourage offenders from committing property offences in order to feed drug habits. However, rehabilitation programmes are also provided for violent offenders, sex offenders and juvenile offenders, among many others. The type of rehabilitation provided depends on both the type of crime which has occurred and the psychology of the specific offender – not all offenders are suitable for rehabilitation, and psychologists and psychiatrists assess offenders to determine if they are suitable for, and will benefit from, rehabilitation programmes. Specific rehabilitation programmes have been suggested for individuals who commit child-related online offences, such as the distribution of child pornography, and these are discussed in more detail in Chapter 6. All rehabilitation programmes need to be carefully carried out, with suitable evaluations and controls, in order to determine their effectiveness.

The aim of restitution is to compensate the victim for the damage done by the offender's actions. For this reason, restitution is best suited to property offences, such as theft and vandalism. One example of the use of restitution involved Jammie Thomas-Rasset (BBC News Online, 25 January 2010), who was fined almost two million dollars in 2009 for sharing songs over the internet (although this fine was later reduced). In restitution cases, damages can be awarded to the victim (such as the music industry) in order to compensate them for any losses incurred. It is also possible that restitution may be a suitable tactic for crimes that occur in virtual worlds. However, restitution is less appropriate for other offences, such as distribution of child pornography.

The goal of incapacitation is to prevent the offender from committing any more crimes. Punishments which aim for this goal include imprisonment, where the offender is prevented from carrying out more crimes because of their incarceration. For cybercriminals, incarceration can take other forms, such as in the case of computer hacker Kevin Mitnick. When he was arrested he was held without bail, as US Magistrate Venetta Tassopulos ruled '… that when armed with a keyboard he posed a danger to the community' (Littman, 1996, as cited by MacKinnon, 1997, p. 17). Mitnick's access to telephones was also severely restricted. In modern society it is very difficult to restrict internet access completely, especially with the advent of internet-enabled mobile technologies such as smartphones. However, variations of such penalties have been considered for cybercriminals. It has been suggested that those who repeatedly download pirated music, videos or games should have their internet connection speed reduced to the extent that it would prohibit further downloading.

> **Activity 1.2 Punishment**
> Discuss the relative merits of deterrence, rehabilitation, restitution and incapacitation as punishments for cybercriminal acts. Consider specific cybercrimes (such as copyright infringement, child-related online offences, hacking, cyberterrorism, etc.). Develop a set of guidelines for one or more types of cybercrime which could be used by a court to determine an appropriate punishment for offenders.

A related responsibility of some forensic psychologists involves risk assessment. In these cases, the psychologist is asked to determine what the probability is of the offender committing further crimes, often for the benefit of parole boards who use the psychologist's report during their decision-making process. Predicting future criminal behaviour is extremely hard, even with the benefit of hindsight. A criminal may be considered to be at high risk of further offending, and so would not be released, but it could not be known with certainty if they would have offended again if they had returned to society. Similarly, an offender who is considered to be at low risk of reoffending and who is released may still reoffend, but avoid detection. When making such assessments, parole boards consider the type of criminal activity involved. For some types of property-related offences it may be preferable to err on the side of releasing the offender, as the consequences of an inaccurate assessment are relatively low. However, if the offender is an online child predator, it may be preferable to err on the side of continuing incarceration, as the consequences of releasing an offender who is still a danger to society are so great.

Summary box 1.5 Punishment, rehabilitation and risk assessment
- Forensic psychologists may be required to develop and implement appropriate rehabilitation strategies for offenders.

- Punishment may involve deterrence, restitution, rehabilitation or incapacitation, or a combination of these devices.
- Appropriate punishment types vary according to the offender and the offence involved.
- Psychologists may be required to assess an offender's risk of recidivism.

Police psychology

Police psychology includes a wide variety of other aspects of psychology, including eyewitness interviewing, suspect interviewing, police training, recruitment procedures and dealing with stress. It can also include topics such as offender profiling, as described above. Many police forces have dedicated cybercrime units (or at least, units which specialise in cybercrime cases alongside related crimes such as fraud). Forensic psychologists can help to identify suitable recruitment and training methods for the police officers who work in these units. However, a key potential support for police investigating cybercriminal cases which could be provided by forensic psychologists involves assistance in dealing with stress, and so this will be the focus of this section.

Stress is a normal part of everyday life for most individuals. At the moment you may be under a certain degree of stress. Perhaps you have to finish an essay for your professor, help your friend to move house, find a solution for a broken printer and manage to pay the rent and bills on time. Individuals vary in their ability to deal well with stress – some feel unable to cope with the smallest of tasks, while others seem to be able to deal with anything that life throws at them. Similarly, police officers can be subject to many kinds of stress (everything from administrative duties to being in life-threatening situations), and they also vary in how well they can deal with these stressors (a stressor is any stimulus which causes stress). Severe stress may result in the police officer experiencing post-traumatic stress disorder (PTSD) or acute stress disorder (ASD). These disorders involve the person having experienced an event involving fear, horror or helplessness, along with additional symptoms such as emotional numbing, heightened autonomic arousal (such as sleep disturbances or startle responses), flashbacks or intrusive memories (American Psychiatric Association, 2000).

Although dedicated cybercrime officers are less likely to be in life-threatening situations than police officers in other units (such as violent crime units), it is still possible that they may develop ASD or PTSD. They may also be at risk of Secondary Traumatic Stress Disorder (STSD), which has been associated with police officers who have been exposed to disturbing images of internet child pornography (Perez *et al.*, 2010). Perez *et al.* also noted that police personnel who experienced STSD and burnout developed other symptoms, such as higher protectiveness of their family and general distrust.

Thankfully, computer software is available which reduces the requirement of police officers to examine each image of child pornography on a suspect's data storage devices (such as computer hard drives and universal serial bus (USB) memory sticks).

However, as new images are produced and distributed, it may still be necessary for cybercrime officers to examine such images to determine the severity of the abuse in the image, or the identity of the victim or perpetrator. Police psychologists can sometimes provide 'stress inoculation training', which helps the officers to deal with the horrendous task of sorting images while protecting their psychological wellbeing. Psychologists can also provide counselling for officers who have been exposed to such images.

Summary box 1.6 Police psychology

- Police psychology considers a number of topics, including police recruitment and training, offender profiling, eyewitness interviewing, suspect interrogation and dealing appropriately with stress.
- Post-traumatic stress disorder and acute stress disorder can occur after an event which caused fear, helplessness or horror. Symptoms include emotional numbing, heightened autonomic arousal, flashbacks and intrusive memories.
- Police officers who investigate cases involving child pornography may be at risk of secondary traumatic stress disorder (STSD) and burnout.
- Police psychologists can provide 'stress inoculation training' and/or counselling for police officers affected by cases.

Cybercrime juries

Juries are frequently portrayed in television programmes and films, so most people are familiar with the concept of what being on a jury involves. In real life, the task of jurors can be quite complex – evidence can be ambiguous, difficult to comprehend or unallowable in court, and the jury is required to sort through all the information in order to reach a verdict. One of the main difficulties in relation to cybercrime juries involves the specialist knowledge which may be required. In addition to understanding the legal terminology of the courtroom, the jury must also familiarise itself with the terminology relating to the specific cybercrime – terms such as 'malware', 'social engineering', 'phishing' and 'advance fee fraud' may be used, and jurors may not be familiar with them before the trial (definitions for each of these can be found in the relevant chapters of this book). Of course, it is not just cybercrime cases that demand specialist knowledge, and it has been argued that it would be better if juries were composed of experts, rather than lay people, although this claim is controversial (Walker, 2001). This lack of understanding of terminology is compounded by the finding that jurors can have poor recall of important information, especially in complex cases such as fraud (Nathanson, 1995).

Evidence presented in cybercrime cases can be confusing for jurors (Carrier and Spafford, 2004; Rogers, 2003; Smith and Bace, 2003). A specific example of potential confusion in cybercrime jurors is suggested by Carney and Rogers (2004). They indicate that some offenders and their lawyers may utilise the 'Trojan defence'.

This defence suggests that the defendant did not intentionally engage in the criminal act, but that they unintentionally installed software on their computer while downloading another file (see 'Trojan horses' in Chapter 4), and it was this software which carried out the offence. Carney and Rogers indicate that a good investigator may be able to determine if the defendant intentionally carried out the crime or not, but it may not be easy to convince a judge and jury of this (Casey, 2002; Smith and Bace, 2003).

It is also interesting to consider how juries make decisions in cybercrime cases. While there are several models of jury decision making, Hastie's (1993) cognitive story model is of specific interest here. This model suggests that jurors create a 'story' of the crime from the evidence presented, and they compare this to a schema (or script) which they associate with a certain criminal activity. For example, a juror's schema for a violent assault may involve a lone individual, innocently walking down a street, who is set upon without cause by another individual or group. However, if the case presented in court doesn't match this schema (perhaps the victim was intoxicated, and insulted the perpetrator), they may be less likely to convict the defendant as they don't accept the act as criminal. It is important to note that jurors can have different schemas relating to the same offence, and so two individuals, given exactly the same evidence, may differ in their tendencies to acquit or convict. The cognitive story model is particularly interesting for cybercrime cases, where many members of the public may have uncertain schemas relating to the offences involved, which may add to their confusion. The 'white hat defence' which is sometimes offered by hackers (the suggestion that they only hacked into a system in order to highlight its vulnerabilities and to report these back to the system administrators) may be a specific example of how an offence does not fit in with a juror's schema for the crime.

Summary box 1.7 Cybercrime juries

- Cybercriminal cases may require juries to familiarise themselves with both legal terminology and terminology relating to the cybercrime itself.
- It has been argued that expert juries may be more appropriate than juries composed of lay people, although this suggestion is not without controversy.

Victims

The victims of many crimes experience negative reactions after their victimisation, and victims of cybercrimes are no different. The reactions experienced vary depending on the type of crime experienced and the coping abilities of the victim, but can include ASD or PTSD, a need for retribution, self-blaming for their victimisation and 'victim blaming', where other people put some or all of the blame for the crime on the victim themselves.

Self-blaming activity occurs when the victim blames themselves for their actions in the lead-up to the criminal event, in the belief that had they behaved differently, they would not have been victimised. For example, a victim of a malware attack may feel that, had they taken more care to update their antivirus software, their computer might still be okay. Similarly, police, friends and family may have little sympathy for the victim, feeling that they should have taken better care of their computer. This 'self-blaming' and 'victim-blaming' can occur for almost any type of crime, and while it is certain that in some cases victims have left themselves vulnerable to attack, such behaviours often shift the focus of blame from the offender on to the victim. Mendelsohn (1974, as cited by Walklate, 2006) has suggested that there is a spectrum of shared responsibility between the victim and the offender. This theory, and similar ones proposed by other researchers, can be quite controversial, particularly in relation to offline sexual assault cases, but it can provide an interesting model for understanding self- and victim-blaming. It should be noted that in many cases victim-blaming is not meant to be malicious – police officers, family members and friends may feel that by chastising the victim for their negligence the victim may learn from their past mistakes. However, the victim may feel more upset by these actions, as the people that they turned to after the crime appeared unsympathetic.

ASD and PTSD can affect victims of crime (Scarpa *et al.*, 2006; Hoyle and Zedner, 2007), with similar symptoms to those mentioned earlier in this chapter. Thankfully, as most cybercrimes are not life-threatening, incidents of ASD and PTSD in victims of cybercrime would seem to be very rare, although there is anecdotal evidence of some distress which has been experienced by victims of crimes in virtual worlds. This is examined in more detail in Chapter 10, but it is important to note that this area requires a great deal more empirical examination before strong conclusions can be drawn.

Finally, victims may experience a need for retribution – a desire that the perpetrator be punished for their actions. There has been some evidence for this in the families of homicide victims (Haines, 1996), but it can also occur in the victims of other crimes, including cybercrimes. Many people have experienced a situation where they feel that

Illustration 1.2 Self-blaming and victim-blaming. Victims of cybercrime may feel that if they had taken more care to protect their computer, they would not have been victimised. Such self-blaming can occur for almost any type of crime.

they have been wronged in some way, and a desire for revenge can be strong. Again, there is some evidence for this among victims of crimes in virtual worlds, and some case studies are presented in Chapter 10.

Summary box 1.8 Victims

- Victims of crimes can experience many consequences, including self-blaming; victim-blaming; acute stress disorder; post-traumatic stress disorder; and a need for retribution.
- Mendelsohn (1974, cited by Walklate, 2006) suggested a spectrum of shared responsibility between the victim and the offender.
- There is some anecdotal evidence of crimes in virtual worlds evoking distress and a need for retribution in victims.

Crime prevention

While it is unlikely that cybercrime can ever be eradicated, it is possible that some crimes could be prevented. Various approaches could be taken to achieve this. For example, Welsh and Farrington (2004) describe interventions that could be used with at-risk groups in order to prevent them from progressing to criminal behaviour. Unfortunately, at present it is quite difficult to predict who will become a cybercriminal, although research in this area is accumulating. It is likely that if a more complete profile of the various types of cybercriminal could be achieved then interventions similar to those described by Welsh and Farrington could be implemented.

Other approaches suggest that potential victims should be educated in how to protect themselves and their property adequately, thus potentially reducing victimisation (see, for example, Farrell and Pease, 2006). Most cybercrime prevention strategies to date have been of this type, most notably with attempts to improve the safety of children online, although Tynes (2007) indicates that it is important that parents allow their children to experience the benefits of the online world while simultaneously protecting their children. Cybercrime prevention is also enhanced by the use of technology in the protection of users and equipment, such as secure log-ins, antivirus software, firewalls and child protection software (that can limit the websites that children visit and the amount of time spent online).

Forensic psychology can help the success of crime prevention strategies by identifying ways in which users can be encouraged to engage in safer online behaviours. LaRose *et al.* (2008) discovered that individuals are more likely to engage in safety behaviours if their personal responsibility and the positive outcomes of safe behaviour online are emphasised. Research from other fields in psychology could also be applied to crime prevention strategies, such as strategies for encouraging individuals to lead healthier lifestyles or social psychological research into persuasion techniques.

Summary box 1.9   Crime prevention

- Cybercrime prevention strategies can involve targeted interventions at potential offenders, victim education strategies and the use of technological protection measures.
- Psychologists can aid in prevention strategies by identifying methods of encouraging users to engage in safer online behaviours.

Forensic psychology – conclusion

As can be seen, forensic psychology can contribute to our understanding of cybercrime in many ways. Investigations and prevention of cybercrimes can be supported by drawing on the research and experience which has built up in forensic psychology over the past few decades. Nevertheless, it is also important that the limitations of forensic psychology are clear to investigators and others involved in cybercriminal cases. Media portrayals of offender profiling tend to promote it as more successful and exact than it is in real life, and it is important that any forensic psychologists working in cybercriminal cases honestly inform other professionals of the strengths and limitations of the field, so that unreasonable expectations and subsequent disappointments can be avoided.

Our attention now turns to an important question in forensic psychology – specifically, why do some individuals become criminals, while others do not?

Theories of crime

There has been a great deal of speculation as to why a person engages in criminal behaviour, often with the hope of identifying a method by which such criminality can be avoided or reduced. However, a single explanation for offending remains elusive. Instead, research findings suggest that criminality results from a variety of different causes, occurring at various levels (from societal levels, through community and social influence theories, to specific individual theories). The following pages will consider some of these theories, with particular focus on social influence and individual theories, as these have the greatest background in psychological theory and research. Some of these theories are currently popular, whereas others have fallen out of favour within the criminological community. Nevertheless, it should be remembered that the theories are not necessarily in competition with each other, and any specific criminality may have arisen from a variety of factors from a number of theories. A brief overview of the levels of explanation of crime will be provided, and then specific theories will be examined, including the social construction of crime, biological theories, learning theories, the complex theory of crime suggested by Eysenck, other trait theories of crime, psychoanalytic theories, addiction and arousal, neutralisation theories, labelling theories, geographical theories and finally routine activity theory.

Levels of explanation of crime

Theories of crime can occur at various levels (Howitt, 2009). These include high-level explanations of crime (such as societal theories and community theories) and explanations of crime that are targeted at more personal levels, such as socialisation influence theories and individual theories. Specific theories of crime might be contained within one level of crime, whereas others consider several levels in their attempts to explain crimes.

Societal, community, socialisation influence and individual theories

The highest-level theories of crime are societal (or macro-level) theories. Howitt (2009) suggests *strain theory* as an example of a societal level theory. At the core of this theory is the inability of all members of society to achieve all of society's goals. For example, it is not possible for all members of society to be wealthy. Those members of society who cannot achieve the goal of wealth through legitimate means may be tempted to become wealthy through criminal or detrimental means, such as theft. The social construction of crime provides a method of applying societal theories to cybercrime, and is examined in more detail below.

The next level of theories of crime involves *community theories*. Perhaps you know of the 'good' and 'bad' areas within your community, and it is often a key variable in people's decisions regarding where to live. Certain areas of cities and towns have higher crime rates than others, and these are generally (but not always) the areas that suffer from economic deprivation. Such geographical distributions of crimes are not confined to within cities – there are often major differences in crime rates between urban and rural areas, and even between countries. Due to the nature of the internet, such geographical distributions are probably not as indicative of cybercrime as they are of other types of crime. However, at an international level, some countries are associated with higher levels of crime than others. This is explored below in the section on geographical theories of crime.

Socialisation influence theories have a strong basis within psychology, particularly the areas of social and developmental psychology. These theories examine how the individual's family, friends and other contacts (such as teachers) affect their likelihood of becoming an offender. They also examine the effects of other influences, such as media (television, computer games, books, internet and other stimuli), on the person. As such, 'observational learning' is a key concept within socialisation influence theories – as humans we learn how to behave in new situations by watching others' behaviours. Similarly, criminal behaviour is often learnt by observing other criminals in action.

Finally, individual theories examine the specific characteristics of the person to determine their likelihood of offending. Reviewing the theories mentioned so far, it is possible that two individuals, while being brought up within the same society, in the same community and with the same socialisation influences, may differ in their eventual criminality. In these cases, it is possible that some specific set of characteristics may determine if a person goes on to display criminal tendencies. These characteristics may be psychological in nature (such as certain personality or cognitive traits) or they may be biological (such as neurological, neurochemical, physiological or genetic). Several individual theories are considered in this chapter.

Summary box 1.10 Levels of explanation of crime

- Theories of crime attempt to explain why crime exists, and who is most likely to become an offender.

- Howitt (2009) suggests that theories of crime can occur at several levels, including societal theories, community theories, socialisation influence theories and individual theories.

Applying theories of crime to cybercrime

There are many different theories of crime, which can be classified at one or more of the four levels of explanation of crime. Here, we will examine some of the most relevant theories of crime in terms of psychological influence and application to cybercrime. Nevertheless, it should be remembered that this is not an exhaustive list of theories, nor can the full complexity of any of the theories be described in detail here. Some key handbooks and collections of classic texts in criminology and forensic psychology (such as Brown and Campbell, 2010; Maguire *et al.*, 2007; Muncie *et al.*, 1996) provide more thorough explanations of each of these theories and should be consulted by the interested reader.

Social construction of crime

Howitt (2009) explains that it is important to consider how crime 'simply is not a static, universal thing that needs no explanation in itself' (p. 78). Society determines what is and is not a criminal act, and an event may be defined as criminal or not depending on a particular set of circumstances. For example, if you take another person's property, it is a criminal act if you do so without their permission, but not if they allow you to take the item. In addition to this, what constitutes a crime varies from jurisdiction to jurisdiction – certain recreational drugs are legally available in some countries, but not in others. The criminality of an action also varies according to the time the act occurs in – consider the prohibition of the distribution of alcoholic drinks in the US during the 1920s. There have been much more recent changes – same-sex sexual activity was decriminalised in Ireland in 1993.

When considering the social construction of crime, cybercrime is a very interesting case. Some cybercrimes were already defined as criminal events due to their similarity to offline counterparts. These types of offences are often considered in the literature to be 'old wine in new bottles', as it is thought that the nature of the crime has not changed, but merely the mechanism by which the crime has been carried out. Offences such as the distribution of child pornography online can be included in this categorisation.

However, not all negative online activities could be classified as criminal quite so easily. For example, the distribution of malicious software or virtual assaults on avatars in online virtual worlds do not fit quite as easily within pre-existing laws. In some cases, laws have had to be developed to deal with such acts, while in others, there is still uncertainty as to how such actions should be considered by legal authorities. Chapter 2 examines the legal situation relating to cybercrime in greater detail.

Biological theories of crime

A 'comparison of the criminal skull with the skulls of normal women reveals the fact that female criminals approximate more to males, both criminal and normal, than to normal women, especially in the superciliary arches in the seam of the sutures, in the lower jaw-bones, and in peculiarities of the occipital region'.

(Lombroso and Ferrero, 1895, p. 28)

The above quote may seem bizarre in the modern context, but at the time of writing it was a relatively common belief that criminals could be recognised by their physiological characteristics. *Phrenology* is a classic example of this theory, and many psychologists and physicians keep a 'Fowler's phrenology head', which attempts to map psychological constructs onto various parts of a person's head. Lombroso (as cited by Jamel, 2008) suggested that criminal brains would differ in shape from those of non-offenders, specifically that they would be less developed and have certain facial characteristics, such as thick lips, a receding chin, a large jaw and an asymmetrical face. Despite the prevalence of phrenology heads in surgeries and offices, they are generally kept only for decorative purposes, as these theories have long been refuted.

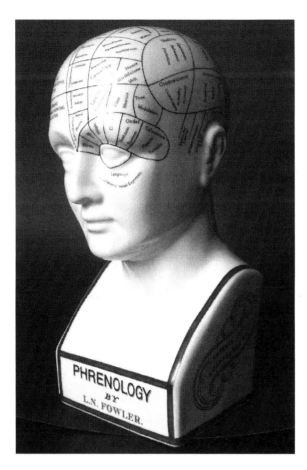

Illustration 1.3 Fowler's Phrenology Head. This attempted to map psychological characteristics onto certain areas of the head, and it was thought that an individual's personality could be read by examining the size and shape of the skull. Some of the characteristics that were supposedly mapped could have related to criminality, such as combativeness, destructiveness, integrity and justice.

Although phrenology is not seriously considered to be a useful tool in predicting criminality, other biological factors may provide more insight. For example, damage to certain structures within the brain may result in deficiencies in planning or changes in personality, which may increase the likelihood of criminal activity, although there are problems in determining a causal relationship and, as such, findings in this field should be interpreted with caution (Jamel, 2008). Similarly, it is possible that unusual neural activity levels in certain areas of the brain may be associated with Antisocial Personality Disorder, which is characterised by aggressiveness, irresponsibility and criminal activity (Davey, 2008, pp. 412–18).

Other possible biological theories examine genetics (for example, males commit more crimes than do females), evolutionary explanations (see Ward and Durrant, 2011 for a review) and levels of neurotransmitters and hormones (such as testosterone). Some researchers have indicated that there may be links between genetics, neural structures and antisocial behaviour (see, for example, Raine, 2008), while others have sought to integrate biological correlates of crime with other criminological theories (see, for example, Armstrong and Boutwell, 2012). The possibility of focusing on biological and physiological risk factors early in life as a method of crime prevention is another potential area for exploration (see, for example, Rocque *et al.*, 2012). However, while there is some evidence that most cybercriminals are male (see the specific literature in each of the chapters of this volume), there is little other research examining the biological construction of those who offend online. As such, it is unknown how useful biological theories are in the explanation of cybercrime.

Learning theories and crime

As with all other skills and behaviours, criminality is learned by offenders. There are many methods of learning a new skill, and a great deal of psychological literature has examined how this can take place. Sometimes we learn via trial and error – we literally learn from our mistakes. While attempts have been made to predict criminality using a variety of learning theories, operant conditioning and observational learning are probably of the most interest here.

Operant conditioning examines how individuals learn behaviours due to the consequences of actions and events. Much of the early work in operant conditioning was completed by B. F. Skinner, who worked mostly with laboratory animals, such as rats and pigeons. He taught these animals to complete different tasks, such as turning in circles or pecking a sign, by rewarding them with food. In a similar way, humans can learn to adapt their behaviours as a result of the consequences of those actions – we learn that if we put a lot of effort into studying for an exam, we are more likely to receive a high grade than if we did not study. This affects our future behaviours – if we wish to receive a high grade in future exams then we are more likely to study for them. Similarly, criminal actions can have high levels of rewards – there may be financial rewards if we steal a person's wallet, or we may experience a release of frustration if we act aggressively. However, the criminal act may also result in punishment – perhaps we will be caught, and may face imprisonment or another penalty. Operant conditioning suggests that offenders will continue to engage in acts that are reinforced and rewarded, while avoiding acts that are punished. The offender may consider the likelihood of being apprehended and punished, and if they consider that to be of low risk, may choose to engage in the behaviour which is assumed to result in high benefit. In some types of cybercrime, such as copyright infringement, the offender may feel that it is unlikely that they will be punished, especially due to the perceived anonymity provided by the internet. At the same time, the perceived rewards are quite high – the offender can obtain the desired video, music or software for free in a short period of time. Rational choice theory is a popular criminological theory which is based on the principles of operant conditioning. It suggests that the offender weighs up the potential costs and benefits of the crime before deciding whether or not to carry it out.

As mentioned earlier, observational learning relates to how learning occurs through observing how other people behave in similar situations, and later imitating that behaviour. Albert Bandura carried out research in this area and demonstrated that children will imitate violent acts conducted by adults if the adult is reinforced for their violence (Bandura, 1965). Research in forensic psychology suggests that criminal behaviour is also learned from others – individuals have been found to be more likely to become criminals if their parents, siblings or peers are also offenders (see, for example, Farrington *et al.*, 2001; Fergusson *et al.*, 2000; Robins *et al.*, 1975; West and Farrington, 1977). Similarly, such social learning seems to be an indicator of a person engaging in some cybercriminal acts, such as virus developers (see Chapter 4) and copyright infringement (see Chapter 8).

Eysenck's theory of crime

Eysenck attempted to develop a theory of crime which combined genetics, personality traits and environmental factors, and examined how each of these types of factors, and the interactions between them, might impact on a person's likelihood of becoming a criminal (Eysenck, 1977, 1987/1996; Eysenck and Eysenck, 1970, 1977). In particular, Eysenck examined extraversion, psychoticism and neuroticism, and suggested that those individuals who had high levels of these three personality traits would be more likely to be involved in criminal behaviour, but that individual differences may occur. Eysenck's theory is quite complex, and encompasses several levels of theorising, but it has been the target of much criticism due to a lack of support by research findings.

Other trait theories of crime

While Eysenck selected psychoticism, neuroticism and extraversion as the traits which he identified as related to criminal activity, many researchers in forensic psychology have examined other personality and cognitive traits which may be related to offending. These include moral development (see, for example, Palmer and Hollin, 1998; Trevethan and Walker, 1989), empathy (see, for example, Broidy *et al.*, 2003; Jolliffe and Farrington, 2004), intelligence (see, for example, Levine, 2008; Lopez-Leon and Rosner, 2010), self-control (see, for example, Baron, 2003; Conner *et al.*, 2008; Holtfreter *et al.*, 2010; Piquero *et al.*, 2007) and impulsiveness (see, for example, Meier *et al.*, 2008).

There is varying support for each of these traits as a correlate or predictor of criminality – some characteristics demonstrate more reliable results than others.

This may be due in part to the differences between offenders – the psychological profile of a fraudster may be very different to the psychological profile of a murderer. Even within the subset of cybercriminals, there may be a wide diversity of traits between offenders – it is likely that there are major differences between, for example, cyberterrorists and distributors of child pornography. Nevertheless, there are some findings regarding the personality traits of cybercriminals, with hackers being found to generally have poor interpersonal relationships (see Chapter 3) and those who illegally download files often having low levels of self-control (see Chapter 8). Of course, it should be remembered that even within these groups, there can be offenders who are exceptions and do not fit the profile created. However, identification of general traits that may be associated with specific cybercriminal types can be useful in the development of crime prevention strategies and rehabilitation of offenders.

Psychoanalytic theories of crime

Psychoanalytic theories of crime often focus on the unconscious struggle between the *id* (an unconscious construct that seeks pleasure and destruction) and the *ego,* which attempts to curtail the *id,* while guided by the *superego* (an internalisation of society's morals and standards). If the superego is not formed properly during childhood, criminal behaviour may occur. However, it has been suggested that psychoanalytic theories do not comprehensively account for criminal activity (Blackburn, 1993), and that crimes which require rational thought and conscious planning, such as white collar crimes, cannot be easily explained by a theory involving unconscious conflict (Kline, 1987). As many cybercrimes require such planning, psychoanalytic theories may not be useful. Nevertheless, there are exceptions, such as online child predators, and De Masi (2007) and Socarides (2004) consider how psychoanalytic theory might explain paedophilic behaviour.

Addiction and arousal theory

Arousal theory suggests that individuals enjoy a certain level of arousal or excitement, and will engage in acts to maintain this level. It helps to explain why some individuals engage in extreme sports, or take part in potentially risky behaviour for enjoyment. McQuade (2006) suggests that arousal theory might be a suitable explanation for cybercrimes such as those of cyberstalkers and hackers, who may experience a psychological thrill from their pursuits.

Similarly, Howitt (2009) considers how criminal behaviour may be an addiction. Firstly, many criminals also have alcohol or substance addictions. Secondly, successful treatments for criminality are often similar to successful treatments for addictions. Finally, Howitt cites research examining joyriders by Kilpatrick (1997) and shoplifters by McGuire (1997) who noted that offenders showed some characteristics of addiction including conflict (knowing that their actions had negative consequences), withdrawal, relapse and tolerance (having to carry out more, or more serious, offences in order to get the same emotional effect). In addition, Howitt suggests that addiction theory may explain why some juvenile offenders persist in their behaviours and become life-long offenders, while most 'age-out' (a similar trend has been noted among cybercriminals such as virus developers). However, there is little evidence to support a relationship between addiction or arousal theory and cybercrime.

Neutralisation theory

People frequently hold a relatively narrow definition of crime, which includes serious offences (such as murder, theft and assaults). However, other offences, while still criminal acts, are often not considered to *really* be crimes by the person. One of the authors (Kirwan) has taught over a dozen groups of students about forensic psychology, and in the first lecture she tests the students to see how they define criminality. At first, the students are asked if they are a criminal. In some cases one or two students will identify themselves as criminals, but in most groups, no-one will consider themselves to be so. The question is then rephrased – the students are provided with a list of activities, and asked if they have ever engaged in any of them. These activities include 'day-to-day' offences, such as driving a car over the speed limit, illegally downloading music or videos, drinking or taking other substances before being of legal age to do so, and even 'borrowing' something from a friend or workplace without the intention of returning it. The exercise demonstrates to students that the definition of crime is much broader than they might think it is, but it also demonstrates *neutralisation theory*. The students have convinced themselves that these crimes are excusable, and not really offences, for a variety of reasons (most often, because they do not feel that their actions really harmed anyone).

Neutralisation theory was initially developed by Sykes and Matza (1957), and it describes how offenders might offer explanations for crimes that they would normally consider to be morally unacceptable. Such excuses can include denying responsibility for their actions (perhaps by suggesting that they had to download a television programme from the internet because it wouldn't be shown locally for several months). Another neutralisation includes denial of injury to the victim – again in the illegal download of the television programme, the offender may suggest that they are not really doing any harm to the makers of the programme. A common neutralisation cited by those who download music illegally is that they are actually helping to launch the career of the musician by spreading the word about their talent. Neutralisations are also common among those who engage in child-related sexual offences; in this case the literature often refers to them as 'cognitive distortions' and further information is provided in Chapter 6. Of course, the justifications provided by offenders do not really excuse the criminal behaviours in most cases, but they allow the offender to carry out the act without reducing their self-image – they can maintain a belief that they are a caring, considerate and law-abiding citizen despite their actions.

Activity 1.3 Neutralisations

It is not just offenders who employ neutralisations. Consider the last time that you used neutralisations to explain or excuse your behaviour. Perhaps you postponed completing an essay for class because you 'deserved a break'? Or maybe you justified an expensive purchase because your friend owned a similar item? Attempt to identify what types of neutralisations might be employed for cybercrimes such as hacking, virus writing and identity theft. Consider Michael's case study at the start of this chapter, and discuss his use of neutralisations – do they excuse his behaviour? Should he still be prosecuted for downloading child pornography?

Labelling theory

The labels that are applied to people impact both how society treats them, and how the person behaves. If you currently hold the label of 'student', you are likely to behave in ways that are in line with that label – you go to classes, read relevant texts, complete coursework and possibly engage in some of the socialising that is commonly associated with student life. Similarly, society will treat you in a certain way because of your 'student' label – people will have a stereotypical image of what you do, how you behave and how you spend your time. If you are a psychology student, you may have experienced a common response from a stranger who has just learned about your chosen course of study – 'Are you analysing me?' The 'label' of 'psychology student' elicits a specific response in many members of society that is frequently inaccurate.

Labelling theory suggests that individuals experience a similar response when given the label of 'criminal'. If they perceive themselves as a criminal, then they may be more likely to engage in further criminal activity. Similarly, society often distrusts those labelled with the term 'criminal', and the person may find it harder to find work. For this reason, many police forces attempt to avoid labelling a young person as an 'offender' following a relatively minor infringement – it is thought that if the label can be avoided, then it is possible that further offending might also be avoided.

Labelling theory has an interesting application in the case of hackers, where many different labels have been associated with various types of hacking activity as those involved attempt to differentiate themselves from each other on the basis of motive or ability. On the other hand, some cybercriminals do not identify themselves as offenders (see the section on neutralisation theory above), and it may be necessary to educate those involved as to the criminality of their actions. A specific example of this involves copyright infringement, and some agencies have developed short video clips, commonly shown at the start of DVDs, which attempt to highlight the criminality of copyright infringement.

Geographical theories

If you think about the city or county you live in, which areas seem to have the highest rate of crime? In general, crime rates tend to be higher in urban areas than rural ones. The geographical distribution of crime has been of interest to many researchers in criminology, and the Chicago School of Sociology found that young offenders tend to live in certain areas within cities (Bottoms, 2007). Geographical theories of crime also examine crime rates in smaller communities, such as within housing estates, and on a much larger scale, by examining which countries are associated with particularly high or low crime rates.

For cybercriminal activity, it is very difficult to examine local levels of crime. However, some trends do seem to be notable at international levels. Symantec regularly releases security reports (see, for example, Symantec, 2011b), which investigate which countries most cybercrime originates from. Countries such as Brazil, China, Russia and the US can regularly be found within the top ten lists of these reports. This may in part be due to the methods by which Symantec captures the data (Whitney, 2010), but may also be indicative of high rates of cybercriminal activity in these countries due to access to computers or the internet. Greenberg (2007) quotes Bill

Pennington of White Hat Security, who suggested that young computer graduates in Russia or China may be engaging in cybercrime for financial reasons. This has yet to be tested empirically, and there may be other reasons why these countries, and others worldwide, are the source of cybercriminal activity.

Routine activity theory

The final theory which we will consider is routine activity theory, outlined by Clarke and Felson (1993). This theory suggests that a crime needs three variables to occur at the same time: a motivated offender, a suitable target and an absence of guardians. If, for example, you have a car (a suitable target) which is left unattended and unprotected (an absence of guardians), a crime still will not occur unless a suitably motivated offender also happens to visit the same location. As such, routine activity theory has some overlap with the geographical theories as motivated offenders are more likely to be present in certain areas of cities and countries.

In a similar manner, a computer is more likely to be hacked if it is seen as a suitable target (perhaps it would be useful because of its processing power, or it is particularly desirable because of the organisation that owns it), is unprotected by guardians (say for example, a lack of adequate antivirus software or a firewall) and is noticed by a motivated offender (perhaps a hacker who wishes to obtain information, or to control the computer as part of a *botnet* – a network of computers that are controlled by a hacker). Routine activity theory can be applied to almost all types of malicious online behaviour, and as such can be very useful in furthering our understanding of how and why a specific cybercrime occurs.

Summary box 1.11 Theories of crime

- The social construction of crime suggests that society determines what is and what is not a criminal event, and this can change across cultures and history.
- Biological theories of crime include phrenology, neural activity levels, neural structures, genetics, neurochemicals, hormones and evolutionary theories.
- Learning theories of crime include operant conditioning and observational learning.
- Eysenck suggested a theory of crime which considered genetics, environmental variables and personality traits, but it has been criticised due to a lack of support by research.
- Trait theories attempt to determine if certain cognitive or personality traits can be associated with criminality.
- Psychoanalytic theories suggest that criminality occurs because of an inadequately developed *superego*.
- Arousal theory suggests that criminal activity fills a need for a certain level of arousal in a person which may be met by extreme sports or other potentially risky behaviours in other individuals.
- It is also possible that criminal behaviour is addictive.
- Neutralisation theory describes how individuals might offer explanations for their criminal behaviour in order to maintain a positive self-image.

- Labelling theory examines how individuals might engage in certain behaviours, or be treated a certain way by society, depending on the 'criminal' label which has been assigned to them.
- Geographical theories examine how crime is distributed at various levels. Some information about the international distribution of cybercrime is available.
- Routine activity theory was outlined by Clarke and Felson (1993). It suggests that criminal events require three variables to occur simultaneously: a motivated offender, a suitable target and an absence of guardians.

Conclusion

It is certain that forensic psychology can add a great deal to our understanding of cybercrime, and the chapters that follow describe research that has been carried out in specific types of cybercrime. Theories of crime can help to explain why cybercrime occurs, although some are of greater use than others, and few have been empirically investigated with a particular focus on cybercrime. It should be remembered that psychological research into cybercrime is still at a relatively early stage and, in many cases, very little empirical work has been completed. It is important that more researchers focus on the psychology of cybercrime so that gaps in current knowledge can be filled and hence forensic psychology can be of greater assistance to cybercrime investigators. Forensic psychology holds huge potential for a variety of areas, including offender rehabilitation, victimology, offender profiling and crime reduction strategies, as well as benefiting juries and police officers in cybercrime cases.

Essay questions

(1) Forensic psychology is often portrayed in the media as mainly involving offender profiling. Describe the other key roles of forensic psychologists, and consider the accuracy of the media portrayal of forensic psychologists.
(2) Compare and contrast statistical and clinical offender profiling.
(3) No single theory of crime can explain why an individual engages in criminal acts, but in combination they can be a powerful predictor of criminality. Discuss.
(4) Different theories of crime are useful for different types of criminality. Consider in light of at least three types of cybercrime.
(5) Crime reduction strategies should focus on society rather than individual criminals. Discuss.

Additional reading

Dozens of excellent texts are available on the topic of forensic psychology, but the following are particularly useful if you'd like to understand the area in more detail:

Brown, J. M. and Campbell, E. A. (eds.) (2010). *The Cambridge Handbook of Forensic Psychology*. New York: Cambridge University Press.

Canter, D. (2010). *Forensic Psychology: a Very Short Introduction*. New York: Oxford University Press.

Holmes, D. A. (2010). *Abnormal Clinical and Forensic Psychology*. Harlow: Pearson.

Howitt, D. (2009). *Introduction to Forensic and Criminal Psychology* (3rd edn). Harlow: Pearson.

Websites

The website www.forensicpsychology.net has a number of useful links relating to several areas of forensic psychology, including crime scene investigations, mental health, capital punishment and cognitive science.

The British Psychological Society's Division of Forensic Psychology website includes information about forensic psychology as a career path, along with details of journals and upcoming events. Visit http://dfp.bps.org.uk/dfp/dfp_home.cfm for more information.

Similarly, Division 41 of the American Psychological Association is the American Psychology-Law Society, with more useful information on careers, publications and events: www.ap-ls.org.

2 Cybercrimes and cyberlaw

Case studies

Mary and Tom met on a social networking site and began a friendship exchanging regular messages. After a number of months Tom suggested an offline meeting. Mary was not keen on the idea but after telling Tom he became quite upset and aggressive and began sending abusive messages to her. Mary became quite distressed and nervous about going online. In the end she had to change all of her online profiles and email addresses and was considered by her doctor to be showing some signs of stress.

John had been playing a massively multiplayer online role-playing game (MMORPG) for a number of months. In addition to investing a good deal of time in gaining a proficiency in the game, John had also spent over £150 on in-game artefacts and additional features. On his most recent visit to the online world he found that some of these goods had been stolen by another player. John was unsure about what if anything he could do about it.

Chapter overview

The first section of this chapter seeks to define the nature of online crime or cyber-crime and look at the ways in which society is responding to it. We go on to look at the response and its multi-faceted nature. Governments attempt to respond with law, corporations with policies and procedures, suppliers with terms and conditions, users with peer pressure and technologists with code. The third section looks at how international laws have evolved through what is referred to as 'soft law' and seeks to draw lessons for the evolution of laws for the internet. The fourth section looks at the more general area of governance, examining how ideas of governance have evolved and how some of the theoretical work in this field may offer guidance for the governance of the internet. The final section examines the emerging role of social networking in online governance.

Online crime

Crime is, unfortunately, an ever-present part of modern society, and the struggle which occurs in every society between those who commit crime and those who seek to prevent, detect or punish criminal activity is always changing, both in the balance of success and the nature of the activities. People are spending more and more time online and using a variety of software and devices to stay in touch and perform activities both for work and pleasure. This increasing time spent online and the growing range of activities, from communication, to financial transactions, to entertainment, has provided the latest areas for this struggle.

Online crime can take many forms and a distinction is normally made between activities such as the theft of goods online, which is clearly a crime in the traditionally understood meaning of the term, private law issues such as disputes between buyers and sellers of online goods and issues of antisocial behaviour or harassment. Certain activities, such as spamming, hacking and copyright infringement, can, depending on severity, target and context, fit into any one of the three categories listed. This typology of private law, dispute resolution or antisocial behaviour is useful in the context of the legal profession as it distinguishes between the types of law that may apply in each case, and, to some extent, the severity of the activity.

Illustration 2.1 Online crime. Crimes online can take many forms, including property crimes and crimes against the person.

Chapter 1 provided an alternative classification scheme which is more helpful when thinking about the importance of technology to the nature of the crime. Technology has always provided new opportunities for individuals to exploit. Each advance in technology that provides such an opportunity is matched by advances in the technology of detection.

The first category is composed of those crimes which existed offline but are now greatly facilitated by the internet. These include misuse of credit cards, information theft, defamation, blackmail, obscenity, hate speech, money laundering and copyright infringement. In the main, comprehensive national laws exist to deal with these issues in an offline environment. With the exception of the cross-border nature of the online version of these activities enabled by the internet, existing legal frameworks are capable of dealing with them.

The second category is made up of crimes that had not existed before the arrival of networked computing and more specifically the proliferation of the internet. These include hacking, cyber vandalism, dissemination of viruses, denial of service attacks and domain name hijacking. National laws have been introduced in many jurisdictions in an attempt to combat these crimes. An overview of the UK law in this area is available at JISC Legal (www.jisclegal.ac.uk).

A third category comes into play when individuals are acting through their online avatars (representations of the user in the form of a three-dimensional model, from the Sanskrit 'avatara' meaning incarnation) or alternate personas. Do these individuals, or their avatars, constitute a new public, and present new issues of governance, both in cyberspace and of cyberspace? Harassing another individual through their online representation may or may not be criminal or antisocial, but there is no doubt that these activities can lead to very real crimes offline.

Activity 2.1 Types of crime

An example of online activity resulting in crime in the real world was the murder of Zhu Caoyuan, a Chinese man who sold a virtual sword won by fellow gamer Qiu Chengwei in the online game Legend of Mir 3. Review this case and consider the reaction of the police to the initial report by Qiu of the theft of his 'property', and how the reaction might be different with a greater awareness of online activity.

Crimes which exist entirely online also have serious negative impacts on their victims. In August 2005 a Japanese man was arrested for using software 'bots' (web robots, or 'bots', are software applications that run automated tasks over the internet) to 'virtually' assault online characters in the computer game Lineage II and steal their virtual possessions. He was then able to sell these items through a Japanese auction website for real money (Knight, 2005). Consider if the crime committed is limited to theft or if there was also a crime committed in the assault. Further examples of such crimes are given at the end of this chapter.

Offensive activities, such as those engaged in by cyberbullies, have had very real effects, with reports of them resulting in depression and suicide (Hinduja and Patchin, 2010a).

This cyberbullying can occur as people become more closely associated with their online persona to the extent that it is viewed, both by themselves and others, as an extension of themselves. These issues and the psychology behind this form of online behaviour are covered in more detail in Chapter 10.

The variety of activities and intents which may be engaged in online has meant that the term cybercrime has come to encompass a range of activities and has not yet achieved a single agreed definition. Definitions include, '*crime committed using a computer and the internet to steal a person's identity or sell contraband or stalk victims or disrupt operations with malevolent programs*', which is used by Princeton University (n.d.). It has also been defined as '*a term used broadly to describe activity in which computers or computer networks are the tool, target, or place of criminal activity. Cybercrime takes a number of forms including identity theft, internet fraud, violation of copyright laws through file-sharing, hacking, computer viruses, denial of service attacks, and spam*', in the *New World Encyclopedia* (n.d.). The IT security company Symantec (n.d.) defines two categories of cybercrime: '*Type I, examples of this type of cybercrime include but are not limited to phishing, theft or manipulation of data or services via hacking or viruses, identity theft, and bank or e-commerce fraud. Type II cybercrime includes but is not limited to activities such as cyberstalking and harassment, child predation, extortion, blackmail, stock market manipulation, complex corporate espionage, and planning or carrying out terrorist activities*'. More succinct definitions include, '*crimes perpetrated over the internet, typically having to do with online fraud*' (*PC Magazine Encyclopedia*, n.d.) or '*crime committed using the internet, for example stealing someone's personal information or introducing harmful programs into someone's computer*' (*Macmillan Dictionary*, n.d.). This chapter takes a broad definition of the term cybercrime and assumes it to cover a variety of activities which may range from those which are clearly breaches of criminal law to those which could more accurately be described as harassment.

Summary box 2.1 Online crime
- Technology has facilitated the commission of some quite traditional crimes such as theft and fraud.
- New crimes such as hacking have also emerged due to the prevalence of technology.
- Cybercrime does not have a single definition but is an evolving concept as dependent on the technology which facilitates it as the activities it involves.

Four responses to cybercrime

A number of approaches to dealing with the issue of cybercrime have been tried. Governments, corporations, individuals and service providers all have an interest in dealing effectively with cybercrime. To date, their activities and initiatives have often been independent of each other; however, their combined effect is largely positive and mutually reinforcing. This section will look at how these four groups have approached the problem of cybercrime.

Government response, the law of the land

There are a number of views about the need for 'cyberlaws'. One argument is that rules for online activities in cyberspace need to come from territorial states (Goldsmith, 1998). Another view is that there is a case for considering cyberspace as a different place where we can and should make new rules. Johnson and Post (1996) were among the first to argue that cyberspace constitutes a new and different space where different rules must apply. Their argument was that in the offline world there is generally a correspondence between borders drawn in physical space, between nation states, and borders in legal space. The point at which one set of laws stops and another starts is normally at the physical border of a country. This correspondence results from four interrelated considerations. The first is the *power* to control a space: law making requires an ability to enforce the law and impose sanctions; this is done by national governments. The second is the *effect* of a law given the proximity of the lawmaker to those affected. A third consideration is the *legitimacy* of the law, or the degree to which the law is implemented with the consent of the governed. Finally, there is the *notice* given to those affected by the law, or the warnings provided to those affected to abide by a given law. The advent of the internet has broken the link between geography and these four principles. How does an individual know where the other individuals, services or institutions might be located or what rules, if any, apply?

Is there a virtual space or cyberspace where traditional legal systems have no jurisdiction, where a new order can be built by the inhabitants of that space? The idea of cyberspace as a place you can go to where new laws might apply is supported by the fact that you must make a decision to go there, normally by deciding to access a computer and enter a password. In this sense there is a boundary you cross to get 'there'. David Post (1996, p. 168) suggested that it may be that cyberspace could signal the 'final days of a governance system relying on individual sovereign states as [the] primary law-making authority, a system that has served us, often for better and sometimes for worse, for the last half millennium'.

The governance of this new virtual space could take a number of forms. A centralised system of control would involve coordination among the existing sovereign powers and some form of multi-lateral agreement or 'Grand Internet Treaty'. The establishment of international governing bodies similar to the World Trade Organization would also be needed. An alternative option would be the decentralisation of law making and the development of processes which do not seek to impose a framework of law but which allow one to emerge. In this case, individual service providers would develop their own systems of governance and standards of behaviour. The law would come from the bottom up as users select the services, products and environment that match their own standards of behaviour and ethics. In this scenario our understanding of justice may change as we see what emerges from un-coerced individual choice (Post, 1996, p. 167).

It should be noted at this point that the growing familiarity with the online world and the growing proportion of the population that is spending time online has undermined this view of the internet as a separate space. This is particularly true among younger users who have never known a world without an online component. Shirky (2009, p. 196) argues that 'the internet augments real world social life rather than providing an alternative to it. Instead of becoming a separate cyberspace, our electronic networks are becoming embedded in real life'.

Different approaches to cybercrime have been tried; for example, the Council of Europe developed a *Convention on Cybercrime* (Council of Europe, 2001) whereas in the US there is a *National Strategy to Secure Cyberspace* (US Department of Homeland Security, 2003). Europe's convention was created to 'pursue a common criminal policy aimed at the protection of society against cybercrime, especially by adopting appropriate legislation and fostering international co-operation'. It deals particularly with infringements of copyright, computer-related fraud, child pornography and violations of network security. The US's national strategy is part of the greater 'Homeland Security' project and is focused on preventing the use of the internet for the facilitation of a terrorist attack.

Private or corporate response, the rules of the game

Cannataci and Mifsud-Bonnici (2007, p. 60) make the case that 'there is developing a mesh of private and state rules and remedies which are independent and complementary'. This language is echoed by Eckersley (2007, p. 81) who talks of the 'mutual enmeshment' of law and politics and the 'constitutive tensions' between the regulative ideals of treaty law and the actual production of treaty law. In terms of the law as users of the internet community experience it they often adopt rules and remedies based on their fitness for purpose. State regulation may be appropriate to control certain activities, technical standards may be more appropriate in other situations and private regulation may be appropriate where access to state courts or processes is impossible. The intertwining of state and private regulation is both inevitable and necessary to provide real-time solutions to millions of online customers and consumers. This should lead to greater collaboration between private groups and states in the development and administration of rules. The mesh of regulation, just like the mesh of a fishing net, is more effective in catching larger participants than smaller ones. Corporate organisations are more likely to comply with regulations than individuals; thus the task of governance is to reduce the gaps in the mesh. Swire (2005, p. 1,975) uses the metaphor of elephants and mice to explain this situation:

[E]lephants are organizations that will be subject to the law, while mice can hope to ignore it. Elephants are large companies or other organizations that have major operations in a country. Elephants are powerful and have a thick skin, but are impossible to hide. They are undoubtedly subject to a country's jurisdiction. Once laws are enacted, they likely will have to comply. By contrast mice are small and mobile actors, such as pornography sites or copyright violators, who can reopen immediately after being kicked off a server or can move offshore. Mice breed annoyingly quickly – new sites can open at any time. Where harm over the Internet is caused by mice, hidden in crannies in the network, traditional legal enforcement is more difficult.

> ### Activity 2.2 Rules of the game
> Review the governance structure of a game like *EverQuest* or *World of Warcraft* from the perspective of the balance of power between the publisher, the developer and the players. Review the analysis of Sal Humphreys (2008) in her paper 'Ruling the virtual world – governance in massively multiplayer online games'. *European Journal of Cultural Studies*, May, **11** (2), 149–71.

Technical response, the law as code

Much of what can or cannot be done online is in the hands of the technologists who have built the network and infrastructure. Sitting on top of this is the software used to create the environments of social networks which are themselves limited by their technical specifications. The computers used to access the internet have further limitations, some by design and others through various security software installed by the user, their employer, parent or, in some cases, the state. The internet is populated with firewalls, antivirus software and restricted domains. It is a web of security that on the one hand offers a system of protection or control and on the other hand presents a challenge to those hackers inclined to see such measures as an anathema to the spirit of the internet.

The choices that are made about what is or is not appropriate behaviour can be made by technologists and designers rather than public representatives or the judiciary. These are normative choices which have far reaching impacts. For example, the design of Facebook made certain normative assumptions about privacy which may be consistent with the thinking of young, liberal, North American IT professionals, but may not align with other sections of society. Some aspects of what can and cannot be done, or even what may be considered right or wrong, will be determined by software engineers. They will find ways to prevent file-sharing or illegal downloading or many other elements of our online activities. Blocking or filtering software has largely removed the need for states to struggle with issues of censorship as they did in the late 1990s. These issues are well discussed by Lessig (2000) in his book *Code and Other Laws of Cyberspace*. If individuals can control the flow of information to their (or their child's) computer there is less need for the state to try the impossible and eliminate it from the web. The challenge for these 'technical governors' of behaviour is their ability to recognise the possibilities of their role.

Whether at national, corporate or end-user level, the option of responding to inappropriate or illegal behaviour through technology rather than regulation offers a lower cost 'soft law' approach which is expanded on later in this chapter. However, unless the technical solutions to, for example, distributing a malicious virus are backed up by some form of legal impediment with clear consequences, they will be viewed as no more than a technical challenge by some.

User response, negotiated law

Private regulations exist in the realm of codes of behaviour agreed among groups of users or laid down by commercial organisations that provide a service or social networking environment. One example of establishing standards of behaviour is online dispute resolution (ODR). The growth of ODR was 'not intended to challenge or displace an existing legal regime but to fill a vacuum where the authority of law was absent' (Katsh, 2007, p. 99). Katsh describes a number of experiments with ODR: a virtual magistrate to aid in disputes between internet service providers (ISPs) and users, an online ombudsman office to offer a general dispute resolution service (run by the University of Massachusetts) and an ODR to resolve family disputes (proposed by the University of Maryland).

The online auction site eBay is an example of a company whose ability to be successful is dependent on the trust of its customers that goods and services will exchange at agreed prices and that buyers and sellers will act in good faith. The feedback rating system goes some way to providing this assurance, but when disputes arise there needed to be an effective process for dispute resolution. eBay engaged an internet start-up, SquareTrade.com, to provide this service. By automating the process and using web pages with forms and options to choose from, rather than an open-ended email system, SquareTrade is able to handle many millions of individual disputes each year.

Social networking sites are also self-governing, either by the collective will of the users or by the use of moderators. Behaviour on such sites that is considered inappropriate by other users causes a reaction and can lead to exclusion. The choice of moderation style is important in influencing the nature of the online conversations and the ethos of the environment. Wright (2006) outlined two broad types of moderation that are used in British and European government-run online discussion forums. These are content moderation, which can be either automated or manual, and interactive moderation, which has a broader remit. Interactive moderation requires a range of roles for the moderator such as replying to messages, encouraging people to join the debate and providing summaries. Interactive moderation is similar to Edwards' (2002) description of the moderator as a 'democratic intermediary'.

There is currently a multi-faceted approach to the control of unacceptable behaviour online. Criminal activity continues to be addressed by national laws, and greater cooperation between states is the best route to all forms of crime that cross national borders. Civil wrongs where possible are addressed through the service provider and in some cases via the civil courts. Other antisocial activity, of the hacking or spamming variety, is tackled by technical solutions where possible, and the cat and mouse game between hackers and the software security industry continues. However, the more we are living and interacting online the more examples we see of attempts to provide online solutions to online problems. At the moment this is largely at the lower end of a scale of cost, or level of serious wrongdoing, but perhaps it gives clues to future solutions. This intertwining of state, private and technical solutions is likely to continue to develop as the de facto model of internet governance.

Summary box 2.2 Responses to cybercrime

- There are a number of ways to respond to online behaviours that are considered unacceptable, whether illegal or not. These include legal, rule based, technical or user-enforced responses.
- The legal route is important particularly for behaviour that has an offline impact.
- Rule-based systems can work well if non-compliance can be detected and suitable penalties or exclusions implemented.
- Technical restrictions can prevent certain behaviour.
- User control can be an important social deterrent.
- No one of these offers a complete solution.
- Taken together they appear to offer an effective response to most online activities.

A soft law approach

In considering a framework of law for the internet, there are lessons to be learnt from international law. In an interconnected world, individual states have less autonomy and it is increasingly important to include non-state actors. There is also a risk of loss of legitimacy as power moves further from individual citizens and states seek to pool authority and sovereignty. One feature of international law is the emergence of soft law as a more effective solution than hard law in many multi-state situations. Hard law is defined as the rules and regulations that make up legal systems in the traditional sense, and soft laws as those which consist of informal rules which are non-binding but, due to cultural norms or standards of conduct, have practical effect. Senden (2004, p. 3) similarly defines soft law as

Rules of conduct that are laid down in instruments which have not been attributed legally binding forces as such, but nevertheless may have certain (indirect) legal effects, and that are aimed at and may produce practical effects.

Hard law can provide a basis for enforcement by setting standards for acceptable behaviour with reputational consequences if breached. A system of centralised enforcement through, for example, an international body like the United Nations Security Council or the International Monetary Fund is also possible. Hard law can also be seen in situations where international commitments are incorporated into domestic law. States may choose the hard law route when (a) the benefits of cooperation are high and the costs of breach are also high; (b) when non-compliance may be difficult to detect; (c) when states wish to form alliances such as the European Union (EU) or North Atlantic Treaty Organization (NATO); (d) when domestic agencies are given power to make agreements with little control from the executive; and (e) when a state is seeking to enhance its international credibility (Abbott and Snidal, 2000, p. 429). However, hard law does entail significant costs and can restrict countries' behaviour and sovereignty. In the context of hard versus soft law, cost refers to the potential for inferior outcomes, loss of authority and reduction in sovereignty.

In the early days of the internet the instinct of governments was to solve the perceived problems of control by hard law. For example in the US the Clinton administration tried on many occasions to pass laws to control pornography online. The Communications Decency Act (1996) was followed by the Child Online Protection Act (1998), which was followed by the Children's Internet Protection Act (1999). All were passed into law; all were challenged in the courts under freedom of speech issues. Only the Children's Internet Protection Act survived the challenges but as it was limited to controlling usage in public libraries, and with libraries given the option to opt in or out, it is effectively redundant. It is this struggle that conventional law making has with the internet that Boyle (1997, p. 189) had previously recognised when he said

Federal judges had come a long way towards recognizing both the technological resistance of the Internet to censorship and the fact that a global net could never be effectively regulated by a single national jurisdiction.

Soft law reduces the cost by limiting one or more of the dimensions of obligation, precision or delegation. Escape clauses can be added, commitments can be imprecise, or delegation to sub-state bodies to facilitate future political change can be added. Rather than seeing these elements as undermining the law, they can be seen as allowing states to enter agreements without threat to sovereignty, allowing for future uncertainty, and lowering the barriers to future, harder legalisation. In choosing between hard and soft law solutions, states face a trade-off between the advantages and disadvantages of both. Soft law can lessen sovereignty cost by offering a range of institutional agreements from which states can choose. Soft law offers an effective way to deal with uncertainty, especially when it initiates processes that allow actors to learn about the impact of agreements over time. Uncertainty presents a major challenge for institutions of international governance and is considered below in the context of Cooney and Lang's (2007) writing on adaptive governance.

Soft law offers techniques for compromise and cooperation between states and private actors. Non-state organisations will normally press for hard law solutions to raise the cost of violation by other parties; however, soft law may be both more achievable (as private actors may lack the ability to enter binding treaties) and also more flexible to changing circumstances.

States and non-state actors can achieve many of their goals through soft legalization that is more easily attained or even preferable ... Soft law is valuable on its own, not just as a steppingstone to hard law. Soft law provides a basis for efficient international 'contracts', and it helps create normative 'covenants' and discourses that can reshape international politics.

(Abbott and Snidal, 2000, p. 456)

States will often opt for a soft law solution if substantive agreements are impossible to attain. Soft law can provide opportunities for deliberation, systematic comparisons and learning (Schäfer, 2006). It may not commit a government to a policy but it may achieve the desired result by moral persuasion and peer pressure. It may also allow a state to engage with an issue otherwise impossible for domestic reasons and open the possibility for more substantive agreements in the future.

The relative legitimacy of hard versus soft laws can depend on the society they are seeking to govern. In the context of online social networks, soft laws have a power and system of enforcement more effective than the hard laws that might attempt to assert legitimacy.

> ### Activity 2.3 Soft law
> Make a list of the environments you spend time in, or activities you participate in, where you feel subject to soft laws; laws which would be difficult to enforce but are followed by social convention. Examples might include social networks, business emails, sports clubs or social gatherings. Can you identify 'laws' or 'norms' you would find difficult to break despite their lacking any force of law?

In considering the appropriate legal framework for the international realm of the internet, the nature of both the activities taking place and the individuals and organisations using the internet needs to be considered. The legitimacy or appropriateness of hard versus soft laws depends on the society they are seeking to legalise. In the context of online social networks, soft laws have a power and potential for support which may make them more effective than the hard laws that might attempt to assert legitimacy. The confluence of states, individuals, businesses and other non-state actors that make up the legal, regulatory and technical web of behaviours that constitute the internet makes it somewhat unique. As Eckersley (2007, p. 80) said,

[T]reaty making is shaped and constrained, on the one hand by the deeper constitutional structure and associated norms of international society, and on the other hand by the particular roles, interests and identities of those State and non-State actors involved in the rule making process.

As McArthur (2008, p. 60) argues, in the global governance arena soft power has become an important means of achieving behaviour-changing outcomes, both within and beyond the proper jurisdictions of nation states. Non-state actors (such as corporations) may exercise power above, below and around the state, so that they may advance political objectives even where they fail to secure regulation and other forms of governmental action (Spiro, 1998, p. 809). This seemingly unstructured mechanism allows non-state actors to govern extra-institutionally.

A second part of the framework for considering law on the internet can be taken from the writing of Cooney and Lang (2007). They describe a need to develop flexible and adaptive international institutions, to respond to rapidly changing global conditions, as well as to changes in our knowledge of the causes of global problems. They also describe the recent development of learning-centred alternatives to traditional command-and-control regulatory frameworks, variously described as 'experimentalist' governance, 'reflexive' governance or 'new' governance. Elements of these approaches contribute to what Cooney and Lang call 'adaptive' governance.

The key elements of this adaptive governance are, firstly, its focus on facilitating continuous learning as a response to uncertainty and systemic unpredictability, redefining the problem and revisiting the question of what constitutes relevant 'knowledge' about a particular problem. Secondly, adaptive governance sees policy making as experimentation. It is a process of 'learning by doing', and treating policy interventions as quasi-experiments. Finally, adaptive governance is an iterative process of review and revision. Monitoring and feedback mechanisms help facilitate learning, not only by fine-tuning the particular policy instruments chosen, but also by drawing attention to relevant knowledge gaps. Policy making is less about the attainment of a single optimal solution and more about providing a forum for the on-going creation of consensual knowledge and agreed processes to guide policy.

Adaptive governance accepts and responds to uncertainty through promoting learning, avoiding irreversible interventions and impacts, encouraging constant monitoring of outcomes, facilitating broad participation in policy-making processes, encouraging transparency, and reflexively highlighting the limitations of the knowledge on which policy choices are based.

(Cooney and Lang, 2007, p. 1)

In common with the thinking demonstrated above when discussing soft law, adaptive governance allows for a wider participation in the formulation of policy and law. Furthermore, it allows for an iterative or progressive approach to policy making and law making. The solution needs to come from state, citizen and corporation; the solution will develop over time as knowledge, systems, and technologies develop.

The identities and interests of States can be shaped by both domestic and transnational discursive practices, and NGOs [non-governmental organisations] are increasingly significant to any understanding of the discursive processes and legitimacy of multilateral agreements.

(Eckersley, 2007, p. 105)

An example of soft law in the area of cyberlaw is the Council of Europe's Convention on Cybercrime (Council of Europe, 2001). In fact what Slaughter (2004, p. 264) describes as the 'vibrant laboratory' of the European Union provides many lessons on how to establish the necessary degree of collective cooperation among a diverse group of states and yet maintain the locus of political power at national level. Another example is the United Nations General Assembly, which initiated a World Summit on the Information Society (WSIS) to offer a further platform for the development of principles and guidelines. The first phase took place in Geneva in 2003 and the second in Tunis in 2005 (World Summit on the Information Society, 2010).

Other areas where a soft law approach has worked in an international context are outlined by Sindico (2006) and include forestry, labour rights and sustainable development. Sindico goes on to describe soft law as a 'pioneer' of hard law. Soft law and voluntary standards in particular are a stage in the creation of legal norms. They are necessitated by the challenge of sustainable global governance. However, in the case of the law of the internet it is unclear if soft law can be seen as a route to hard law.

The particular prevalence of non-state actors in the creation and management of the virtual space and the uniquely strong position of technical standards and rules in the governing of that space make the route to a hard law solution non-linear at best and opaque at worst.

Perhaps the main soft laws, if they can be called that, are the very technical standards that underpin the internet itself. These are set out in the requests for comments (RFCs) run by the Internet Engineering Task Force (IETF) but have largely emerged as technical standards from discussions between various parties, rather than being decreed in the form of hard law. This is quite a peculiar situation given that under present law the definition of nearly every product is formally set down in hard law regulation.

These ideas of soft law and adaptive governance offer further lessons to the notion of a structure of laws for the internet. Systems of informal rules may not be binding but have effect through a shared understanding of their benefits. Adaptable law is flexible and open to change as knowledge develops. Agreements include state and non-state actors, and involve both the citizen and business. Finally, soft law offers lessons on continuous learning in a changing environment, resulting in an evolving system of laws.

Summary box 2.3 Soft law and adaptive governance

- International law has shown that a soft law approach using guidelines and norms may be more effective than a hard law or regulatory approach.
- A system of adaptive governance, where policy making is not definitive but experimental and governance is seen as a learning and changing process, is suited to online governance.
- In some fields, soft law has been used as a precursor to hard law. This may not be a possible route for the regulation of online behaviour due to the inherent dynamic of change online.

Governance

The World Bank sets out a definition of governance as the interplay of four elements: policy making, bureaucracy, an executive and a strong civil society.

Good governance is epitomized by predictable, open, and enlightened policymaking (that is, a transparent process); a bureaucracy imbued with a professional ethos; an executive arm of government accountable for its actions; a strong civil society participating in public affairs; and all behaving under the rule of law.

(World Bank, 1994, p. vii)

Is it possible that the internet and its virtual worlds could be governed? A centralised system of control involving coordination among the existing sovereign powers is one governance option. However, the structure of international society is anarchic, in the sense that there could be no world government to enforce international legal norms (Eckersley, 2007, p. 81).

[W]orld government is both infeasible and undesirable. We need more government on a global and a regional scale, but we don't want the centralization of decision making power and coercive authority so far from the people actually governed.

(Slaughter, 2004, p. 8)

It does not seem likely that a 'grand internet treaty' could be agreed between different independent states with different cultures, values, norms and traditions. At the 2005 International Summit on the Information Society in Tunis, internet governance was defined as:

the development and application by governments, the private sector, and civil society, in their respective roles, of shared principles, norms, rules, decision making procedures and programmes, that shapes the evolution and utilization of the Internet.

(Working Group on Internet Governance, 2005, p. 4)

The decentralisation of law making and the development of processes which do not seek to impose a framework of law but which allow one to emerge is one way in which governance may evolve. Service providers would develop their own systems of governance and standards of behaviour. The law would come from the bottom up as users select the services, products and environment that match their own standards of behaviour and ethics. In the example cited previously of the stolen sword in the game Legend of Mir 3, strong internal governance either through user-agreed ethics or technical restrictions could have provided the 'victim' of theft with some opportunity for redress. It could also have provided some form of punishment, perhaps through the exclusion of the perpetrator of the theft. This might have been sufficient to address the sense of loss and helplessness that presumably led to the subsequent offline crime. Our understanding of justice may change as we see what emerges from un-coerced individual choice (Post, 1996).

The appropriate legal or ethical framework in one context or virtual environment may be quite different in another. MacSíthigh (2008) argues that the increased availability of user-generated content is influencing the development of cyberlaw. As individuals and businesses develop more content, services and applications, the ability of the state to keep up with appropriate legislation or even guidelines is limited. MacSíthigh lists several examples of self-regulation and co-regulation of activities online. For example, a joint government/industry group like the Broadband Strategy Group in the UK has established guidelines for British media producers. In other cases, governments have drafted codes of behaviour for industry groups which are observed on a voluntary basis (MacSíthigh, 2008, p. 86).

Foucault wrote about power as being a function of surveillance, our behaviour being influenced by the knowledge that all of our actions online can be recorded, monitored or directed. In this sense technical solutions offer part of the solution to governance of the internet. 'Power is not ensured by right but by technique, not by law but by normalization, not by punishment but by control' (Foucault, 1978, p. 138). This control may be exercised by the state but is often in the hands of the commercial organisations that design and develop the technologies we use. As an example of this Yang (2006) describes the situation in China where the internet both provides the most fundamental channel and dynamic of online activism in China and raises the bar of political control. He argues that the internet is not a completely free realm and that the regime of internet control in China has evolved along three axes. The first is social and political control (arresting a cyber-dissident or assigning bulletin board managers to censor posts), the second is technological control (filtering of keywords and blocking of websites) and the third is psychological control. According to Yang, the first two kinds of control, when widely known to internet users, have the effect of a panopticon. A panopticon is a type of building designed to allow an observer to see all the occupants of an institution without them being able to tell whether or not they are being watched. This concept was invoked by Michel Foucault (1975) as a metaphor for modern 'disciplinary' societies and their pervasive inclination to observe and normalise. By accustoming citizens to the idea that they are always watched, the agents of control may induce self-disciplined and conformist behaviour.

The way in which we are increasingly living our lives online and leaving digital fingerprints wherever we go is a phenomenon so recent that we do not yet know the full implications. Each time we download an app to our phone that requires our location or some other information, we exchange our privacy for the convenience or utility offered by the software. Our personal history in pictures, text messages, blogs, profiles, films and so on will remain behind us indefinitely and take on a life of its own. Governance by surveillance is all the more powerful a concept with so much of our lives now digitally recorded. Carroll and Romano (2011) and Massimi et al. (2010) have looked at what happens to our data after we die and how digital artefacts might be passed on in the same way as physical ones. In the near future passwords may be left in wills to those who come after us and systems designed to span multiple lifetimes.

Activity 2.4 A digital life

Consider the number of digital environments that you engage in, from online banking and shopping to social networks and online games. What would a list of those activities reveal about the way you live your life? What record of your life and activities will remain after you and how will you pass on those digital records in your will? Make a list of all those you consider worth retaining and those you would prefer disappeared.

It is important when thinking about how the online citizen may be governed to consider the relationship between governments and technology. The first serious attempt by governments to embrace new technologies as a method for improving governance was as part of the New Public Management (NPM) agenda of the late 1980s and early 1990s. NPM was about breaking up monopolistic public-service structures. It sought to use incentives to influence activities and adopted private sector management techniques. This appealed to the Thatcher and Reagan administrations in the 1980s who blamed 'Big Government' for the global economic downturn of that time (Evans, 2009, p. 38). NPM administrative reform was market based, competence based and with an emphasis on deregulation and governance. These four categories of changes came from the view that a public organisation could be analysed in the same manner as a firm.

NPM led to the first steps being taken by governments towards using technology under the term eGovernment. This was driven by the desire to improve efficiency and to replicate private sector management practices. Inevitably the starting point in the use of technology was in service delivery. Existing processes were replicated in new and more efficient ways, mostly by putting repetitive tasks, like form filling and information provision, online. Few, however, were making use of the additional functionality of the technology to do new things. Morison and Newman (2001, p. 1) put this well when they state, 'It may be that any efficiency gains that are made by reinventing government and viewing it as just another provider are at the expense of an opportunity to use technology to more fundamentally reinvent democracy and re-work the relationship between citizen and state'.

Communications technologies available through the internet offer the state new ways of engaging the public. The expansion of the use of communications technologies has led governments to move beyond the efficiency mantra of NPM, and alternative ways of thinking about governance have emerged. These have included network governance, Public Value Management (PVM) and Digital-Era Governance (DEG). NPM was based on the principles of disaggregation, competition and incentivisation. Dunleavy *et al.* (2005) make the case that a range of information technology-centred changes are leading to reintegration, needs-based holism and digitisation in a move they call Digital-Era Governance (DEG). The reintegration of functions into government, the building of holistic needs-oriented structures and the progression of the digitalisation of administrative processes combine to reverse some of the changes introduced by NPM.

The first wave of eGovernment was focused on the back office: systems were automated, tasks were simplified and some processes were put online but essentially the system remained unchanged. The growth of the internet and the capabilities of Web 2.0, in terms of social networking technologies, mobile computing and the general pervasiveness of the online life of the nation, represents opportunities for structural changes in the way public services are understood, accessed and delivered. Although the term Web 2.0 suggests a new version of the World Wide Web, it does not refer to an update of any technical specifications, but rather to cumulative changes in the ways software developers and end-users engage with the web. Specific features of Web 2.0 applications include interactive information sharing, interoperability, user-centred design and collaboration. Examples of Web 2.0 applications include web-based communities, hosted services, social networking sites, video-sharing sites, wikis, blogs, mashups (combining data from multiple sources to provide a new service) and folksonomies (from taxonomy or collective tagging) or categorisation. A Web 2.0 site allows its users to interact with other users or to change website content, in contrast to non-interactive websites where users are limited to the passive viewing of information that is provided to them. Large-scale switchovers to the use of email and the evolution of websites from 'shop windows' to the core of the service are examples of this. Two trigger points in this evolution may be: firstly, the point at which the electronic version of every file is considered the authoritative version and a hard copy only printed as needed; and secondly, the point at which a government agency no longer 'has' a website but rather 'is' a website (Dunleavy *et al.*, 2006, p. 153).

Technology allows for the reintegration of services so that, for the citizen, a single point of engagement is possible with state services. This holistic approach should allow reduction in the duplication of information and form filling as the citizen can enter information once, and go to a single source to be directed to the service needed. Hood (1983, cited in Dunleavy *et al.*, 2005) argued that it was not sufficient for governments just to deliver services, but they needed to actively do *information seeking* to establish needs. The two-way dialogue, made possible by changes in the digital era, brings this concept of a connected citizenry ever closer.

For these digitisation changes to be effective and truly cost-saving in both time and resources they need to run instead of conventional administrative processes and not in parallel to them. This movement to DEG would thus need to be driven by a combination of incentive and removal of traditional channels. Governments will have to actively manage the displacement of service users to the new electronic channels (Dunleavy *et al.*, 2005, p. 487).

Activity 2.5 A governmental one stop shop
Consider the advantages of having all of your data and interactions available through a single portal. Do the advantages of efficiency, and joined-up government services, outweigh the potential disadvantages? Does sharing of medical data lead to better healthcare or higher insurance premiums?

This concept of governance is both in its early stages of development and yet at a tipping point in terms of public demand/readiness to accept these kinds of changes to the way they engage with the state. The level of citizen engagement is higher and the combining of services in a more holistic approach to service delivery will result in an outcomes approach rather than an inputs or outputs approach. The reliance on electronic engagement will provide a wealth of comprehensive data on the level of citizen/state engagement, and the evaluation of performance may be limited by the quantity of data rather than the lack of it. In parallel with the development of service delivery technologies, advances in data mining and data gathering technologies may address this evaluative issue. Much work has been done on user surveys, customer forums and online dispute resolution in the private sector from which evaluators in the public sector can benefit.

What all of these alternative views of governance have in common is an attempt to broaden out the governance structure to a range of government and non-government actors. The technologies available through Web 2.0 innovations allow for new ways for the state to communicate with citizens. It is clear that many parts of both traditional government and the general population are not yet quite ready for this leap of faith but it is equally clear that this is the direction in which governance is moving.

Summary box 2.4 Governance

- The governance of the internet is unlikely to take the form of some 'Grand Internet Treaty'.
- It is more likely that a framework of governance will emerge and may vary depending on the nature of the activity engaged in.
- The digital tracks of all of our online activity are likely to lead to changes in our behaviour.
- The relative merit of enhanced services and the consequent impact on privacy creates a dichotomy in which we trade convenience for privacy.

Social networking

Social networking is changing the distinction between traditional notions of media and modern forms of communication, by blurring the lines between personal messages and publicly available forums. This gives a public voice to individuals and allows for an engagement with society that was not previously accessible. Shirky (2009) sees the capacity of social networks to facilitate group forming as a key benefit.

A desire to be part of a group that shares, cooperates, or acts in concert is a basic human instinct that has always been constrained by transaction costs. Now that group forming has gone from hard to ridiculously easy, we are seeing an explosion of experiments with new groups and new kinds of groups.

(Shirky, 2009, p. 54)

He further argues that this 'wiring of humanity' lets us treat free time as a shared global resource, and lets us design new kinds of participation and sharing that take advantage of that resource (Shirky, 2010, p. 27). The use of these technologies is not limited to younger, more technology-aware users nor is it limited to affluent western societies. According to Sunstein (2007, p. 17), 'in both the domestic and in the international context, that problem [the digital divide] seems likely to diminish over time, as new technologies, above all the internet, are made increasingly available to people regardless of their income or wealth'.

According to the International Telecommunication Union (ITU, 2011), one-third of the world's population of 7 billion people are using the internet. Developing countries have increased their share of the world's total number of internet users from 44 per cent in 2006, to 62 per cent in 2011. The explosion in mobile phone use has been driven not only by developed countries, but by developing nations. Again, according to the ITU, there are over 5.9 billion mobile-cellular subscriptions, global penetration is 87 per cent overall and 79 per cent in the developing world. Mobile broadband subscriptions have grown 45 per cent annually over the last four years and today there are twice as many mobile broadband as fixed broadband subscriptions. The mobile phone is fast becoming the device of choice for access to the internet, leaving laptop and desktop computers behind. Hamadoun Touré, the Secretary-General of the ITU, speaking in February 2010, said,

Even the simplest, low-end mobile phone can do so much to improve health care in the developing world, good examples include sending reminder messages to patients' phones when they have a medical appointment or need a pre-natal check-up, or using SMS messages to deliver instructions on when and how to take complex medication such as anti-retrovirals or vaccines. It's such a simple thing to do, and yet it saves millions of dollars and can help improve and even save the lives of millions of people.

(UN News Service, 2010)

Flexible, cheap and inclusive media offer opportunities to do all sorts of things we once did not or could not do. In a study by the Pew Research Centre, those using social networks were 2.5 times more likely to attend a political rally or meeting, 57 per cent more likely to persuade someone to vote and 43 per cent more likely to say they would vote (Evangelista, 2011). The increase in political engagement is suggested to stem from the fact that Facebook members tend to become more aware of issues from those in their network who are politically active. It acts as a 'social sharing machine', increases the visibility of issues and 'speeds up that collective action model'.

The literature shows us that governance should be considered in its broadest sense. The advances in social networking technologies are providing us with the tools to rebuild social capital and encourage group working. This in turn is providing the opportunity to build civic engagement and introduce the skills of governance at a local level. These technologies are no longer the sole preserve of younger or better-resourced individuals but are rather becoming universally available.

The digital divide based on age is also narrowing. Technology once requiring advanced and specialised knowledge to understand and operate is becoming better and simpler to use. Advances in our understanding of human computer interaction and usability engineering, combined with the natural progression of technology from novel to normal, is reducing this divide. In the 1920s one used to have to be a skilled mechanic to drive a car and in the 1970s a programmer to use a computer. Today communication tools are becoming second nature to the most novice of user, young or old. As the digital divide diminishes, the acceptability of using technology for democratic engagement becomes more practical and more acceptable. The more people online, the larger the size, scale and efficiency of the communication 'market' (Couldry, 2007, p. 390).

The growth of social networks has been rapid and shows no signs of slowing. Sites aimed specifically at children include HabboHotel, Club Penguin and Barbie.com. These sites have users numbered in the hundreds of millions worldwide. Facebook, with a user population of 845 million as of December 2011, has more than 483 million daily active users (Protalinski, 2012). Social networks have also expanded the market for online interaction. The massive growth in computer games initially drove boys and young males to their laptops for interaction with their peers in massively multiplayer online role-playing games (MMORPGs). What gaming achieved for many young men, social networking has achieved for young women. Social networking is of course gender neutral but because it appeals to many young women more than gaming does, there is massive growth in the use of information and communications technology (ICT) in that segment. Gamers remain mostly male, although there is now growth in female participation in gaming. These issues are well discussed by Mazzarella (2005).

> ### Activity 2.6 A connected life
> Make a list of all the devices that your smartphone has replaced (address book, music player, watch, etc.). Make a list of the social networks you are registered with and the length of time since you last checked them. How would losing your phone and social networking connections impact on your daily life?

The greater connectedness of citizens, the increasing proportion of time spent on social networking sites and the growing range of activities engaged in has meant that these sites have become targets for the cybercriminal. Malware (computer viruses, worms, spyware and other malicious software) is discussed in detail in Chapter 4. Social networks have provided a new delivery mechanism for its distribution. Identity theft and online fraud, which are considered in Chapter 5, are also facilitated by the huge amounts of information now provided by individuals through their social networking activities. Social networks have also provided a new platform for cyberbullying and cyberstalking, Chapter 7 investigates both. All of these negative activities were previously carried out by email or text message or, in the case of malware, by hiding code within legitimate software or on portable storage devices. Social networks have provided a new platform and a wider audience to these activities.

However social networks have provided at least as many opportunities as they have risks. Individuals have become more responsible for the production and management of their own social and political identities. Young people enjoy unprecedented levels of freedom to define and manage their self-identities. This places increasing strains on governments to appeal to highly personalised political preferences that are hard to address, much less satisfy, than the broad group or class interests of an earlier era. Individual citizens, particularly younger ones who have grown up in this new environment, feel that their personalised expectations of politics are perfectly reasonable and often find that politics and politicians either ignore them or are far off the mark in their communication appeals (Bennett, 2008, p. 13).

Tapscott (2009, p. 245) points out that the 'net generation' are often portrayed as caring only about themselves and popular culture. This, he claims, is not true; they are demonstrating their engagement by their increase in volunteering. Through volunteering young people are seeking to address some of the most difficult problems such as poverty and global warming as well as local community issues. Tapscott also believes that young people do not feel powerless, citing a number of studies to support this view. Even the level of engagement by young people in conventional political activity is not always recognised. In the US John Della, the director of polling for the Harvard Institute of Politics, analysed the 2004 presidential election. He points out that while as a percentage the under 30s are not voting in the same numbers as the over 65s, because they greatly outnumber the over 65s they represent a much bigger voting bloc in absolute terms (cited in Tapscott, 2009, p. 247).

Human beings are innately social beings. As we are increasingly interconnected through social networks this is providing us with opportunities to express this social dimension and to be active in our many communities. As the concept of community has grown in our understanding of governance, social networking has been both supporting and reinforcing this behaviour. The growth in the perceived importance of self in the minds of younger voters and their desire, and increasing ability, to build and contribute to communities is providing them with a sense of identity as an actualising citizen. These new, younger, citizens are developing networks of trust and confidence in virtual spaces which are informing their behaviour in their communities and informing their sense of the polis.

The ability of social networks such as Facebook and others to facilitate the formation of groups and communities and to enable them to act collectively and promote communication is a critical extension of this process of enabling community governance activities. Research from Canada (Bernard, 2009, cited in Clarke, 2010, p. 7) showed that, despite low levels of voting among younger citizens, a large number were engaging in political activities on social networking sites. Around 52 per cent had started or joined a Facebook group or cause, 47 per cent went online to debate issues and 39 per cent had forwarded emails about causes. Research in the UK also shows that young citizens were more likely to use the internet to find information about politics and social causes (Di Gennaro and Dutton, 2006, cited in Clarke, 2010, p. 7). Bennett (2008, p. 8) argues that digital media provide young people with an important set of tools to build social and personal identity and to create the online and offline environments in which they spend their time.

It is important to expand our conception of politics and the political, as young people, both wittingly and unwittingly, push those bounds through their application of digital technologies. The politicians and public officials who represent the official world of politics to young people must learn more about their citizenship and communication preferences and how to engage with them. Young people themselves can better learn how to use information and media skills in ways that give them stronger and more effective public voices (Bennett, 2008, p. 10).

Benkler (2006) sees the nature of the internet as a democratising force. He sees it changing how individuals can interact with their democracy and experience their role as citizens.

The network allows all citizens to change their relationship to the public sphere. They no longer need to be consumers and passive spectators. They can become creators and primary subjects. It is in this sense that the Internet democratizes.

(Benkler, 2006, p. 272)

Social networking technologies provide the tools to build social capital and encourage group working. This, in turn, is providing the opportunity to build civic engagement and introduce the skills of governance at a local level. As we are increasingly interconnected through social networks this is providing us with opportunities to express this social dimension and to be active in our many communities. Younger citizens have a desire, and increasing ability, to build and contribute to communities. This is providing them with a sense of identity as an actualising citizen developing networks of trust and confidence in virtual spaces which are informing their behaviour in their communities.

Young, active citizens are finding new ways to engage through volunteering and networked digital media. Social networks have provided numerous examples, big and small, of young people's energy and desire to engage with each other and their communities to effect change. Digital media and social networking are both facilitating existing volunteering activities and opening up possibilities for community and social engagement in ways that were impossible before.

Summary box 2.5 Social networks

- Social networks have blurred the distinction between private and public communication.
- The combination of social networks and the mobile phone has provided a constant connectedness between a vast number of people who are in continuous communication.
- This pairing of technology has diminished the digital divide but also opened up the possibilities for cybercrime on a larger scale.
- The risks associated with storing so much personal information online and being in constant connection with the internet are matched by many positive and socially constructive benefits.

Conclusion

The internet continues to grow both in terms of functionality and number of participants. The amount of time spent by participants online also continues to grow. As we spend an increasing proportion of our day online and perform an increasing number of tasks there, the concept of a cybercitizen is a real and meaningful one. As cybercitizens, we need a framework of laws, rules or guidelines to maintain a sense of order online. Some of this framework is growing organically and some will be imposed. As governments increasingly see opportunities to engage with us online the emphasis may be on the latter. It is important to maintain this understanding of the way our actions will be monitored and restricted as we proceed to engage with the remaining chapters in this book.

Essay questions

(1) Online behaviours can be controlled in many different ways, and by different agencies. Describe these methods of control, with consideration to the circumstances under which behaviours should be managed by different entities.
(2) Which technologies have altered the relationship between citizen and state?
(3) What are the advantages and disadvantages of being constantly available to our network of friends on social networks?

Additional reading

Brooke, H. (2011). *The Revolution will be Digitised*. London: William Heinemann.
This book examines the balance between freedom and security and asks if privacy can still exist in an online world. It considers if the internet is empowering individuals or facilitating censorship, surveillance and oppression.

Hands, J. (2011). *@ is for Activism*. London: Pluto Press.
This book examines how politics has been changed by digital media, online social networking and mobile computing. It includes case studies on the antiwar and global justice movements, peer production, user-created TV and 'Twitter' activism.

Henman, P. (2010). *Governing Electronically*. New York: Palgrave Macmillan.
Using Foucault's governmentality approach, the nature of technology and government is examined in this book. Henman argues that information technology is more than just a tool for politicians and policy makers, but contributes to the nature of policy, power and citizenship.

Loader, D. and Mercea, D. (2012). *Social Media and Democracy: Innovations in Participatory Politics*. Oxford and New York: Routledge.
This book brings together a wide range of authors to examine the interaction between social media and politics. It provides an analysis of the importance of social media in civic engagement.

Websites

An overview of UK online law is available at JISC Legal: www.jisclegal.ac.uk.
Examples of online crime:

BBC News (31 March 2005). Game theft led to fatal attack. *Technology*. Retrieved from http://news.bbc.co.uk/1/hi/technology/4397159.stm.

(14 November 2007). 'Virtual theft' leads to arrest. *Technology*. Retrieved from http://news.bbc.co.uk/2/hi/technology/7094764.stm.

Emigh, J. (24 October 2008). Online gamer arrested for 'virtual murder' in Japan. *Betanews*. Retrieved from www.betanews.com/article/Online-gamer-arrested-for-virtual-murder-in-Japan/1224888499.

Guardian, The (24 October 2008). Japanese woman faces jail over online murder. Retrieved from www.guardian.co.uk/world/2008/oct/24/japan-games.

Irish Times, The (10 October 2008). Woman faces jail for hacking her virtual husband to death. Retrieved from www.irishtimes.com/newspaper/frontpage/2008/1025/1224838828960.html.

Morris, S. (14 November 2008). Internet affair leads to couple's real life divorce. *The Guardian*. Retrieved from www.guardian.co.uk/technology/2008/nov/14/second-life-virtual-worlds-divorce.

Reuters (30 March 2005). Gamer gets life for murder over virtual sword. *CNET*. Retrieved from http://news.cnet.co.uk/gamesgear/0,39029682,39189904,00.htm.

Truta, F. (18 January 2008). Russia – gamer kills gamer over gamer killing gamer . . . er, in-game! *Softpedia*. Retrieved from http://news.softpedia.com/news/Russia-Gamer-Kills-Gamer-over-Gamer-Killing-Gamer-Er-In-Game-76619.shtml.

3 | Hackers

Case studies

Former hacker Kevin Mitnick has made a career from advising on computer security and has authored a number of books on hacking, with a particular focus on social engineering methods (see, for example, Mitnick and Simon, 2002, 2005). He has admitted to breaking into the computer systems of several organisations, including the University of Southern California, Motorola, Fujitsu and Sun Microsystems. He used a variety of methods of infiltration, including social engineering, where he impersonated employees of some of the companies he victimised. He was sentenced to almost four years in prison, along with severely restricted access to computers for a further three years (US Department of Justice, 1999).

Adrian Lamo has also experienced a lot of publicity due to his hacking activities. His attempts to improve the security of firms led to mixed responses from the companies involved – some were highly appreciative of his efforts, while others filed lawsuits against him (see Mitnick and Simon, 2005). Probably his most famous hack involved infiltrating the *New York Times* private network and using their subscription to the search tool Lexis-Nexis, although he has had many other interesting hacking experiences (Kahn, 2004). More recently, Lamo has been in the news for turning in US military analyst Bradley Manning, after Manning reputedly 'boasted' to him about passing on confidential information to whistle-blowing website Wikileaks (BBC News Online, 7 June 2010).

Hacking victims are not restricted to companies. In 2011, the *News of the World* newspaper ceased publication after it emerged that journalists at the long-running publication had engaged in hacking of the voicemail accounts of approximately 800 mobile phone users (BBC News Online, 10 December 2011). These mobile phone users included several celebrities, but also some victims of serious crime and their families. In many cases the hacking of the voicemail accounts required little skill, as the users had not changed the voicemail passwords from their default settings.

One of the most interesting hackers from a psychological perspective is Gary McKinnon, who hacked into ninety-seven US government computers, including the US Navy and NASA (National Aeronautics and Space Administration), between 2001 and 2002, using the online name 'Solo'. His declared motive was 'to prove US intelligence had found an alien craft run on clean fuel' (BBC News Online, 28 July 2009, para. 3). McKinnon's actions do not seem to be those that most individuals would take – his hacking became an obsession, with consequences for other aspects of his life: he lost his job and girlfriend, and eventually stopped eating properly and neglected his personal hygiene. In hindsight he indicated that he 'almost wanted to be caught, because it was ruining me' (Boyd, 2008). McKinnon, a British citizen, is at the time of writing continuing to fight extradition to the US, despite admitting to the hacking charges, as it was feared that his mental health would be at risk if he was extradited. McKinnon has been diagnosed as having Asperger's Syndrome, an Autistic Spectrum Disorder, one of the symptoms of which can be the development of restricted, repetitive patterns of behaviour, interests and activities. McKinnon denies that his hacking was malicious in nature, or that it caused damage costing $800,000, although he faces up to seventy years in prison if convicted in the US, where prosecutors claim that he completed 'the biggest military computer hack of all time' (BBC News Online, 31 July 2009). This case is of particular interest due to the diagnosed nature of McKinnon's psychological status, to which his defence say the authorities in the UK have not given proper consideration. They suggest that if he was to be extradited, McKinnon would suffer 'disastrous consequences' and that he should be tried on lesser charges in the UK in order to protect his mental health (BBC News Online, 31 July 2009). They indicate that there is 'clear, uncontradicted expert evidence' that the stress of extradition could result in psychosis and suicide (BBC News, 9 June 2009), and later they indicated that he was suffering from 'very severe depression' (BBC News, 10 December 2009). While McKinnon may not be the most typical of hackers, his case is of particular interest due to the role that his psychological disorder may have played in the origin of his crimes, and the considerations that may need to be taken with regard to his punishment due to the psychological effects he may suffer.

Chapter overview

There have been many fictional representations of hackers, from movies such as *WarGames*, through to the iconic *Matrix* series. It appears that hackers have caught the imagination of viewers, but they have also proven to be popular with researchers. Indeed, it seems that no other type of cybercrime has received the level of interest among psychological researchers that hacking has. Nevertheless, in many cases this research is limited in scope, either only examining a small number of hackers, or being largely based on theoretical work.

This chapter will examine the research to date on hacking and hackers, though it should be considered that these terms are contentious, and have different meanings in different contexts. Indeed, there is a massive nomenclature associated with hacking, and labels vary according to whether or not the activity is malicious in nature, the methods used to achieve the goal and the skill level of the hacker, among many other factors. And so the first part of this chapter will examine some of these naming conventions, as well as attempting to gain an understanding of the level of hacking activity which occurs. The chapter will then attempt to examine the main methods which hackers use in order to achieve their goals. These methods can be technical or non-technical in nature, and many rely on a flaw in judgement on the part of a computer user. Next, the motives of hackers will be examined, which can vary from political causes, to vengeance, to financial reasons, to the relief of boredom, and many others. The psychological profile of hackers will then be described, considering aspects such as ethical position, personality traits and interpersonal relationships. These interpersonal relationships have particular importance for the subsequent section, examining hacking groups. The final two sections of the chapter will examine potential methods by which hackers may be punished, and potential prevention methods.

Definitions and prevalence rates

Before considering the psychology of hackers, it is necessary to understand that there has been a lot of contention regarding the use of the term 'hacking' itself, and different groups use it to describe different individuals. There are also many other terms that are used in the hacker sub-culture, and some of the most common of these will be examined here. In addition, an attempt will be made to determine the prevalence of hacking attacks, although this is an extremely difficult task to achieve for many reasons, including potential lack of awareness of victimisation, and the methods used to gather the statistics.

Hacking definitions

While we often think of hacking as a relatively recent activity, Levy (1984) suggests that it began in the late 1950s. He indicates that the first hackers were based at a few US universities at a time when computers were rare. These original hackers were motivated to use and improve computer technology, and many suggest that without them computers would not be as widespread as they are today. This use of the term hacking to describe legal activities is still prevalent, with many using the term to describe any attempt to improve or alter technology. In the early 1960s, the first incidents of hacking as a nuisance activity were noted, sometimes resulting in financial abuses, and the term 'hacking' to describe a criminal activity started to become established. When this occurred, the original, law-abiding hackers attempted to differentiate themselves from the criminal element by labelling the latter group 'crackers'. However, despite several attempts to invent such terms that allow differentiation, the vast majority of the general public and media sources still use 'hacking' to denote an activity where an individual gains unauthorised access to a computer system.

This is compounded by the lack of consistency in what those who are engaged in illegal activities call themselves. Sterling (1992) states that 'Nobody who hacks into systems willingly describes himself … as a "computer intruder", "computer trespasser", "cracker", "wormer", "darkside hacker" or "high-tech street gangster"' (p. 56), and suggests that most of these individuals instead choose to call themselves 'hacker'.

This is further compounded by a lack of consensus in academic literature regarding the relative definitions of hacking and cracking. For example, Simpson (2006, as cited in Tavani, 2011, p. 179) differentiates between the two by defining a hacker as anyone who 'accesses a computer system or network without authorisation from the owner' and a cracker as a hacker who has 'the intention of doing harm or destroying data', while many other authors use the term 'hacker' for both groups.

Another important distinction involves 'white-hat', 'black-hat' and 'grey-hat' hackers. The term 'white-hat' is used for those who enjoy working with computers, and who may infiltrate the systems of other individuals or groups, but who do not cause malicious damage in the process. In some cases 'white-hat' hackers are also termed 'ethical' hackers, but this designation is more commonly applied to company employees or consultants who are specifically tasked with finding exploits in order to make the system more secure, rather than external individuals who infiltrate a system without the prior permission of the organisation. It should be remembered that some 'white-hat hackers' who are not 'ethical hackers' are still involved in criminal activity, despite their intention not to cause malicious damage. This is because the attempt to gain unauthorised access to the computers or networks of other people or groups is still illegal in many jurisdictions, even if no damage is caused. Some white-hat hackers attempt to justify the infiltration by contacting the individual or group and warning them of the flaw in their security system. In fact, it has been reported that Adrian Lamo would offer to fix the security flaw he uncovered at no charge if the hacked organisation was appreciative of the information he provided (Kahn, 2004).

On the other hand, 'black-hat' hackers have the specific intent of carrying out some form of damaging action or of gaining unauthorised access to information or software without the intention of aiding the organisation to improve their security. A third group are the 'grey hat' hackers, a term used to describe hackers who search for exploits, but only disclose these exploits to the system administrators under certain circumstances, often in the hopes of monetary reward. In some cases, grey-hat hacking is used to describe a malicious attack that is orchestrated against an ethically dubious organisation or individual. For example, if a hacker perceives that a company is not treating its employees fairly, they may feel that the company deserves to have its system infiltrated.

Illustration 3.1 White, black and grey hat hackers. Some distinctions between hackers use the terms 'white hat', 'black hat' and 'grey hat' to distinguish between those who engage in different types of activities, or who have different motives.

This nomenclature could be of the utmost importance for the hacker involved. Bryant and Marshall (2008) suggest that labelling theory could be applied to hacking terminology. Described in more detail in Chapter 1, labelling theory is a sociological theory of crime, which suggests that once a person is named or defined in a certain manner, consequences flow from this. One of these consequences is the possibility that the definition can become a means of defence or adjustment to the societal reaction to them (Rock, 2007). It is therefore possible that once an individual has been assigned the term 'hacker' (or 'cracker' or 'black-hat' or any of the other terms discussed above), then the individual begins to alter their behaviour accordingly in order to fit in with the label assigned to them. As such, the media usage of the term 'hacker' to include mainly those who hack for malicious reasons may have an impact on those who term themselves hackers, but whose hacking activities lie primarily within the original definition of the term – they may change their behaviours and engage in more criminal or malicious activities due to this labelling.

In addition to the high-level distinctions between hackers and crackers, and white-hats, black-hats and grey-hats, several researchers have suggested further classifications of hackers. These are outlined in Table 3.1. Many of these classifications have overlaps, for example, Rogers' (2000) 'newbies' are quite similar to Chiesa et al.'s (2009) 'script kiddies'. Most distinctions within many classification systems refer to the experience levels, methods and motives of each type of hacker.

As well as these categorisation systems, other authors have identified additional types of hacker. For example, Taylor (2001) suggests the 'Microserf' who was or still is associated with hacker groups but who now work within corporate structures, and 'hacktivists' whose actions are motivated by political drive. Warren and Leitch (2009) also identify 'hacker-taggers' – who leave a 'tag' on a website that they have hacked. They do not aim to interfere with the function of the website, or to steal data, they simply aim to leave their 'tag' on the website. For example, they may leave the website they have hacked as it was, but include a single line saying 'This website is owned by (name)'. Warren and Leitch (2009) suggest that based on their research, hacker-taggers are very competitive, with a strong desire to succeed. They also exchange information among themselves regarding successful defacements but cause minimal or no damage to the websites. They could be individual hackers or groups, and they rely upon media reports to cause political damage or embarrassment. This type of behaviour could potentially be compared to 'tagging' in graffiti culture (see Halsey and Young, 2002 for a description of the importance of tagging in graffiti).

Activity 3.1 Classifications of hackers

Identify the overlaps between the various categories of hacking mentioned above (consider those mentioned in the text, along with those outlined in Table 3.1). Using this, develop an overall classification of hackers. For each category, attempt to determine if most hackers in this category would be willing to self-categorise themselves into the same category, or if they would identify themselves as belonging to a different group.

Table 3.1 Categories of hackers

Researcher(s)	Category	Definition
Marc Rogers (2000)	Newbie/tool kit	'Persons who have limited computer and programming skills. These persons are new to hacking and rely on already written pieces of software, referred to as tool kits, to conduct their attacks. The tool kits are readily available on the internet.'
	Cyber-punks	'Persons who usually have better computer skills and some programming capabilities. They are capable of writing some of their own software albeit limited and have a better understanding of the systems they are attacking. They also intentionally engage in malicious acts, such as defacing web pages and sending junk mail (known as spamming). Many are engaged in credit card number theft and telecommunications fraud.'
	Internals	'Disgruntled employees or ex-employees who are usually quite computer literate and may be involved in technology-related jobs. They are able to carry out their attacks due to the privileges they have been or had been assigned as part of their job function.'
	Coders	Rogers does not provide a specific definition for this group, but they are seen to be hackers with high skill levels.
	Old guard hackers	'Appear to have no criminal intent although there is an alarming disrespect for personal property... [They embrace] the ideology of the first generation hackers and appears to be interested in the intellectual endeavour.'
	Professional criminals	'Professional criminals and ex-intelligence operatives who ... specialize in corporate espionage, are usually extremely well trained, and have access to state of the art equipment.'
	Cyberterrorists	Again, Rogers does not provide a specific definition of this group.
Raoul Chiesa et al. (2009, pp. 52–6)	Wannabe lamer	Found 'practically anywhere on the net, as they are constantly and publicly asking for help of various descriptions'.
	Script-kiddie	'Their specialty is using tools developed by others to carry out violations they can boast about.'

Table 3.1 *(cont.)*

Researcher(s)	Category	Definition
	The '37337 K-rAd iRC #hack 0-day exploitz' guy	'Characters who would do anything to become "famous" … they are willing to use "brutal methods" to get where they want to be. These aren't hackers who explore; rather, they use what is already available … They have at their disposal real attack weapons, tools to exploit 0-day vulnerabilities, which are still unknown.'
	Cracker	'Originally, cracker meant someone who removed the protection from commercial software programs. Recently, the term has started to appear in the papers and on mailing lists and has started to mean "violent" hackers, i.e. hackers who are happy to become a nightmare for system administrators, deleting files and causing permanent damage.'
	Ethical hacker	'They enter your system, explore it quickly … and they'll even let you know about it, sending you report mails or suggestions once they have finished exploring … often, they are naïve and speak about their actions publicly, taking for granted that they haven't done anything wrong.'
	Quiet, paranoid and skilled hacker	'Possibly the most devious of the non-money motivated hackers … this hacker is paranoid, so it will be very difficult to detect his presence and virtually impossible to find him.'
	Cyber-warrior	'Mercenaries who have acquired very great skills … keep a low profile … they do it for money or for ideals.'
	Industrial spy	'Money is the motivation … they are highly skilled, with lots of experience … insiders are part of this category.'
	Government agent	'They have a good hacker background and are employed for espionage, counterespionage, and information monitoring of governments, individuals, terrorist groups and strategic industries.'

For the purpose of conciseness, the high-level term 'hacker' will be used throughout this chapter, with specific indications where the research cited differentiates black-hat, white-hat and grey-hat hackers. Nevertheless, it should be remembered that the individuals involved in the research that follows may choose to define themselves differently, or they may be described differently by their victims or law-enforcement personnel.

Summary box 3.1 Hacking definitions and nomenclature

- Hacking is thought to have existed since the late 1950s, but was originally used to describe legal activities such as the exploration of the potential of computers.
- Malicious hacking probably began in the early 1960s.
- Various terms have been introduced to try to distinguish between the criminal and non-criminal types of hacking, but most media sources and the general public still use the term 'hacking' to describe a criminal activity.
- Hackers can be differentiated by the use of the terms 'white-hat', 'black-hat' and 'grey-hat', depending on their ethical perspective and whether or not they cause malicious damage.
- Many companies employ 'ethical hackers' to test the security of their systems with their consent.
- Various sub-categories of hacker have been identified, including 'script-kiddies', 'cyberterrorists', 'wannabe lamers' and 'internals'.
- Labelling theory may have implications for hackers, as non-malicious hackers may feel that they are identified as criminals by others, and so may change their behaviour accordingly.

Types of hacking attack

There are several types of damage that a hacker can inflict on a computer system or website.

For many, the 'typical' hacking attack involves the *intrusion* of a system, which may involve accessing classified information or leaving behind malicious software. In December 2011, the activist group Anonymous allegedly stole thousands of emails, passwords and credit card details from Stratfor, a US-based security organisation (BBC News Online, 26 December 2011).

Some hackers engage in *defacement* of a website or system, as occurred with the US House of Representatives website just before President Obama's State of the Union address in January 2010. In these cases, the hackers change the content or appearance of the website or system, often with the intent of embarrassing the organisation involved.

One of the most famous types of hacker attack is a denial of service (DoS) attack. This occurs where a hacker floods the system or website with requests, to the extent that the system cannot cope with the demands and is unable to handle legitimate requests from users.

In June 2011, the UK Serious Organised Crime Agency (SOCA) website was allegedly the victim of such an attack, suspected to be organised by the hacking group LulzSec (BBC News Online, 20 June 2011). This type of attack is designed to prevent legitimate users from accessing the website, and is often used to embarrass the victim, rather than to access any classified information. A slight variation on the DoS is a distributed denial of service (DDoS) attack, where the hacker uses a botnet (a remotely controlled collection of systems) to flood the system with requests.

While there are several other, lesser known, types of attack, Bryant and Marshall (2008) suggest that the likelihood of a hacking attack being successful depends on six major elements. These are the hacker's experience and expertise, their freedom to move through the network, the nature of the attack, the victim's experience and expertise, the guardianship of the victim (such as firewalls) and the guardianship of the hacker (measures designed to stop them from acting beyond their home network). Bryant and Marshall suggest a formula which may illustrate the interaction between these factors. However, the high number of unknowns for this formula, combined with the relatively small amount of information it provides about the hacker themselves, may mean that it provides little assistance to the investigators.

Activity 3.2 Types of hacking attacks

Examine the news reports from the technology sections of online newspapers and magazines and identify any cases of hacking that have occurred in recent months. Identify the victim, the suspected perpetrator(s) and the type of hacking attack. What do you think motivated this attack? Did the type of attack reflect the motive involved?

Known prevalence rates

As with many other types of crime, it is impossible to know the true extent of the problem of hacking. However, there have been several studies and reports in this area. Rantala (for the US Department of Justice, Bureau of Justice Statistics, 2008) in a survey of 7,818 businesses that responded to the National Computer Crime Survey in 2005, found that few businesses that detected an incident reported the cybercrime. The proportion of businesses that experienced a cyberattack (such as viruses, denial of service, vandalism or sabotage) or computer security incident (such as spyware, hacking, port scanning and theft of information) seems to be small, at 6 per cent and 12 per cent respectively.

The Computer Security Institute (CSI) computer crime and security survey (2011) reported on incidents between July 2009 and June 2010, and found that 16.8 per cent of respondents had experienced DoS attacks (down from a high of 32 per cent in 2005), with 11.4 per cent having experienced password sniffing (compared to a high of 17 per cent in 2009/10). A further 7 per cent had experienced website defacement (compared to a high of 14 per cent in 2009/10). System penetrations by outsiders were reported by 11 per cent of companies. These statistics indicate that hacking victimisation varies considerably from year to year, but there appears to be an overall downward trend. This variation could be explained by a number of factors, including changes in security settings, changes in actual rates of hacking attempts and changes in policies regarding reporting and recording of such offences. Another possible complicating factor is that the companies who responded to the survey tended to have a higher interest in security, and as such the results do not reflect a truly random sample of the population. It is unknown how many companies who had been the target of such attacks did not respond to the survey or report their victimisation.

Overall, it is extremely difficult to determine how much hacking activity occurs, partially due to difficulties in completing a methodical survey of the extent of the problem, and partially due to some victims' preference not to admit to being victimised for the sake of avoiding negative publicity. It is also possible that some victims are never aware of the fact that they have been targeted, or if they are, they manage the problem privately (through the use of protection software or fixing/replacing their equipment) and do not report the event. In addition to this, attempts to determine hacking prevalence among private individuals (rather than companies and organisations) are rare, and so we have very limited information about these victims. As such, it can be expected that the true extent of hacking activity far exceeds what is recorded and reported by official agencies. This is a common problem when attempting to determine the actual rates of many types of crime, and is referred to as the 'dark figure' in criminological literature.

Activity 3.3 Prevalence of hacking attempts among non-organisations

Devise a strategy for determining how prevalent hacking attempts are on private individuals, rather than organisations. Consider sampling methods as well as other methodological issues (for example, how would you control for users being unsure if they had been the victim of a hacking attempt or not?).

Summary box 3.2 Types of hacking attack and known prevalence

- There are different types of hacking attack. These include:
  - infiltration
  - defacements
  - denial of service (DoS) and distributed denial of service (DDoS).
- It is difficult to determine exactly how much hacking occurs, and it is expected that there is a high 'dark figure' of hacking.
- The most recent figures from the Computer Security Institute indicate a drop in hacking levels.
- Statistics regarding non-corporate hacking victimisation are rare.

Methods of hackers

There are a number of different methods by which hackers infiltrate systems. Various security organisations attempt to keep track of emerging methods through a variety of means. For example, the international 'honeynet' project (www.honeynet.org) monitors hacking attempts by placing computers or networks with limited or no security patches (honeypots) on the internet. These honeypots are designed to allure hackers, whose methods can then be monitored.

A hacker named Dustin (as cited by Mitnick and Simon, 2005, p. 126) suggests that there are four main methods that hackers use to infiltrate systems: technical entry into the network, social engineering, dumpster diving and physical entry. The first of these, technical entry into the network, reflects the common perception held among the general public of what hacking is – a hacker who sits at their computer, gaining access to the network of the target from a remote location. A hacker may use a variety of tools and techniques to do this, including (among many others) 'port-scanning' to obtain a list of all applications and services running on a computer, which will assist them in devising a strategy of attack. They may also engage in 'packet-sniffing', capturing network traffic and potentially intercepting unencrypted data or 'pinging', which allows a hacker to determine if a system is present on a network. Furnell (2010) also lists a number of technical tools that hackers can employ, including vulnerability scanners (that search for known security holes) and password crackers. Computer viruses and other malware can also be used to cause considerable damage to the systems of home users and organisations. These are considered in more detail in Chapter 4.

Social engineering involves using deception to persuade people to assist in the penetration of the network. For example, a hacker may call a receptionist at a company, saying they are from an IT support company and need the administrator's password to try to correct a bug in the system. Social engineering could also include eavesdropping on conversations between employees of a company to find out useful information, or 'shoulder surfing' – covertly watching an employee enter their user-name and password with the intention of using that information in a hacking attempt later. Variations on social engineering include 'phishing' and 'pharming' (Sanders-Reach, 2005), which are discussed in more detail in Chapter 5 as they are frequently used for identity theft. Some interesting descriptions of actual attacks and social engineering methods that are used are provided in Mitnick and Simon (2002) and Hadnagy (2011).

Dumpster diving refers to a method involving searching the rubbish bins of a person or company for useful items. This may include scraps of paper with user names and passwords, old computer hard drives which may still have sensitive information on them, or even confidential files that may have been discarded without being properly shredded.

Illustration 3.2 Shredding documents can help to prevent infiltration by dumpster diving.

Finally, 'physical entry' occurs when the hacker manages to enter a building directly and carry out the hack from the inside. Sometimes, this could be as simple as getting through a lax security system and finding a vacant computer terminal which has been left logged on. In some cases, physical entry is enabled by social engineering methods. For example, a potential hacker may try to gain access to an area of a building that is normally restricted by swipe card access. If the hacker times their attempt well, they may be able to follow a legitimate employee through the door, with the employee often inadvertently holding the door open for the intruder.

These methods indicate that the hacker does not necessarily need to have advanced technical skills in order to complete a successful attack. Social engineering and physical entry tactics do not require any specific computer skills, and can be some of the most effective means of accomplishing a task.

Summary box 3.3 Methods of hackers

- Organisations such as the honeynet project monitor the methods used by hackers so as to improve security.
- Hackers use many different methods to achieve their goals, but these can broadly be defined in terms of four categories:
  - technical entry into the network
  - social engineering
  - dumpster diving
  - physical entry.
- Not all these methods require the hacker to have advanced technical skills, but many hackers will use a variety of methods to achieve their goals.

Motives of hackers

Understanding cybercriminals' motivation may help to improve security measures (Lafrance, 2004). There has been a considerable volume of written work in this area to date, which can broadly be separated into theoretical work and empirical work.

Theories regarding hacker motives

Several researchers have put forward theories which attempt to explain the reasons why hackers do what they do. These are listed in Table 3.2

It is clear from the lists of potential motives outlined in Table 3.2 that several authors have proposed overlapping motives, particularly in relation to curiosity, status in a social group and need for power. Despite these taxonomies and theories, Calcutt (1999) suggests that 'there is no discernible motive force which drives their [crackers'] existence' (p. 60). He suggests that their activities are relatively random. Nevertheless, some authors have attempted to examine hacker motives in light of

Table 3.2 Theorised motives of hackers

	Suggested motives
Taylor (1999)	Feelings of addiction Urge of curiosity Boredom with the educational system Enjoyment of feelings of power Peer recognition in the hacking culture Political acts
Kilger (n.d., as cited by Spitzner, 2003); Kilger *et al.* (2004)	Money Ego Entertainment Cause (basic ideology) Entrance to a social group Status
Lafrance (2004) – insider hacking	Economical profit Revenge Personal interest in a specific file External pressure from people or organisations outside of the company (such as organised crime or a family member)
Fötinger and Ziegler (2004)	Deep sense of inferiority – power achieved through hacking may increase self-esteem
Schneier (2003)	Not for profit To satisfy intellectual curiosity For the 'thrill' To see if they can Reputation Respect Acknowledgement Self-actualisation
Bryant and Marshall (2008) – early hackers	To prove themselves against the authorities of the network, with little malicious intent Self-esteem Peer recognition
Bryant and Marshall (2008) – later hackers	Depended on type of hacker For example, cyberterrorists motivated by ideals; professional criminals motivated by profit; internals were disgruntled

specific psychological theories. For example, Taylor (2003) proposes that 'psycho-sexual theories suggest that hacking provides men (and especially young, pubescent men) with a cathartic outlet for their frustrations and a biological urge to dominate' (p. 130). Taylor goes on to explore the psycho-sexual theory in depth, using quotes from hackers to support the suggestion that the final moments of a successful hack have some orgasmic qualities for the hacker.

Rennie and Shore (2007) also attempted to apply psychological theory to the actions of hackers, specifically using Ajzen's (1985, 1991) 'theory of planned behaviour' and

Beveren's (2001) 'flow theory'. The 'theory of planned behaviour' has been used in a variety of contexts to both explain and predict behaviours, as well as targeting strategies for changing behaviour. 'Flow theory' attempts to explain absorption in a particular activity, where the experience itself is desired, rather than any specific end goal, and is a common explanation for excessive internet activity. When experiencing flow, users feel concentration, curiosity, intrinsic interest and control (Shernoff *et al.*, 2003). The emotions reported by hackers are similar to those reported by other people experiencing flow (Rennie and Shore, 2007), and some of the motives offered as explanations by hackers (such as intrinsic interest and curiosity) would also seem to be supported by flow theory. Rennie and Shore (2007) indicate that flow theory therefore explains the progression of the hacker career, but it on its own cannot provide a complete model for computer crime. As such, they propose an advanced model of hacker development, incorporating other factors, such as ideology, vandalism and career, to predict the eventual type of individual which emerges, such as penetration testers, hacktivists and cyberterrorists. They indicate that flow theory explains the development of hackers from script-kiddies or newbies to experienced and skilled hackers. They indicate that an important method of dealing with the problem is to address it early, and to reduce the likelihood that teenagers will start hacking behaviours in the first place.

Empirical work examining hacker motives

Having considered so many different theoretical approaches, it is worth considering the empirical work in this area, although it is very sparse in comparison to the theoretical writings.

Fötinger and Ziegler (2004) describe a study conducted by the German Federal Bureau of Criminal Investigation (the Bundeskriminalamt or BKA). Following a large-scale hacking attack on an internet provider in the area of Münster, Germany in 1999, the BKA issued questionnaires to the hackers involved, resulting in data from 599 hackers. In this study, it was found that the hackers claimed that they were motivated primarily by 'trial and error' – honing their skills (33.1 per cent of respondents) or economic reasons (51.3 per cent of respondents). Woo *et al.* (2004) carried out a content analysis of 462 defaced websites, and concluded that about 70 per cent of the defacements could be classified as simple pranks, while the rest had a more political motive. Bernhardt Lieberman (2003, as cited in Fötinger and Ziegler, 2004) interviewed a total of forty-two hackers. He found that hackers considered the 'intellectual challenge' and a wish to 'learn about computers and computing' to be their primary motivations. 'Breaking the law' and 'to achieve notoriety' were listed as their lowest-rated motivations. These findings are contradictory to both the public perception and the opinions listed in many articles and books on the subject.

Chiesa *et al.* (2009) describe several motives cited by hackers, including intellectual curiosity, love of technology, fun and games, making the personal computer world safer, fighting for freedom, conflict with authority, rebelliousness, spirit of adventure and ownership, boredom, fame-seeking, anger and frustration, political reasons, escape from family and/or society and professional reasons. Kirwan (2006) found that the motivations of hackers were very wide-ranging, and little in the way of consistent patterns could be observed. There were no clear differences between the cited motivations of white-hats and black-hats, despite the fact that discrepancies were expected due to the presence of criminal intent in black-hat hackers. She found that the motivations cited in online interviews with hackers were often quite vague, with hackers often citing 'commendable' reasons for their actions (such as to protect their friends' systems, or because they were passionate about computers), whereas those motives indicated by a content analysis of hacker bulletin boards were much more specific, and included the 'darker' side of hacking-related activities, such as unlawfully accessing another person's files.

Based on the literature to date, it appears that hackers have quite a wide range of motivations for their actions. However, it should be remembered that some researchers (such as Voiskounsky and Smyslova, 2003) were unable to uncover reliable trends in hacker motivation, and so the research to date must be considered with caution. Part of the reason for this is that in most cases we must rely solely on the stated responses of cybercriminals to questions regarding motivation – there is a strong possibility that they are replying in what they perceive to be a socially acceptable way, and as such the results may be subject to bias.

Summary box 3.4 Motives of hackers

- While a considerable amount has been written regarding the motives of hackers, much of this has been theoretical in nature, with relatively little empirical work.
- Many different motives for hacking have been proposed. Some of the most commonly proposed motives include peer-recognition, curiosity, need for power, alleviation of boredom, self-esteem and financial reasons.
- Attempts have been made to apply psychological theories, such as flow theory, the theory of planned behaviour and psycho-sexual theories, to hacking motives and behaviour.
- Not all studies have resulted in conclusive findings regarding the motives of hackers.
- In most cases, we are dependent on hackers to self-report their motives for hacking, which may result in biased information as they may be more inclined to respond in a socially acceptable manner.

Profile and personality characteristics of offenders

As mentioned in Chapter 1, psychological profiling can be of assistance in some criminal investigations. Donato (2009) examines the potential of profiling for computer hacking, and suggests that it might be useful. However, Donato's proposed methodology does not allow for much psychological insight into the hacker involved, focusing more on using clues to establish the technological prowess of the hacker based on the mistakes they make during the attack. Little attention is placed on social engineering techniques, or on determining the hacker's psychological makeup. Similarly, it does not invoke the 'ghosts of hackers past' – most methods of offender profiling are based at least in part on an analysis of what types of evidence were left behind by offenders with certain characteristics, and Donato generally overlooks this. It is likely that the first step in creating reliable offender profiles of hackers involves investigating the psychological and demographic characteristics of previous offenders, so that new clues can be matched up to previous scenes of cybercrimes. While Donato's idea that criminal profiling can be applied to hacking behaviours is sound in principle, it appears that a great deal more background work to identify the common characteristics of these offenders is needed before it can realistically be used as a tool to aid investigations.

Demographic characteristics

When considering the profile of hackers, it is useful to initially attempt to ascertain demographic characteristics, such as gender and age. Certainly, the media-induced stereotype of hackers is that of young males. Bissett and Shipton (1999) describe the common media stereotype of the computer hacker. He is 'an evil genius, usually male, usually acting alone, and employing fiendish cunning at the computer terminal to outwit a faceless bureaucracy or establishment' (p. 905). Similarly, Murphy (2004) suggests that the common perception of a malicious hacker 'is that of a gifted but socially inept teenager. Generally they are visualised as male' (p. 12). Levy (1984) wrote that, at that time, there had never been a star quality female hacker, and that most of the males existed as bachelors. Bissett and Shipton state that, at their time of writing, there was only one female member of the hacker group 'Cult of the Dead Cow', although there was also a female white-hat hacker (Meinel, 1998). Indeed, Bissett and Shipton suggest that the language and images used in the 'Cult of the Dead Cow' all suggest adolescent or young adult male activity. Young *et al.* (2007) indicated that when they attended a DefCon conference (a large hacker convention), it appeared that most of the hackers were between 12 and 28 years old.

Kabay (1998) indicates that while the participants in public hacker meetings are predominantly young people, some computer criminals have been people in their thirties. He also points out the lack of knowledge concerning personality profiles of cybercriminals, and while he suggests that the writing in hacker publications seems 'uniformly immature' it cannot be verified if this trait is representative of the hacker population as a whole. Turgeman-Goldschmidt (2011) interviewed fifty-four hackers, of whom only three were female. The age of the hackers she interviewed varied from 14 to 49 years, with an average age of 24. Almost three-quarters of these hackers had twelve or more years in education, with a similar number having above average income levels.

In the Bundeskriminalamt (BKA) study cited by Fötinger and Ziegler (2004) only 35 of the 599 hackers who responded were female. On average, the females were found to be consistently older than the males (male average was 22.2 years, female average was 34.7 years). The females also only used approximately half the number of hacked accounts that the males did (average 6.8 for females, with 14.1 for males). Overall, 72.2 per cent of the alleged criminals lived with their parents when the crimes were committed. The BKA also suggests that most hackers have middle or higher education, and are often students or trainees using the computer in their spare time.

In the UK, the Home Office (2005) reports the findings of the Offending, Crime and Justice Survey (OCJS), which asked participants to self-report their hacking behaviours. They found that 0.9 per cent of internet users said they had used the internet to hack into other computers, with males more likely than females (1.3 per cent versus 0.5 per cent), and younger people (aged 10–25) more likely than older people to admit to hacking behaviours.

While many hackers are suspected to be either in full-time education or unemployed at the time of their highest activity levels, there are numerous hackers who have later progressed to more reputable professions, often in the IT security field. However, companies are advised to think carefully about hiring a former hacker, both for security and for client confidence reasons (see Cushing, 2001 for further discussion of this phenomenon taken from the corporation's perspective).

Overall, it would appear that the evidence concerning the demographic characteristics of hackers supports the general stereotype of young males, but that there are exceptions to this, and there have been many cases of female hackers.

Summary box 3.5 Demographic characteristics of hackers
- The media stereotype suggests that hackers are mostly young males.
- While there are some exceptions, most research to date supports this stereotype.
- Hackers have also been found to have good educational levels.
- Other findings suggest that hackers are sometimes students or trainees, and can have above average income levels.

Ethical positions

One of the most popular areas of research and discussion within the psychology of hackers involves an examination of their ethical positions. Some researchers suggest that many hackers subscribe to a common code of ethics, but that this has changed somewhat over time. One of the initial theories relating to this dates from Levy's (1984) work.

The hacker ethic
In 1984, Levy suggested several key characteristics of the 'hacker ethic'. These include that:

(1) Access to computers, and anything which might teach a person something about the way the world works, should be unlimited and total. This suggests that hackers feel that computers should not be limited to the wealthy or the privileged, but that all should be able to access them. Given the relative shortage of computers at the time, this was a difficult goal to achieve. Hackers also had a relatively narrow view of this principle – while many felt that they should be allowed access to the computers of others, they were not as eager to allow others access to their own systems.

(2) All information should be free and available to the public, and secrecy should be avoided. Evidence of this principle can be seen in the hacking activities of Gary McKinnon, who felt entitled to access confidential government documents.

(3) Mistrust authority – promote decentralisation. According to Levy, hackers felt that the best way to support the free dissemination of information was to reduce bureaucracy.

(4) Hackers should be judged by their hacking, and not by any other characteristic that they might exhibit or possess. This would include characteristics such as qualifications, race, position, gender or age. Indeed, the very nature of the internet, and particularly the popular uses of the internet in the early 1980s, allows an individual to keep these characteristics well hidden.

(5) The creation of art and beauty using computer technology is possible and should be encouraged. This may include traditional forms of artistic work, for example graphics or music, but a well-written piece of code in itself could be considered beautiful by some hackers. This was especially so at the time, as processing power was limited. If code could be written elegantly, then it allowed more tasks to be achieved by the system.

(6) Computers can change one's life for the better. They may provide focus, make the hacker more adventurous or enrich their life.

While the hacker ethic noted by Levy in 1984 seems admirable on the surface, much of it is oriented to the best interests of the hackers themselves. They indicate that computers and information should be free to all, when it seems unlikely that they would be willing to share some of their own resources in this regard. While the principle indicating that hackers should be judged by their hacking prowess rather than any other criteria seems well intentioned, outsiders cannot help but feel that they are also being judged by their lack of hacking prowess. Regardless, Levy's hacker ethic was not to last.

Mizrach (n.d., circa mid-1990s) carried out a content analysis of twenty-nine online documents in order to determine how widely accepted the hacker ethic was, and if it had changed since Levy's description in 1984. He determined that there was a new hacker ethic which has some continuity from the previous one. Mizrach indicates that this new hacker ethic evolved like the old one, informally and by processes of mutual reinforcement. He indicates that the new hacker ethic contains some ambiguities and contradictions. The new hacker he identified has ten main principles:

(1) 'Above all else, do no harm' – similar to the Hippocratic oath of the medical profession, this suggests that computers and data should not be damaged if at all possible. Mizrach here questions whether there is an ethical dilemma if the hacker inadvertently causes damage to a system.

(2) 'Protect privacy' – Mizrach indicates that this in some ways contradicts the original hacker ethic, that all information should be freely available.

(3) 'Waste not, want not' – that computer resources should not be wasted, and that it is ethically wrong to keep people out of systems when they could be using them. Mizrach here uses the example of a person's car – if the car is borrowed, filled with fuel, returned with no damage and perhaps even a few suggestions as to how the performance can be improved, and the owner never misses it, is the act unethical? Mizrach indicates that there is a double-standard here, as most hackers are very possessive over the use of their own systems.

(4) 'Exceed limitations' – always attempt to exceed the known limitations of technology or software.

(5) 'The communication imperative' – that people have the right to communicate and associate with their peers freely.

(6) 'Leave no traces' – avoid leaving any indication that the hacker was present, and avoid calling attention to the hacker or their exploits. This is necessary to protect the hacker themselves, the information they have gathered and other hackers from being apprehended.

(7) Share!' – share information with as many people as possible.

(8) 'Self-defence' – against a possible 'big brother' situation due to the growing power of government and corporations – the ability to hack effectively reduces the likelihood that these large organisations will affect citizens too much.

(9) 'Hacking helps security' – it is right to find security holes, and then tell people how to fix them. This principle has a number of ethical problems, which are outlined in more detail below.

(10) 'Trust, but test' – the hacker must constantly test the integrity of systems and find ways to improve them. This may extend to testing the systems that affect the hacker. For example, if the hacker suspects that their confidential information is being held by an agency (perhaps a government department), they may feel that they have the right to test the security of that system against intrusion by others. This principle is again clearly a double standard – it is likely that other people's information will be held on the same databases and will be available to the hacker if they are successful in their intrusion attempt.

Mizrach also outlines a number of activities that hackers should not engage in according to the new ethic, including profiting from hacking, not adding to the body of hacker knowledge, damaging systems (with or without the use of viruses), excessive selfishness, theft (especially from small organisations), bragging, spying and turning in other hackers to the authorities. He also outlines the consequences of breaking the hacker ethic, indicating that this results mostly in anathema or social ostracism.

In the 1990s analysis, Mizrach suggested that the hacker ethic had changed for several reasons. Firstly, there was far more computing power available then than when the original hacker ethic was formed. Secondly, there was a belief that society had changed for the worse. Thirdly, there was a belief that the computer industry had discarded the original hacker ethic. And finally, it was felt that there had been a generational change – that young hackers then were qualitatively different to hackers of a previous generation.

Chiesa *et al.* (2009) summarise the hacker ethic into four main points – do not damage penetrated systems, do not modify the information present on the invaded computer (except the log file to erase evidence of the intrusion), share information and knowledge with other members of the underground and supply a service by sharing accesses that should be free to all (pp. 171–2). Similarly, Tavani (2011) attempts to summarise the hacker ethic by suggesting that many hackers 'have embraced, either explicitly or implicitly, the following three principles' (p. 180) – that information should be free, that hackers provide society with a useful service and that activities in cyberspace do not harm people in the real world. Tavani goes on to explain the problems with these three principles, at least in theory. For example, he suggests that, in many cases, hackers are probably aware that there are limits to the appropriate freedom of information (if all information were free, then privacy would be compromised and the integrity and accuracy of information would be questionable). In addition, while non-malicious hackers can be beneficial for society, this does not mean that all hacking activity is acceptable. Tavani cites Spafford (2004), who indicates that, in some cases, hacking activity could be considered ethical, despite the fact that computer break-ins cause harm. Spafford gives an example of a case where medical data was required in an emergency to save someone's life – in this case Spafford believes that a break-in to this computer would be the ethical thing to do.

Subscription to the hacker ethic and justifications for breaches

As the hacker ethic appears to be a very dynamic concept, it is difficult to determine exactly whether or not the modern hacker subscribes to it completely. Nevertheless, some hackers (particularly white-hat hackers) do appear to hold their ethical principles in high regard. Lieberman (2003, as cited in Fötinger and Ziegler, 2004) questioned hackers on their subscription to the hacker ethic (as outlined by Levy, 1984), and found that although many hackers agreed with most of the principles involved, only 7 per cent indicated that privacy was not important to them. Lieberman suggests that hackers do not extend that belief to those whose computers they attack, accusing them of a highly hypocritical approach. As with many codes of practice, it is to be expected that some members of the community will not adhere to them. It is evident that at least some hackers do not subscribe to any version of the hacker ethic, and even for those who do, it must be remembered that there are many loopholes within the principles which allow certain unethical and/or illegal behaviours to be completed without retribution from the hacking community.

Activity 3.4 Case studies and the hacker ethic
Starting with the case studies at the beginning of this chapter, attempt to determine if the hacker involved appeared to subscribe to either Levy's or Mizrach's hacker ethic. Use reliable sources from books or the internet to seek further evidence to support your conclusion. Consider whether the ethical principle involved justifies the hacker's activity.

Marc Rogers (as cited in Fötinger and Ziegler, 2004) suggests that hackers tend to minimise or misconstrue the consequences of their activities, rationalising that their behaviour is really performing a service to the organisation or society as a whole. Post (cited in Fötinger and Ziegler, 2004) suggests that hackers share a sense of 'ethical flexibility' – the serious consequences of hacking can be more easily ignored as human contact is minimised over the computer. Young *et al.* (2007) also found that the hackers had a high level of moral disengagement, and disregard any negative consequences of hacking by blaming the victims.

So is it possible for ethical hacking to exist? Richard Spinello (2000) indicates that even though many hackers maintain that hacking is for fun and not damaging, and even though many of them consider even looking for personal information such as credit card numbers as immoral and unethical, any act of trespassing is unethical, even if there is no attempt to gain personal information. He indicates that 'people should not go where they do not belong, either in real space or in cyberspace' (p. 179). He does not argue that searching for personal information is more 'wrong' than simply 'looking around', but concedes that 'this does not excuse the latter activity'.

When this rationale is extended to the offline world, the ethical implications become clearer. If an individual succeeds in evading all the security guards and precautions which protect the sensitive areas of an important building (for example, the White House), and then proceeds to search through important or confidential documents, but does not actually steal or change anything, it is still clear that their action is unethical, and there would be little hesitation in prosecuting the offender. Even if an intruder makes their way into a person's home, just to have a look around without causing any damage, it is still clearly an unnecessary invasion of privacy. It is also unlikely that the homeowner would forgive that intruder, even if they were to offer an explanation of how they had managed to overcome the household security, so that the homeowner could then improve their protection measures. Similarly, it is unlikely that the curators of the White House would hire their intruder as a security expert to prevent further invasions. Yet these are common perceptions among the hacker community – that it is acceptable to intrude in order to determine the effectiveness of security, and that the victim should be grateful, to the extent of offering financial reward in the form of employment, for the infringement. These beliefs are supported by the evidence that many former hackers have gone on to hold careers in the IT security field, whether employed by major software developers or freelancing, as in the case of Kevin Mitnick.

Chiesa *et al.* (2009) cite examples of how 'ethical hackers', such as Ethical Hackers Against Paedophilia (EHAP), have attempted to display the positive sides of hacking. This organisation uses unconventional, yet legal, tactics to try to combat paedophilia online. Whether or not their activities could truly be considered ethical requires an in-depth evaluation of their techniques. In doing so, it must be remembered that behaviours do not necessarily become ethical simply because of the person or group affected, no matter how despicable their actions have been. Similarities can be drawn between this type of behaviour and others where people behave in what may be unethical ways in order to achieve what they feel is an ethical objective, for example the defacement of the websites of research laboratories that engage in animal testing by animal rights activists.

Summary box 3.6 – Ethical principles of hackers

- Various authors have suggested that most hackers subscribe either consciously or unconsciously to a code of ethics.
- The first such 'hacker ethic' was proposed by Levy (1984).
- Several other authors have proposed more recent codes of ethics, including Mizrach and Tavani.
- While the hacker ethics generally appear positive, it is unclear exactly how many hackers truly subscribe to them, and even for those who do, there appear to be several loopholes within the principles.

Interpersonal relationships

Interpersonal behaviour has been studied in various areas of criminal psychology for some time, although there has been relatively little research to date regarding the interpersonal relationship skills of hackers. Lieberman (2003, as cited in Fötinger and Ziegler, 2004) gave hackers a questionnaire on social anxiety and social avoidance, and found that the answers given go against the stereotyped image of hackers as loners who are incapable of social interaction. Lieberman also found that many hackers had normal romantic relationships and sex lives. Similarly, Woo *et al.*'s (2004) study indicated that hackers are not the lonely, isolated individuals sometimes portrayed in the media but are members of an extensive social network.

Contradicting these findings, Chesebro and Bonsall (1989) suggest that hackers eschew social contacts and Turkle (1984) suggests that hackers regard the computer as an extension of the self and as a friend. She suggests that the computer is employed to create a self-contained reality and to substitute for direct face-to-face interactions with other human beings. She indicates that 'The hacker culture appears to be made up of people who need to avoid complicated social situations, who for one reason or another got frightened off or hurt too badly by the risks and complexities of relationships' (p. 216). In empirical research, Turgeman-Goldschmidt (2011) noted that 78 per cent of her sample of hackers were single, with only 13 per cent being married, although most of the hackers in her sample were in their twenties, and so a relatively high proportion of unmarried individuals is to be expected.

Murphy (2004) suggests that malicious hackers are 'loners with poor self-esteem and a greater ability to interact with computers and technology than with other people' (p. 12). Then again, Murphy also suggests that the hackers may be more socially cognisant than previously thought, at least as far as the organised hacking groups on the internet are concerned. He also suggests that hackers, in particular white-hats, are as likely to form romantic relationships and have children as the rest of society. Kirwan (2006) found that hackers indicated weaker relationships with family members than a control group of non-hacker computer users. In addition, the control group demonstrated higher levels on a measure of interpersonal relationships than the hacking group. However, no clear differences were found between the interpersonal relationships of the 'white-hat' and 'black-hat' groups. These findings were given additional support by the findings of a content analysis of hacker bulletin boards, which suggested that, while hackers appear to be capable of forming close relationships, they also appear to be more likely to have difficulties in those relationships than 'normal' computer users. Nevertheless, it was also found that many of the case study hackers (both white-hat and black-hat) were involved in romantic relationships. Chiesa et al. (2009) found that hackers often have difficult relationships with parents, often with an absent father. They found that parents of hackers didn't seem to care about what their children did with their computers. Chiesa et al. also noted that the hackers tended to be loners, with few other friends. The friends they did have are normally other hackers, who they didn't know in real life, and most people that they did know offline were not aware of their hacking activities.

As such, the findings regarding the interpersonal skills of hackers are varied. Basing conclusions on the empirical work, it would appear that hackers have interpersonal skills which might be slightly inferior to the population as a whole, but that a sweeping conclusion cannot be made describing all hackers.

Other personality characteristics

In addition to the research on motives, ethics and interpersonal relationships, some researchers have examined other personality characteristics of hackers. For example, Woo (2003) found that hackers who strongly endorsed nationalism showed higher aggressiveness scores than hackers with lower levels of nationalism. Woo also found links between high levels of narcissism and high levels of aggression among hackers. On the other hand, Platt (1994) visited hacker conventions, and found that the delegates were much more trusting and mild-mannered than he had expected. He felt less threatened by them than by 'normal' teenage males, and even noted that they showed 'an amazing degree of naïve trust' (p. 1), at least as far as other delegates were concerned. Fötinger and Ziegler (2004) suggest that hackers are task-oriented rather than time-oriented. They suggest that hackers are more likely to hold nocturnal habits, because there are fewer distractions at night. Bachmann (2010) examined rational decision-making processes and pronounced risk propensity in 124 hackers who attended a hacking conference in Washington, DC. He found that hackers had a higher need for cognition and higher risk propensity than the general public, and that they preferred rational thinking styles over intuitive approaches. They also enjoyed solving complex problems more than the general public. Interestingly, the hackers with the highest preference for rational decision making were also those who were more successful in their hacking attempts. Those with the highest risk propensity behaviours engaged in more attacks, but reported less success.

Summary box 3.7 Interpersonal relationships and other personality characteristics of hackers

- While some authors suggest that hackers have inferior interpersonal relationship skills, some empirical work indicates that hackers are capable of forming long-term relationships. However, these relationships may be slightly weaker than those of non-hackers.

- Hackers have also been found to be nocturnal in nature and task-oriented. There are conflicting findings regarding aggressiveness.
- Bachmann (2010) found that hackers preferred rational thinking styles over intuitive approaches, and they had higher risk propensity than the general public. These factors also influenced their success rates in hacking attempts.

Hacker groups versus lone hackers

While some hackers prefer to work alone, there has been a growing trend of news reports describing the activities of hacker groups, such as Anonymous and LulzSec. Hacker groups sometimes engage in 'hacktivism' which 'draws on the creative use of computer technology for the purposes of facilitating online protests, performing civil disobedience in cyberspace and disrupting the flow of information by deliberately intervening in the networks of global capital' (Gunkel, 2005, p. 595).

Chiesa *et al.* (2009) discuss how some hackers may prefer to work alone as they feel more secure – the less people know about their hacking behaviour, the less likely they are to be uncovered. Chiesa *et al.* go on to describe how hackers may initially seek mentors while they are learning necessary hacking skills, but may later prefer to seek information independently. However, it is possible that some lone hackers may form temporary collaborations with others who have required skills for a specific task.

Chiesa *et al.* (2009) indicate that some adolescents who start hacking may join a group because they are attracted to the underground world. They suggest that being part of a hacker group may be important for personal identity development, providing a sense of belonging and offering a sense of protection. The new hacker may develop 'a feeling of well-being that comes from being accepted by the other members of the group' (p. 163). Finally, they suggest that the greatest advantage of being part of a group is the element of shared responsibility, leading to a greater sense of safety. However, Chiesa *et al.* note that some hacker groups will set minimum skill requirements for entry, and may require members to maintain a level of activity within the group to retain membership.

Summary box 3.8 Hacker groups versus lone hackers
- Some hackers prefer to work alone. One potential reason for this is an increased feeling of security. Lone hackers may form temporary alliances with other hackers as required.
- New hackers may seek out a more experienced hacker to act as a mentor. These hackers may later prefer a more solitary existence.
- Hacker groups may provide important psychological supports for members, particularly in terms of a sense of shared responsibility, feelings of belonging and personal identity development.

Punishment

Brenner (2006) indicates that in the US, depending on the type of hacking activity engaged in, offenders can be fined, imprisoned for up to ten years, or both. This imprisonment can be extended to up to twenty years for repeat offenders. Brenner describes how most US states tend to use a two-tiered approach, distinguishing 'simple hacking' (gaining unauthorised access to a computer) from 'aggravated hacking' (gaining unauthorised access to a computer that results in the commission of some further criminal activity), explaining that these states generally consider 'simple hacking a misdemeanour and aggravated hacking a felony' (p. 84). However, some states use a single statute for both activities, while others, such as Hawaii, use up to five different classifications.

Tavani (2011) suggests that most involved would 'support legislation that would distinguish between the degrees of punishment handed to those who are found guilty of trespass in cyberspace' (p. 206). Tavani goes on to indicate that in real-world counterparts of these activities (such as breaking and entering), a distinction would normally be made between offenders who have engaged in different degrees of criminal activity. For example, an offender who picks a lock but does not enter a premises would normally receive a lesser sentence than the offender who enters the premises but does not steal or damage anything, but who in turn would receive a lesser sentence than the offender who commits burglary.

There are a variety of methods by which hackers can be punished. While imprisonment is one of the most commonly cited punishments, fines can also be implemented. As mentioned earlier in the case of Gary McKinnon, it is also possible to be extradited, and in some cases the hacker's access to technology may be limited. Nevertheless, it has yet to be fully determined if any of these punishments can act as an appropriate deterrent for hackers. Young *et al.* (2007) surveyed hackers and other attendees at a DefCon conference in Las Vegas. They found that even though hackers perceive that they would be subject to severe judicial punishment if apprehended (thus demonstrating the effectiveness of the US government in communicating the seriousness of illegal hacking), they continued to engage in illegal hacking activities. The hackers felt that there was a low likelihood of this punishment occurring. This is of note, as severity of punishment has little effect when the likelihood of punishment is low (Von Hirsch *et al.*, 1999) whereas increased likelihood of punishment has been found to work as a deterrent (Killias *et al.*, 2009). Young *et al.* (2007) also found that hackers perceived high utility value from their hacking activities, perceiving the gains from hacking to outweigh the potential losses. It seems likely that until this is reversed hackers are unlikely to reduce their offending behaviours.

Summary box 3.9 Punishment
- A variety of punishments have been used to penalise hackers, including fines, imprisonment, extradition and limiting access to computers.

- While hackers seem aware of the severity of potential punishments, this does not seem to act as much of a deterrent. This is possibly because hackers do not perceive punishment to be a likely outcome, and they perceive the benefits from hacking as outweighing the potential losses.

Prevention methods

Rennie and Shore (2007) indicate that several controls are required to combat hacking. These include the intervention of parents and peers to teach children about the criminal nature of hacking and reduce its perceived attractiveness. Police patrols that identify the early signs of hacking behaviours in a potential offender would also be required, and supplemented with the use of formal warnings and acceptable behaviour contracts. Rennie and Shore also indicate that the availability of hacker tools needs to be curtailed, so that the script-kiddies commencing their hacking careers find it too difficult to begin, and hence are not subjected to the flow experience. Finally, this needs to be supported by increased system security that would reduce the effectiveness of the hacking scripts and tools, which would also prevent the flow experience.

In any effort to increase security against hacking behaviours a two-pronged approach is required – those methods that focus on improving the security systems themselves (such as better encryption and firewall software) and those methods that focus on the human element in security. No amount of technological improvements in safety will solve the problem if social engineering techniques are still effective. Users need to be made aware of how to ensure that systems remain secure, and how passwords and other confidential information should be protected. Simple safeguards such as ensuring that computers are not left logged in when unattended, doors to computers which hold critical information are locked and training is given on how to create secure passwords, could reduce the opportunities available to hackers.

> ### Activity 3.5 Defending systems against social engineering
> Imagine that you have been asked by an organisation to train their employees about the dangers of social engineering in hacking attempts. Design an awareness and/or training strategy to educate users about how social engineering can result in weaker security systems. Include specific suggestions as to how users can reduce the likelihood that they will fall victim to social engineering tactics.

Summary box 3.10 Prevention methods
- The prevention of hacking requires several approaches in order to be successful.
- Attempts can be made to identify young people who are at risk of becoming hackers, and intervention programmes can be developed.

- The availability of hacker tools can be restricted.
- Organisations and individual computer users can be educated about suitable methods to protect their systems, including both technological protection methods (such as firewalls) and reducing susceptibility to social engineering techniques.

Conclusion

While hackers have caught the public and academic imagination in ways that many other types of cybercriminals have not, there is still relatively little reliable empirical knowledge about them. What does exist is often contradictory, and it is difficult to develop an overall picture of what a hacker is like. The problems inherent in studying hackers are probably partly to blame for this – it is often difficult for researchers to find hackers to participate in their research, and even when they do so, it is uncertain as to whether or not these hackers share the characteristics of other hackers who are more reclusive. Indeed, Kabay (1998) indicates that although there are a considerable number of popular books published in this area, it is unknown whether the hackers profiled in these sources are representative of the rest of the hacker population. Researchers also face difficulties in gaining the trust of hackers, and in ensuring that the research participant is actually an active member of the hacking community. From the perspective of users, it is important that adequate protection measures are used to ensure security, especially in large companies and organisations. Overall, while a considerable amount is known about the psychology of hackers, there are many gaps in the research, and much of the theory which has been put forth in the area needs to be empirically investigated before it can be considered reliable.

Essay questions

(1) Hackers use a variety of methods and techniques to attain their goals. Describe each of these, indicating how different techniques suit different motivations and technological skill levels.

(2) There is considerable disagreement as to the nomenclature used within hacking circles and by researchers of hackers. Identify the most common nomenclature and taxonomies of hacking, and evaluate their effectiveness at describing different types of hackers.

(3) Hackers cite a wide range of motives for their behaviour, but it is difficult to find consistent patterns. Critically evaluate the theoretical and empirical literature examining hacker motives.

(4) Some authors believe that many hackers subscribe to a hacker ethic. Describe the various ethical principles that it has been suggested that hackers subscribe to, and using case studies of actual hackers, determine if there is support for the existence of these principles.

(5) Hackers have poor interpersonal skills. Discuss.

Additional reading

Books and articles

The Hacker Profiling Project (HPP) is an Institute for Security and Open Methodologies (ISECOM) project: www.isecom.org/projects/hpp.shtml. Their book outlines some of the key findings from the early stages of their research:

Chiesa, R., Ducci, S. and Ciappi, S. (2009). *Profiling Hackers: the Science of Criminal Profiling as Applied to the World of Hacking.* Boca Raton, FL: Auerbach Publications.

Several articles and book chapters attempt to analyse the psychology of hackers, and the potential for psychological profiling in hacking investigations. These include:

Donato, L. (2009). An introduction to how criminal profiling could be used as a support for computer hacking investigations. *Journal of Digital Forensic Practice*, **2**, 183–95.

Furnell, S. (2010). Hackers, viruses and malicious software. In Yvonne Jewkes and Majid Yar (eds.), *Handbook of Internet Crime*. Cullompton, UK: Willan Publishing (pp. 173–93).

Young, R., Zhang, L. and Prybutok, V. R. (2007). Hacking into the minds of hackers. *Information Systems Management*, **24**, 281–7.

Websites

The Computer Security Institute publishes an annual report which outlines the known rate of computer crime among businesses. This report can be freely downloaded at http://gocsi.com/survey.

Christopher Hadnagy is the lead developer of www.social-engineer.org – a website which compiles information about social engineering methods and strategies.

The Honeynet Project website (www.honeynet.org) provides information on this important research which helps to improve online security through the use of honeypots that tempt hackers to infiltrate their systems.

4   Malware

Case studies

'Cookie monster' was an early computer virus type program. This relatively benign virus would prevent the person from using the computer by requesting a 'cookie' at regular intervals. If the user typed in the word 'cookie', the message would disappear, only to reappear a while later requesting another treat. The 'cookie monster' virus was an irritation, but it spread slowly and was relatively benign as it did not damage the computer, nor steal data from the user.

More modern viruses can have considerably more serious consequences. An example of malware with much more serious potential is the Stuxnet worm, first detected in June 2010. In September of that year it was revealed that the worm had infected computers at Iran's first nuclear power station (BBC News Online, 2010). The Stuxnet worm specifically targets systems used to manage utilities such as water, oil rigs and power plants. It is a highly tailored worm, and is thought to be the first worm designed to target such facilities. Instead of using the internet to distribute itself it infects Windows via portable memory devices such as universal serial bus (USB) keys. Because of this it can target systems that are not connected to the internet for security reasons. Once infected, the worm can reprogram the software which gives instructions to industrial machinery, such as motors and coolers, telling them to turn on or off at given signals.

Chapter overview

Most computer users have heard of a computer virus, but they are only one of many types of 'malware' or 'malicious software'. The methods by which malware has been developed and distributed have changed over the three decades since the first viruses appeared, and this is partly as a result of social engineering tactics and responses to emerging technologies. This chapter starts with definitions of malware and an attempt to determine the prevalence of malware. Different types of malware will then be defined, and a brief history of some of the most famous malware will be presented. Production and distribution methods of malware will be described, and then the motives, profile and personality characteristics of offenders will be outlined. Finally, the chapter will close with some suggested methods of preventing malware infection.

Definitions and prevalence rates

It is important to start by defining malware, and some key terms relating to malware distribution and behaviour, such as 'payload' and 'in the wild'.

Edgar-Nevill and Stephens (2008) define malware as 'any piece of software devised with malicious intent' (p. 91). The term is taken from the phrase 'malicious software' and is used to describe any software program that spreads from one computer to another and that interferes with computer operation. Kramer and Bradfield (2010) indicate that while malware is intuitively considered to be 'software that harmfully attacks other software, where to harmfully attack can be observed to mean to cause the actual behaviour to differ from the intended behaviour' (p. 105), this definition is insufficient. They claim that this is because the 'intended behaviour' is infrequently defined, and so a more accurate definition of malware needs to also consider the concept of 'software system correctness' (p. 105).

'In the wild' refers to how widespread the malware is. Malware such as viruses is not always released, and may be developed as a 'proof of concept' which could remain limited to a small network of computers or devices. When a piece of malware escapes or is intentionally released so that it spreads to unsuspecting users on other systems, it is considered to be 'in the wild'.

'Payload' is what the malware will actually do. In the 'cookie monster' example above, the payload refers to the application's demand for a 'cookie', thus preventing the user from continuing their work. The payload for the Stuxnet worm appears to be the program's ability to gain access to systems within the industrial plant. Furnell (2010, p. 189) identifies three main categories of payload, each of which is likely to be underpinned by different types of motive. These categories of payload are:

- damage and disruption (such as corrupting or deleting files);
- stealing information (such as using a keylogger to capture information, or copying files to the computer); and
- hijacking systems (enabling remote control of the system, perhaps to create a botnet – a distributed network of computers controlled by an unauthorised user).

Prevalence

Despite the relatively long history of malware, the problem seems to still be growing. Symantec (2011a) recorded over 3 billion malware attacks in 2010, with over 286 million variants of malware. They noted a 93 per cent increase in web-based attacks over 2009, with 42 per cent more mobile vulnerabilities noted.

> **Activity 4.1 Malware prevalence – geographical trends**
> Take a look at the McAfee Global Virus Map (http://home.mcafee.com/
> VirusInfo/VirusMap.aspx).
>
> Malware prevalence rates are not uniform globally. What areas of the world
> have the highest infection rates? What areas have the lowest rates? In your
> opinion, what causes such discrepancies in malware infection rates?

This increase in risk is also reflected by the 2010/11 Computer Security Institute (CSI) survey (CSI, 2011). The CSI survey indicates that 67.1 per cent of businesses claim to have been the victim of a malware infection. When compared to other threats, such as denial of service, password sniffing or financial fraud, malware infection was found to be the most prevalent incident. McAfee and the National Cyber Security Alliance (McAfee–NCSA, 2007) found that viruses are also a major problem for home users, with over half of surveyed homes having experienced a virus, and 44 per cent believing that they were currently infected with spyware.

Summary box 4.1 Definitions and prevalence rates
- The term 'malware' is derived from 'malicious software'.
- Malware generally spreads from computer to computer, and interferes with the normal functioning of those computers.
- A 'proof of concept' refers to a program (malware or otherwise) which is created to determine if the proposed functionality is feasible.
- 'In the wild' refers to malware which has spread.
- 'Payload' refers to what the malware actually does.
- Furnell (2010) suggests that there are three different types of payload – damage and disruption, stealing information and hijacking systems.
- Malware is a growing problem, with a high proportion of businesses and home users being victimised each year, and a large number of new threats being identified annually.

Types of malware

When most computer users think of malware, they think of computer viruses. While these are probably the best-known type of malware, there are many others, including worms, Trojan horses, spyware, keyloggers, logic bombs and rootkits. As well as these, there are also virus hoaxes that can cause destruction through the actions of users who follow the instructions contained in the hoax. Definitions of all types of malware can vary from researcher to researcher, and so those definitions which appear to be most commonly used are described below, and are summarised in Table 4.1. It is important to remember

Table 4.1 Types of malware

Type	Definition
Virus	A self-replicating program which needs some form of human action to run and propagate.
Worm	A self-replicating program which does not need a file to travel in, and has the capability to travel autonomously, without any human action required.
Spyware	A type of malware which collects information about the computer user, forwarding it to the creator of the spyware or a third party.
Trojans	Appears to be benign or useful software but once installed causes damage to the system, or allows another individual to gain control of the computer.
Logic bombs	Software that checks for certain conditions in a computer system and then executes when they arise.
Rootkits	Replaces the process management capabilities of a system with the intention of hiding the malware which is installed.
Hoaxes	Falsely warns of virus threats. This may result in lost work hours or damage to a system as a user unwittingly deletes an essential system file or downloads a real virus which they believe to be the solution to the threat.

that each type of malware is not necessarily independent – Edgar-Nevill and Stephens (2008) indicate that there can be 'blended attacks', where several types of malware are used in combination. However, the differences, at least from the victim's perspective, can be minor. Bocij (2006, p. 33) indicates that for most users malware types such as viruses and worms are very similar, and can have virtually the same effect on their systems.

Activity 4.2 Types of malware

Have you ever been the victim of a malware attack? If so, do you know which type of malware it was (virus, worm, Trojan, etc.?). Take a look at the websites of anti-malware companies (such as McAfee, Symantec and Sophos) and identify which of the current malware threats fall into each of these categories.

A *virus* is a self-replicating program, similar to the viral infections that cause human illness. In the same way as biological viruses need a host, computer viruses need a file to spread from one computer to another. While many individuals and organisations use the term 'virus' as a catch-all term for several types of malware, most definitions of computer viruses indicate that a true virus needs some form of human action to run and propagate, while other types of malware may not. This human action may be as simple as opening an infected document running an infected program.

A *worm* is very similar to a virus as it also spreads from computer to computer but, unlike a virus, it does not need a file to travel in, and most definitions agree that worms have the capability to travel autonomously, without any human action required. As such, worms are capable of both self-replication and self-transmission, and can send out thousands of copies of themselves. Tavani (2011, p. 177) indicates that worms can spread more quickly than viruses, as they do not need a human operator. He provides the example of the 'Code Red Worm'. This worm became prevalent in 2001, using a vulnerability in the Microsoft NT 4.0 operating system. It was designed to infect systems on days one to eighteen of a given month, and then activated its payload on the nineteenth day, when it would target additional computers. It would then lie dormant until the end of the month.

Spyware is a type of malware which collects information about the computer user, forwarding it to the creator of the spyware or a third party. This can put personal and corporate data at risk by divulging passwords, bank account details and browsing history. Furnell (2010) indicates that spyware always has the same objective – to invade privacy. This distinguishes it from other forms of malware which are less predictable in what they aim to do. Thompson (2005) indicates that as well as the privacy problems, spyware can also significantly slow down a computer, resulting in lost work hours. A specific type of spyware involves *keyloggers,* software devices that monitor the keystrokes of the user, such as passwords, usernames and confidential documents and correspondence, and then sends out a copy to the person who distributed the virus.

Trojan horses or *Trojans* are named after the ancient military tactic of the Greek soldiers who created a giant wooden horse, which they left outside the gates of the city of Troy after a lengthy siege. The Greek army then pretended to sail away, while the Trojans brought the horse inside the city walls as a victory trophy. Unknown to them, there were Greek soldiers hiding inside the horse, who crept out during the night and let the remainder of the Greek army inside the city. In malware terms, a Trojan horse will, at first glance, appear to be some type of benign or useful software, such as a picture or useful application. But once installed, the Trojan horse causes damage to the system or allows another individual to gain control of the computer. In some cases, the Trojan horse may still appear to perform the promised useful function. This is especially the case for Trojans with spyware payloads, where the distributor of the program would prefer if the user did not discover the spyware software.

Tavani (2011) indicates that a *logic bomb* is a piece of software that checks for certain conditions in a computer system and then executes when they arise. As such, it may form part of another piece of malware which determines when the payload executes. A *rootkit* replaces the process management capabilities of a system with the intention of hiding the malware which is installed. It is 'used to hide the installation of any files and other system details that should not be present on a victim's computer'

Illustration 4.1 Types of malware. Many types of malware exist, one of which is a 'Trojan horse'.

(Stephens, 2008, p. 127). If a rootkit is used in a malware program, and the user proceeds to check the status of their system, they will see a false projection of the true nature of their system, which may hide the malware from view.

While not necessarily including an actual software application, *virus hoaxes* can still cause problems by taking up user time and effort or by persuading users that a file on their system is a virus and must be deleted, while the file is actually important for the efficient running of the system. One of the first known hoaxes emerged in 1994, and was known as 'Good Times'. It warned of a virus with the power to erase a recipient's hard drive, and encouraged the reader to forward the warning to all their friends. The 'Good Times' virus did not actually exist, but the hoax did succeed in using up system resources, bandwidth and user time and effort as it was widely distributed by well-meaning users. More recently, hoaxes have become more sophisticated, sometimes using a pop-up message or other ploy to indicate to a user that their system has been scanned and a virus or vulnerability has been detected. These messages then direct the user to a website which offers a patch for the vulnerability or a file which will remove the virus. If the user downloads this file, they are unwittingly installing real malware on their system. In other cases users have received phone calls from individuals pretending to be customer support representatives of major software organisations. These 'representatives' are actually fraudulent, but they use social engineering tactics to persuade users to turn on their computers and pass control of their system to the representative, who may then instal malware onto their system.

There are many other types of software that can constitute components of malware files. Information about these is available through the websites of reputable anti-malware providers, and through academic journals such as the *Journal in Computer Virology*. Links to these sources are available in the online resources for this chapter.

Summary box 4.2 Types of malware

- While viruses are probably the best known type of malware, there are many other types, including worms, Trojans, spyware, logic bombs and rootkits.
- These types of malware are not necessarily independent, and several can exist within one piece of malware.
- Virus hoaxes can also cause disruption due to lost work hours or unintentional deletion of essential system files.

A brief history of malware

Due to its underground nature, it is difficult to say with certainty when the first malware was developed. Bocij (2006) suggests that while computer viruses have existed for some time, with 'naturally' occurring versions appearing as early as 1974 as part of programming glitches, most references to computer viruses did not appear until the early 1980s. Illustration 4.2 describes the timeline of some of the most famous malware of the past three decades, though it is far from an exhaustive list. Early malware focused on computers, but more recently malware has been developed which targets mobile phones. Most recently, malware has specifically targeted social networking sites and smartphones.

1982	• Elk Cloner • Targeted Apple operating systems and spread via floppy disc. It was not destructive, but it did display a poem about itself every fiftieth time that the contents of the disc were run.
1985/86	• ©Brain • First IBM-PC virus. This virus was designed to infect any computer running a pirated copy of software which was legitimately written and distributed by the creators of the virus.
1988	• Worm created by Robert Morris, a graduate student at Cornell University • Significantly damaged internet activity and was important as it demonstrated that cybercrime could have a significant disruptive effect on internet users.
ca. late 1980s	• Cascade virus • Had a payload that made text fall down the screen and land in a heap at the bottom.
1988	• Stoned or Marijuana virus • Displayed the message 'Your computer is stoned. Legalize Marijuana'.
1998	• HPS virus • Activated on Saturdays and flipped uncompressed bitmap files horizontally.
1999	• Melissa virus • Infected thousands of computers using Microsoft Outlook, causing an estimated $80 million in damage.
2000	• 'I love you' virus • Infected millions of computers by persuading users to open an infected attachment which pretended to be a love letter to the recipient.
2001	• 'Anna Kournikova' • Virus that posed as an attachment, appearing to be an image of a Russian tennis player.
2003	• 'Slammer' virus • Reputedly caused a large-scale denial of service on the internet, crashing computers at a nuclear power plant and disrupting a major bank's ATM network.
2004	• 'Cabir' • First known mobile phone virus. Thought to be a proof of concept, as it trasmittted only by using Bluetooth and simply displays the word 'Caribe' on the phone's screen when turned on.
2008	• 'Conficker' • Allows the distributor to use the computer as part of a remote controlled 'botnet' (a collection of infiltrated computers).
2008	• 'Koobface' • Worm which targets users of social networking sites and spreads by sending messages to a user's social networking contacts. These messages direct the contact to a third-party website, where they download an infected file.
2009	• 'Ikee' worm • First worm known to infect 'jailbroken' iPhones. • Changed the phone wallpaper to a picture of 1980s pop singer Rick Astley.
2010	• 'Stuxnet' • High-profile worm targeting equipment in industrial plants, most famously an Iranian nuclear power plant.

Illustration 4.2 Timeline of malware. A far from definitive list of high-profile malware, listed chronologically since the early 1980s.

As can be seen in the chart, some earlier malware producers demonstrated an interesting sense of humour in the payloads of their code. An example of this is the Cascade virus, which made all the text on the screen fall and land in a heap at the bottom. More recent computer-based malware shows less humour, but some early smartphone malware, such as the 2009 'ikee' worm, has occasionally demonstrated a return to such humour. This may be because the earliest malware written for devices was more of a proof of concept, and the malware developer may have more interest in drawing attention to the existence of the malware than those who develop malware for more established platforms, who may prefer to remain covert.

Also of note through the timeline is the use of social engineering to persuade victims to engage in behaviours that would infect their system. An example of this is the 2001 'Anna Kournikova' Trojan that appeared to be a photograph of a beautiful Russian tennis player. Similarly, some of the malware that targets social networking site users plays on people's desires for sociability – a wish to see and 'like' videos and links that friends share. In addition to this, these types of malware often rely on people's tendencies to trust links, videos and files that their friends have shared, feeling that if their friends have posted information about these resources, then they are more likely to be safe.

Summary box 4.3 A brief history of malware

- The earliest malware probably appeared in the mid-1970s, but was an unintentional result of programming glitches.
- The earliest known virus to appear in the wild was called Elk Cloner, and it targeted Apple operating systems from 1982.
- Malware has developed over the years, and now targets mobile phones, smartphones and social networking sites.
- Malware has made use of social engineering strategies to persuade users to engage in behaviours that will infect their systems.

Methods of malware production and distribution

There are two elements to malware as a cybercrime. Firstly, the malware must be developed, and secondly, it must be released into the wild.

While early malware developers produced their code from scratch, advanced programming skills are no longer required for development. Many malware development kits can be cheaply and easily obtained (Ollmann, 2008). Yar (2006, p. 32) describes how one of these development kits was used to create the 'Anna Kournikova' Trojan. The author admitted that it was his first attempt to create malware, and it only took a minute to prepare, due to a toolkit called the 'Vbs Worm Generator'. This toolkit allowed users to custom design a worm with a variety of destructive payloads. Despite the ease and speed with which malware can be created using such a development kit, custom programs are still sometimes preferred. This is because custom programs are less likely to be detected by antivirus software, and so are more likely to achieve their goal, and propagate more widely.

Once the malware has been developed, it must then be distributed. Furnell (2010) indicates that distribution methods can be linked to whatever new service is in favour with the online community. Historically, early viruses were spread via floppy disk. As such, it could take a long time for an infection to spread. In the late 1990s transmission by disk was frequently eschewed as infection via email became the preferred method. This was a faster method of transmission due to the increased popularity of email at that time and because a physical infected disk did not need to be present – the malware could spread through the email or an attachment instead.

Infection methods have continued to progress to other popular services, such as instant messaging, peer-to-peer sharing and social networking sites (Furnell, 2010). Collins (2006) lists several methods by which computer viruses and malware can be contracted, including opening email attachments, opening files, accessing webpages with malicious code, downloading software from the internet and sharing infected drives. As can be seen with Stuxnet, virus writers who are targeting offline systems are now returning to virus propagation by disk, specifically USB keys. After a piece of malware is produced, it may remain an active threat for a long time, as the original writers or others produce new variations of the program so as to bypass the security updates released by antivirus software products (Furnell, 2010).

Furnell (2010) reports the importance of social engineering in infecting systems, as the propagation system may still require user input to be successful. He indicates that many viruses have been linked to notable dates, such as Christmas, Valentine's Day or April Fool's day, as by doing so, virus writers and distributors feel that they have better chances of success. For example, a user may not feel that an attachment labelled 'Merry Christmas' which is received from a friend or family member is a threat, provided of course that the email is received in December. But this is not the only social engineering method that malware developers and distributors employ.

Rusch (2002) indicates that malware developers and distributors make use of several key social psychological principles when preparing the program in order to ensure that users are more likely to run the application or distribute the file. He indicates that people's use of heuristics (rules of thumb) to shorten decision-making time may play an important role. Because of a reliance on heuristic decision making, the more similar an application looks to a requested or useful file, the more likely a person is to open it without proper evaluation of the potential risk. Rusch also indicates that it is possible that users place too much trust in online sources and information, especially when the sender utilises friendly language and language that suggests that the recipient knows them. He also lists other reasons why people may be more likely to accept and open a malware program, such as claims of authority in the email (perhaps suggesting the email is from a trusted source such as a well-known corporation or public body or that the email has already been scanned for viruses).

As stated above, malware which targets social networking sites also takes advantage of social psychology in several ways, including exploiting a person's trust in their friends, and their desire to keep abreast of popular trends and internet memes. In addition to this, some malware utilises other human desires to encourage propagation. This can include greed. For example, in the hours following the death of Steve Jobs, several scams appeared on social networking sites promising to give away large numbers of iPads, iPhones and other Apple products in his memory. When a user clicked on these scam messages they unknowingly downloaded malware. These scams played on both human greed and the trust that people had in Apple as a major company.

Summary box 4.4 Methods of malware production and distribution

- While malware which is produced from scratch is preferred due to its potential ability to evade anti-malware software for longer, malware production kits are easily available.
- Methods of distribution of malware have varied over time and have taken advantage of popular online services.
- Early malware was distributed on floppy disks. Distribution via email then became popular. Modern malware uses a variety of means to propagate, including peer-to-peer sharing, webpages, email, instant messaging, social networking systems and USB disk drives.
- Much malware takes advantage of social engineering in order to encourage propagation and infection.

Motives of malware producers and disseminators

As with most types of crime, there is no single motive that explains all malware production and distribution. In many cases, the best indicator of motive is the payload (Furnell, 2010). It is also probable that there has been a change in motive over time – while originally virus writers claimed to write because of curiosity or altruistic reasons (such as discovering system vulnerabilities), there now appears to be a higher proportion of malware producers who are concerned with financial gain (Bocij, 2006). It should also be noted that the action of infecting a computer may not be the desired end result in itself – instead the infection may actually be a means to an end. Furnell (2010) states that 'it used to be a question of what the malware would do *to* the user's system or data, but it has increasingly become a case of what might be done *with* it' (p. 189). Furnell indicates that this distinction is important – in the first instance the damage, however extensive, is limited to the system. Files may be deleted or corrupted, and the system may become unusable, but the damage goes no further. However, if the system is compromised it may be used to acquire data about the user or others. In this case, the system is less obviously infected, and may be used for other purposes, such as distributing spam or being used as a 'zombie' or 'bot' in a denial of service attack.

Setting aside the potential motive of creating a bot, other possible motives for malware development and dissemination include desire to complete an intellectual challenge, boredom, social factors and vengeance. It is also possible that malware development may share some motives with vandalism, and this is explored towards the end of this section.

Financial motives

A malware developer may have financial motives, and Bocij (2006) suggests that virus writers gain financially from their work in two main ways – extortion and paid employment. In some cases, the virus writer may threaten to make confidential information (such as customer accounts) public, unless the company pays a sum of money. Bocij also suggests that virus writers may wish to gain paid employment either from antivirus software manufacturers or from other criminals who hire them to create custom viruses. In addition to these, malware developers may profit financially by using spyware to collect information about the user, such as bank account details, usernames, passwords or other personal information that makes them vulnerable to identity theft. This information may be used directly by the malware developer, or may be sold on to a third party, in some cases to an organised crime gang or a terrorist group, but in many cases stolen credit card details are easily purchasable by any internet user.

Intellectual challenges and avoiding boredom

Financial motives are easy to understand from a psychological perspective, but they do not seem to explain all malware development. For example, Thompson (2004) indicates that while the best virus writers can spend hours working on programs, they often have little interest in spreading them to the wild. His interview with a virus writer called 'Philet0ast3r' uncovered that the developer was afraid of being caught by the police and had ethical principles which prevented him from distributing the code. Thompson concludes that virus writers complete their acts for the intellectual challenge. He suggests that most virus authors are initially victimised by another virus, and as a result of this event become curious as to how they work. Bocij (2006) reflects Thompson's theory, and agrees that some viruses are created as a test of knowledge or out of curiosity – a form of proof of concept.

Another potential motive for virus writing may be as simple as alleviation of boredom, with malware producers seeking to gain enjoyment from the activity. The virus writer 'Philet0ast3r', in his interview with Thompson (2004), describes developing a virus which installed two chatbots (artificial agents who engage in conversations) on the infected computer, making them appear in a pop-up window. The chatbots hold a nervous conversation, visible to the user, where they wonder if the computer's antivirus software will find them. This aspect of 'fun' can also be seen in some of the more humorous payloads described above. Nevertheless, it cannot be denied that many malware programs are not created simply to entertain the developer. This is evident from some of the more sinister payloads which have been observed to date.

Just because a malware developer is motivated by alleviation of boredom or intellectual curiosity does not mean that their work will not appear in the wild. Thompson

(2004) describes how many virus writers post their code to the internet, for others to examine and copy and potentially disseminate. Thompson suggests that some of the malware developers who upload their code feel that they are not accountable for the actions of those who disseminate their viruses – that they have an interest in writing the programs, and that it is not their responsibility if others disseminate them. This can seem like a shallow defence though as, according to Thompson, security professionals suggest that virus writers are aware that by publishing the code on the internet, it will be picked up by a 'script-kiddie' (a person who cannot write good code themselves, but who will use code created by others). Thompson indicates that the original malware developer may be pleased to see the virus in the wild, even though they did not release it themselves. Nevertheless, some malware developers do claim to send a copy of the virus they wrote to the antivirus companies before they circulate it on the internet, to ensure that it cannot be used for negative purposes. Again Bocij (2006) echoes this, and indicates that some virus writers see their work as a service to heighten security.

Social factors

As with other types of cybercrime, it is possible that malware development may in part be driven by a developer's need for attention or peer recognition. Thompson (2004) indicates that virus writers get a thrill when their work appears on an antivirus company's website as a new 'alert'. He also indicates that peer acceptance is important, and that the virus writers he spoke to often work in groups, publish online magazines together and email their work to their friends. Bocij (2006) also indicates that peer recognition is important. He suggests that a virus writer experiences an increase in status if they create a particularly well-written or widespread program, especially if the virus becomes notorious and is discussed in the media and online.

Vengeance

Another potential motive for malware development involves vengeance against other people or organisations. For example, Thompson describes a virus writer called Vorgon who created a worm which targeted those companies who did not give him a job. Bocij (2006) describes how some virus writers will fight among themselves, or with others involved in computer security. He cites the example of a female virus writer called 'Gigabyte' who targeted Graham Clueley, a professional in the antivirus industry. He tells how Gigabyte became angry about Clueley's disparaging remarks about virus writers, and about how he perpetuated the stereotype of the male virus writer. She went on to release several viruses that specifically attempted to ridicule Clueley through the form of games and quizzes that users with infected computers were forced to partake in.

Vandalism

When comparing malware development to other types of crime, it seems to share many characteristics with vandalism (Bocij, 2006). For example, those malware applications that write messages on users' screens could be seen as comparable to engaging in non-artistic types of graffiti.[1] Destructive malware, such as damaging or deleting files, could be seen as similar to intentionally scratching a car or puncturing tyres. Bocij suggests that virus writers and vandals may therefore share motives for their behaviours, and proposes that some of these include 'boredom, misplaced anger, or an urge to rebel against authority' (p. 50).

Goldstein (1996) describes how the central behaviour of vandalism is aggression – intentional physical or psychological injury – and lists three potential theories of vandalism proposed by the literature – the 'enjoyment theory', the 'aesthetic theory' and the 'equity-control' theory.

The enjoyment theory suggests that vandalism has an intrinsic reward. The vandal gains satisfaction from the activity, which they may not be able to find through other activities such as schoolwork. A similar situation may be evident in malware developers – those who are capable of producing complex and effective code may not feel that they are being sufficiently challenged in school, and as such seek fulfilment elsewhere. In this sense, malware development may have similar origins to other types of juvenile delinquency, a theory which is supported by the evidence that many virus writers 'age-out' of the activity as they get older (see the work by Sarah Gordon below).

The aesthetic theory suggests that vandalism is motivated by a desire to enjoy the artistic qualities of the object, such as novelty, organisation and complexity. This may explain those involved in aesthetically appealing graffiti, who may be attempting to create artistic content while simultaneously leaving evidence of their presence in a given location. The malware developer may also be seeking to develop artistic content, although in their case the artistry may be expressed through a well-written piece of code. Another aspect of the aesthetic theory suggests that vandals may be motivated by a desire to take away the aesthetic qualities of a place or object, reducing it to a lesser state. Again, this may be applicable to malware developers, who wish to witness their creation reduce a previously functioning system to a worthless piece of equipment.

The final theory – equity-control theory – suggests that if a person perceives themselves to be in an inequitable situation, with little ability to modify the existing arrangements, they are more likely to engage in vandalism. The destruction or damaging of another's property appears to be a solution to resolving the inequity through quick and cheap means that are not beyond the vandal's control. This theory suggests that those who perceive themselves as having high inequity and low control are more likely to be engaged in vandalism. The equity-control theory may also be an appropriate psychological explanation for malware production, as it would appear to fit well with the vengeance motive described above. There is also empirical support for this model with educated samples (see, for example, DeMore *et al.*, 1988, who found support for the equity-control theory in university students). However, as with the enjoyment and the aesthetic theories, there have not yet been studies examining the equity-control theory's applicability to malware development.

> ### Activity 4.3 Vandalism and malware
> - Examine the list of malware in Illustration 4.2. Discuss how the theories of vandalism could be used to explain each of these. Are there any examples in this list that cannot be explained by a theory of vandalism?

Given the apparent success in applying theories of vandalism to malware development, it is worth considering the empirical research examining the characteristics of vandals. For example, Martin *et al.* (2003) studied a community sample of 2,603 adolescents and found that those who engaged in vandalism were more likely to experience a number of other problems, including family, parental, behavioural and psychological difficulties. These included increased reports of depression, anxiety, hopelessness, risk-taking behaviours and low self-esteem. The adolescent vandals also had higher levels of family pathology, parental overprotection, parental criticism and drug use. It would be interesting to examine the characteristics and backgrounds of malware developers in a similar fashion in order to determine how similar malware development is to vandalism, but a study of this scale examining malware developers has not yet been completed. Nevertheless, some preliminary work attempting to profile virus writers has been completed, and is discussed below.

Summary box 4.5 Motives of malware producers and disseminators
- Several motives of malware producers and disseminators have been suggested, and it is thought that these may have changed over time.
- Some malware developers may be motivated by financial reasons, while others may be motivated by intellectual challenges, alleviation of boredom, social gains or vengeance against a person or organisation.
- It is possible that malware developers and distributers might have similar motives and psychology to those who engage in vandalism. Psychologists have used three main theories to explain vandalism – the 'enjoyment theory'; the 'aesthetic theory' and 'equity-control theory', and these can be applied to malware development and distribution. However, it is not known if these can explain all malware cases, and there is limited empirical information available about the psychology of vandalism.

Profile and personality characteristics of offenders

Compared to hackers, there has been very little work which attempts to determine the profile and personality characteristics of malware developers. In particular, there is an extreme paucity of empirical work in the area, and what little has been done is now quite dated. Nevertheless, the work of Sarah Gordon (1993, 1994, 1996, 2000) has been innovative and crucial in providing some insights into the psychology of malware developers.

Gordon's initial work (1993) attempted to describe the mind of a male virus writer called 'Dark Avenger'. In this paper, Gordon indicates that privately, virus writers display frustration, anger and general dissatisfaction, but also some evidence of conscience, and indicates that during an interview with Dark Avenger, he demonstrated sorrow for his actions. Dark Avenger described his reasons for writing viruses, which mostly related to curiosity and interest in the concept of virus distribution. Unfortunately, the paper does not allow for inferences to be drawn regarding other virus writers as it is mostly a transcription of an interview between Gordon and a single virus writer.

Gordon (1994) then went on to describe four types of virus writers using data she had gathered using mixed methods research. She indicates that it is important that the heterogeneity of virus writers be considered, that virus writers vary with regard to circumstances, skills, personality and ambition. In this regard, Gordon (1994) identified four main types of virus writer – a young adolescent, a college student, a professional and a mature, reformed ex-virus writer. She particularly focused on moral development, and examined the virus writers in light of Kohlberg's (1969) moral development theory. Kohlberg's theory suggests that there are six stages of moral development through which children and adults can progress during their lives. Progressing through the levels depends on the extent to which moral standards are internalised and self-accepted moral principles are developed. It is interesting to note that it is possible to reach the highest levels of Kohlberg's stages and still be engaged in criminal activity, depending on how the individual rationalises their actions. However, it is generally accepted that criminals normally remain limited to the early stages of the model. Gordon (1994) identifies adolescent virus writers as being ethically normal and of average or above average intelligence. These virus writers showed respect for their parents and understood right from wrong, but typically did not accept responsibility for the effects of their viruses. The college student virus writers also appeared to be ethically normal, and again were not concerned about the results of their actions. The adult virus writers were the smallest group, and appeared to be below the level of ethical maturity normal for their age. The ex-virus writers were ethically normal, and indicated that they had ceased their virus writing because of lack of time or boredom with the activity. They generally seemed to be socially well adjusted and undecided about the ethical acceptability of virus writing. Gordon described four case studies, including one example from each group, and she concludes that the four individuals are different in personal characteristics, with each being at an appropriate stage of development for their age, excepting the adult virus writer's lower moral development stage. The small sample involved in this early research allows few conclusions to be made, but it did illustrate that not all virus writers are the same, and that there is variation in age, income, education, location and social interaction, among other characteristics.

Gordon continued her research in a second paper relating to the heterogeneity and characteristics of virus writers (1996). Again she emphasises that all virus writers are not the same, and indicates that it is impossible to draw conclusions about the psychology of virus writers as if they were a homogeneous group. In this study, she follows up on three of the cases described in the earlier (1994) paper. She found that the adult virus writer continued to distribute viruses, and that the adolescent had moved on from just virus writing to also becoming involved in virus distribution. However the college student had stopped writing viruses. These findings supported Gordon's theory that virus writers 'age-out', becoming more likely to give up virus writing as they become older. This is similar to research findings relating to other types of crime, with most individuals who are involved in crime as children and young adults being unlikely to become lifetime persistent offenders (see, for example, Farrington, 1990).

Gordon (1996) discusses the particularly interesting case of the student who had given up virus writing. She indicates that he previously had said that he wrote viruses primarily for his own personal learning, and that it was acceptable as long as it was not harmful. The student had subsequently been confronted by a user who had been victimised by one of his viruses. This initiated a change in his perspective so that he then publicly stated that virus writing was wrong for both himself and other people, regardless of intent, and that he would no longer write viruses. While this is just one case study, it is of interest to note the change in perspective of the virus writer when forced to consider the consequences of his actions. It suggests that if virus writers were more aware of the consequences, then perhaps fewer would continue with the behaviour. Gordon (1996) also suggests that as virus writers become older, peer pressure becomes less important, and morality develops, until they retire from virus writing. As such, she indicates that for most virus writers, as for most juvenile offenders, the antisocial activity eventually ends on its own. Unfortunately, as new generations discover viruses, younger individuals start to replace those who have aged out. On approaching the 'next generation' of virus writers, Gordon found that while they initially appeared to be more aggressive and technologically advanced than earlier virus writers, they were generally similar in skill level to their predecessors. However, there were exceptions, which she classified as the 'new age virus writers', who were older, generally employed, and more private. Gordon suggests that as these virus writers are already older, they are less likely to 'age-out'. Nonetheless, again Gordon's work is mostly based on a small number of participants, and it is difficult to assess whether these findings can be generalised to a wider sample of virus writers.

In 2000, Gordon considered the impact of high-profile legal intervention, such as arrests and visits by law enforcement personnel, on the virus writing communities. She suggests that for the adults who continue to write viruses, it is not the law that is important, but the individual's perception of likelihood of prosecution. Gordon concludes that laws have some limited effect for some individuals, but that laws that are considered to infringe an individual's freedom of speech (or freedom to write viruses) could result in a backlash in the US. She therefore suggests that any aggressive legislation relating to virus writing would be unlikely to have any positive impact on reducing the problem.

While Gordon's research is interesting, there has been relatively little large-scale evaluation of the psychological profile of computer virus writers. In addition, most of her work relating to the psychology of virus writers is now quite dated. Other authors, such as Bocij (2006), have reviewed some of the early literature relating to virus writer characteristics and indicate that the traditional stereotype of the socially inept teenager who writes viruses as a form of revenge against society may have some truth behind it. Nevertheless, Bocij suggests that current malware producers are now somewhat older than they were in the 1990s, with most being in their twenties rather than teenagers. He also suggests that there has been an increase in female virus writers.

The most relevant study of recent years was completed by Rogers, Siegfried and Tidke (2006) who investigated self-reported criminal behaviour, including virus writing and virus use, among students. They found that 88 per cent of their sample of seventy-seven students was classified as computer criminals, and that introversion was a significant predictor of engaging in computer criminal behaviour. Other personality characteristics, such as internal moral choice, social moral choice, hedonistic moral choice, conscientiousness, neuroticism, openness to experience and agreeableness were not found to be predictors of cybercriminal behaviour. Unfortunately, Rogers, Siegfried and Tidke's (2006) study does not differentiate between different types of computer criminal – as well as being involved in computer viruses, the students were classified as computer criminals if they guessed passwords, used another person's password without permission, looked at or changed other people's files without permission, obtained another person's credit card information without permission or used a device to obtain free telephone calls. Therefore, it is difficult to be certain that introversion is directly linked to virus writing or virus use, as the other types of computer criminal may have skewed the results. Rogers, Siegfried and Tidke (2006) do not report what percentage of the group was involved in virus writing or virus use. They also admit that these findings were in contrast to an earlier study completed by Rogers, Smoak and Liu (2006), which found that there were differences between self-reported computer criminals and non-criminals on moral choice and exploitive/manipulative behaviours.

Overall, the empirical psychological research relating to the characteristics of virus writers is remarkably limited, especially given the comparatively massive library of work which has been done examining the psychology of computer hackers. A satisfactory, recent empirical study of malware developer psychology remains elusive. Nevertheless, there has been some research which has examined how psychology can influence a user's intention to engage in safe online behaviour, which will now be examined.

Summary box 4.6 – Personality and profile of malware offenders

* Very little work has been completed which attempts to describe the personality and profile of malware developers and distributors.

- The most detailed work in this area was completed by Sarah Gordon, although this is now quite dated.
- Gordon noted that virus writers displayed frustration, anger and general dissatisfaction, but also an element of conscience.
- She described four categories of virus writer: the young adolescent, the college student, the adult virus writer and the ex-virus writer. All showed normal moral development, except for the adult virus writer.
- Gordon noted that virus writers tended to 'age-out', with most (but not all) giving up virus writing as they get older. This is a similar trend to other types of juvenile delinquency.
- Gordon also indicated that virus writers' perception of likelihood of prosecution was important.

Prevention methods

The most common preventative measure taken against malware is antivirus software, which should be used in conjunction with firewall software for intrusions. Most antivirus software can both detect viruses and delete them. In some cases it can also repair damaged files, and remove infected sectors of disk drives. However, anti-malware software cannot always catch every threat, simply because there is always a risk that a system could become infected before the anti-malware software has been updated. Malware is constantly evolving so that it has the opportunity to release its payload before it is detected by antivirus software, and Furnell (2010) describes how some malware also actively defends itself against anti-malware software. It can do this by blocking access to the antivirus vendor's website in order to prevent security updates and by changing system configurations so that the antivirus does not run automatically on start up.

Because of these advances in malware, the human element in security is increasingly important. According to Huang *et al.* (2010), 'no matter how well designed, security methods rely on individuals to implement and use them' (p. 221). From this perspective, psychology can provide some insights into the behaviour and attitudes of potential victims. For example, Lee *et al.* (2008) indicate that individual internet users play important roles in preventing the distribution of malware – if they open email attachments or download infected software, it puts them and others at risk. Lee *et al.* (2008) emphasise the importance of people's cognitive appraisal of threats in generating a motivation to protect themselves, and they apply this to anti-malware. They use the example of protection motivation theory, devised by Rogers (1975, 1983), which proposes that there are six main components that influence the intention to protect the self from a threat. These components, along with their application to malware infection prevention, are outlined in Table 4.2.

Table 4.2 Protection motivation theory and malware infection prevention

Component	Applied to malware	Sample cognition
Perceived severity of the threatened event	Beliefs regarding the payload and damage the malware can do to the system	'A virus could destroy all my files, so it is important that I protect my system'
Perceived probability of the threat	Person's belief that they are likely to be victimised	'Computer viruses are very common, and if I am not adequately protected, it is extremely likely that I will be victimised'
Perceived response efficacy of preventative measures	Person's belief that anti-malware software will be effective	'Antivirus software is regularly updated, and it is unlikely that I will be infected with a virus before it is identified by the software'
Perceived self-efficacy in using preventative measures	Beliefs regarding ability to properly maintain anti-malware software or engage in other preventative measures	'There is no point in me downloading antivirus software as I will never remember to update it'
Potential rewards	Expectations of maintaining a malware-free system	'If I keep my antivirus software up to date, my data will be secure'
Potential costs	Sacrifices the person may have to make to prevent infection	'Antivirus software is too expensive, and it will slow down my operating system'

Activity 4.4 Rogers' protection motivation theory and malware infection cognitions

Using the sample cognitions in Table 4.2 as a guide, develop further examples of sample cognitions for each of the six components of protection motivation theory. Identify how these cognitions could be used to persuade computer users and professionals to engage in safer anti-malware behaviour.

Consistent with this theory, Lee *et al.* (2008) found that a number of variables predicted intention to adopt virus protection behaviour in a sample of college students. These variables included perceived self-efficacy in using virus protection measures, perceived response efficacy of virus protective measures, positive outcome expectations of virus protection measures, prior virus infection experiences and perceived vulnerability to virus threats. Conversely, they found no significant relation between perceived severity of virus attacks and negative outcome expectancies on intention to adopt protective measures. They conclude that in order to increase security, it is important to both increase individuals' awareness of the likelihood of virus attacks and also conduct interventions to increase self-efficacy and response efficacy beliefs.

Several other studies have examined the variables that predict users' intentions to engage in safer online behaviour. Huang *et al.* (2010) found that six factors characterised people's perceptions of threats to information security. These factors were knowledge, impact, severity, controllability, awareness and possibility, and bear strong similarity to the variables identified by Lee *et al.* (2008). Huang *et al.* (2010) also found that the user's computer experience had a significant effect on perception of information security, with experienced users having more knowledge about threats and feeling that it would be easier to reduce the effects of the threats.

In the same vein, Ng *et al.* (2009) used the Health Belief Model to study users' computer security behaviour. The Health Belief Model was developed by Rosenstock (1966) and is used in psychology to predict both health behaviours and responses to treatment in ill patients. It proposes that behaviour results from a set of core beliefs, including susceptibility to illness, severity of illness, the costs and benefits involved in carrying out the behaviour and cues to action (such as the perception of symptoms). In later forms of the model, other core beliefs have been added, such as health motivation and perceived control. With relation to computer security behaviour, Ng *et al.* (2009) found that perceived susceptibility, perceived benefits and self-efficacy explain email-related security behaviour. However, the Health Belief Model has several criticisms, which may also apply to computer security behaviour. These include that it focuses a great deal on conscious processing of information – it is possible that computer users do not consider online security in such detail.

Ng and Rahim (2005) used the theory of planned behaviour to investigate users' intention to practise home computer security. The theory of planned behaviour suggests that the stronger a person's intention to behave in a particular way, the more likely they are to actually do so (Ajzen, 1988, 1991). Ng and Rahim (2005) tested to see if home computer users intended to regularly update their antivirus software, as well as backing up critical data and using a personal firewall. They found that attitude and subjective norm were associated with intentions. Other important factors found to influence home users were perceived usefulness, family and peer influence, mass-media influence and self-efficacy.

These factors are not just useful for predicting the security intentions of personal computer users. Similar studies have been completed with business executives. For example, Lee and Larsen (2009) found that the intention of the executives of small and medium-sized businesses to adopt anti-malware software was predicted by their appraisal of the level and type of threat involved, as well as their appraisal of how well they would cope with an infection. Lee and Larson also noted that there was considerable variance between the executive's intent to adopt and whether or not they actually adopted the software, with this variance caused by social influence from key stakeholders and variables specific to the situation, such as budget and support matters. Similar variables affect intentions of security professionals. Lee and Larson (2009) also found that intent to adopt anti-malware software by information security experts and information technology intensive industries was primarily affected by threat appraisal and social influence, as well as vendor support. In contrast, intent to adopt by non-information security experts and non-information technology intensive industries was more influenced by coping appraisal and budget issues.

In order to encourage safer online behaviour, it is important to understand how users view malware. Wash (2010) used qualitative research to identify mental models of security threats used by home computer users when choosing security software, and four conceptualisations of malware emerged. He found that while all his participants had some mental model of the effects of malware, they tended to use the term 'virus' as a catch-all term for malicious software. He found that some participants had very under-developed models of viruses, knowing that viruses cause problems but being unable to really describe these problems adequately. Others saw viruses as 'buggy software' rather than as code specifically written for malicious purposes. A third group saw viruses as intentionally annoying pieces of software, but rarely had well-developed ideas of what the virus writer was like. A final, fourth group felt that viruses were created to support criminal activities, with identity theft as the ultimate goal. Only a small number of participants recognised multiple types of virus. Wash's research suggests that most computer users have a limited understanding of the full complexity of malware, and this may result in faulty cognitions with regard to online security. If users have greater awareness of the phenomenon of malware, they may be more capable of better security decisions.

Despite the regularity with which threat appraisal determines intent to engage in online security behaviours, there is evidence to indicate that we are probably not capable of accurately judging threat appraisal. Campbell *et al.* (2007) found that students believed that positive internet events were more likely to happen to them and negative internet events were less likely to happen to them compared to the average student. Interestingly, heavy internet users were more optimistic than light users were, despite increased time spent online.

Lee *et al.* (2008) propose several measures which may both improve online security and increase users' intention to take preventative measures to protect their systems. These measures include appropriate standardisation of antivirus software applications, such as a requirement to include antivirus software with all new personal computers and the use of filtering technology on all email applications. Lee *et al.* (2008) also suggest other methods of improving security, including guidelines for public notification, and a legal requirement for website proprietors to reveal the risk of virus infection from downloading files from their website. Lee *et al.* (2008) also suggest that automated warnings each time a user tries to open an attachment or download a file could be beneficial, especially if they were coupled with an automated check of the recency of the current version of the user's antivirus software. These warnings may be particularly useful with the increased popularity of smartphones.

Johnston and Warkentin (2010) indicate that one method of influencing user intentions to engage in online security involves 'fear appeals'. These are fear-inducing arguments incorporated into persuasive communications. They found that fear appeals do impact on user intentions to engage in safer behaviours, but this is not consistent across all users – the effects of self-efficacy, response efficacy, threat severity and social influence identified earlier in this section also had an impact on compliance. It is therefore important that any prevention interventions consider a wide variety of user characteristics in order to ensure maximum impact.

Summary box 4.7 Prevention methods

- The most common prevention methods for malware infection involve technological interventions, such as antivirus software.
- However, these are only effective when used properly, and psychology can provide insights into successful use of such interventions.
- Researchers have applied various psychological theories to predict use of technological interventions. These include:
  - Rogers' protection motivation theory;
  - Rosenstock's health belief model;
  - Ajzen's theory of planned behaviour.
- Factors found to determine likelihood to take preventative measures include:
  - perceived self-efficacy in using virus protection measures;
  - perceived response efficacy of virus protective measures;
  - positive outcome expectations of virus protection measures;
  - prior virus infection experiences;
  - perceived vulnerability to virus threats;
  - perceived susceptibility;
  - intention to engage in preventative measures;
  - perceived usefulness;
  - family and peer influence;
  - mass-media influence.
- It should be remembered that people tend to believe that they are more likely to experience positive events, and less likely to experience negative events than average.
- Many methods are available which would encourage better online security.

Conclusion

While very little is known about the psychology of malware developers, a considerable volume of research has examined user intentions to engage in online security. As a result of this, it is probable that some effective intervention strategies could be developed which would encourage users to engage in safer behaviours. Malware has developed significantly over the past three decades, infecting a wider variety of devices using a greater number of methods. Some researchers are starting to consider what may occur in the future, should there be wider use of technological implants by humans. For example, Gasson (2010) describes how he was implanted with a radio frequency identification (RFID) device which was infected with a computer virus. These RFID devices have previously been implanted in individuals to allow access to secure areas in government buildings or VIP areas in nightclubs. Gasson argues that RFID devices have evolved to the extent that they should be considered simple computers, and so the potential repercussions of human infection with computer viruses need to be evaluated from moral, ethical and legal perspectives. While this is a fascinating area of research, it would seem that we still have some time to consider such potential infections, and the bulk of our efforts should be focused on heightening security behaviours in response to current threats, such as malware on social networking sites and smartphones.

Essay questions

(1) Malware developers appear to 'age-out' in a similar fashion to other juvenile delinquents. Compare and contrast the psychology of malware developers and juvenile delinquents.

(2) Education of users is more effective than antivirus software. Discuss.

(3) Describe the evolution of computer viruses, including how viruses can now be found on mobile devices and social networking sites. Evaluate the role psychology has played in this evolution.

(4) Is malware development a type of vandalism?

(5) While Sarah Gordon's work examining the psychology of virus writers is quite dated, it is still relevant to malware today. Discuss.

Additional reading

Books and articles

While dated, Sarah Gordon's work on the psychology of virus writers is still fascinating reading. Her articles include the following:

Gordon, S. (1993). Inside the mind of the Dark Avenger. *Virus News International* (January 1993). Abridged version retrieved from www.research.ibm.com/antivirus/SciPapers/Gordon/Avenger. html.

(1994). The generic virus writer. Presented at the 4th International Virus Bulletin Conference, Jersey, 8–9 September. Retrieved from http://vx.netlux.org/lib/asg03.html.

(1996). The generic virus writer II. In *Proceedings of the 6th International Virus Bulletin Conference*, Brighton, UK, 19–20 September. Retrieved from http://vx.netlux.org/lib/static/vdat/epgenvr2.htm.

(2000). Virus writers: the end of the innocence? In *Proceedings of the 10th International Virus Bulletin Conference*, Orlando, FL, 28–29 September. Retrieved from www.research.ibm.com/antivirus/SciPapers/VB2000SG.htm.

Other articles and book chapters of specific relevance to malware include:

Furnell, S. (2010). Hackers, viruses and malicious software. In Y. Jewkes and M. Yar (eds.), *Handbook of Internet Crime*. Cullompton, UK: Willan (pp. 173–93).

Kramer, S. and Bradfield, J. C. (2010). A general definition of malware. *Journal in Computer Virology*, **6**, 105–14.

Ollmann, G. (2008). The evolution of commercial malware development kits and colour-by-numbers custom malware. *Computer Fraud and Security*, **9**, 4–7.

Websites

Symantec provides several online resources of interest to those who wish to know more about malware. Their collection of whitepapers relating to online security is updated regularly and can be browsed at www.symantec.com/business/security_response/whitepapers.jsp.

Symantec also host 'Connect', an online resource of articles and communications. The articles in the 'Security' section are of particular interest to those who wish to know more about malware. See www.symantec.com/connect/security/articles.

McAfee includes interesting and useful information about virus threats, virus hoaxes and antivirus tips. Particularly interesting is their interactive global virus map, which allows users to track different types of virus activity over different timeframes, see http://home.mcafee.com/VirusInfo/VirusMap.aspx.

Similarly, Sophos includes a vast quantity of interesting information in its threat analyses section, at www.sophos.com/en-us/threat-center/threat-analyses.aspx.

Endnote

1 It should be noted that there are many graffiti artists who make public spaces more aesthetically pleasing through their work, and these are not included in this comparison with malware developers. Graffiti can be considered by many as true artistic works, and some graffiti artists have become famous due to their creations.

5 | Identity theft and fraud

Case studies

Deirdre was alarmed to receive an email from her friend Steven, saying that he had been travelling abroad and had his wallet stolen. He desperately needed some cash to tide him over until he could get home, and he begged her to send him £500 to cover his expenses and pay his hotel bill. He promised to reimburse her in full once he got home. While Deirdre wasn't particularly close to Steven, she was eager to help, and hated to see her friend in distress. She sent him the money, following the instructions in his email. A week later she rang Steven to make sure that he had got home all right, only to discover that he had no idea what she was talking about. Steven's email account had been hacked by a fraudster, who had sent the begging email to every account in his address book.

James checked his email, and found that one of his favourite online shops had sent him a message to tell him that his account had been compromised. He needed to log in to his account immediately to check what had happened, and to avoid any more losses. James clicked on the link in the email in a panic, bringing him to the homepage of the online store, where he entered his login details. At this point an error message appeared, asking him to try again later. James emailed the online store, and waited for a response. When they responded they advised him to cancel his credit card, as it was likely that he was the victim of identity theft. The website he had entered his details on was a fake, created by fraudsters, with the intention of getting access to his account.

Chapter overview

Fraud isn't a new phenomenon. It has existed in some form for hundreds of years, and some examples of offline fraud are provided below for comparison purposes. But the widespread use of the internet has meant that it has been identified by fraudsters as a potential new method of identifying and targeting victims. Initiating an online fraud is cheaper and easier than trying to do so offline; less effort is wasted on targeted individuals (or 'marks') who do not fall for the fraud, and there may be a perception by the offender that they are less likely to be apprehended due to the relative anonymity of the internet. This chapter will attempt to determine what fraud and identity theft are, and how much of these crimes exist online. Descriptions of offline frauds will be presented, with indications of how some of these have migrated to online fraud. The methods of attack used by fraudsters and identity thieves will be described, and attempts will be made to identify what elements of human psychology make us vulnerable to online fraud. The effects of fraud on the victim will be considered, along with possible methods of helping users to avoid being victimised.

Definitions and prevalence rates

While both identity theft and fraud are considered and described in this chapter, and in some cases they occur in the same crime, they have different characteristics. Fraud refers to the use of trickery for some gain, often financial. Identity theft refers to the use of someone else's documentation or personal information, again generally for financial gain. Other types of 'identity theft' can occur online – anyone who has left their social networking site logged in and later found that a friend or relation has used the opportunity to post embarrassing comments on their profile will likely feel some form of identity infringement. However, this type of activity is often done as a prank, or in more negative cases, as a form of bullying (see Chapter 7), but rarely involves financial losses, and so these cases won't be considered in depth here.

Fraud comes in many different types. Some fraudsters target individuals, promising goods or services where the descriptions do not match reality (evident in some cases of online auction fraud). In other cases a fraudster might suggest to their potential victim that they stand to gain significant amounts of money by complying with the fraudster's requests (such as in lottery fraud or advance fee fraud). Other types of online fraud

Illustration 5.1 Identity theft. Identity theft involves the use of someone else's documentation or personal information, often for financial gain. However, other types of online impersonation can occur.

specifically target organisations, such as 'click-fraud', which may seek to deplete a company's advertising budget by repeatedly clicking on advertisements.

McQuade (2006) defines identity theft as 'acquiring and then unlawfully using personal and financial account information to acquire goods and services in someone else's name' (p. 69). Smith (2010) indicates that while it is not a new criminal activity, it is facilitated by information technology. New technologies make it easier to access personal information and to fabricate important identity documents.

Marshall and Stephens (2008) describe how people are required to present some kind of 'trusted token' to either validate their identity or confirm that they have the authorisation to complete the action they are attempting. In offline contexts, this can include a credit card or identification card, such as a passport. In online contexts, such physical 'trusted tokens' are less frequently used (though there are some cases where organisations require scanned copies of such physical documents). More frequently used 'trusted tokens' online involve passwords. The interactions which are most vulnerable to identity theft and fraud online tend to require more trusted tokens than those that are not. For example, for most email accounts, a user requires only their email address and a single password to access the information. However, for online banking, it is common that three or four trusted tokens are required (such as an account number, date of birth and a password). Use of credit cards online can require even more information – the credit card number, cardholder's name, expiration date and card code verification (CCV) number are normally the minimum information required, but other trusted tokens, such as the cardholder's address and a verification password, may also be required. As identity theft often involves the fraudulent presentation of such trusted tokens, Marshall and Stephens argue that identity theft should really be considered 'authority fraud'.

Activity 5.1 'Trusted tokens' and online security

List your online accounts under the following headings: banking; shopping; email; social networking sites; other. For each account, identify how many pieces of information you must provide as 'trusted tokens'. Which accounts need the most trusted tokens? Which accounts need the fewest? Does the number of trusted tokens required match the risks involved should someone gain unauthorised access to your account? How could the number of trusted tokens be increased?

As with many other types of online crime, it is impossible to know exactly how much fraud and identity theft occurs. However, these types of offences are probably the cybercrimes which most users have some kind of experience of – most people have received an email which attempted some kind of fraud, or tried to get the reader to disclose some trusted tokens in the way of personal information. Online fraud and identity theft have reached a level of prevalence where many resources have been developed for both personal and corporate users advising them on how to improve their security (see, for example, Archer *et al.*, 2012; Collins, 2006; Lininger and Vines, 2005; Mintz, 2012).

While identity theft and fraud are recognised as significant problems, it is still likely that many individuals and organisations are victimised or targeted without their experiences ever being reflected in estimates of crime rates. Smith (2010) indicates there are several reasons why it is very difficult to determine the true extent of the problem of identity theft. These include:

- a lack of clarity regarding the definition of the concepts involved;
- fear by victims of reporting the offence as criminals may implicate them in the criminal event (this may be especially true for victims of advance fee fraud scams who may have inadvertently been involved in money laundering activities);
- fear of secondary victimisation, where a user feels feel that they may be blamed by others for activities which could be seen as having enabled their victimisation.

Yar (2006) also suggests several reasons why the true extent of internet fraud is not known, including:

- victims may not report the crime due to the loss of relatively small amounts of money – they may feel that it is more trouble to report than it is worth;
- the victim may be embarrassed that they were deceived;
- the victim may not know who to report the crime to;
- the victim might also feel that it is unlikely that they will get their money back, so there is little point in going to the trouble of reporting it.

Levi (2001) indicates that victims may not be asked about their victimisation, or are unaware of their victimisation, which may also result in underestimation of the extent of the problem. It is also probable that many potential victims would not report the event if they received an email suspected to be fraudulent, but they were not deceived into losing any money.

Despite these difficulties in calculating the true levels and costs of identity theft and fraud, there are some estimates available from a number of sources. The UK National Fraud Authority (NFA) estimated in their 2012 report that fraud loss against the UK amounts to approximately £73 billion per annum, although not all of this occurs online. Of this, the private sector is the most severely hit (at £45.5 billion), followed by the public sector (at £20.3 billion) and individuals and not-for-profit sectors (at £6.1 billion and £1.1 billion respectively). Using a large-scale survey in December 2011, they found that 10 per cent of participants had been a victim of fraud within the previous two years. The NFA reported that online banking fraud losses alone amounted to £35 million in 2011, but that this was a reduction on the previous year, probably due to customers using better protection systems and security measures brought in by banks.

Smith (2010), based on a review of several studies regarding the extent of identity theft, estimates that losses for major countries are in excess of £1 billion annually per country, although it should be noted that much of this identity theft occurs offline. Jewkes (2010) cites a 2007 US Federal Trade Commission report that indicated that over a twelve-month period, 8.3 million Americans had been victims of identity theft.

She also cites a report by the credit-checking agency Experion, covering the same time period, that reported a growth of 69 per cent in identity theft in the UK.

A specific strategy used by identity thieves and online fraudsters involves 'phishing' (a description of which is provided below). The Anti-Phishing Working Group (APWG) is the global association which attempts to eliminate fraud and identity theft resulting from phishing and related incidents. Their Phishing Activity Trends Report for the first half of 2011 indicates that unique phishing email reports from customers exceeded 20,000 per month, with approximately 30,000 unique phishing websites detected per month. Over 300 brands were hijacked by phishing campaigns every month, with the US being the country that hosted the most phishing websites. About 70 per cent of URLs contained some form of target name (Anti-Phishing Working Group, 2011).

Despite the inability to accurately assess the extent of identity theft and fraud online, the statistics above clearly indicate that it is a severe problem. However, these are not new offences, and offline versions of these crimes have existed for many years.

Summary box 5.1 Identity theft and fraud definitions and prevalence

- Fraud refers to the use of trickery for some gain, often financial.
- Identity theft refers to the use of someone else's documentation or personal information, again normally for financial gain.
- Fraud has many different types, and can target individuals, companies, public sector and not-for-profit groups.
- New technologies make it easier for fraudsters and identity thieves, but these types of offences are not new.
- Identity theft often involves the unauthorised use of some kind of 'trusted token', such as a password, account number, or other information or documentation.
- It is difficult to know exactly how much identity theft and fraud occurs, as there are several reasons why they may not be reported, including fear or embarrassment on the part of the victims, or a lack of awareness of who to report the offence to.
- However some organisations, such as the UK National Fraud Authority and the Anti-Phishing Working Group, publish regular updates on the extent of such problems.

Similar offline offences

While online fraud is obviously a relatively new offence, many types of online fraud are derived from offline frauds that have existed for many years. For example, some travelling salesmen sold potions that claimed to have medicinal properties. These potions were advertised as having the ability to cure many different types of illnesses and maladies, and in many cases the fraudster used an accomplice, who pretended to be an audience member who had been healed by the potion. This encouraged many other members of the audience to invest in the potion. By the time these customers discovered that they had been deceived, both the fraudster and their accomplice had moved on to another town. A modern online equivalent of this fraud is 'pharma-fraud', which is discussed in more detail below.

Other famous types of fraud include Ponzi schemes and pyramid schemes. Both of these rely on the recruitment of new members to the schemes in order to provide returns to early investors. While the early investors may then make a profit, the schemes eventually run out of new recruits, and most of those who joined later in the scheme lose all their investment.

Employment fraud targets some of the most vulnerable members of society, persuading them that they can earn significant amounts of money through adminis-trative or production work carried out at home. These victims are persuaded to pay a fee upfront in order to cover expenses or provide materials, but the nature of the scheme means that they seldom make their initial investment back. If payment is made, it often involves fake cheques, or the use of fake bank accounts (often as part of a larger money laundering scheme). Advertisements for such employment schemes are common online.

Finally, lottery frauds can occur offline. A victim discovers that they have won a prize on a scratchcard, but in order to claim the prize they must call a premium rate phone line to submit their details and discover which of the many prizes on offer they have actually won. The call can often last for some time, and towards the end of the call the victim discovers that they have won a relatively worthless prize (such as a small sum of money, or a piece of costume jewellery). The fraudsters make their profit through the charges on the premium call. Many similar lottery frauds occur online, often involving a degree of identity theft as the user divulges confidential information. In other cases, online lottery scams require the 'winner' to forward an administrative fee in advance of receiving their winnings (which never arrive).

The above are just some of the types of offline fraud that can occur – there are many more. However, other types of fraud occur mostly online, and these are considered in the next section.

Summary box 5.2 Offline fraud schemes
- While online fraud is relatively new, offline fraud has existed for centuries.
- Offline fraud can take a variety of forms, including the selling of fake medicines, Ponzi schemes, pyramid schemes, employment fraud and lottery fraud.

Methods of attack

Clough (2010) describes how 'the internet is a paradise for those who prey upon the gullible, the greedy or the vulnerable' (p. 183). There are several advantages to carrying out identity-related crime in online environments, as outlined by Jaishkankar (2008).

These include that it is easier to carry out such crimes online, it can occur faster and they can occur across international boundaries. Several different strategies are used for online identity theft and online fraud. In some cases, the offender may use information available online to target a specific victim, while in other cases the offender has many targets, and they utilise a broad approach in the hope that some will fall for the scheme. In some cases the offenders use social engineering strategies, attempting to persuade the victim to part with money or useful information, generally involving some kind of trickery. Table 5.1 gives an overview of several of the main methods of attack, with some of the more common attack methods described in more detail in the sections that follow.

Social networking site fraud

Social networking sites (SNS) are a very popular method of keeping in touch with friends and family. Individuals create profiles on these websites that can include a lot of personal information. This disclosure of information can leave the individual at risk of several types of cybercrime, including stalking and online child predation. However, for the purposes of this chapter, the focus here will be on identity theft and fraud. It may be that the user includes so much personal information on their profile that they are vulnerable to identity theft – it may be easy to determine the answers to key security questions, such as date of birth, telephone number and mother's maiden name, based only on the content of an individual's profile. However, there are also several examples of frauds occurring on social networking sites. Social networking site fraud takes a variety of forms, but most commonly attempt to persuade users to click on particular links, visiting specific websites or installing specific applications. The outcomes of clicking on these posts vary – in some cases users are persuaded to complete online forms providing sensitive information, in others users allow the scammers to have access to personal information from their SNS profiles. The scams can also surreptitiously install malware onto the user's computer, which may then be used for further cybercrime, such as the creation of a 'botnet' (a network of computers controlled by a hacker to engage in a particular action, such as an attack on a specific website or system). In some cases, the victim is persuaded to provide so much information that they are at risk of identity theft.

These frauds use a variety of methods to persuade users to comply with their requests. For example, they are regularly linked to recent events (in October 2011, posts appeared on Facebook advertising free iPads in memory of Steve Jobs, within hours of his death). They take advantage of human emotions such as fear, greed, guilt and compassion. A common variety of these schemes involves an application which indicates that, once installed, it will provide the victim with information about which of their friends views their profile the most often – thus manipulating human curiosity, and also possibly romantic attraction. Another variation of the fraud adds an image to a victim's photo albums, while simultaneously tagging several of their contacts in the image. When these contacts are drawn to the image by this tagging, they also run the risk of infection. Other versions of the fraud simply suggest that they are a link to a video that the user might want to see – when the user clicks on the link, they are

Table 5.1 Overview of methods of online fraud and identity theft

Social networking site fraud[*]	Takes a variety of forms, but most commonly attempts to persuade users to click on particular links, visiting specific websites or installing specific applications. The outcomes of clicking on these posts vary.
Online dating fraud[*]	An offender joins an online dating site and pursues a potential victim, often under an alias. They persuade the victim to send them money, sometimes repeatedly.
Conference fraud[*]	A potential victim is 'invited' to a fake international event, and required to pay some expenses upfront.
Phishing[*]	Emails directed at a user to obtain personal information, such as passwords and account details.
Advance fee fraud[*]	The potential victim is persuaded to part with some money upfront, with the promise of a large return that never materialises.
Keyloggers	Keyloggers monitor the keystrokes of users. They can be either hardware or software devices, and can log the passwords, usernames and other confidential information of users. These logs can then be sent back to the potential identity thief.
Dumpster diving	Searching the rubbish bins of a person or organisation in order to obtain useful items of information, such as passwords, bank details, memory devices, or even the hard drives of computers. This is a difficult and time-consuming activity, that must be carried out locally to the victim (Wall, 2007), and in many cases there is no guarantee of obtaining the required information. As such, it is generally only used for highly targeted attacks that are expected to have a high yield.
Help-desk attacks	May involve calling a help-desk, pretending to be a targeted victim, in the hope of finding out information which may be used in an identity theft attack. Alternatively, an offender may attempt to eavesdrop on a genuine call to a help-desk by an individual. Another common attack type involves an offender calling a potential victim directly, indicating that there is a problem with their computer or account, and offering to help them to fix the problem. During the call the potential victim may provide the caller with personal information, or may permit the fraudster to have control of their computer, perhaps allowing them to add a keylogger to the system.
Internet auction fraud	In some cases, a paid-for item may never be delivered. In others, a product may be misrepresented, or be a stolen item. Product inauthenticity (for example, where a product is advertised as being a designer label, when in fact it is a forgery) can also come under the descriptor of such fraud. Shill bidding can occur on some auction sites, where fake bids are placed in order to increase the price. However, many auction sites are aware of these scams, and use a variety of mechanisms, including customer satisfaction ratings, to reduce these problems.

Table 5.1 *(cont.)*

Lottery fraud	A user may arrive at a website to find an advertisement indicating that they have won a prize, or they may receive an email suggesting that they have won a competition. The user is either convinced to part with enough personal details to allow the criminal to complete an identity theft, or they are required to pay a processing fee to cover administrative costs. If they do eventually receive a payout from the lottery, it is likely to be of little or no value.
Pharma-fraud	Pharma-fraud involves the advertisement of medicines online. In a similar manner to the traditional offline medicinal scam described above, the victim is urged to pay for a 'miracle cure' medicine that can resolve many kinds of problems, from hair-loss to sexual dysfunction. In some cases the product never arrives, while in others a worthless placebo, or unregulated substance, is delivered instead.
Charity fraud	Charity and disaster relief frauds involve emails or websites that urge a potential victim to make a donation to a specific cause. In many cases they are linked to a specific event, such as an earthquake, hurricane or other natural disaster. The potential victim is asked to make a donation to those affected by the disaster, often by supplying their credit card details. In some cases, the victim will find that as well as losing the money donated, their account will also be charged with other losses.

* These topics are described in more detail later in the chapter.

prompted to allow an application to have access to some of their settings. When this access is granted, the video does not appear, but a new post appears on their wall, suggesting that they have viewed and intentionally shared the video. Finally, the posts are generally propagated during the victimisation process – when the victim allows the scam to access their SNS settings, it often posts a copy of itself as an update to their profile. This suggests to other users that the victim has endorsed the application as being legitimate. The victim is often unaware of this update until they are informed of its presence by other users.

Online dating fraud

In a similar manner to the SNS frauds above, potential offenders may create profiles on online dating websites with the hope of gathering information about suitable victims (Finch, 2007). This information may later be used to engage in identity theft. However, it is also possible that online dating fraud takes on an additional edge, as it impacts on the emotional wellbeing of the victim.

Whitty and Buchanan (2012) examined online dating fraud, indicating that it became apparent in about 2008. They describe the 'online romance scam' as a situation where a criminal 'pretend[s] to initiate a relationship through online dating sites then defraud[s] their victims of large sums of money' (p. 181). Rege (2009) describes some of the methods by which some fraudsters may attempt to carry out the scam. The scam may start by the development of an online relationship with the victim, which may last for a lengthy period of time. At some point during the scam, the perpetrator asks for money from the victim by describing a difficult situation that they are in, such as unexpected medical bills. In some cases the offender may start by asking for relatively small amounts of money, but this can escalate over time, and may result in significant amounts of cash. Whitty and Buchanan specifically attempted to examine the extent of such fraud in the UK, estimating that 230,000 British citizens may have fallen victim to the crime. They indicate that victims needed more support and advice when reporting their victimisation.

Conference fraud

Conference fraud refers to scams where the targeted individual is invited to an international event. Often these events are academic conferences, but they may also involve other types of occasion, such as the movie event depicted in Box 5.1.

Box 5.1 Sample conference fraud email

Hello,

Magic Movies cordially invites you to a movie anniversary event holding in DUBAI, 20th July, 2012. And you are entitled to a cash benefit of $2.4 million dollars, because you are selected by your email as a resident in community of our operational base. You can receive payment on or before the event. For inquiry, reply with your full name & phone number.

Con-grants! You won the $2.4 million dollars & Event Ticket.
Magic Movies®. ©2012.

These frauds work in a variety of ways, but often involve payment of some kind for a related expense, such as a hotel reservation (as is the case in the conference fraud email in Box 5.2).

Box 5.2 Conference fraud email depicting an attempt to defraud the victim by requiring them to book a room in a fake hotel (in the original, a well-known hotel brand was mentioned – this has been changed to 'Sleepytime Hotels' in order to protect their brand identity)

United Nations World Conference on the Impact and Implications of the Global Financial and Economic Crisis on Sustainable Development & Climate Change Proposals for an Integrated Global Response to the Crisis.

Dear Invitee, Nonprofit/NGO Colleague,

On behalf of the organizing and scientific working committee, the United Nations invites you to a Four-day summit of Economists, Educationists, Administrators, Manufacturers, Researchers, Non-Governmental Organizations, Religious Leaders, Community Organizations, individuals from the Public and Private Sector to assess the worst global economic down turn since the Great Depression. The aim is to identify emergency and long-term responses to mitigate the impact of the crisis, populations, and initiate a needed dialogue on the transformation of the international financial architecture, taking into account the needs and concerns of all countries of the world.

Registration to this Summit is absolutely "free" and strictly for invited individuals and organizations only. As an invitee, you have received a registration code UN/WFEC/002761/2012/UK with the invitation letter, which grants you access to the registration form. The United Nations General Assembly will sponsor free travel costs and all-round flight ticket for all participant. Invited participants will only be responsible for their hotel accommodation and feeding cost at the hotel. The Sleepytime Hotel has been officially designated to accommodate all participant for this unique and prestigious global financial and economic crisis summit.

Important Dates:

Submission of Paper Presentation and Proposals – Immediately.

Submission of Registration form and Proof of Accommodation from Sleepytime Hotels – Immediately.

Registration Closing Date – As set by the United Nations.

Register Now!

Summary box 5.3 Social networking site fraud, online dating fraud and conference fraud

- Social networking site fraud can involve a variety of techniques.
- Potential identity thieves can gather personal information from profiles.
- Users can be persuaded to allow applications designed by fraudsters to have control of aspects of their accounts.
- Users can be persuaded to provide fraudsters with personal information in exchange for perceived benefits, such as the ability to see who has been viewing their profile.
- SNS fraud is often perpetrated by posting content and links to the victim's profile.
- Online dating fraud occurs when a criminal pretends to initiate a romantic relationship with a victim through an online dating site, only to later persuade the victim to send money to them.
- Conference frauds invite the email recipient to a seemingly important occasion or event, but indicate that they can only attend if they follow certain guidelines, such as by reserving a room at a specific hotel.

Phishing

Phishing refers to emails that are directed at a user to obtain personal information, such as passwords and account details. A potential identity thief will send out large numbers of such emails, generally claiming to be from an organisation that would have legitimate reasons to access such information. These organisations can include online shops, online auction sites, online payment systems, revenue commissioners, banks and other financial institutions. In some cases the phishing emails are accompanied by company logos, and email addresses are used that may appear similar to those actually used by the organisation. There are several strategies that a phishing email may use.

The first of these involves the creation of fear in the victim. This strategy is often used in emails that pretend to be from a tax collection agency, banks or online payment systems. The emails often suggest that account information has already been compromised, and that the user needs to contact the organisation immediately. Many such phishing emails direct a user to a fake website, and the redirection of an internet browser to a false website is often termed 'pharming'. In many cases the user will be unaware that they are not at the actual website of the organisation, and will fill in personal details as normal. The fake websites may have various levels of sophistication – in some cases the website will be a close copy of the target site, with practically full levels of functionality. In other cases the fake website may have many broken links, and few functioning webpages. Box 5.3 provides an example of such a phishing email from a banking service.

Box 5.3 Phishing email from a banking service

You have 1 important mail alert!

We strongly advise you should update your account and resolve the problem.

Click here to proceed

Failure to do this will lead to your account been suspended or de-activated.

Thanks for your co-operation.

Yours Sincerely

Many of the individuals who receive this email will not have an account with the specific bank or organisation involved, and so will easily recognise it as a scam. However, a significant number of the recipients are likely to hold such an account, and it only takes a small number of these to fall for the scam in order for the fraudsters to achieve a profit.

Not all these schemes rely on fear – some schemes attempt to convince the potential victim that they are due a refund, or some other positive outcome. Box 5.4 includes the text from a phishing email that pretended to be from an online shop, describing how the recipient is due a refund.

Box 5.4 Phishing email from an online store, offering a refund

Dear Customer,

Our record shows that you have a refund slated for your account due to charges made against your account by us. We do apologise for this mistake which was caused by errors from our system.

This transaction cannot be completed due to the errors present in your account information.

You are required to click on the LOGON below to fix this problem immediately. Please note, it will take 3 working days to credit your account with the refund.

Log On

Please do not reply to this message. For questions, please call Customer Service. We are available 24 hours a day, 7 days a week.

While phishing by email remains the most common strategy in many countries, in some cases the fraud has been perpetrated using text (or SMS) messages. In these cases the attack is called 'smishing'. Phishing using telephone calls (or any other medium that uses voice) is called 'vishing'.

While many phishing attacks involve sending the same information to a wide group of potential victims, some attacks target specific individuals. These attacks are termed 'spear-phishing', and in these cases the fraudster may invest a great deal of time and effort in learning details about the target individual and those around them. A specific sub-type of spear-phishing involves 'whaling', which targets high-level executives of organisations. In these cases, the offender attempts to infiltrate the executive's computer in order to find out confidential information about the organisation.

In recent years, a variation on standard phishing attacks has emerged. In these cases a fraudster gains access to a person's email account, either through a traditional phishing scheme (where the phishing email appears to be from the email provider), or through the use of a keylogger or other information gathering method. The fraudster then sends emails to all the contacts in the address book of the user, pretending to be the email account holder. They pretend that they are in financial difficulty, often in a foreign country, and in desperate need of assistance. Excuses that are often used include lost credit cards, or medical emergencies, as in the email in Box 5.5 below. If a person responds to these emails, the perpetrator will often continue the correspondence in the hope of persuading the contact to transfer cash.

Box 5.5 Phishing email using a hacked email account and contact list

Hello,

How are you? I do hope that you receive this email in good health. Am presently in London (United Kingdom) to be with my ill Cousin, whom is a student here. She's suffering from a critical uterine fibroid and must undergo a hysterectomy surgery to save her life. I am deeply sorry for not writing or calling you before leaving, the news of her illness arrived to me as an emergency and that she needs family support to keep her going, I hope you understand my plight and pardon me.

So I want to transfer her back home to have the surgery implemented there because hysterectomy surgery is very expensive here, Am wondering if you can be of any assistance to me, I need about $1000 to make the necessary arrangement. I traveled with little money due to the short time I had to prepare for this trip and never expected things to be the way it is right now. I'll surely pay you back once I get back home, I need to get her home ASAP because she is going through a lot of pain at the moment and the doctor have advised that it is necessary that the tumor is operated soon to avoid anything from going wrong. I'll reimburse you at my return.

Summary box 5.4 Phishing

- Phishing refers to emails that are directed at a user to obtain personal information, such as passwords and account details.
- Phishing scams often rely on the potential victim's fear or greed.
- Phishing which is distributed by text messaging is referred to as 'smishing'.
- Phishing which occurs using voice is referred to as 'vishing'.
- The redirection of an internet browser to a false website is often termed 'pharming'.
- 'Spear-phishing' occurs when phishing is targeted at specific individuals.
- 'Whaling' is a type of phishing that targets high-level executives of companies.

Advance fee fraud

In advance fee fraud (or '419 schemes'), the potential victim is often coerced through the promise of financial gain, but in order to obtain this money, they are persuaded to provide a sum of money upfront. These schemes are also sometimes known as 'Nigerian scams', as many examples involve the potential fraudsters masquerading as wealthy Nigerian individuals. However, it is not uncommon for the fraudsters to profess to be from many other countries. For example, Box 5.6 below includes the text from an advance fee fraud email which pretends to be from Scotland.

Box 5.6 Sample advance fee fraud

I got your contact from the international web site directory, prayed over it and selected your name among other names due to it's esteeming nature and the recommendations given as a reputable and trust worthy person who can benefit my worth all desire. I am married to Late Mr. Henry W. Ninmer of West Coast Mining Limited General Manager UK, since his death I have been battling with both Cancer of the lungs and fibroid problems. While he was alive, he deposited a substantial amount of money worth Five Million British Pounds Sterling with a Financial Institution here in the

Glasgow, UK where he works as a manager in West Coast Mining Limited UK which I inherited after his death.

My worries now reason of contacting you are that my doctor notified me recently that I have less than one month to live due to my unfortunate ailment. I decided to hand over this funds to a devoted (God) fearing individual that will utilize this money for charity purpose and to help the needy, orphans, disables, less privillages the way I am going to instruct them. Having known my health condition I decided you to donate this money to a good charity organizations and orphanage homes in your country. I also took this decision because I am a widow and my husband relatives are not honest with my husband when he was alive, they are enemies of progress and don't have the fear of God in them and I have to avoid them from having any idea about this money.

I took this bold decision to contact you personally as a foreigner for assistance so that the money can hand over to you as my foreigner partner once my pastor present you to the safe keeping company where the money was deposited, because I have handed all the relevant document including the deposit certificate to my pastor. Please my dear in the Lord use this money as I directed you since I can not come over due to my hearth and I have helped some people right here in my country including my church. Contact my pastor, Rev. Daven Morgan so that he shall direct you to where the money was deposited and explain in full details all you need to know about this matter. Please I want you and your family to always pray for my healing and always be prayerful to God in all the days of your life.

God works for those that work in His Vineyard. Pls contact my pastor, Rev.Daven Morgan to help and assist you

Yours faithfully,

Mrs. Amelia Lemke Ninmer

There are many variations on advance fee fraud attacks. In some cases, the victim is asked for bank details, in some, they may find themselves inadvertently laundering money for the fraudsters. Some schemes suggest that the email recipient might be entitled to a large inheritance from a recently deceased individual who shares their last name, while in others the email pretends to be from a minor who is seeking a guardian to care for them (and their vast fortune!). Edelson (2003) describes several other common themes used in such frauds, including a banker trying to close the account of a dead customer, and the fraudster pretending to be the relative of a military or political individual who has died.

While most experienced internet users would recognise such scams with relative ease, it must be remembered that they remain popular because it only requires a small number of recipients to fall for them in order for the fraudsters to benefit substantially. For example, Zuckoff (2006) describes how a well-educated psychotherapist fell for an advance fee fraud scheme, eventually finding himself charged with bank fraud, money laundering and possession of counterfeit cheques.

Activity 5.2 Identifying online fraud schemes

Search through your email accounts and identify any fraud emails that you may have received (remember to check your spam filter). Identify which of the fraud emails that you have received fit within each of the categories outlined above. Do any of the emails fit within more than one category?

Summary box 5.5 Advance fee fraud

- Advance fee frauds are sometimes called '419 scams' or 'Nigerian scams'.
- In these scams the mark is persuaded to part with some money upfront (often allegedly for administrative costs), with the promise of a large return.
- There are many variations of advance fee fraud emails.

Human susceptibility to online fraud and identity theft

Many of the schemes described above are very familiar to regular users of the internet, and yet they continue to be popular among fraudsters. If they were not successful, at least occasionally, these scams would not be as common as they are. There are several reasons why internet users are susceptible to these scams, and many of these reasons rest in human psychological processes, especially decision making.

To begin, the fake websites used in phishing and pharming attacks can be very persuasive. Dhamija *et al.* (2006) showed twenty websites to participants, some of which were fake. Most of the participants were deceived by those websites considered to be good quality. Almost a quarter of the participants relied only on the website content to establish its authenticity, without looking at the website address or security indicators to validate its author. These behaviours are explained by long understood processes in human decision making. For example, Payne (1980) examined how the salience (or attention-attracting properties) of a cue (a specific element in a person's perceptual field) can affect how well it will be attended to and weighted when making a decision. In online fraud, a large logo or a personalised message could be considered a salient piece of information, and these cues can therefore increase the confidence in a user that an email is legitimate.

The tone of the message may also play an exaggerated role when users attempt to determine its legitimacy. Griffin and Tversky (1992) found that evaluators, forming impressions of an applicant on the basis of letters of recommendation, tended to give more weight to the tone or enthusiasm of the letter (a salient feature) than to the credibility or reliability of the evidence. This can be applied to fraud as it may be that users will pay more attention to the content of the fraudulent email than to establishing its true source.

Another potential influence on decision making is the projected authority of the offender. Marshall and Stephens (2008) and Yar (2006) describe how if an individual looks and behaves in a manner that we would expect them to, given their self-description, then we tend to accept them to be who they say they are. In other words, if we receive an email that appears to be from our bank's customer service department, and the language and tone used in the email is consistent with how we believe that source would behave, we are more likely to believe that the sender is indeed who they say they are. Tversky and Kahneman (1974) discuss the representativeness heuristic, where individuals are assumed to draw conclusions by evaluating the extent to which the evidence provided corresponds with the information that they have about that situation which is stored in long-term memory. As such, if the person views a fraudulent email and finds that it includes the logo for their bank, appears to be official in nature, and refers to them by name, this may be quite representative of their personal construct of what a letter from their bank looks like. As such, they might be more likely to interpret the email as coming from their bank, and hence follow the instructions in it.

This 'projected authority' has a second potential impact on our behaviour – Marshall and Stephens (2008) describe how, as the email often seems to come from an individual or entity which holds some authority (such as a bank, revenue commissioners or other entity), there may be a suggestion of potential threat if the authority figure is unhappy with the recipient's response. The potential victim may feel that if they are perceived as being unhelpful, then there may be negative consequences for them later.

Another possible influence on how the email recipient makes a decision is the implication of a need for an urgent response. Many fraud emails, particularly phishing emails, imply that the user needs to respond urgently, either to benefit from the promised gain, or to avoid penalties. Time pressure is a key influence on human decision making (see, for example, Svenson and Maule, 1993), and when urged to respond quickly, users are more likely to miss certain items of information that may dissuade them from replying.

Another possible impact on human susceptibility to online fraud involves the writing styles in advance fee fraud emails. Holt and Graves (2007) completed a qualitative analysis of over four hundred fraudulent email messages, and found that multiple writing techniques were used to encourage responses. These included the use of critical and serious tone in the subject line (such as 'Urgent Attention' or 'Payment Agent Needed'). Others included cordial greetings (such as 'Hello Friend') which may make the recipient feel emotionally linked to the sender. Holt and Graves found that 75 per cent of messages gave no indication of how the sender chose the recipient, though a small number of messages indicated that they had found the recipient through an online search for 'reliable and honest' people. Most messages requested confidentiality and a rapid response, with half of the emails requesting personal information, sometimes bank account details. However, some messages simply sought an indication of whether or not the recipient would help them. This may be an attempt to get a 'foot in the door', hoping that once the individual has committed themselves to helping the scammer, then they will be more likely to follow this with further information and action later.

Nhan *et al.* (2009) examined similar suspect unsolicited emails and found that 'relationship-building social engineering methods' (p. 452) were preferred to direct requests for sensitive information. They found that scammers rarely requested bank account or social security numbers in initial emails. They also discovered that the scammers tended to pose as financial institutions and reputable companies. Holt and Graves indicate that some emails also use links to news stories in order to help to support their claims, while others use religious language, presumably in the hope of evoking an emotional or spiritual response. They also found that spelling, typographical and grammatical errors were very common (present in over 80 per cent of emails), and indicate that these errors may actually be included on purpose, in order to reinforce the belief that the sender is a foreigner.

It is possible that once a user has begun to interact with a fraudster online, they may begin to recognise that they may be vulnerable and have made an error in engaging with the individual. However, they may still continue to engage with the fraud due to a psychological state called 'cognitive dissonance' (Festinger, 1957). Cognitive dissonance is an aversive motivational state where the person holds two or more thoughts that are inconsistent with each other. For example, if they have already sent money to the fraudster during an advance fee fraud, they may feel regret that they have done so, while simultaneously retaining hope that they will see a return on their money. During cognitive dissonance, the person will try to alter one of the two cognitions in order to reduce ambivalence. As they have already invested money in the scheme, the victim may choose to reject the thought that they have been defrauded, even though it is the more likely outcome, in order to justify their previous actions to themselves. Cognitive dissonance can explain why an individual who has already lost significant amounts of money to a fraudster appears unwilling to accept the possibility that they have been scammed and will never see their money again.

Finally, it is also possible that once we reach the conclusion that an email is genuine, it is more difficult to change our minds. Einhorn and Hogarth (1978) describe 'confirmation bias', a tendency for people to seek information and cues that confirm their tentatively held hypothesis or belief, and not seek those that support an opposite conclusion. Due to this bias, any ambiguous cues in the email will be interpreted in a manner that supports the favoured belief. This puts users at risk of only attending to the information that confirms that the sender of the email is who they claim to be, and ignoring other information (such as spam warnings from legitimate sources) which is in opposition to their conclusion. To make matters worse, Bremmer *et al.* (1996) noted that people in general are overconfident in their state of knowledge or beliefs, becoming unlikely to seek additional information (which may refute the hypothesis) even when it is appropriate to do so. As such, potential victims of fraud or identity theft may not liaise with their bank to see if the email was legitimate before clicking on the link provided.

Some researchers have attempted to integrate several psychological mechanisms into a single model to explain phishing vulnerability. For example, Vishwanath *et al.* (2011) propose an integrated model which explains much of the susceptibility to phishing victimisation. They specifically note that many phishing attempts are only peripherally processed, and that simple cues in the email are processed by the user.

This highlights the importance of the salience of cues mentioned above. Vishwanath *et al.* also noted the importance of urgency cues in provoking a reaction by the intended victim, emphasising the importance of time-sensitive responses described above.

Lastly, some researchers have attempted to determine what demographic groups are most at risk of victimisation. Sheng *et al.* (2010) found that women were more susceptible than men to phishing attempts. Similarly, Jagatic *et al.* (2006) found that females were more likely to fall for spear-phishing attacks. With regard to age, Sheng *et al.* (2010) found that those aged between 18 and 25 years were most susceptible.

Activity 5.3 Identifying tactics used in fraud emails

Using the emails that you identified in Activity 5.2, examine each email to determine which of the strategies described above appear in each. Do the emails include multiple strategies?

Summary box 5.7 Human susceptibility to online fraud and identity theft

- There are several reasons why humans may be susceptible to seemingly obvious attempts at fraud.
- Many of these are based on the psychology of human decision making.
- The salience of certain cues in emails may make a user more likely to believe the sender is from a legitimate agency.
- Projected authority of the sender is a key factor in a decision as to whether or not to comply with a fraudulent email, particularly if the potential victim feels that the sender may be unhappy with a lack of cooperativeness.
- Advance fee fraud emails use a wide variety of tactics to engage the recipient, including serious tone, cordial greetings, typographical errors and 'foot in the door' techniques.
- Cognitive dissonance occurs when an individual holds simultaneous but conflicting views and seeks to eliminate one. This may explain why an individual who has already lost money during a fraud may continue to engage with the fraudster.
- Confirmation bias describes how individuals seek information that confirms a tentatively held hypothesis, and thus may explain why individuals do not notice cues that would disconfirm such a belief.

Effects on victims

If online fraud or identity theft does occur, there can be several effects on the victim. These effects can take several forms, most notably financial effects and psychological effects.

In many cases the financial effects of identity theft are frustrating and inconveniencing, but relatively short-lived (see, for example, Winterdyk and Thompson, 2008). This is because banks or credit organisations will often cover any losses. However, this cover is less frequently extended to cases of fraud, and so many victims can find themselves at substantial loss.

There may also be psychological effects of victimisation. While these are obviously less severe than would be expected for other types of cybercrime victimisation (such as cyberstalking or child predation), some writers have suggested that victims of phishing scams may develop symptoms similar to post-traumatic stress disorder (PTSD), particularly in relation to embarrassment and depression (Carey, 2009). Similarly, Sharp et al. (2004) completed an exploratory study of the impact of identity theft on victims by examining thirty-seven victims using focus groups and questionnaires. Sharp et al. found that the majority of participants experienced increased maladaptive psychological and somatic symptoms, particularly those with unresolved cases.

Some victims of online fraud and identity theft may also experience secondary victimisation, where family, friends and authorities may place some blame on the victim for their experience. While obviously somewhat controversial, this is a common occurrence in many types of crime (see, for example, Amir, 1971; Grubb and Harrower, 2008; Klinger, 2001), and there is also some evidence that secondary victimisation may occur in identity theft cases (Kirwan, 2009a).

Summary box 5.8 Effects on victims
- Identity theft and online fraud may have a variety of effects on victims – including both financial and psychological effects.
- Often banks or credit organisations cover losses relating to identity theft.
- Some authors and researchers have suggested that phishing and identity theft may have psychological effects on victims. These include embarrassment, depression and other maladaptive psychological and somatic symptoms.
- Some victims may also experience secondary victimisation.

Prevention methods

There are several methods by which the risks of online fraud and identity theft can be reduced. However, the growing diversity of online behaviours also means that the work of the identity thief has become easier. Important identifying documentation, such as birth certificates and household bills, can be obtained online relatively easily. Similarly, as more individuals switch to online shopping and online banking it is easier to apply for credit and use credit cards without ever entering a physical 'bricks and mortar' location.

Marshall and Stephens (2008) suggest that a key method of reducing crime is to raise public awareness of the risks, while encouraging users to protect the details of their financial accounts. Finch (2007) argues that users must also be encouraged to protect other personal information online. The importance of choosing strong

Illustration 5.2 Choosing strong passwords. The strength of passwords is important in preventing identity theft and fraud, and users often engage in bad password management behaviours.

passwords should also be encouraged, as users tend to engage in bad password-management behaviours because of the 'convenience–security tradeoff' (Tam *et al.*, 2009). It is easier to remember a simple password, and to use the same password for multiple online accounts, rather than engage in safer behaviours such as choosing different complex passwords for each account.

Some researchers have attempted to identify specific methods of preventing identity theft. For example, Wang *et al.* (2006) suggest several key mechanisms for accomplishing this, including education and guidance that informs users on how to check if they have been the victim of identity theft, and what to do if they are victimised. These educational materials may take the form of government materials, pamphlets and websites. Another prevention mechanism involves companies educating their customers about the risk (such as a bank indicating on its online banking system that it will never email users asking for personal details). More severe penalties could also be implemented for convicted identity thieves, and better background checks could be carried out on individuals in companies and organisations who would legitimately handle personal information. Finally Wang *et al.* suggest that newer technologies, such as biometrics and smart cards, could also be useful prevention methods, although Smith (2007) indicates that such methods are not foolproof, and particular care needs to be taken when issuing such biometric identifiers to individuals to prevent identity theft occurring at this stage.

Davinson and Sillence (2010) evaluated a training program, 'Anti-Phishing Phil', in order to determine its effectiveness at improving safe online behaviours. This programme adapted a model used in health psychology normally used to encourage healthier behaviours in individuals. The programme increased users' intentions to protect themselves online, with an increase of secure behaviour noted at a seven-day follow-up. However, Davinson and Sillence note that these changes occurred regardless of information type or training provided, and suggest that the improved security may be due to simply providing warning information, thus raising awareness of risks. This suggests that a complex intervention strategy, targeted to individual users, may not be required in order to change user behaviour.

> ### Activity 5.4 Prevention methods
> Using the suggestions outlined above as a starting point, devise a public awareness campaign that would help to reduce identity theft or online fraud. Consider how the information would be disseminated, along with the most important information that you want users to remember. Design materials to disseminate the information (such as websites, emails, posters, pamphlets, advertisements, etc.).

Summary box 5.9 Prevention methods
- Identity theft and online fraud has been enabled by the growing diversity of online behaviours.
- Several methods of preventing these crimes have been suggested. These include:
  - improving public awareness of risks;
  - encouraging users to protect details of financial accounts;
  - encouraging users to choose strong passwords;
  - encouraging companies to inform their customers about risks;
  - imposing more severe penalties for offenders;
  - using newer technologies such as biometrics.

Conclusion

There are many methods by which identity theft and online fraud occur, and while many seem obvious to experienced internet users, sufficient numbers of individuals still fall for them to make them worthwhile for offenders. Potential fraudsters and identity thieves employ a wide variety of tactics to encourage users to engage in the scam, and many of these tactics rely on well-established psychological mechanisms. Victimisation can result in both financial and psychological consequences, and it is important to establish effective prevention methods.

Essay questions

(1) Describe the types of online fraud that can occur. Explain the methods used in each type of fraud, with particular focus on social engineering tactics.
(2) How does cognitive psychology inform our understanding of why internet users are vulnerable to online fraud and identity theft?
(3) Why might a victim of fraud avoid reporting the crime? How can victims of fraud or identity theft be encouraged to report the offence to the authorities?
(4) There is some literature available regarding the psychology of offline fraudsters. Does this literature have relevance to the psychology of their online equivalents?

Additional reading

Books and articles

The articles below offer insights into various types of fraud and identity theft offences from psychological and criminological perspectives:

Holt, T. J. and Graves, D. C. (2007). A qualitative analysis of advance fee fraud e-mail schemes. *International Journal of Cyber Criminology*, **1** (1). Retrieved from www.cybercrimejournal.com/ thomas&danielleijcc.htm.

Jaishkankar, K. (2008). Identity related crime in cyberspace: examining phishing and its impact. *International Journal of Cyber Criminology*, **2**, 10–15.

Li, S. H., Yen, D. C., Lu, W. H. and Wang, C. (2012). Identifying the signs of fraudulent accounts using data mining techniques. *Computers in Human Behaviour*, **28**, 1,002–13.

Nhan, J., Kinkade, P. and Burns, R. (2009). Finding a pot of gold at the end of an internet rainbow: further examination of fraudulent email solicitation. *International Journal of Cyber Criminology*, **3**, 452–75.

Whitty, M. T. and Buchanan, T. (2012). The online romance scam: a serious cybercrime. *Cyberpsychology, Behavior and Social Networking*, **15**, 181–3.

Winterdyk, J. and Thompson, N. (2008). Student and non-student perceptions and awareness of identity theft. *Canadian Journal of Criminology and Criminal Justice*, **50**, 153–86.

Websites

The UK National Fraud Authority website includes reports and statistics regarding fraud (including online frauds) in the UK: www.homeoffice.gov.uk/agencies-public-bodies/nfa.

Fraud and internet crime in the UK can be reported to the ActionFraud website at www.actionfraud. police.uk.

The website of the Anti-Phishing Working Group (APWG) provides useful information about phishing rates and scams, as well as a crimeware map and other resources: www.antiphishing.org.

'Stop. Think. Connect' is a website designed to help internet users stay safer online and was created by a coalition of private companies, as well as non-profit orgnisations and government organisations. It includes information on research and surveys, as well as general advice for internet users: www.stopthinkconnect.org.

The US Federal Bureau of Investigation provides practical tips on avoiding fraud on its website: www.fbi.gov/scams-safety/fraud/internet_fraud/internet_fraud.

The Internet Crime Complaint Centre (IC3) is a US governmental website which accepts complaints from victims: www.ic3.gov/default.aspx.

Child predation and child pornography online

Case studies

Emily is thirteen years old, and has just joined a popular social networking site. She's very excited – her friends have been using the site for a while, but she's only just been allowed to create a profile. She finds her classmates online and contacts them using the social networking site. Several other people contact her, including Graham, whom Emily doesn't know, but who seems to be a friend of one of her classmates. Graham starts sending her messages, complimenting her photos and chatting about her favourite bands and television programmes. Graham says he's sixteen years old, and Emily is flattered by his attention. After they've exchanged a few messages, Graham starts flirting with Emily, and asks her to visit him at his house. Emily has never had a boyfriend, and doesn't want to upset Graham by refusing to go – besides – Graham is cute, and funny, and pays more attention to her than anyone else in her life. Nevertheless, she feels a little unsure, and decides to bring a friend with her when she goes to see him. When Graham answers the door, Emily realises that he's at least five years older than he said he was, and looks nothing like his photograph. She and her friend run away, but they don't tell anyone what happened.

Deborah is seven years old, and is spending the summer holidays with her uncle and his family. While she enjoys spending time with her cousins, she is uncomfortable around her uncle, as he touches her, and she's not sure if this is normal or not. Her uncle says that it's okay, and to prove it, he uses his computer to find pictures of other little girls who are being touched in a similar way. Deborah notices that the other girls seem to be smiling, and there are lots of pictures of different girls. Deborah starts to think that perhaps her uncle's behaviour is normal.

Chapter overview

The scenarios above are both fictional, but are based on experiences typical of real victims of these crimes. Many parents are very nervous about allowing their children to use the internet, and predatory behaviour and online child pornography are understandably near the top of the list of their fears. Child sex offending has been the focus of a substantial amount of academic research, with many studies attempting to understand these offenders and develop suitable intervention and/or rehabilitation strategies. When examining this research, it should be noted that while female child sex offenders do exist, it seems that the majority of offenders are male, and many research studies cited in this chapter focus solely on male offenders.

This chapter firstly considers the nature of paedophilia, examining some of the theories that have been proposed which may explain why some people show these tendencies. In particular, it describes 'cognitive distortions' – 'attitudes and beliefs which offenders use to deny, minimize or rationalize their behaviour' (Murphy, 1990 as cited by Blumenthal *et al.*, 1999, p. 129), noted by many authors as a common occurrence in such offenders. The chapter goes on to examine both online child predators and online child pornography in more detail. The psychology of both perpetrators and victims of both types of offence will be described, and suggestions will be made for potential methods of making the internet a safer environment for children and adolescents.

Paedophilia

Paedophilia is defined by the American Psychiatric Association's (2000) *Diagnostic and Statistical Manual of Mental Disorders* (*DSM*) as having several specific characteristics. These include experiencing intense and recurrent sexually arousing fantasies over a minimum of six months, or urges or behaviours that involve sexual activities with a prepubescent child or children. The individual must be at least sixteen years of age, and at least five years older than their victims, and other symptoms, such as impairment in social or occupational functioning, must be evident. It should be noted that this description has been subject to some critique (see, for example, Blanchard, 2009), particularly in relation to the criteria relating to disruption or distress. Blanchard also suggests that the *DSM* needs to consider more thoroughly the inclusion of individuals who are attracted to pubescent children who have not reached sexual maturity (or 'hebephiles').

There has been considerable research interest in the psychology of paedophiles, and several efforts have been made to understand why some individuals show paedophilic tendencies. Many of these efforts have focused around the childhood of paedophiles, as Sheldon and Howitt (2007) note that in many cases paedophiles seem to be aware from a very young age that they are sexually oriented towards children. Some of the most influential models which attempt to explain paedophilia are Finkelhor's (1984, 1986) 'four preconditions model of paedophilia', Hall and Hirschman's (1991) 'quadripartite model' and Ward and Siegert's (2002) 'pathways model'. Several of these models utilise the concept of *cognitive distortions* within their explanations, so this concept will be considered first, before proceeding to a description of each of the three models.

Cognitive distortions

Cognitive distortions in forensic contexts are 'offence-supportive attitudes, cognitive processing during an offence sequence, as well as post-hoc neutralisations or excuses for offending' (Maruna and Mann, 2006, p. 155). They are basically the excuses and rationale that an offender provides themselves (and sometimes others) with, which allow them to justify their behaviour to themselves – though it should be noted that such justifications are rarely recognised as adequate by society as a whole. Nevertheless, cognitive distortions are frequently noted in criminals (regardless of whether or not their crime is sexual in nature) and have also been noted in non-criminal populations.

Cognitive distortions can occur among both contact child sex offenders (those who abuse children directly) and offenders who view and collect child pornography, but do not engage in contact offending. Several common cognitive distortions among these groups have been noted (see, for example, Burgess and Hartman, 1987; Quayle and Taylor, 2002; Sheldon and Howitt, 2007; Taylor and Quayle, 2003; Ward and Siegert, 2002), including:

- a belief that the child is enjoying the experience;
- a belief that it is normal for children to engage in sexual behaviour;
- a belief that children who are abused to create child pornography are willing participants;
- a belief that sexual abuse is an appropriate way to teach children about sexuality;
- a belief that, as the video or image of the abuse already exists, further viewing of the material does not harm the child or society;
- a belief that as long as the offender does not carry out the abuse themselves, or pay for any pornographic materials, then they are not doing any harm;
- a belief that the perpetrator is entitled to sex with an individual to whom they are physically attracted, whether or not that person is a child;
- a belief that they have no control over their behaviour;
- a belief that sex with adults can be dangerous, but that children are not a threat;
- a belief that the current western age of consent is a recent and culturally defined phenomenon, and that historically sexual activity with minors was the norm.

It is of course relatively easy to dispute these beliefs. For example, Taylor and Quayle (2003) describe how the trauma of the victim does not end following the production of the pornography, but is maintained for as long as the record exists. This is exacerbated by the widespread dissemination of such material online, making it virtually impossible to remove all copies of the material.

Activity 6.1 Challenging cognitive distortions

Examine the list of cognitive distortions above. What other cognitive distortions could be held by paedophiles and collectors of child pornography? For each cognitive distortion listed, explain why it is an inadequate excuse for the relevant offending behaviour.

Summary box 6.1 Paedophilia and cognitive distortions

- Paedophilia is defined in the American Psychiatric Association's (2000) *Diagnostic and Statistical Manual of Mental Disorders* (*DSM*) as having several symptoms, including experiencing intense and recurrent sexually arousing fantasies over a

minimum of six months, or urges or behaviours that involve sexual activities with a prepubescent child or children.
- This definition has been critiqued by several authors.
- Hebephilia is an attraction to pubescent children who have not reached sexual maturity.
- Cognitive distortions are excuses and rationale that an offender provides themselves (and sometimes others) with, which allow them to justify their behaviour to themselves.
- Cognitive distortions can occur among both contact child sex offenders (those who abuse children directly) and offenders who view and collect child pornography, but do not engage in contact offending.
- Several common cognitive distortions among these groups have been noted, but these are relatively easily refuted.

Finkelhor's four preconditions model

Finkelhor's (1984, 1986) 'four preconditions model of paedophilia' assumes that child sex offending has several causes, and that four preconditions need to be present for a sexual assault to occur. These are:

- The motivation to commit the crime. For example, the offender may believe that other sources will not sexually satisfy them, or are unavailable to them. Therefore, the offender feels that the child is the only source of sexual gratification available to them.
- Overcoming internal inhibitors. Finkelhor suggests that paedophiles, like the rest of society, are socialised to inhibit sexual approaches to young people. The paedophile must overcome these internal inhibitors in order for the abuse to occur. They may utilise drugs or alcohol to reduce their inhibitions, or they may use some of the cognitive distortions described above to excuse their behaviour to themselves.
- Overcoming external inhibitors. At this stage, the paedophile must overcome the external inhibitors that society puts in place to protect children. Very young children are normally protected by parents or caregivers for the majority of the time, and paedophiles with a preference for this group may need to target family members. As children get older, they become more independent, and are more likely to interact with people outside their immediate family, including contacts that they may make online. As children grow older, they are less carefully protected, and as such, fewer external inhibitors need to be overcome by a predator.
- Overcoming the victim's resistance. This final stage of the preconditions model requires the paedophile to overcome the victim's resistance, generally through a grooming process. This may involve the use of treats or gifts, or simply focusing attention on a child. The child is often gradually introduced to sexual activities, and child pornography images and videos may be used to persuade the child that the behaviours are normal.

Finkelhor's model is useful in understanding the process of offending, but it does not explain why an individual would be sexually attracted to children (Ward *et al.*, 2006). As such, other explanations for this attraction are required.

Hall and Hirschman's quadripartite model

Hall and Hirschman (1991) identified four factors in offending behaviour, but suggested that different offenders could have different dominant factors. These four factors are:

- Affective dyscontrol. This refers to an inability to identify and manage emotions. An individual experiencing affective dyscontrol may confuse a reduction in loneliness when a young person is present, with sexual attraction.
- Personality problems, such as attachment difficulties. These may be formed during early childhood experiences with parents or other adults.
- Physiological sexual arousal, which has been noted in many studies of child sex offenders.
- The presence of cognitive distortions (as described above).

According to this model, different paedophiles will experience different anomalies, and so the treatment approach used should vary according to the dominant factor in the specific offender (Ward, 2001).

Ward and Siegert's pathways model

Ward and Siegert (2002) felt that previous models of sexually offensive behaviour were insufficient, and so developed a model that integrated the best elements of several previous models. They felt that a tendency to committing a sexual offence derives from a combination of developmental experiences and environmental factors. Ward and Siegert suggested that there are four different pathways to becoming a paedophile, and so there are four different types of paedophile.

- The use of cognitive distortions (as described above).
- The presence of deviant sexual scripts. All individuals develop understandings of how sexual relationships should develop and the types of sexual behaviour that are acceptable. These are developed through socialisation, but in some cases deviant scripts are established. This may be due to being prematurely sexualised, or it may be due to difficulties in differentiating sex and intimacy.
- Intimacy deficits. These may be caused by insecure attachment styles, preventing the offender from forming satisfying adult relationships, and potentially causing loneliness and social isolation.
- Dysfunctional emotional regulation. The offender may express anger and punish partners through the abuse of children. Alternatively, the offender may use sexual activities to calm their mood.

Ward and Siegert (2002) finally suggested that a fifth pathway could involve dysfunctions across multiple areas. As with Hall and Hirschman's model, the treatment of the offender depends on the pathway involved. Middleton et al. (2006) considered the Ward and Siegert model in relation to possession of internet child pornography, and found that most offenders could be assigned to either the intimacy deficits or emotional dysregulation pathways, although about 40 per cent of the sample showed deficits on multiple pathways. While there are some problems with this research (as outlined by Elliott *et al.*, 2009), and Bryce (2010) suggests that it is possible that some internet-related contact offenders may not be classifiable to the identified pathways, Middleton *et al.*'s finding is supported by Quayle *et al.* (2006) who also indicate that 'for some offenders, but not all, accessing images on the Internet may function as a way of avoiding or dealing with difficult emotional states' (p. 10).

Summary box 6.2 Models of paedophilia

- Several efforts have been made to understand why some individuals show paedophilic tendencies.
- Many of these efforts have focused around the childhood of paedophiles.
- Some of the most influential models which attempt to explain paedophilia are:
  - Finkelhor's (1984, 1986) 'four preconditions model of paedophilia':
    - assumes that child sex offending has several causes, and that four preconditions need to be present for a sexual assault to occur:
      - the motivation to commit the crime;
      - overcoming internal inhibitors;
      - overcoming external inhibitors;
      - overcoming the victim's resistance.
  - Hall and Hirschman's (1991) 'quadripartite model' also identified four factors in offending behaviour, but suggested that different offenders could have different dominant factors. These four factors are:
    - affective dyscontrol;
    - personality problems;
    - physiological sexual arousal;
    - the presence of cognitive distortions.
  - Ward and Siegert's (2002) 'pathways model' suggests that there are four different pathways to becoming a paedophile, and so there are four different types of paedophile:
    - the use of cognitive distortions;
    - the presence of deviant sexual scripts;
    - intimacy deficits;
    - dysfunctional emotional regulation;
    - a fifth pathway could involve dysfunctions across multiple areas.

Child predation online

Parents often fear that young children will be pursued online, but in many cases, victims of online predators are adolescents. There is also normally a gradual 'grooming' of the adolescent in order to prepare them for a sexual encounter, and the adolescent is frequently aware of (and consents to) the sexual nature of the contact in advance of its occurrence. In many cases, online predation seems to bear more resemblance to statutory rape than paedophilia (Wolak *et al.*, 2008), and predators are frequently honest about their sexual interests in the encounter. While there has been a lot of media interest regarding the possible dangers of child predation on the internet, it is not necessarily a new type of offence (Wolak *et al.*, 2008). However, it can be argued that the internet can provide an easier route for predators to encounter and engage with children and adolescents.

Wolak *et al.* (2006) found that about one in seven young internet users had received unwanted sexual solicitations, which is bound to worry any parent. However, the number of youths who received *aggressive* solicitations (where the predator attempted to make offline contact) is much smaller, at about 4 percent of young internet users. Similarly, Bryce (2010) notes that the 'prevalence of online sexual exploitation is relatively small given the wider context of sexual offending against young people in society' (p. 322). As such, while it is right for young people and their parents to be wary of possible online predators, such fears should not overshadow the awareness of risks relating to offline predators.

The predation process online

Predators use a variety of online technologies and communication mechanisms to identify and communicate with potential victims. Malesky (2007) indicates that three-quarters of men who perpetrated or attempted to perpetrate contact sexual offences against minors using the internet monitored chatroom dialogue. Approximately half of these men reviewed online profiles to identify victims. Similarly, Mitchell *et al.* (2010) found that social networking sites can be used by online predators to find out information about the victim, disseminate photographs, communicate with the victim, identify a potential victim and even communicate with the victim's friends. The risks are not limited to social networking sites – Wolak *et al.* (2006) noted that some predators used online gaming and online dating websites to target victims.

Yar (2006) suggests that online child sexual abuse can take two forms:

- In some cases, the abuse remains 'virtual', with the communication occurring only online. The youth and the offender discuss sexual activities, often engaging in masturbatory behaviour. This type of abuse may involve webcams, or swapping photographs. Even if the youth and the offender never meet, the predator may still be convicted of child sexual abuse in some jurisdictions, as inciting a child to engage in such behaviour can be illegal (Yar, 2006).
- The second form involves using the online communications as a preparation for later physical contact, and is sometimes termed 'grooming'. The offender may start with the behaviours outlined in the first form above, but may also request to meet at an offline location. This form of abuse refers to the 'aggressive solicitations' described by Wolak *et al.* (2006) above.

The grooming process is often gradual. Edgar-Nevill (2008) describes several steps that may be involved in the grooming procedure. Once the offender has targeted a victim, they develop an online profile, which may or may not involve deception regarding the offender's age (for example, Wolak *et al.* (2004) found that only 5 per cent of offenders pretended to be teenagers). Edgar-Nevill indicates that the offender will attempt to move communications to a private channel as quickly as possible (for example, switching from posting on their social networking site profile to using instant messaging), and the messages will become more frequent and personal. The predator uses the conversations to develop the victim's empathy and trust, and the victim may begin to enjoy the attention. The predator may then ask the victim to take a specific action, such as using a webcam or meeting in person. Wolak *et al.* (2008) suggest that most victims who meet their online predator do so with the expectation of engaging in sexual activity.

Dombrowski *et al.* (2004) note a similar process to Edgar-Nevill's description, again suggesting that the victim may find the attention appealing. Dombrowski *et al.* also note the escalation of predation from communication, to gifts or pictures, and then to overt communication about sexuality. Dombrowksi *et al.* suggest that the predator may use pornographic material to desensitise the youth to sexual content, and that the offender may use a variety of techniques to ensure that the victim does not discuss the sexual activity, including psychological manipulation. For example, the offender may suggest that if the victim discloses the relationship to a parent or guardian, then the caregiver may restrict their use of the internet, or prevent the victim from meeting the predator (whom they have come to trust).

O'Connell (2003) describes how an online predator assesses the risks involved in pursuing a relationship, especially when they reach the stage of asking the victim to meet offline. This may involve asking the victim about the security measures that their parents put in place in order to prevent sexual predators. The offender may choose to end the relationship before physical contact is made.

Activity 6.2 Protecting youths from online predators

Considering the methods used by online predators above, as well as the age profile of their likely victims, devise a strategy for informing youths and parents about the risks of online predators. While doing this, consider how parents can balance feeling that their child is protected without being overly restrictive of their online interactions.

Comparison to offline predation

While considering the techniques used by online predators above, it should be noted that they appear to be different to the techniques used by offline offenders. This appears to be primarily due to the difference in the likelihood of the victim knowing the offender beforehand. Similarly, much of the literature regarding non-internet paedophilia refers to younger children, while online predators are more likely to target adolescents.

For offline offences, children are in the most danger in private locations, such as their home, and are more likely to know or trust the perpetrator (Elliott *et al.*, 1995).

Online predators are less likely to know their victims in advance (Wolak *et al.* (2006) indicate that online predators only knew their victims in 14 per cent of cases).

Nevertheless, there are some similarities between online and offline predators. For example, in most cases violence is not used, and in both techniques, the minor is frequently made to feel special and deserving of attention by the offender, which is exploited by the predator when they proceed to initiating sexual advances.

It is likely that increased presence online may make youths more accessible to predators, allowing more opportunities for predators to be alone with victims, and allowing offenders to find victims more easily (Wolak *et al.*, 2008). This is exacerbated by the ability to have rapid and private communications through the internet, which aids the predator. It is also possible that adolescents may have a higher tendency to talk about more personal matters with strangers in online contexts, than if they met them face to face, thus potentially leading to rapid development of feelings of intimacy between the predator and the victim, and resulting in faster progression to sensitive topics such as sex (Wolak *et al.*, 2008).

Summary box 6.3 The predation process online

- In many cases, victims of online predators are adolescents rather than younger children.
- There is normally a gradual 'grooming' of the adolescent in order to prepare them for a sexual encounter.
- In many cases the adolescent is aware of (and consents to) the sexual nature of the contact in advance of its occurrence.
- Predators use a variety of online technologies and communication mechanisms to identify and communicate with potential victims.
- Predators use online conversations to develop the victim's empathy and trust, and the victim may begin to enjoy the attention.
- Pornographic material may be used to desensitise the youth to sexual content, and the offender may use a variety of techniques to ensure that the victim does not discuss the sexual activity.
- These techniques appear to be different to the techniques used by offline offenders, probably due to the difference in the likelihood of the victim knowing the offender beforehand.
- Adolescents may have a higher tendency to talk about more personal matters with strangers in online contexts than if they met them face to face, thus potentially leading to faster progression to sensitive topics such as sex.

The psychology of online child predators

Due to the apparent preference for adolescents among internet child predators, it may be that the psychological models describing paedophiles are not relevant to our understanding of their behaviour. As younger children are not as accessible online (they visit fewer websites, and are more likely to be supervised during their online activities), it would seem that online predators more closely fit the definition of hebephiles (those attracted to pubescents who have not reached sexual maturity) than paedophiles. This is an interesting point – hebephiles are not restricted to online predatory behaviours, but recognising the distinction between paedophiles and hebephiles may be of importance for those who investigate and rehabilitate online child predators.

Hines and Finkelhor (2007) describe how adult men who pursue adolescent girls offline are likely to have feelings of inadequacy and arrested psychosocial development, as well as lower levels of education and increased likelihood of criminal history. However, it is possible that there is a difference between online and offline hebephiles. Lanning (2001a) indicates that hebephiles may have a variety of motives and reasons for their behaviour, including impulsivity, anger, curiosity and a desire for power. Nuñez (2003) suggests that hebephilic behaviour may be a wish to relive adolescent experiences or to seek admiration from victims.

Wolak *et al.* (2008) indicate that online predators tend not to be impulsive, aggressive, violent or sadistic, with abductions being rare. The predators appear to be patient enough to develop relationships with their victims before meeting them, and seem charismatic enough to persuade the victim to meet them of their own free will.

The psychology of the victims of online child predators

Many studies have examined the characteristics of the victims of offline sexual offenders. Some of the risk factors that have been identified include physically attractive youths with low self-esteem (Elliott *et al.*, 1995) and youths from dysfunctional families or impoverished backgrounds (Kenny and McEachern, 2000). Most victims of online solicitations are female, and when boys are targeted it is usually by males (Wolak *et al.*, 2004, 2006). Wolak *et al.* (2006) found that the vast majority (over 80 per cent) of victims were fourteen years of age or older, with the most aggressive and distressing solicitations concentrated among the older teenagers.

Mitchell *et al.* (2007) describe how youths who send personal details to strangers, or who talk to strangers online about sex, are more likely to receive aggressive sexual solicitations. Wolak *et al.* (2008) describe how youths who had a history of either physical or sexual abuse, rule-breaking behaviour, depression or social interaction problems were also at higher risk.

Parents of adolescents frequently worry about the amount of personal information that their children post online. Wolak *et al.* (2008) found that posting personal information online on its own does not appear to be particularly risky, and that interactive behaviours, such as communicating with strangers about sex, appear to place adolescents at higher risk. Other activities that they note may increase risk include interacting with unknown people online, friending unknown people on social networking sites, seeking pornography online and being rude or nasty online.

It seems that most youths deal fairly well with online predation, with two-thirds removing themselves from the situation, either by leaving the website or the computer or by blocking the predator (Wolak *et al.*, 2006). Other methods of dealing with the incident included confronting the predator, warning them, telling them to stop, or ignoring them. In over half of cases, the youth did not tell anyone about the incident. While most youths (66 per cent) said that they were not particularly upset or frightened by the event, some did have stronger emotional reactions, especially in cases where attempts were made to meet the victim offline. Some of these youths reported symptoms of stress, avoiding websites or internet applications, pervasive thoughts about the incident, irritability, agitation and embarrassment.

If the victim does meet the offender and engage in sexual activity, they may experience more extreme symptoms. While there is very little research examining the effects of such an encounter, there are many negative outcomes associated with sexual abuse generally, including 'delinquency, depression, substance abuse, guilt, post-traumatic stress disorder' (Bryce, 2010, p. 335), as well as evidence of negative effects continuing much later into life (Dombrowski *et al.*, 2004).

Summary box 6.4 The psychology of online predators and their victims

- The psychological models describing paedophiles may not be relevant to internet child predators due to their preference for adolescents.
- Some of the characteristics which may describe online predators include feelings of inadequacy, arrested psychosocial development, lower levels of education, increased likelihood of criminal history, impulsivity (although there is some disagreement regarding this), anger, curiosity, a desire for power, a wish to relive adolescent experiences, a wish to seek admiration from victims and possibly patience.
- Most victims of online solicitations are female, and when boys are targeted, it is usually by males.
- The majority of victims are over fourteen years of age.
- Youths who send personal details to strangers, or who talk to strangers online about sex, are more likely to receive aggressive sexual solicitations.
- Most youths seem to deal fairly well with online predation, but some experience severe psychological distress.

Improving the safety of children online

There are several potential methods of improving the safety of children online. These include preventative measures, such as technological tools that can be used to monitor and restrict online behaviour, as well as educational strategies, that can provide young people with the skills that they require to manage their online behaviour safely into the future. Policing techniques can also be utilised to apprehend offenders, both through the impersonation of youths online, and through technological detection of language indicative of sexual predators. Finally, some research has been done which attempts to determine potential rehabilitation strategies for offenders.

With regard to educational strategies, it is important that these are primarily targeted at the right age group (adolescents instead of younger children), and they ideally should be targeted at the potential victims themselves, rather than their parents or caregivers (Wolak *et al.*, 2008). This is to increase the probability that the potential victims pay closer attention to the message. Wolak *et al.* (2008) also emphasise the importance of good sex education for adolescents generally, and focusing prevention strategies on the interactive aspects of internet use, rather than on posting of personal information. However, Bryce (2010) concludes that a significant number of young people engage in perilous online behaviours, even when they are aware of the risks involved. To combat this, Bryce suggests that educational strategies need to place more emphasis on the potential negative consequences of these behaviours. It is also preferable that prevention methods are targeted at youth behaviours, rather than the specific online locations they frequent, so that potential victims can use the knowledge in all aspects of their online behaviour (Mitchell *et al.*, 2010). Nevertheless, it should be noted that while psychoeducational internet safety interventions may increase internet safety knowledge, users might still continue to engage in risky online behaviour (Mishna *et al.*, 2011).

Dombrowski *et al.* (2004) describe how technological methods of child protection are insufficient, as they can be circumvented by both predators and children, and so these must be used in conjunction with psychoeducational methods. One potential method which could be used involves the development of contracts of internet use, agreed by both adolescents and caregivers, dictating acceptable online behaviours in relation to time spent online, locations visited online and the types of online interactions permitted.

Other methods of improving online security are employed by police forces. Mitchell *et al.* (2005) found that police impersonation of juveniles online led to a quarter of all arrests for internet sex crimes against minors. Nevertheless, it is possible that the offenders caught during such operations may be qualitatively different to other offenders – they may be less experienced, and Mitchell *et al.* note that there appeared to be some demographic differences between these offenders and those apprehended by other means.

McGhee *et al.* (2011) used communication theories and computer science algorithms to create a program to detect online sexual predation. While their program was not completely accurate (it achieved 68 per cent accuracy), it may provide a method of identifying online predators that might otherwise have been missed.

Once apprehended, it is possible that attempts may be made to rehabilitate online child predators. There are a wide variety of treatment programmes available for child sex offenders, including surgical castration, medications and cognitive-behavioural approaches, and there seems to be a positive effect on offenders undergoing treatment (Schmucker and Lösel, 2008). Some of these programmes target the cognitive distortions outlined above, while others focus on emotional dysregulation or social skills deficits. While the diversity of online predators should be recognised, Wolak *et al.* (2008) indicate that most of these approaches are likely to be applicable to online offenders.

Finally, Livingstone (2009) makes a valid point when arguing that 'online risks do not merit a moral panic, and nor do they warrant seriously restricting children's internet use, especially as this would deny them many benefits' (p. 178). While it is important that children and adolescents be protected online, it is also important to ensure that they reap the full benefits of online life. To place unnecessary restrictions on a child's internet access does not ensure the child's safety, but rather makes it more likely that the child will not be able to deal with such an encounter effectively if they are unfortunate enough to experience it. Nevertheless, it must be remembered that many children experience horrific sexual abuse, and in some cases photographic or video records of this abuse are circulated online. The phenomenon of child pornography distribution and collection online will be considered in the remainder of this chapter.

Activity 6.3 Developing a contract of internet use

Draft a sample contract of internet use, suitable for a young adolescent (aged 13–14 years). Consider what elements of online behaviour should be covered by the contract, and what you feel an acceptable amount of time is for such an individual to spend online daily. When you have finished, consider whether or not the same contract would be suitable for an older teenager (aged 16–17 years) or a younger child (aged 9–10 years).

Summary box 6.5 Improving the safety of children online

- Educational strategies should be primarily targeted at adolescents instead of younger children, and they ideally should be targeted at the potential victims themselves, rather than their parents or caregivers.
- It is also preferable that prevention methods are targeted at youth behaviours, rather than the specific online locations they frequent.
- Technological methods of child protection are insufficient, as they can be circumvented by both predators and children.
- Police impersonation of juveniles may lead to arrests, but it is uncertain whether those apprehended are representative of most online predators.
- There are a variety of rehabilitation programmes used for sex offenders generally, many of which may be applied to online child predators.
- It is important that any precautions that are taken do not prevent the child or adolescent from reaping the full benefits of online life.

Child pornography online

Sheldon and Howitt (2007) indicate that, at least in terms of convictions, internet child pornography is the major activity that constitutes internet-related sex crimes. Child pornography is not a new offence, but the development and distribution of such images and videos have been facilitated by the emergence of new technologies, such as webcams, digital cameras, smartphones and photo-editing software, as well as by the development

Table 6.1 The ten levels of child pornography content outlined by COPINE

Level 1: Indicative	Non-sexualised pictures, such as bathing costumes. May be collected from commonly available sources.
Level 2: Nudist	Naked or semi-naked children, taken at legitimate nudist settings. May include photographs taken during bath time.
Level 3: Erotica	Surreptitiously taken photographs of naked or semi-clothed children.
Level 4: Posing	Naked or semi-clothed children are deliberately posed, but not in sexualised postures.
Level 5: Erotic posing	The child appears in a provocative or sexualised posture, in varying degrees of nakedness.
Level 6: Explicit erotic posing	Images that emphasise the child's genital areas.
Level 7: Explicit sexual activity	Sexual activity involving children, such as touching, masturbation or oral sex, but adults are not seen in the image.
Level 8: Assault	Involves a record of the child being assaulted by an adult using their fingers.
Level 9: Gross assault	Images may include penetrative sex, masturbation, or oral sex with an adult.
Level 10: Sadistic/bestiality	The child is subjected to pain or there is sexual activity with an animal.

of a greater number of methods of distributing such material, such as via social networking and file-sharing sites. Before the popularity of the internet, child pornography was more limited – images tended to be manufactured and traded locally, and distributors needed a considerable amount of quite specialised equipment to develop and copy the images (Wortley and Smallbone, 2006). Today, images and video can be made with less equipment, less expense and in higher quality, and the material is easily duplicated and distributed. Gathering a collection of child pornography is now easier and cheaper than before, and the offender may also have a sense of anonymity due to the online nature of the offence (Quayle *et al.*, 2006). Nevertheless, police forces are becoming increasingly adept at identifying offenders, and so this sense of anonymity is often misplaced.

Ratings of material

Adult pornographic material varies greatly in terms of content, style and essence, and child pornography also varies greatly. Attempts have been made to develop systems by which such child pornography can be rated, with notable research being conducted by the Combating Paedophile Information Networks in Europe (COPINE) project in University College Cork (Taylor *et al.*, 2001). The COPINE project described ten levels of content, listed in Table 6.1. Of these the first few levels would be unlikely to lead to prosecution (Jones, 2003).

Table 6.2 UK 'SAP' scale (Sentencing Guidelines Council, 2007, p. 109)

Level 1	Images depicting erotic posing with no sexual activity.
Level 2	Non-penetrative sexual activity between children, or solo masturbation by a child.
Level 3	Non-penetrative sexual activity between adults and children.
Level 4	Penetrative sexual activity involving a child or children, or both children and adults.
Level 5	Sadism or penetration of, or by, an animal.

Another rating scale is used by the UK's Sentencing Advisory Panel (SAP). Their five-point scale is outlined in Table 6.2.

Summary box 6.6 Ratings of child pornography materials

- Child pornography is not a new offence, but the development and distribution of such images and videos have been facilitated by the emergence of new technologies.
- Offenders may have a false sense of anonymity due to the online nature of the offence.
- The Combating Paedophile Information Networks in Europe (COPINE) project (Taylor *et al.*, 2001) described ten levels of content of child pornographic materials.
- Another rating scale is used by the UK's Sentencing Advisory Panel (SAP).

Background and psychology of child pornography offenders

Before considering the psychology of child pornography offenders, it is important to consider that there may be several different types of such offender. For example, there may be considerable differences between a person who collects such images, without ever engaging in a contact offence, and a person who creates and/or distributes the images. There may even be differences between individuals who distribute the images – some may do so in order to expand their own collection through swapping with others, while some may do so for financial gain, as collectors pay for images. The complexity of these offenders is illustrated by Krone (2004), who suggests a typology of internet child pornography offenders. This typology is outlined in Table 6.3. It should be noted that these categories are not mutually exclusive – some offenders may be classified under more than one category.

While Krone's typology is useful for classification purposes, it does not explain the psychology behind each type of offender, or the potential evolution of an offender from one type to another. Indeed, a key question examined in the literature attempts to determine if the viewing and collection of child pornography is a stepping-stone to contact offences.

Some studies have attempted to create a profile of internet child pornography users. Researchers have generally found users of internet child pornography to be mostly

Table 6.3 Krone's (2004) typology of internet child pornography offenders

Browsers	Save images of child pornography that they happen across, but do not interact with other offenders.
Trawlers	Actively seek out images, and may network with other offenders.
Secure collectors	Engage in high levels of security behaviours and may be members of secure child pornography rings. Their collecting may become obsessional.
Non-secure collectors	Use non-secure sources and open content. Engage in high levels of networking, but do not employ security strategies.
Physical abusers	Sexually abuse children and may record these abuses for personal use, but also seek other child pornography online.
Producers	Create child pornography for the purpose of disseminating it to others, rather than for personal use.
Distributors	Disseminate abuse images, sometimes just for financial reasons.
Private fantasisers	Create digital images using electronic means, such as photo-editing software, for personal use.
Groomers	Send child pornography to other children to try to initiate a sexual relationship with them.

male (Frei *et al.*, 2005; Seto and Eke, 2005; Webb *et al.*, 2007), though other researchers, such as Siegfried *et al.* (2008), have found that a substantial minority of internet child pornography users were female. With regard to age, Wortley and Smallbone (2006) found that offenders are most likely to be between the ages of 26 and 40, while Siegfried *et al.* (2008) found that 80 per cent of users were under 35 years of age. Other findings relating to the characteristics of internet child pornography users include:

- they are more likely to be white (Babchishin *et al.*, 2011; Wortley and Smallbone, 2006);
- they are more likely to be single, and never married (Siegfried *et al.*, 2008);
- they may experience some symptoms of internet dependence (Blundell *et al.*, 2002; Schneider, 2000);
- they are generally well educated and/or in employment (Burke *et al.*, 2002; Frei *et al.*, 2005; O'Brien and Webster, 2007; Riegel, 2004; Siegfried *et al.*, 2008; Wolak *et al.*, 2005).

As with many other types of offender profiling, the description above is problematic as it describes many individuals who are not offenders, as well as those who are. Similarly, it does not describe all offenders – some individuals who do not fit the profile still engage in criminal activity. It is therefore important to remember that the findings above may not always be useful in criminal investigations.

It has been noted that offenders often search for specific types of images or videos (Quayle and Taylor, 2002; Steel, 2009). It is possible that searches for such specific material may relate to pre-existing sexual fantasies. It is also possible that material could be created to fit existing requests by potential users (Lanning, 2001b).

Some research has also examined the personality of internet child pornography users. Siegfried *et al.* (2008) found that users had higher levels of exploitive-manipulative amoral dishonesty (EMAD) traits, and lower scores on internal moral choice than non-offenders, suggesting that they did not have the same personal moral compass that most individuals do. Therefore, they may recognise child pornography as illegal and socially unacceptable, but they may not believe that it is immoral for them personally. Laulik *et al.* (2007) found that internet sex offenders seemed to experience deficits in interpersonal functioning and affective difficulties, along with correlations between time spent accessing child pornography and some psychological difficulties, such as schizophrenia, borderline features and depression. There have been some conflicting findings however – for example, Wall *et al.* (2011) did not find that internet child sex offenders had particular difficulties with emotional avoidance.

Other studies have noted differences between internet sex offenders and contact sex offenders (for example, Webb *et al.*, 2007), particularly in relation to ethnicity and age, but not in relation to personality or mental health functioning. Reijnen *et al.* (2009) found no specific differences between child pornography offenders and other types of offender on a number of psychological traits. Similarly, Elliott *et al.* (2009) compared internet and contact sex offenders, finding that contact offenders had more cognitive distortions and cognitive impulsivity, while internet offenders had higher scales on fantasy and underassertiveness. Bates and Metcalf (2007) found that internet offenders were more likely to respond in socially desirable ways than contact offenders, and had lower scores on sexualised attitudes towards children. Both Burke *et al.* (2002) and O'Brien and Webster (2007) found higher intelligence scores in internet offenders than contact offenders. Babchishin *et al.* (2011) found that online offenders had greater victim empathy, greater sexual deviancy and lower impression management than offline offenders. Research studies such as these suggest that contact offenders and internet only offenders may have qualitatively different personality types.

Summary box 6.7 Child pornography offenders

- There may be several different types of child pornography offenders, including various types of collectors, producers and distributors.
- Krone (2004) suggested a typology of nine different types of internet child pornography offenders.
- Researchers have found users of internet child pornography to be mostly male, white, single, never married, experiencing internet dependence, well educated and/or in good employment.
- Offenders often search for specific types of images or videos, which may relate to pre-existing sexual fantasies.
- Several differences have been noted between the psychology of internet child pornography offenders and contact offenders.

Psychology of child pornography victims

It is important to consider how internet child pornography victims are affected by their experience. Here we will not consider the psychological effects of the actual sexual abuse itself, which have been covered in detail by other sources (see, for example, Hillberg *et al.*, 2011; Maikovich *et al.*, 2009; Maniglio, 2009), but instead will focus on the effects of the continued existence and distribution of the material on the abuse victim.

Silbert (1989) outlines how the victim's initial psychological distress can last for many years. This is partly due to the existence of the permanent record of the abuse (Calcetas-Santos, 2001). Taylor and Quayle (2003) also emphasise this, indicating that the abuse continues for as long as the pornographic material exists. With the advent of distribution via the internet, it is now next to impossible to ensure that all copies of the material are destroyed – the images and videos are cheaply and easily copied and distributed worldwide. A victim may always be left wondering if the material remains in existence. Because of this, the victim may encounter symptoms in addition to those that are a direct result of the abuse itself. Silbert (1989) noted that victims' initial feelings of shame and anxiety intensified as time passed, and victims may also experience feelings of deep despair, worthlessness, hopelessness, difficulties in forming normal sexual relationships as adults, and a distorted model of sexuality.

Taylor and Quayle (2003) noted that, at that time, there had been little empirical research examining the long-term effects on victims of internet child pornography, and unfortunately relatively little has been completed since then, especially when compared to the research gathered on the offenders themselves. Leonard (2010) noted that victims of internet offending may experience additional confusion, particularly as a result of their compliance with directions from the perpetrator on how to behave when the pornography is staged. It should be noted that even aside from research examining the psychological effects on victims, there is relatively little information available about the demographic characteristics of children who appear in internet child pornography. Quayle and Jones (2011) completed one of the few studies in this area, and found that there were approximately four times as many female victims as male victims, and ten times as many Caucasian children as non-Caucasian children.

Summary box 6.8 Victims of online child pornography

- It is thought that there may be differences between the psychological reactions of victims of internet child pornography and those of children who have been abused but pornography has not been developed and distributed.
- This may be partly due to an inability to ensure that all copies of the material have been destroyed.
- In addition to symptoms experienced due to the abuse itself, victims may experience many other types of psychological distress.
- There has been very little research to date examining the effects on victims of such abuse.

Punishment and rehabilitation of child pornography offenders

Considering the severity and harm that can be caused by those that develop, circulate and collect child pornography online, it is important to consider how these offenders should be treated, and if rehabilitation is possible.

Firstly, it should be considered how many offenders are likely to continue to use child pornography after they are apprehended. Endrass *et al.* (2009) found that only 3 per cent of a sample of users had reoffended with a violent and/or sex crime at a six-year follow-up. A slightly larger group (nearly 4 per cent) had reoffended with a non-contact sex offence. As such, Endrass *et al.* conclude that it is unlikely that such criminals would reoffend, and this finding might suggest that the development and implementation of a treatment programme for internet child pornography users may not be the most appropriate use of available funds. A similar relatively low recidivism rate was found by Eke *et al.* (2011), who obtained data for registered male child pornography offenders at an average follow-up time of 4.1 years. Eke *et al.* (2011) found that while 32 per cent of offenders had carried out some form of further crime, only 4 per cent were charged with new contact sex offences with an additional 2 per cent charged with historical contact sex offences and 7 per cent charged with a new child pornography offence. Nevertheless, it should be remembered that these low recidivism rates do not necessarily mean that the child pornography users have not reoffended – it is possible that they have adapted their use of technology in order to reduce the likelihood of apprehension.

> **Activity 6.4 Dedication of resources to the rehabilitation of child pornography offenders**
> Given the relatively low recidivism levels noted in child pornography offenders, should funds and resources be dedicated to rehabilitating offenders?

Reducing the likelihood of reoffending is not always the primary goal of punishment, and public perception of the severity of the offence can influence how an offender is treated. Lam *et al.* (2010) examined how university students perceived the offence of child pornography. The offence was considered more severe when younger victims were targeted, and male offenders were considered to be at a higher risk of recidivism. Similarly, there seem to be high levels of public support for sex offender treatment generally (Mears *et al.*, 2008). On the other hand, authors such as Berlin and Sawyer (2012) have suggested that severe penalties associated with accessing internet child pornography should be reconsidered in some cases, arguing that many such offenders pose relatively low risk to the community.

Despite the importance that is placed on dealing with sex offenders, to date most assessment and treatment programmes used for internet child sex offenders have tended to be adapted from generic sex offender programmes, and while differences between contact and non-contact offenders have been noted, there have been suggestions that there is enough overlap of predisposing factors to suggest that similar assessment tools can be used for both groups (Middleton, 2004, 2009). One example of a more specific rehabilitation programme is the internet sex offender treatment programme (i-SOTP; Middleton, 2008). The i-SOTP aims to prevent both further viewing behaviours and escalation to contact offending, through a series of twenty to thirty sessions. The i-SOTP has been accredited for use in the community by the National Probation Service of England and Wales and has been found to be effective in improving socio-affective functioning and decreasing pro-offending attitudes (Middleton *et al.*, 2009).

Summary box 6.9 Punishment and rehabilitation of child pornography offenders

- Internet child pornography offenders appear to have low levels of recidivism.
- There is therefore some debate as to whether or not resources should be dedicated to their rehabilitation.
- Most assessment and treatment programmes to date have been adapted from generic sex offender programmes.
- But these may not be appropriate due to the differences between contact and non-contact offenders.
- Middleton and colleagues developed the i-SOTP to prevent further viewing behaviours and escalation to contact offending, and it has been found to be effective.

Conclusion

Child-related online offending is an extremely serious issue, and has been the subject of a great deal of research to date. Unfortunately there are still many significant gaps in our knowledge, including a full understanding of the effects of such victimisation on the children involved, and an evaluation of the best methods of encouraging young people to engage in safer online behaviour in order to avoid predators. From the literature to date, it would also seem that perpetrators of internet-related child sexual offences are somewhat different to other child sex offenders, and so a greater understanding of these differences may be beneficial in tackling these problems in a more effective manner.

Essay questions

(1) Evaluate how well theories of paedophilia explain online child pornography and online child predation.
(2) Education, rather than technological interventions, is the best method of protecting children and adolescents from online sexual predators. Discuss.
(3) Online child pornography collectors are substantially different to contact offenders. Discuss.

Additional reading

Books and articles

There are many excellent sources which provide additional information about both online child predators and child pornography.

Wolak, Finkelhor and Mitchell have prepared many articles examining online child predators, with one of the most accessible being:

Wolak, J., Finkelhor, D., Mitchell, K. and Ybarra, M. (2008). Online 'predators' and their victims: myths, realities, and implications for prevention and treatment. *American Psychologist*, **63**, 111–28.

Similarly, Siegfried, Lovely and Rogers' study provides a psychological analysis of online child pornography behaviour:

Siegfried, K. C., Lovely, R. W. and Rogers, M. K. (2008). Self-reported online child pornography behaviour: a psychological analysis. *International Journal of Cyber Criminology*, **2**, 286–97.

Sheldon and Howitt's book *Sex Offenders and the Internet* (published in 2007 by Wiley) describes many types of online sex offenders, including both child pornography offenders and paedophiles.

Finally, Livingstone's book *Children and the Internet: Great Expectations, Challenging Realities* (published in 2009 by Polity) considers both the positive and negative elements of children in online environments.

Websites

The National Centre for Missing and Exploited Children maintain 'NetSmartz' (www.netsmartz. org), which provides information and resources for children, teenagers, educators and parents and guardians about staying safe online. They cover a wide variety of issues, including predators and inappropriate content, as well as social networking, sexting and file-sharing.

In the UK, the Serious Organised Crime Agency (SOCA) is affiliated with the Child Exploitation and Online Protection Centre (CEOP) (www.ceop.police.uk). This website also offers advice and resources for parents and children of different ages.

The Federal Bureau of Investigation provides help and advice for parents at www.fbi.gov/stats-services/publications/parent-guide.

7 Cyberbullying and cyberstalking

Case studies

Christina was happy in school until a new girl, Emma, started in her year. Emma made friends easily, and soon was the most popular girl in the class, but she took a dislike to Christina. Emma began to bully Christina in school – regularly calling her names and insulting her. Christina realised that she was no longer being invited to social events with her former friends, and she spent more and more time alone. While her classmates remained her 'friends' on social networking sites, they often sent her bullying messages, or posted nasty comments about her on their profiles. Christina was particularly upset when one person whom she had considered to be a good friend posted information that Christina had told her in secret on the public pages of the social networking site. The bullying soon extended to receiving text messages on her mobile phone, often from numbers that she did not recognise. While Christina tried to remain positive, she found herself becoming more and more introverted and depressed.

Alex had dated Sarah for three months during their first year in university, before breaking it off with her. He thought that they could remain friends, but over time it became apparent that she was stalking him. She commented on every post that he made on social networking sites, and sent him repeated emails and text messages asking to get back together. When Sarah started to show up at parties and events that he was attending, Alex realised that she was using a calendar on a social networking site to figure out where he would be. She also used his online profile to determine what subjects he was taking, and could regularly be found outside the lecture theatre just before or after his classes. She also monitored his location check-ins using his smartphone, and would show up nearby. Eventually Alex blocked her from his social networking account, and changed his mobile phone number so that Sarah couldn't reach him.

Chapter overview

Cases of cyberbullying with horrific consequences appear all too regularly on the news. Real life cases of victims such as Ryan Halligan, Megan Meier and Jamey Rodemeyer, who committed suicide due to the bullying they experienced, demonstrate the importance of understanding and tackling this serious issue. While receiving considerably less attention from the media and academic research, cyberstalking can also cause great distress to victims. Cyberbullying and cyberstalking are not always criminal events, but they can involve actions that are criminal in nature, such as direct threats. This chapter provides an overview of both of these areas, examining definitions, methods, comparison to offline equivalents, traits of perpetrators, effects on victims and potential solutions.

Cyberbullying

We shall first turn our attention to cyberbullying, which has received a considerable amount of attention from researchers. As mentioned above, not all cyberbullying is criminal in nature, but Jewkes (2010) indicates that cyberbullying occupies 'a grey area between social harms and illegal acts, depending on their severity and the legal jurisdiction in which they take place' (p. 526).

Definitions and prevalence

Many definitions of cyberbullying have been offered. Hinduja and Patchin (2009) define cyberbullying as 'willful and repeated harm inflicted through the use of computers, cell phones, and other electronic devices' (p. 5). Willard (2007, p. 1) defines cyberbullying as 'sending or posting harmful material or engaging in other forms of social aggression using the Internet or other digital technologies' while Shariff and Gouin (2005) describe cyberbullying as consisting of 'covert, psychological bullying, conveyed through the electronic mediums' (p. 3). Bhat (2008) cites Hazler's (1996) description of bullying, which suggests that bullying occurs when the victim is being harmed by the physical, verbal or socio/emotional actions of the bully, when there is a power imbalance between the victim and the bully and when the actions are repeated over time. Bhat (2008) indicates that cyberbullying 'involves the use of ICT to intimidate, harass, victimise or bully an individual or a group of individuals' (p. 54). More recently, Langos (2012) has indicated that the 'repetition, power imbalance, intention and aggression, regarded as essential criteria of traditional face-to-face bullying' (p. 285) should retain their importance in the definition of cyberbullying.

It is important to note that many of the above definitions either implicitly or explicitly refer to the bullying being carried out wilfully. It is of course possible that an activity is perceived as bullying by the target or a third party, but was never intended to hurt. O'Sullivan and Flanagin (2003) examine this in relation to another disruptive online activity – flaming. Flaming describes antagonistic or aggressive online communications, often in public settings such as bulletin boards and forums. They propose that all online communications can be categorised depending on how they are intended by the sender, and how they are interpreted by the receiver and a third party. For example, if a sender intends to send a flame, both the receiver and a third party might recognise the aggressive intention if it is sufficiently obvious. However, either the receiver, the third party or both may fail to recognise the communication as a flame if it is too subtle, or if it contains reference to in-group material that a third party may not be familiar with. Similarly, a sender may not intend a message to be aggressive, but it may be interpreted as a flame by the receiver, third party or both, because of poor choice of language or tone, use of sarcasm or diverging cultural norms. This framework can also be applied to cyberbullying cases – the sender may or may not intend the communication to be hurtful, and the receiver and/or third party may or may not accurately interpret the sender's intention. It is possible that some bullying instances are never recognised by the victim as intentional transgressions, and it may be that some victims wrongly interpret online communications as bullying, when they were sent without the intention of causing harm. O'Sullivan and Flanagin recognise that their framework could inform analysis of other negative and harassing online behaviours, and it is likely that it could apply to some cyberstalking cases as well as cyberbullying ones.

O'Sullivan and Flanagin's framework also highlights a problem for many researchers of cyberbullying – that it is difficult to ascertain exactly how much cyberbullying exists. Different statistics may be obtained, depending on how the research is completed. If asked whether or not they have been cyberbullied, a person may indicate that they have, although their 'bully' may see the interaction very differently. It is important to note that the absence of intent by the 'bully' does not necessarily lessen the painful reaction of the 'victim' – unintentional hurt is still hurtful. Similarly, a third-party researcher examining online interactions may see bullying where it does not exist, or may miss subtle forms of bullying interaction. As such, care should be taken when interpreting statistics relating to both cyberbullying and cyberstalking.

Activity 7.1 Interpreting online communications

Consider a time when an online communication that you sent was misinterpreted by the recipient. What aspects of the message led to the miscommunication? If a third party had seen the message, would they have agreed with your intended meaning, or your recipient's interpretation? If you have enough examples of such communications, try creating a log so as to identify the most common causes of such miscommunications. Remember to include messages that you have received and misinterpreted, as well as those that you sent.

As well as misinterpretation of intent, there are many other reasons why it is difficult to be certain how much cyberbullying exists. A victim may feel shame or embarrassment because of their victimisation, or a fear of the repercussions of reporting such events (for example, having to face their bully, or a fear that their parents will take away their mobile phone and/or internet access in an attempt to prevent further victimisation). Despite these limitations (and possible under-reporting), studies examining cyberbullying rates portray a worryingly high prevalence. For example, Smith et al. (2006) found that 22 per cent of British participants had been cyberbullied, and United Press International (2008) found that more than 40 per cent of US teenagers had been victimised. Kowalski and Limber (2007) found that 11 per cent of students had experienced cyberbullying during the past couple of months, while the Pew Internet and American Life Project (Lenhart, 2007) found that 32 per cent of teenagers had experienced online harassment, including receiving threatening messages or having embarrassing pictures posted online. Hinduja and Patchin (2010b) found that about 20 per cent of teenagers had been a victim of cyberbullying, while Dehue *et al.* (2008) found that 16 per cent of children had engaged in cyberbullying, with 23 per cent being victimised.

Another problem in determining cyberbullying rates is that different researchers use different definitions. For example Wolak *et al.* (2007) found that 9 per cent of 10–17 year-olds had experienced online harassment over the previous year, but they did not classify most of these as cyberbullying due to the lack of aggression, repetition or power imbalance. Wolak *et al.* suggest the term 'online harassment' (p. S51) to describe these incidents instead.

While most studies determining the rate of cyberbullying have understandably focused on school-age children and teenagers, adults may also be victims or perpetrators of such activity. However, there are far fewer studies examining the rate and impact of cyberbullying among adults. One of these, completed by Privitera and Campbell (2009), found that 34 per cent of individuals in the workplace had been bullied face-to-face, and 10.7 per cent had been cyberbullied. All of those who were cyberbullied were also victimised face-to-face.

Summary box 7.1 Cyberbullying definitions and prevalence

- Many definitions have been offered for cyberbullying.
- Several of these definitions explicitly or implicitly indicate that the bullying behaviour is intentional, although hurt may still occur when it is not the sender's intent to cause harm.
- Comments made online may be misinterpreted by both receivers and third parties, which may affect the determination of prevalence of cyberbullying.
- Victims of cyberbullying may also avoid reporting their experiences due to fear of repercussions or feelings of shame or embarrassment.
- Studies examining cyberbullying have found wide discrepancies in reported prevalence.
- Cyberbullying can also occur among adults, although this has not been examined as widely as cyberbullying in teenagers and children.

Methods of cyberbullying and comparison to 'traditional' bullying

In the early days of the internet, cyberbullying was difficult, if not impossible. Few people had access to the technology, and there were far fewer ways of contacting individuals online. The wide variety of technologies that are now available within most western civilisations has made it much easier for potential cyberbullies to reach their intended victims. The popularity of mobile phones, social networking sites, video-sharing sites, file-sharing sites, email, instant messaging, location tagging, blogging, micro-blogging and web publishing software has resulted in a wide variety of methods of creating and disseminating hurtful content to a victim and a wider circle of individuals (such as classmates, friends, family and colleagues). Possibly the most frequently used technology currently popular among young users is social networking sites (SNS). As SNS encompass many other types of online communication (including photo and video sharing, as well as sending personal and public messages), they provide many opportunities for cyberbullying behaviours. This section examines what online technologies are used in cyberbullying, and how cyberbullying differs from offline, or 'traditional', bullying.

A wide variety of cyberbullying methods has been identified by many researchers, including Bhat (2008), Dehue *et al.* (2008), Hinduja and Patchin (2009), Jewkes (2010), Kowalski and Limber (2007), Lenhart (2007), Mitchell and Finkelhor (2007), Smith *et al.* (2006) and Wolak *et al.* (2007). Some of the most common forms of cyberbullying are listed in Table 7.1.

There are similarities and differences between cyberbullying and traditional (or offline) bullying. Some research suggests that there are differences between cyberbullies and traditional bullies, although overall it seems that in many cases cyberbullying is another tool used by traditional bullies as part of a larger strategy. For example, Raskauskas and Stoltz (2007) found that students' roles in traditional bullying were similar to cyberbullying.

Two factors that may contribute to differences between cyberbullying and traditional bullying are anonymity and disinhibition. The anonymity found online can make it easier to engage in cyberbullying, while also making it harder for parents and teachers to fully investigate a case (Kowalski and Limber, 2007; Li, 2007). This anonymity may also mean that the victim does not know who their bully or bullies are, which may add to their trauma as they are uncertain as to who they can trust (Shariff, 2005).

The related concept of online disinhibition refers to the tendency by individuals to carry out certain behaviours online that they would not in face-to-face environments. In some cases this can have a positive effect – a user may engage in altruistic behaviours online, or may feel more comfortable disclosing information during therapies conducted in online environments. However, online disinhibition may also be negative, with the effect that cyberbullies 'do not have to deal with the immediate emotional, psychological or physical effects of face-to-face bullying on their victim' (Hinduja and Patchin, 2009, p. 22). This release from traditional constraints of conscience may mean that the bully is inclined to say or do far more hurtful things online than they would in an offline context. It may also mean that the bullying continues for longer than it would offline, as the bully does not have to deal with any guilt that may arise from seeing the effects of their behaviours on the victim first-hand. Indeed Bhat (2008) suggests that cyberbullies may not realise the serious effects that their actions are having on the victim – they may think that they are engaging in a relatively harmless prank. If a similar prank occurred face-to-face, the evidence of hurt on the victim's face might prevent any furthering of the behaviour. Willard (2007) also notes the possible contribution of online disinhibition to the actions of a cyberbully. It is possible that the presence of anonymity and online disinhibition may

Table 7.1 Common cyberbullying methods

Social ostracism	Exclusion from groups or activities. Can notably occur on social networking sites, where a victim may be excluded from a circle of friends, ignored by other users, or blocked by bullies.
Disparaging public comments	Can be made on social networking site profiles, or other online settings such as webpages, forums, bulletin boards or in chatrooms. When disparaging comments are made about a victim on an SNS it has the added consequence of being visible to a wide group of the victim's contacts and friends, which may add to the humiliation.
Creation of hurtful/embarrassing content	Dedicated websites or pages on SNS can be created which specifically target the victim. Photographs or videos intended to hurt or embarrass the victim may also be created and posted in public settings. As almost every mobile phone also includes a camera, surreptitious photographs or videos can be taken of a victim, which can be immediately uploaded to social networking sites if the handset is a smartphone. The photos or videos may also be modified to increase embarrassment before they are uploaded.
Sharing of confidential information	A victim's former confidante may share a previously disclosed secret with a wider audience, and may publicly post the secret online. A specific variation on this can involve 'sexting', where a person may have shared naked or explicit photographs of themselves with a trusted other, only to find that these were later shared with a much wider group of people.
Impersonation	An additional method by which cyberbullying can be carried out involves impersonation online, commonly involving the hijacking of their SNS profile in order to make it appear as though they are posting embarrassing messages or uploading inappropriate photos or videos. While such SNS impersonations are often completed as practical jokes, without the intent to bully, they can also be carried out maliciously. In some cases the perpetrator may change the password on the account, making it very difficult for the account holder to remove the embarrassing content.
Sending harassing communications	Text messages, picture messages, leaving voicemails, calling the victim, instant messaging, emails, other forms of synchronous or asynchronous online communications.
Name calling, ridiculing, gossiping and spreading of rumours	This behaviour may take place in a wide variety of public or private online settings.
Voting or rating websites	Posting photographs or information about a victim to one or more websites where visitors judge aspects of a person's attractiveness. A public judgement that the victim is 'not attractive' may add to the victim's emotional reaction (Hinduja and Patchin, 2009).
Online gaming and virtual worlds	A victim may find that their avatar is repeatedly picked on or ostracised in an online game or virtual world. For example, a victim may play a first-person-shooter type online game, but their bullies pick on them by repeatedly killing their character. Crime in virtual worlds is considered in more detail in Chapter 10.
'Happy-slapping'	An incident of a person being physically bullied is recorded and distributed, perhaps using a video-sharing website or social networking site.

explain why some people may engage in cyberbullying who would not take part in traditional bullying. For example, Twyman *et al.* (2009) found that almost two-thirds of cyberbullies/victims were also traditional bullies/victims, but that some online bullies were not traditional bullies, which they attributed to online disinhibition.

A third difference between cyberbullying and traditional bullying may be reflected in the size of the potential audience. Bullying which occurs online may be visible to a much wider audience than bullying in face-to-face settings (Kowalski and Limber, 2007; Shariff, 2005). Any content which is posted online can also be easily copied and forwarded (Hinduja and Patchin, 2009; Lenhart, 2007). Of course, some types of bullying behaviour involve both traditional and cyberbullying aspects, such as happy-slapping, where an incident of a person being physically bullied is recorded and distributed, sometimes on a video-sharing website or social networking site.

A final potential difference between cyberbullying and traditional bullying is the greater number of options available to bullies to contact the victim, and therefore the greater proportion of time that bullying can take place (Hinduja and Patchin, 2009). Historically, if a person was being bullied in a school environment, they could at least take refuge in their home or other social settings. As most young people carry mobile phones, they are also vulnerable to cyberbullying at any time or place. There is a constant link between the bully and the victim.

Summary box 7.2 Methods of cyberbullying and comparison to 'traditional' bullying

* The wide variety of online technologies has made it much easier for potential cyberbullies to reach their intended victims.
* Technologies used in cyberbullying include mobile phones, social networking sites, video-sharing sites, file-sharing sites, email, instant messaging, location tagging, blogging, micro-blogging and web publishing software.
* Common methods of cyberbullies include:
  - social ostracism;
  - disparaging public comments;
  - creation of hurtful/embarrassing content;
  - sharing of confidential information;
  - impersonation;
  - sending harassing communications;
  - name calling, ridiculing, gossiping and spreading of rumours;
  - voting or rating websites;
  - online gaming and virtual worlds;
  - happy-slapping.
* Some differences between cyberbullying and traditional bullying include:
  - perceived or actual anonymity;
  - online disinhibition;
  - size of the potential audience;
  - greater potential contact between the victim and the bully.

Traits of cyberbullies

Several studies have attempted to examine the traits and motives of cyberbullies. Some research (such as Dempsey *et al.*, 2011) suggests that technology provides new tools for already aggressive youths, and so cyberbullies and traditional bullies may be very similar.

One possible difference between traditional bullies and cyberbullies may relate to gender. For example, Kowalski and Limber (2007) found that traditionally, boys are more likely to be the bully, but online, girls are more likely to engage in bullying behaviours. Similarly, Li (2007) found that while over half of cyberbullies were male, females preferred to use electronic communications to bully others. Conversely, Hinduja and Patchin (2008) found that gender and race were not significantly related to engaging in or being the victim of cyberbullying, and Ybarra and Mitchell (2004) found that males and females were equally involved in cyberharassing others.

It has been suggested that those who are victims of traditional bullying may be more likely to engage in cyberbullying (Ybarra and Mitchell, 2004) while other factors found to be positively correlated with cyberbullying include computer proficiency, amount of time spent online, school problems and substance abuse (Hinduja and Patchin, 2008). Twyman *et al.* (2009) found that both cyberbullies and victims of cyberbullying were more likely to spend greater amounts of time on the internet, instant messaging, social networking or emailing.

Other traits that may be associated with cyberbullies include impulsiveness, quickness to anger, heightened perception of hostility in the actions of others, greater likelihood of holding rigid beliefs, reduced empathy and greater use of aggressive actions to protect their image (Bhat, 2008). In particular, Bhat indicates that impulsivity may be especially important in cyberbullies, as the perpetual accessibility of the internet allows actions to be taken quickly in retaliation to any real or imaginary offence against the bully. Stress may also be an indicator of both traditional and cyberbullying (Patchin and Hinduja, 2011). Steffgen *et al.* (2011) noted that cyberbullies had lower empathy levels than non-cyberbullies, and cyberbullies were more afraid of becoming victims of cyberbullying.

Finally, with regard to motive, Strom and Strom (2005) suggest that this is to threaten, humiliate or harm the victim, as well as creating fear and helplessness in them, while Bhat suggests that it is the same as for offline bullying – 'to embarrass, threaten, shame, hurt, or exclude the victim' (2008, p. 58). Cyberbullies may 'seek implicit or explicit pleasure or profit through the mistreatment of another individual' (Hinduja and Patchin, 2009, p. 17) or cyberbullying may be motivated by intolerance, as some attacks are carried out on minority groups (Lenhart, 2007).

Summary box 7.3 Traits of cyberbullies

- Some studies have suggested that females are more likely to engage in cyberbullying, but findings are inconsistent across researchers.
- Other characteristics that may be common among cyberbullies are:
  - victimisation of traditional bullying;

- ○ increased time spent with technology;
- ○ offline problems, such as school problems and substance abuse.
- Certain characteristics, such as impulsiveness, perception of hostility, holding rigid beliefs, reduced empathy and increased aggression.
- It is likely that cyberbullies have similar motives to traditional bullies.

Victims of cyberbullying

With regard to research on victims of cyberbullying, this has taken two main directions – examining which individuals may be more prone to cyberbullying victimisation, and attempting to determine what the effects of such victimisation are on the individuals.

Several researchers have found that girls are more likely to be victims of cyberbullying (Kowalski and Limber, 2007; Lenhart, 2007; Li, 2007; Smith *et al.*, 2006). Lenhart (2007) found that teenagers who share their thoughts and identities online, those who used social networking sites and those who used the internet daily were more likely to be targets of cyberbullying. However, with the increased popularity of all of these activities since Lenhart's study, it is unlikely that these are useful predictors of victimisation anymore. Kowalski and Limber (2007) found that almost half of victims did not know who their cyberbully was, and so it seems that the perceived anonymity discussed above is real, at least in some cases.

The consequences of cyberbullying can be severe. They can be psychological, emotional and/or social in nature, and in some cases can last for years (Patchin and Hinduja, 2006). Both cyberbullies and cybervictims have more suicidal thoughts and are more likely to attempt suicide (Hinduja and Patchin, 2010a). Emotional responses in victims of cyberbullying can include anger, hurt, anxiety, sadness and fear (Beran and Li, 2005), while Burgess-Proctor *et al.* (2009) indicate that victimisation may prevent the individual from exploring the more positive aspects of online life. Beran and Li (2005) suggest that academic work may also be affected by victimisation.

It is possible that different types of cyberbullying could have different effects on victims. For example, Smith *et al.* (2006) found that participants perceived picture/video clip and phone call bullying to have the most serious impact, while chatroom, instant messaging and email bullying were perceived as having the least impact. While this is very interesting research, further exploration with examination of more recent technologies (such as SNS) needs to be conducted. Menesini *et al.* (2011) have gone some way to addressing this by determining that the severity of different cyberbullying acts can be represented along a continuum. Menesini *et al.* (2011) suggest that the less severe acts are silent or prank phone calls and insults on instant messaging, while the most severe acts are unpleasant images on websites and content depicting intimate or violent scenes. Boulton *et al.* (2012) found that undergraduate students considered cyberbullying to be worse than verbal traditional bullying, but not as severe as physical traditional bullying.

Summary box 7.4 Victims of cyberbullying

- Research suggests that victims of cyberbullying are more likely to be females.
- Consequences of cyberbullying can be severe.
- Consequences can be psychological, emotional and/or social in nature.
- In some cases, victims of cyberbullying are more likely to attempt suicide.
- It is possible that different types of cyberbullying could have different effects on victims.

Possible solutions to cyberbullying

Several potential solutions to the problem of cyberbullying have been suggested. These tend to have two main approaches – preventative measures and attempts to deal appropriately with specific cyberbullying incidents that have already occurred. In some cases these responses have been formal, involving the intervention of schools or police, while in other cases informal measures can be taken by the victim and/or their parents.

Many authors have offered suggestions for preventing and/or responding to cyberbullying (see, for example, Bhat, 2008; Brown *et al.*, 2006; Dehue *et al.*, 2008; Hinduja and Patchin, 2009, 2010b; Kowalski and Limber, 2007; Li, 2007; Mesch, 2009; Microsoft, 2009; United Press International, 2008; Willard, 2007). A brief summary of some of these suggestions is provided below:

(1) Appropriate monitoring of children's use of the internet.
(2) Educating children about cyberbullying and the harm it can inflict.
(3) Setting-up of appropriate guidelines for children's use of technologies.
(4) Putting internet-enabled devices in central locations in the home.
(5) Discussing children's online activities with them.
(6) Ensuring that children feel comfortable reporting bullying to a parent.
(7) Informing children about appropriate and inappropriate online behaviours.
(8) Using contracts outlining appropriate internet and mobile phone use.
(9) Limiting younger children's online activities to those considered appropriate by an adult.
(10) Teaching older children that others online are real people, who will experience emotional reactions to bullying.
(11) Encouraging schools to take an active role to prevent and combat cyberbullying.
(12) Development of character traits such as empathy, and the teaching of social skills.
(13) Displaying signs near computers at home and in schools to ensure that children are reminded about acceptable online behaviour.
(14) Reviewing bullying and harassment policies in schools.
(15) Encouraging children to have a say in the development of policies in the area.
(16) Evaluating policies to ensure that they are achieving their goals.
(17) Indicating to children what the consequences would be if they engage in cyberbullying.

(18) Blocking communication with cyberbullies, if it does occur.

(19) Discussing cyberbullying events with appropriate others, which may include parents (of both the victim and the bully), teachers, police, school administrators, the internet service provider and any particular online site involved. It may not be necessary to involve all of these parties.

(20) Considering the use of tracking or filtering software if a child is found to be a bully.

(21) Considering limiting a bully's access to the internet and other technologies.

While many of these suggestions seem appropriate in theory, the increasing prevalence of smartphones may reduce the feasibility of suggestions regarding limiting internet use. In the long term, it is probably best to focus on psychoeducational tactics, such as educating children about appropriate online use, and encouraging open discussion about online experiences.

Activity 7.2 Managing cyberbullying in schools

Imagine that you have been approached by a headteacher in a school who is worried about a growing cyberbullying problem among the students, especially those aged 13–14 years. Prepare a strategy for dealing with the problem. Consider which of the suggestions above you might include, as well as if you have any suggestions of your own to add. Who would you involve in the strategy?

Summary box 7.5 Possible solutions to cyberbullying

- Solutions to the problem of cyberbullying can be preventative, or an attempt to manage an existing cyberbullying problem.
- Many suggested solutions for cyberbullying involve reducing or limiting a child's internet access, an approach which has become increasingly difficult due to the increased prevalence of smartphones.
- Other approaches are psychoeducational in nature, involving teaching appropriate online skills and suitable reactions to cyberbullying incidents.

Cyberstalking

Like bullying, stalking can also be seen as a repeated engagement in threatening or harassing behaviours (Ashcroft, 2001). However, there is significantly less research examining cyberstalking than there is on cyberbullying. For this reason, this section of the chapter relies more on what has been discovered about offline stalkers, with attempts to determine if these findings are applicable to cyberstalkers. Some authors (such as Roberts, 2008) have argued that cyberstalking is similar to many offline forms of stalking, and that many offenders use elements of both, rather than exclusively using one or other type.

Definitions and prevalence

The definition of cyberstalking is difficult, as researchers fail to agree on the definition of the term even without the 'cyber' prefix, and in some cases use other terms, such as 'obsessional harassment', 'obsessional following' and 'obsessional relational intrusion' (Häkkänen-Nyholm, 2010).

One of the first to write about cyberstalking was Ashcroft (2001), who defined cyberstalking as 'the use of the Internet, e-mail and other electronic communication devices to stalk another person' (p. 1). Later, Mishra and Mishra (2008) defined cyberstalking as 'when a person is followed and pursued online. Their privacy is invaded, their every move watched. It is a form of harassment and can disrupt the life of the victim and leave them feeling very afraid' (p. 216). Other definitions of cyberstalking include 'the persistent and targeted harassment of an individual via electronic communication such as email' (Yar, 2006, p. 122) and 'the use of information and communications technology (ICT) in order to harass one or more victims' (Bocij, 2006, p. 160). Interestingly, Bocij notes the importance of intent in cyberstalking, but contrary to many of the definitions of cyberbullying, Bocij indicates that there need not be the intent to cause distress in order for an incident to be considered cyberstalking.

A major problem in determining the rates of cyberstalking is that in many cases a victim may be unaware that they are being stalked. Their awareness of the stalker varies according to which definition is used – if a definition which considers only harassment is used, then the victim must be aware of the actions. However, if a broader definition of stalking is used, such as monitoring movements, a person may not be aware of their stalker. They may not realise that someone is closely watching what photographs they share online, where they check-in using their smartphones, or who else they regularly interact with. This variation in definitions of cyberstalking also causes problems when attempting to quantify the extent of the problem using large-scale studies.

Even if a person is aware of their stalker, they may not report it. Ashcroft (2001) suggests that this may be for one of two reasons – they may feel that the behaviour is not criminal in nature, or they may feel that law enforcement agencies will not take them seriously. Similarly, Joseph (2003) suggests that victims may not consider the act to be dangerous, and so may not report it.

Despite the limitations above, there is some limited research which attempts to determine the prevalence of cyberstalking. Spitzberg and Hoobler (2002) found that almost one-third of university students reported experiencing unwanted computer-based pursuit, which was generally considered harassing, but relatively harmless. The voluntary organization Working to Halt Online Abuse (WHOA, 2012) indicated that they receive approximately fifty to seventy-five online harassment or cyberstalking cases per week. Reyns et al. (2012) found that 40.8 per cent of college students had experienced cyberstalking victimisation, while 4.9 per cent had perpetrated cyberstalking.

Parsons-Pollard and Moriarty (2009) indicate that while it is difficult to say with certainty, partly because of rarity of reporting, it appears that rates of cyberstalking are increasing. There are many reasons why a victim might not report cyberstalking. Reyns and Englebrecht (2010) found that variables such as seriousness of the offence, the offender having a prior record, fearfulness and acknowledgement of the incident as stalking increased the likelihood that the victim would report the cyberstalking.

Lyndon *et al.* (2011) asked 411 college students about how they used the popular social networking site Facebook after a romantic relationship had ceased. Over half had looked through their ex-partner's photographs to find pictures of them with their new partner, and 58.6 per cent had posted poetry or music lyrics in their status to try to get back together with their former partner. Almost a third updated their status to make their ex-partner jealous, and over 30 per cent posted poetry or music lyrics to taunt or hurt their ex-partner. Far fewer engaged in more harassing activities such as creating a false Facebook profile of their ex-partner (3.6 per cent), using Facebook to spread false rumours about the ex-partner (3.6 per cent) or posting embarrassing photographs of their ex-partner (4.2 per cent). However, 14.6 per cent had written inappropriate or mean things about their ex-partner on a friend's wall, and 7.5 per cent had posted nasty or spiteful comments on a photo of their ex-partner.

Lindsay and Krysik (2012) carried out a replication of an earlier study by Finn (2004) to determine the change in cyberharassment among college students over time. Lindsay and Krysik (2012) found that over 43 per cent of students had experienced harassment, compared to just over 16 per cent in Finn's (2004) study.

Summary box 7.6 Cyberstalking definitions and prevalence

- Relatively little research has examined cyberstalking.
- Various definitions of cyberstalking exist, some of which use harassment as a measure (the reaction of the victim), while others focus more on the behaviours of the stalker. The role of intent also varies by definition.
- Victims may not report cyberstalking due to a lack of awareness of its occurrence, a feeling that it is not severe or a feeling that law enforcement will not take them seriously.

Methods of cyberstalking

Cyberstalking can be seen in two ways. Firstly, it could refer to the use of technologies to enable offline stalking behaviours (such as using a person's check-ins on a social networking site to determine their physical location, and then following the person there). Secondly, cyberstalking could mostly remain online, using computer-mediated communication to monitor a person's movements and communicate with them, with physical contact being limited (although a stalker may send their target offline gifts or messages).

Mishra and Mishra (2008) subdivide cyberstalking into 'direct' and 'indirect' forms. Direct forms involve contacting the victim (perhaps through text messages, emails,

Table 7.2 Common cyberstalking behaviours

Public distribution of offensive online messages	On social networking sites, forums, websites, or other online settings.
Damage to files or equipment	Through sending vast quantities of spam or malware.
Physical assault	Generally considered rare.
Threats	Threats can include threats to the victim directly, or threats to commit suicide if the victim does not respond to the stalker.
False accusations about the victim	For example, the posting of false advertisements about the victim. In some cases, the stalker may use an online forum to suggest that the victim is advertising sexual or other services, in some cases posting the victim's home or work address in the post.
Sending of abusive messages directly to the victim	Obscene, violent, insulting or indecent messages.
Gathering information about the victim	Perhaps through the use of keyloggers (see Chapters 3 and 4), online profiles, or hacking email accounts.
Encouraging others to harass the victim	A stalker may encourage viewers of online content to take action against the victim by making it appear as if the victim has negative personality traits.
Ordering goods or services for the victim	May cause embarrassment by sending potentially humiliating products to the victim's workplace.
Attempting to meet the victim	Often by appearing at locations where the victim is expected to be.
Leaving objects for a victim to find	Such as surveillance photographs, symbolic objects, or other items, where they know that the victim will be (possibly because of information gathered from monitoring online information).
Identity theft and impersonation	Using data collected online to impersonate the victim for financial or personal gain. A stalker may impersonate a victim, creating online accounts in their name, or hacking their existing accounts. See Chapter 5 for more information on financial identity theft.
Use of sites that promote retaliation and revenge	These sites often offer anonymity to the stalker
Use of information brokerage sites	These sites offer access to personal information, such as workplaces, dates of birth, social security numbers, etc. which a stalker may use to gather information about their victim.

phone calls, etc.) while indirect cyberstalking involves using the internet to display messages more publicly, such as via webpages or social networking sites.

Some potential cyberstalking behaviours have been noted by researchers (see, for example, Bocij, 2006; Clough, 2010; Finn and Atkinson, 2009; Lyndon *et al.*, 2011; McQuade, 2006; Mishra and Mishra, 2008; Philips and Morrissey, 2004; Pittaro, 2007, 2011; WHOA, 2012; Wykes, 2007). Several of these are listed in Table 7.2.

> **Activity 7.3 How vulnerable are you to online stalking?**
> What information is available online about you that might make you vulnerable to cyberstalkers? Consider the information that you make available on social networking sites as well as other profiles. Remember that a potential stalker may be someone who you currently consider to be a friend. What items of information are available about you that could enable the behaviours listed in Table 7.2 to be completed?

Some researchers have noted that cyberstalking frequently escalates over time (WHOA, 2012), while others have noted that cyberstalking may be related to an offline abusive partner who uses technology to monitor their communications and movements (for example, Finn and Atkinson, 2009).

It is possible that the same characteristics of the internet which may enable cyberbullying could also enable cyberstalkers. For example, the anonymity provided by the internet has been noted as enabling cyberstalking by Ashcroft (2001), Philips and Morrissey (2004) and Wykes (2007). Similarly, the disinhibition phenomenon described above in relation to cyberbullying may also relate to cyberstalkers, as they become more comfortable expressing their emotions and desires directly to the victim (Meloy, 1998).

Philips and Morrissey (2004) also note that the nature of the internet may mean that cyberstalking incidents can occur over much larger geographical distances than offline stalking. This may result in a victim thinking the stalking is less serious, and Yar (2006) does suggest that cyberstalking is more likely to remain at a distance (p. 129), with the predator and victim less likely to meet in real life. Nevertheless, both Yar and Philips and Morrissey indicate that online stalking, even over a distance, may progress to offline stalking, with the potential for physical harm.

A final aspect of online interactions that may impact on cyberstalking is 'electronic propinquity' (Finn and Banach, 2000), where 'people feel in proximity to each other online despite the physical distance' (p. 248). It is also possible that potential cyberstalkers may misinterpret the meaning of messages they receive, developing idealised perceptions of the individual. This is similar to the established concept of 'hyperpersonal communication' which has long been noted in computer-mediated communication, where users of such communication feel emotionally closer than if contact was made offline (see, for example, Henderson and Gilding, 2004; Walther, 1996, 2007).

Summary box 7.7 Methods of cyberstalking

- Cyberstalking may remain online, or may be used as part of a strategy which also involves offline stalking aspects.
- Cyberstalking may involve direct messages to the victim, or indirect messages about the victim (Mishra and Mishra, 2008).
- Some behaviours which cyberstalkers engage in include:
  - public distribution of offensive online messages;
  - damage to files or equipment;

- physical assault;
- threats;
- false accusations about the victim;
- sending abusive messages directly to the victim;
- gathering information about the victim;
- encouraging others to harass the victim;
- ordering goods or services for the victim;
- attempting to meet the victim;
- leaving objects for a victim to find;
- identity theft and impersonation;
- use of sites that promote retaliation and revenge;
- use of information brokerage sites.
- Cyberstalking may escalate over time, and may involve an offline partner.
- Anonymity (or perceived anonymity) may facilitate cyberstalking.
- Cyberstalking may occur over large geographical distances.
- 'Electronic propinquity' and 'hyperpersonal communication' may affect the perceptions the cyberstalker holds about their relationship with the victim.

Traits of cyberstalkers

There is limited information about the traits of cyberstalkers, and so information about offline stalkers will also be examined, in an attempt to determine if cyberstalkers may hold similar traits.

Joseph (2003) suggests that cyberstalkers and traditional stalkers share a common motive – 'a desire to exert control over their victims and engage in similar types of behaviour to accomplish this end' (p. 106). Ashcroft (2001) agrees, also highlighting the desire for control, whether the stalking occurs online or offline.

Much research suggests that the victim and stalker are already acquainted, sometimes having had a previous relationship (see, for example, Dimond et al., 2011; Joseph, 2003; WHOA, 2012), with Ashcroft (2001) suggesting that in many cases cyberstalking commences when the victim tries to break up a romantic relationship with the stalker. Nevertheless, not all cyberstalking occurs between former romantic partners, and victims can also be stalked by friends, work colleagues, neighbours, family members or other online acquaintances, as well as strangers (WHOA, 2012). In some cases, cyberstalking or cyberharassment can occur between current partners (see, for example, Burke et al., 2011; Melander, 2010). There also appears to be evidence that the majority of cyberstalkers are men (see, for example, Joseph, 2003; WHOA, 2012; Yar, 2006).

Several classification systems have been proposed for offline stalkers. Zona et al. (1993) proposed three types of stalker:

- erotomanics – feel that they are loved by the person they stalk, despite a lack of a previous relationship. These are usually females who focus on celebrities;
- love obsessional – frequently (but not always) believe that they are in love with the person they are stalking, with delusions sometimes deriving from psychotic illness. These tend to be males;

- simple obsessionals – where a prior relationship exists between the stalker and their victim, though this may be a professional or personal relationship, rather than a romantic one. These are equally likely to be of either gender.

Zona *et al.* (1993) found that most stalkers were either love obsessionals or simple obsessionals – erotomanics were rare. Meloy (2000) indicates that most stalkers are simple obsessionals, with about a quarter being love obsessionals and only a small minority being erotomanics.

Mullen *et al.* (1999) differentiated between five types of stalker. These are:

- rejected stalkers – who pursue a former intimate partner, and are often motivated by reconciliation or revenge;
- intimacy-seeking stalkers – who believe that a romantic relationship is destined to happen;
- incompetent stalkers – who are not in love with the victim but are trying to establish contact with them;
- resentful stalkers – who are seeking revenge and wish to scare the victim;
- predatory stalkers – who use stalking as a method of preparing to sexually assault the victim.

Mullen *et al.* (1999) noted that delusional disorders were common among the stalkers, particularly the intimacy-seeking stalkers.

Mishra and Mishra (2008) suggested a typology of cyberstalkers, proposing three different types:

- a common obsessional cyberstalker – who previously had a relationship with the victim, which they refuse to let go of;
- a delusional cyberstalker – who may be suffering from a mental illness that leads them to the false belief that they have a romantic relationship with the victim, possibly a celebrity or those in the helping professions such as teachers or doctors;
- a vengeful stalker – who is angry at their victim because of a perceived indiscretion.

McFarlane and Bocij (2003) proposed four types of cyberstalker:

- vindictive cyberstalkers – who are particularly malicious, and prone to threatening and harassing their victims. They may make use of technology, such as disruptive malware;
- composed cyberstalkers – who target victims in a calmer way, but still with the purpose of causing distress through a variety of threatening behaviours;
- intimate cyberstalkers – who due to infatuation aim to establish a relationship with the target, with whom they may or may not be personally involved;
- collective cyberstalkers – consisting of multiple stalkers who target the same victim.

It has been proposed that stalkers generally may have extreme emotional dysregu-lation, and are more likely to be substance abusers, to experience depression, to be more angry and jealous and to have had poor emotional attachments to their parents (Douglas and Dutton, 2001). Alexy *et al.* (2005) also noted that cyber-stalkers were more likely to include threats of suicide, which may elicit feelings of guilt in the victims. Häkkänen-Nyholm (2010) summarises research on stalkers, indicating that those who are in clinical and forensic settings often have a variety of psychological disorders, including substance abuse, mood disorders and personality disorders.

Summary box 7.8 Traits of cyberstalkers

- There is limited research on the traits of cyberstalkers, but their motives are thought to be similar to offline stalkers – specifically regarding control over their victim.
- Cyberstalking often (but not always) occurs between former romantic partners.
- Cyberstalkers are more likely to be males.
- Some classification systems for stalkers have been proposed:
  ○ Zona *et al.* (1993) proposed 'erotomanics', 'love obsessionals' and 'simple obsessionals';
  ○ Mullen *et al.* (1999) proposed 'rejected', 'intimacy seeking', 'incompetent', 'resentful' and 'predatory' stalkers;
  ○ Mishra and Mishra (2008) proposed a typology of cyberstalkers, including 'common-obsessionals', 'delusional' and 'vengeful'.
  ○ McFarlane and Bocij (2003) proposed four types of cyberstalker, including 'vindictive', 'composed', 'intimate' and 'collective'.
- It is thought that stalkers may experience emotional dysregulation and other psychological and social problems.

Victims of cyberstalking

As with the section examining the victims of cyberbullying above, this section will attempt to determine both the characteristics of victims of cyberstalking, and the effects that stalking has on them.

The literature to date suggests that the majority of victims are female (see, for example, Bocij, 2006; Joseph, 2003; Moriarty and Freiberger, 2008; Reyns *et al.*, 2012; WHOA, 2012; Yar, 2006) but there is some evidence to suggest that this difference is not as pronounced as it is for offline stalking, with a greater relative proportion of males becoming victims of cyberstalking. Alexy *et al.* (2005) even found that male students were statistically more likely than female students to have been cyberstalked, normally by a former intimate partner.

WHOA (2012) found that the majority of victims of cyberstalking who completed their survey were Caucasian (over 80 per cent) and single (53 per cent), but Bocij (2006) found that three-quarters of his sample were married or cohabiting with a partner. He found that over 40 per cent did not know the identity of their harasser. Reyns *et al.* (2012) found that non-whites, non-heterosexuals and non-singles experienced disproportionally more cyberstalking. Finn and Banach (2000) suggest that those who seek help and advice online may put themselves at a higher risk of cyberstalking, due to the large amount of personal information revealed.

Reyns *et al.* (2011) examined how routine activities theory (described in Chapter 1) might help to explain cyberstalking. When they studied 974 college students, they found that the theory (when adapted to online behaviours) could help to predict which students became victims. As predicted by the theory, 'online exposure to risk, online proximity to motivated offenders, online guardianship, online target attractiveness, and online deviance' (p. 1,149) all predicted cyberstalking victimisation. They noted that behaviours such as adding strangers as friends (increased virtual proximity), engaging in deviant activities (such as harassing others) and engaging with deviant peers could all be important factors in risk of victimisation. Lindsay and Krysik (2012) found that in a college sample, increased time on social networking sites, owning an internet-connected phone and having ever sent a 'sext' message predicted cyberharassment.

Yar (2006) suggests that even if the cyberstalker and their victim never actually meet, the victim may still suffer psychological harm, and that some of the reactions that victims of offline stalking undergo (such as fear, anxiety and making adjustments to their normal lives) may also be experienced by victims of cyberstalkers. Philips and Morrissey (2004) suggest that cyberstalking victims can experience annoyance, distress, trauma and even fear for their lives, as well as a feeling that they are in some way responsible for the events. As mentioned above, the victim may feel particularly guilty if the cyberstalker threatens suicide. Häkkänen-Nyholm (2010) describes how much of the research to date indicates a variety of effects on stalking victims, including 'general disturbance, affective health, social health, resource health, cognitive health, physical health, behavioral disturbance, and resilience' (p. 565). However, other research, such as Sheridan and Grant (2007), has found that cyberstalking had no significant psychological or medical impact on victims. It is likely that the effect on the victim will depend a great deal on the length of the stalking experience, and the nature of the stalker's activities.

Summary box 7.9 Victims of cyberstalking

- The majority of cyberstalking victims are female, although there is a higher proportion of male victims than for offline stalking, and some research has found a majority of male victims.
- There are mixed findings regarding the marital status of victims.
- It is possible that those who seek help and advice online are at higher risk of cyberstalking, due to the amount of information they disclose.
- Victims of cyberstalking can experience a wide range of distressing emotions, but some research indicates that the effects can be minimal.

Possible solutions to cyberstalking

As with cyberbullying, several suggested responses to cyberstalking have been proposed. In some cases these are contradictory – for example, Joseph (2003) suggests that a victim should delete emails with inappropriate content and block emails from certain harassers. However, it may be more appropriate to keep all messages in case they are needed as evidence for police or courts (Philips and Morrissey, 2004). Also, Ashcroft (2001) indicates that victims of cyberstalkers should not block the stalker's communications as it is possible that a threat may be sent which the victim (and/or police) should be aware of. Other advice offered to victims of cyberstalkers (by authors such as Joseph, 2003; Philips and Morrissey, 2004; and Pittaro, 2007, 2011) includes:

- avoiding retaliation or engaging with the stalker– which would reward the harasser with a response (and hence reinforce the behaviour according to Pittaro, 2011);
- informing the stalker that their communications are unwanted, and asking them to stop;
- reporting the incident to the administrator of the website or service it occurs on;
- saving communications from the offender to use as evidence;
- being careful of including personal information on public profiles;
- being cautious of meeting in real life people that they first encountered online;
- logging off if a situation becomes hostile;
- reporting the incident to the police.

Häkkänen-Nyholm (2010) describes a typology of coping responses outlined by Cupach and Spitzberg (2004). Five types of responses were identified, including:

- 'moving with' – attempting to negotiate with the stalker;
- 'moving against' – such as threatening the stalker;
- 'moving away' – such as changing email and physical addresses and common habits;
- 'moving inward' – such as denial or substance abuse;
- 'moving outward' – such as prosecution or restraining orders.

Of these, 'moving away' tactics are considered to be the most necessary and effective, while 'moving with' strategies are likely to fail, and 'moving against' strategies can escalate the intensity of the interaction.

The roles of the police, internet agencies and rehabilitative services should also be considered. Ashcroft (2001) indicated that law enforcement officers should receive training in dealing with cyberstalking cases in order to increase their sensitivity concerning the impact of the situation on the victim. Parsons-Pollard and Moriarty (2009) suggest that 'law enforcement agencies are ill equipped to handle [cyberstalking]' (p. 435). Ashcroft also recommends that internet service providers offer suitable support for victims. Reyns (2010) argues that situational crime prevention may be effective in reducing the problem of cyberstalking. Pittaro (2007, 2011) proposes that if potential cyberstalkers were aware of the risks of apprehension and punishment, they might be deterred from committing these acts, using the assumption of rational choice theory as outlined in Chapter 1. He suggests that as the risk of detection and prosecution is exceptionally low, there is little deterrent effect. The reliability of this argument is uncertain, however, as depending on the type of cyberstalker, they may not feel that they are actually committing an offence, and so may not recognise the need to avoid prosecution.

Sheridan and Davies (2004) indicate that stalkers vary in their response to attempted interventions – while some respond well, others will 'view police interference as a challenge to overcome whilst still maintaining control of the victim' (p. 206).

As such, although stalkers may be treated similarly from a legal perspective, it is important that rehabilitative measures consider the psychology of the stalker when devising strategies to reduce recidivism.

Activity 7.4 Responses to cyberstalking

Prepare an information sheet for internet users, outlining what steps they should take if they discover that they are being victimised by a cyberstalker. Consider what actions they should take, as well as providing advice on how they should decide if the activity is serious enough to warrant reporting to law enforcement personnel or internet agencies.

Summary box 7.10 Possible solutions to cyberstalking

- While advice varies, victims of cyberstalking are generally advised to keep communications from stalkers, avoid retaliation, report the incident, inform the stalker that their communications are unwanted, be careful of including personal information on public profiles and log off if a situation becomes hostile.
- The roles of law enforcement agencies and internet agencies are also important in managing cyberstalking.
- It is likely that stalkers will vary in their responses to attempted interventions, and so responses should be tailored appropriately.

Conclusion

Both cyberstalking and cyberbullying are problems that many individuals face online, with both being amplified by the increased use and functionality of smartphones and social networking sites. One of the greatest areas of research potential is the examination of the effectiveness of interventions and preventative strategies for both cyberstalking and cyberbullying. In addition, greater empirical research is required for most aspects of cyberstalking, and for cyberbullying in the workplace. Both cyberbullying and cyberstalking can be used in addition to their offline equivalents, but it is possible that these activities may be attractive to some individuals who would not bully or stalk offline. It is of particular interest to determine with certainty what types of individuals are attracted to only the online aspects of these activities, possibly due to the anonymity and disinhibition aspects described above.

Essay questions

(1) Can cyberbullying be considered an extension of traditional bullying, or is it qualitatively different?

(2) The disclosure of personal information through social networking sites enables cyberstalkers. Discuss.

(3) What role does online disinhibition play in the occurrence of either cyberbullying or cyberstalking?

(4) Does the nature of online communication result in cyberstalkers misinterpreting the meaning of their victim's messages, as proposed by Finn and Banach (2000)?

(5) How important is the role of intent in the definition of cyberbullying or cyberstalking?

Additional reading

Books and articles

Patchin and Hinduja's edited book *Cyberbullying Prevention and Response: Expert Perspectives* (published in 2012 by Routledge) provides a selection of views by cyberbullying experts on the legal, social and educational aspects of cyberbullying prevention and management.

Reyns, Henson and Fisher apply routine activities theory to cyberstalking in the following article:

Reyns, B. W., Henson, B. and Fisher, B. S. (2011). Being pursued online: applying cyberlifestyle-routine activities theory to cyberstalking victimisation. *Criminal Justice and Behaviour*, **38**, 1,149–69.

Ménard and Pincus attempt to determine the predictors of cyberstalking:

Ménard, K. S. and Pincus, A. L. (2012). Predicting overt and cyber stalking perpetration by male and female college students. *Journal of Interpersonal Violence*, **27** (11), 2,183–207. Available at http://jiv.sagepub.com/content/27/11/2183.

Tokunaga reviews much of the research available on cyberbullying in the following article:

Tokunaga, R. S. (2010). Following you home from school: a critical review and synthesis of research on cyberbullying victimization. *Computers in Human Behaviour*, **26**, 277–87.

Websites

The Cyberbullying Research Centre (www.cyberbullying.us/) includes both scholarly research articles and resources to prevent and respond to cyberbullying.

Working to Halt Online Abuse (WHOA: www.haltabuse.org) provides guidance and support for victims of cyberharassment and cyberstalking.

The National Centre for Missing and Exploited Children maintains 'NetSmartz', which provides information on cyberbullying (among many other threats to children online) at www.netsmartz.org/Cyberbullying.

8   Digital piracy and copyright infringement

Case studies

Brenda loves to listen to upcoming bands online. When she finds a new band that she likes, she joins their fan pages on social networking sites, downloads images of them to use as backgrounds on her phone and laptop, and writes positive reviews about them on her blog. However, as she has limited income, she doesn't actually buy their music, either on CD or as a download – instead she finds their music on file-sharing websites and downloads it for free. While she knows this is wrong, she justifies it by telling herself that she introduces the artists to a new group of fans via her blog, and that in the long run, they'll make money from her actions.

Greg enjoys films and the latest television shows. Rather than pay for a subscription to a television service, or buy box-sets, he prefers to download the content from the internet. While he knows that this is illegal, he feels that it's unlikely that he'll be caught. Even if he is, he thinks that he probably won't be punished because all of his friends also download copyrighted work from the internet, and he feels that they can't all be prosecuted. He thinks that anyone who pays for a television service, and then watches the programmes with advertisements, is an idiot, as he can download an ad-free version from the internet within hours of the programme first being aired.

Chapter overview

There are offences that many individuals carry out at some point in their lives – perhaps driving a little too fast, taking stationery supplies from the workplace, engaging in under-age drinking or smoking, or perhaps even using illegal or controlled substances. We tend to think of these as 'victimless' crimes, because we cannot easily identify any individual who is being harmed by these actions. Of course, this is not to say that there are no victims of these offences – such as the company whose supplies are being taken, or those whose health or safety is put at risk by the actions of the offender. But because these victims aren't easily identifiable, many individuals feel that these crimes do not do any harm.

Similarly, most people do not consider themselves to be cybercriminals because they do not hack, create malware, prey on children online or commit fraud. But many internet users do engage in an online, supposedly 'victimless' crime – copyright infringement through piracy of music, film, television programmes, books or software.

Several high-profile file-sharing services have been the subject of major news stories in recent years, such as 'Kazaa', 'Napster', 'The Pirate Bay' and 'Limewire' (David, 2010; Jewkes, 2010; Yar, 2007).

This chapter examines online copyright infringement, with particular focus on illegal file-sharing of music, video and software. Definitions of key terms will be provided, and the various methods used during illegal file-sharing and piracy will be outlined, along with a historical view of how copyright infringement has developed over time. The psychology of offenders will be examined, including demographic characteristics and motives, as well as the psychological characteristics that such offenders seem more likely to exhibit, and the methods by which they explain their behaviours, particularly neutralisations. Potential solutions will be considered, including the key methods by which deterrence may be achieved, as well as an attempt to identify the most effective form of punishment available.

Definitions

Many different terms are used when describing the illegal distribution of copyrighted material. For example, Bryant (2008) uses the terms 'illegal file-sharing' and 'commercial music piracy' to describe the transmission of files and the creation of physical discs such as CDs or DVDs respectively. Other authors, such as Hill (2007), use less differentiation, defining digital piracy as 'the purchase of counterfeit products at a discount to the price of the copyrighted product, and illegal file-sharing of copyright material over peer-to-peer computer networks' (p. 9).

Intellectual property (IP) law and protection are used as the basis for legal and economic uses of the term 'piracy' (Yar, 2006, p. 65). Stephens (2008) describes intellectual property rights (IPR) as 'encompassing the privileges accorded to the creators and owners of creative work (IP) including inventions, designs, software, music, films, and written works' (p. 121). Such privileges can include the prevention of reproduction without the copyright holder's permission (Stephens, 2008), although Stephens also notes that some consumers argue for 'fair use' of the content. This 'fair use' is open to interpretation – but for example, consider the case of a customer who buys a music CD through a legitimate source, such as a high street store. They may wish to have easy access to the music in their car, as well as in their home, and they may make a copy of the CD to keep in their glove box. They might want to make a digital copy in mp3 format to keep on their portable music player, but they later might buy a new device that doesn't read mp3 files, and so they need to copy it to a different format. If they also want to use one of the files as a ringtone on their mobile phone, they may need to make a new version of the file again, in a third format. The consumer may need to purchase four further copies of the same music track in order to legally possess this content, even though they paid for the first CD, and would only ever listen to one version at a time. It is interesting to note that many companies are now beginning to recognise this desire by consumers to have multiple copies of a digital product, and many DVDs now include a version of the film or television programmes that can be directly installed onto a portable media player or computer.

Illustration 8.1 Cost of piracy. It is difficult to estimate the exact cost of digital piracy. Some copyright infringers argue that digital piracy may actually help a music artist's career.

Organisations created to protect copyright holders regularly publish information about the costs and prevalence of copyright infringement. Bryant (2008) indicates that 'industry-based organizations may have a particular interest in emphasizing the seriousness of the problem' (p. 23), understandably so, as the welfare and employment of their members are at risk. While there is little doubt that piracy activity is a very common problem (Yar, 2007), in reality it is very difficult to accurately estimate the true cost of piracy for several reasons, as outlined by Yar (2006). For example, overall piracy rates are 'often extrapolated from detection and conviction rates' (p. 72), thus meaning that levels of policing activity by law enforcement or other bodies may impact on the estimates of piracy rates. Increased levels may reflect increased policing efficiency and activity, rather than an increase in offending behaviour. Another problem with estimations occurs because many agencies quantify the extent of the problem in financial losses, based on the 'legitimate product price'. This presumes that each illegal copy of the file replaces a legitimate purchase, which is not necessarily true. For example, a person may download an illegal copy of a movie. Many estimates of piracy costs assume that the person would otherwise have paid for a cinema ticket, or bought the movie on DVD or Blu-Ray. While certainly true for some users, it probably does not apply in every case – not every instance would directly replace a real sale, as some individuals may download the content as it is free, but would not pay the full price for it. It should also be considered that dilution of product value is another important consideration in copyright infringement (Wall and Yar, 2010). If the product has unrestricted use, it is likely to have a lower value than if the number of copies is more limited.

Activity 8.1 Copyright infringement statistics
- Search online for the latest statistics involving copyright infringement. Some useful organisations which may provide reports include:
  ○ British Phonographic Industry (www.bpi.co.uk);

- British Software Alliance (www.bsa.org);
- International Federation of Phonographic Industries (www.ifpi.org);
- International Intellectual Property Alliance (www.iipa.com);
- Motion Picture Association of America (www.mpaa.org).

Some researchers have argued that illegal music downloading may not always have a negative impact on sales and income. For example, Peitz and Waelbroeck (2006) suggest that illegal music downloaders may use 'sampling' to find products and artists that better suit their own tastes, and that those downloaders may be willing to pay more once they have found their preferred content. While it is certainly true that some users may later purchase content that they have sampled online, not all downloaders do this. Also, many legitimate digital music retailers offer potential customers the opportunity to listen to short clips of tracks to allow them to sample the music before paying for it.

Yar (2006) describes how some recording artists can profit more from illegal downloading, as the more users who listen to their music, the higher the potential ticket sales for concerts, where musical artists often make a higher proportion of income rather than through the sales of CDs and legitimate downloads. There have even been some musicians who distribute their work freely online with this specific purpose. However, this does not take into account other potentially invisible victims. Many record labels reinvest the income from music purchases into the development of new artists, and bypassing legitimate purchase of content may impact on the incomes of technicians, engineers and other professionals who helped to develop the content.

Wall and Yar (2010) indicate that illegal music downloading may actually help to promote music culture, thus expanding the market, particularly with regard to sales of older works. They suggest that it is possible that sales of CDs have remained constant, or perhaps even risen, and that the introduction of authorised content download websites has been very successful. There is some support for this theory. LaRose and Kim (2007) found that downloading intentions had no impact on CD or online pay music purchases. Oberholzer-Gee and Strumpf (2007) found that downloads have a negligible effect on sales, but this study has been criticised, and most studies have found some negative relationship between illegal file-sharing or peer-to-peer systems, and legitimate sales (Liebowitz, 2006; Zentner, 2004).

Summary box 8.1 Definitions
- Many terms are used, such as copyright infringement and illegal file-sharing.
- Hill (2007) defined digital piracy as 'the purchase of counterfeit products at a discount to the price of the copyrighted product, and illegal file-sharing of copyright material over peer-to-peer computer networks' (p. 9).
- This chapter mainly considers music, film and software piracy, although there are other forms, such as text and design copyright infringement.
- The extent of 'fair use' of content is often debated – a person may legitimately want several copies of a file, but all for personal use.

- While regular statistics on the extent and cost of digital piracy are released, it is very difficult to obtain truly accurate figures.
- There are some arguments that illegal music downloading may eventually have a positive impact on sales, perhaps because of sampling, concert attendance or the sale of older works.
- But most studies suggest that there is a negative relationship between digital piracy and legitimate sales.

Methods of copyright infringement

Copyright infringement is not a new offence. David (2010) cites how Henry Fuesli's 1781 painting 'The Nightmare' was pirated very soon after its first authorised reproduction (pp. 1–2). Even Charles Dickens experienced piracy, as his works were transmitted to the US via telegraph without his permission or royalties payments (Jewkes and Yar, 2010, p. 3). There is some irony in the fact that most of Dickens' works are now legally available as free downloads for eReaders (electronic reading devices), while new authors experience copyright infringement of their books on the same devices. More recently, illegal copying of material has taken many forms, but it has become much easier to copy greater quantities of material due to the digitisation of content (Bryant, 2008).

In the 1980s, dual deck tape recorders provided the means by which people could copy both music cassettes and software cassettes, which could store the software for many home computers of the time. Bryant (2008) cites how the British Phonographic Industry (BPI) launched a campaign in the early 1980s saying that 'home taping is killing music'. 'VHS' format video cassettes could also be copied in a similar way, either by using the relatively rare dual deck video recorders, or by connecting two single video recorders. However, this form of analogue copying of music, software and film was restricted in a way that modern digital copying is not. Serial copying of the tapes resulted in a significant deterioration in quality (Bryant, 2008). A copy of an original recording looked or sounded acceptable (at least when the limitations of the medium were taken into account). But a copy of a copy was much less tolerable, and any subsequent copies were practically unusable. A second problem with analogue copyright infringement related to the time taken to prepare the copy – in some cases the copy had to be made in real time, and so, for example, if a person wanted to copy a 45-minute audio tape, it required 45 minutes to prepare each copy.

When CDs and DVDs became the preferred formats for content the digital nature of the files meant that deterioration of quality was much less of a problem, and files could be copied much faster. Copying CDs became quite popular in the 1990s, but Bryant (2008) indicated that in most cases people only circulated these copies to their families or friends, or made 'back-up' copies of their own music collection. Nevertheless, many pirated CDs were created for sale as well. Video piracy lagged behind, hampered by the later production and popularisation of DVDs, as well as the relatively low memory of recordable DVDs compared to commercial DVDs (meaning that it was much more difficult to transfer the content from a commercial DVD to a copy,

Illustration 8.2 Analogue media. Analogue media took longer to copy, and was more prone to quality degradation, than digital media.

than it was to do so for a CD). DVDs were also more likely to include copy protection software, which an offender would need to overcome in order to make a pirated copy.

As previously mentioned, some computer games and software which was stored on cassette tape could be copied using dual deck tape recorders. When software started to appear on CD-ROM, some programmes were included in their entirety on the disk, which could then be easily copied (Stephens, 2008). To attempt to avoid this, systems were introduced which required additional information, normally in the form of a product key, which was required to install the software. This product key (normally a list of letters and numbers) was provided either within the packaging of the software, or via communication with the company. Sometimes the same product key could activate multiple versions of the software, and so piracy adapted to simply including a copy of the key with the illegal disk. Even if the software was designed so that the product key could only be used once, there were still methods of getting around this – 'keygens' (key generators) were developed which mimicked the mathematical algorithms which were used to create legitimate product keys. The keygen therefore created a new and unique product key which would still be accepted by the software. Another strategy involved software that had been installed as a trial version – in some cases this software included code which deactivated the product when the trial period ended. This code could sometimes be overwritten, thus preventing the deactivation.

Up until now, we have considered offline methods of copyright infringement. However, the internet has provided new means of distributing pirated copies of music, text, video and software. One of the key differences involves the widespread nature of the distribution online (Yar, 2007). While illegal markets for offline distribution were not uncommon, much piracy which occurred before the popularisation of the internet and digital content was restricted to exchanges between friends, acquaintances and family members. The internet greatly expanded people's networks, and hence the pool of resources. Previously, if a person wanted a pirated copy of the latest album by their favourite artist, they had to wait until a friend bought it (and was willing to let them copy it), or they had to go to a place where pirated copies of albums were sold. The nature of the internet means that it is much more likely that somebody, somewhere has already copied the album and made an illegal copy available on a file-sharing network.

There are several other methods by which the internet enables piracy (Yar, 2006). These include:

- reduced cost of materials (for example, there is no need to buy discs or tapes);
- soft copies of content can be distributed more quickly than if discs were required;
- unlimited copies can be made from a single file hosted on the internet;
- problems associated with the distribution of physical media are circumvented (such as problems of confiscation and border controls);
- reduced risk of detection, as the distributor has higher anonymity (or at least, perceives that they do);
- the point of distribution can be located in a country where there is little enforcement of copyright laws, therefore reducing the likelihood of prosecution.

Bryant (2008) also notes that the increased speed of the internet enables online piracy and copyright infringement – greater upload and download speeds make distribution of files considerably more appealing. This is further enabled by reducing file sizes using compression techniques (such as converting a song into 'mp3' format, which takes up minimal space and can be quickly and easily transferred). This ability to upload and download not just music but entire films or television series with relatively small file sizes has greatly increased the volume of online content, to the extent that new release (and sometimes pre-release) movies can be found on the internet. One consequence of this is that there are now considerably shorter gaps between initial releases of films and airings of television programmes in their home country, and release dates in other countries. This is in the hope that viewers will not download the programme, and will instead wait for a higher quality airing on television.

Summary box 8.2 Methods of copyright infringement

- Copyright infringement is not a new offence, and works have been illegally copied for centuries.
- Audio and video cassette tapes were illegally copied, but this often required real-time copying, and the quality of the content degraded significantly if copies of copies were made.
- The introduction of CDs and DVDs meant reduced degradation of quality and faster copying speeds, but some problems still remained for those engaged in piracy, such as storage capacity on recordable DVDs and copyright protection measures embedded in the discs.
- Software provided on CD-ROM could also be copied, and although a variety of mechanisms were introduced to attempt to reduce piracy, many of these have been overcome through the use of 'keygens' or other coding techniques.
- Online digital piracy has resulted in wider distribution methods and expanded pools of available content.
- The internet has several advantages for those involved in copyright infringement, including reducing the need for physical media, faster distribution methods, lower risk of border controls and confiscations, reduced file sizes and reduced risk of detection.

Psychology of offenders

As mentioned, copyright infringement is probably the cybercrime in which many people are most likely to engage and, as such, it is relatively easy to research these offenders. This is particularly true of content downloaders, who seem to be considerably more common than content suppliers or uploaders. In considering the psychology of these offenders, we will first attempt to uncover if there are any demographic characteristics that describe such offenders. The motives of offenders will be analysed, before considering what personality traits (particularly self-control) and societal factors (such as social learning theory) can do to inform our understanding of such offenders. This section will describe the neutralisations (or justifications) that these offenders use to explain their actions, before considering how some theories of decision making and behaviour have been applied to digital piracy.

Demographic characteristics

Several studies have attempted to identify the demographic characteristics of those involved in intellectual property violations. Piquero (2005) reviewed much of this literature. While she found that some studies indicated that males were more likely to perpetrate such offences, other studies found no gender difference. She also noted that older college students were more likely to engage in piracy than younger college students, but that overall, younger individuals were more likely to engage in these behaviours than older individuals were. Yar (2007) also noted that while piracy activity is conducted by people from many social classes, there seems to be a particular problem among younger people.

Over one-third of students commit some form of software misuse or piracy (Cronan *et al.*, 2006), with those students who are more familiar with computers, and those completing computer-related courses of study, reporting the most misuse. Similar to Piquero, Cronan *et al.* found that students in higher years of courses were also more likely to engage in software misuse.

Motivations

While there have been proposed links between piracy and terrorist groups, it is unclear to what extent this applies to online copyright infringement (Yar, 2007), or how many of those engaged in online piracy have links to terrorist organisations. It is likely that a significant proportion of those involved in online illegal file-sharing do not have terrorist links, and so this chapter will focus on these individuals. Cyberterrorism will be considered in more detail in Chapter 9.

Higgins (2007) identified motivation as an important factor in illegal download-ing behaviours. Bryant (2008) suggests that those who illegally download content are motivated by both the opportunity to collect the content without paying for it, but also the opportunity to access the content immediately, without having to leave their home (pp. 2–4). When music piracy first became popular online, there were very few sources where legitimate copies of songs could be accessed – it was difficult to download music both instantly and legally. This has since changed – major online retailers such as iTunes and Amazon provide the opportunity to access music files, instantly, legitimately and from the comfort of the customer's own home. But the presence of these major retailers has not eliminated music piracy, and so other motives, most likely price, must still be a major explanation of downloader activity. Hsu and Shiue (2008) found that many consumers were not willing to pay the full retail price of non-pirated versions of software in Taiwan, and that these were more likely to use pirated versions. Factors such as social norms, source reliability and the presence of technical support were cited by those who were willing to pay more, but prosecution risk seemed to have little effect. Conversely, Liao *et al.* (2009) found that prosecution risk did have an impact on intention to use pirated software.

If downloader activity can be explained by financial motives (and, to a lesser extent, accessibility), this does not help to understand the actions of those who upload files (Becker and Clement, 2006). While some file-sharing networks require users to upload files in order to utilise their service, many do not. Becker and Clement (2006) found that some uploaders may be motivated by reciprocity – a feeling that they have benefited (or will benefit) from the service, and that they should give something back. It would therefore seem that there is a social aspect to file-sharing, which will be considered later in this chapter. However, it should be remembered that many users of these services never upload any content.

As previously mentioned, most individuals who commit 'victimless' crimes do not consider themselves to be criminals. In a similar vein, Bryce and Rutter (2005) found that most internet users view piracy behaviours as morally acceptable and a useful method for saving money. They discovered that 27 per cent of people had downloaded music tracks, and 18 per cent had downloaded entire albums, in the previous year. The major barrier they identified to legal downloading was a lack of access to credit cards, which may help to explain why younger users are more likely to commit such offences. The motivations cited by Bryce and Rutter's participants included range of choice, convenience, cost and being able to access music that was not otherwise available in the offender's country. They did not see any major risks in downloading, except the possibility that the file would not work properly, or that they may inadvertently download malware. Reasons given for not copying music included preference for the legitimate version, fear of poor product quality, lack of guarantee and potential links with organised crime.

Interestingly, while many other types of cybercrime seem to be facilitated by anonymity and online disinhibition, Hinduja (2007) found that the reduced sense of self, and subsequent reduced feelings of responsibility for actions, did not seem to influence participation in illegal file-sharing. No link was found between those who prefer anonymity and pseudonymity online and likelihood to engage in software piracy. This is an interesting finding, but further research is required to see if it can be replicated, and if it applies to other forms of piracy, such as music and video.

Summary box 8.3 Demographic characteristics and motivations of offenders

- Older college students seem more likely to engage in copyright infringement than younger college students, but overall, younger people are more likely to perpetrate such offences.
- Greater familiarity with computers seems to be correlated with higher likelihood of offending.
- It has been suggested that motivation for digital piracy is a combination of reduced cost and immediate access. As legitimate forms of immediate access are now available, while piracy remains, it would seem that reduced cost is the dominant factor.
- Uploaders may be motivated by reciprocity (Becker and Clement, 2006), although their motivations are not as well understood, and many users never upload content.
- Other potential motives include range of choice, lack of access to credit cards, convenience and being able to access content that was not otherwise available.
- Online anonymity has not been linked to software piracy.

Self-control and social learning theory

As with many types of criminal behaviour, it is likely that it is a combination of factors that leads an individual to illegally download material. Higgins *et al.* (2006) suggested that low self-control may be a factor in predicting who would engage in digital piracy, but that individuals need to learn the behaviours from others, and so social learning theory (see Chapter 1) is also important. We will consider the roles of both of these factors in turn.

Low self-control is a fairly stable characteristic through life, and has been linked to criminal behaviour (Gottfredson and Hirschi, 1990). Individuals with low self-control tend to be impulsive, insensitive, risk-taking and fail to consider the long-term consequences of their actions (Higgins *et al.*, 2006), and links have been demonstrated between low self-control and downloading behaviours (Higgins *et al.*, 2012). Malin and Fowers (2009) found that adolescents' attitudes towards internet piracy were related to low self-control. LaRose *et al.* (2005) also found that downloading behaviour was linked to deficient self-regulation.

Low self-control, combined with learning deviant models from offending peers, may initiate or increase an individual's involvement in crime. As the behaviours are learned from peers, this may also help to explain why individuals involved in piracy do not consider it to be morally wrong. Further support for the role of social learning theory was found by Morris and Higgins (2010). Similarly, D'Astous *et al.* (2005) found that a person's intention to swap music online depended on their perception that important others in their lives wanted the piracy to be committed, and a belief that they would be able to do so – both of which can be linked to social learning theory. The study by Malin and Fowers (2009) also found that attitudes to internet piracy were related to affiliation with deviant peers.

Summary box 8.4 Self-control and social learning theory

- Low self-control is a relatively stable personality characteristic which has been linked to criminal behaviour. It is characterised by impulsivity, insensitivity, risk-taking and failing to consider long-term consequences of behaviour.
- Several researchers have found links between low self-control and digital piracy.
- Deviant behaviours may also be learned from peers, which may help to explain why offenders do not see it as morally wrong.
- Social learning theory, and belief about other people's perceptions of offending, seem to be important predictors of offending behaviour.

Neutralisations and ethical positions

Neutralisations were described in Chapter 1, and are a similar phenomenon to cognitive distortions described in Chapter 6. Neutralisations are basically techniques that offenders use to reduce the guilty feelings that offending creates. Sykes and Matza (1957) originally defined five types of neutralisation:

- Denial of responsibility – offenders refuse to accept responsibility for their actions, perhaps suggesting that they were forced into the action because of matters beyond their control.
- Denial of injury – offenders suggest that the victim was not injured, or that they could afford the financial loss.
- Denial of victim – offenders see the victim as deserving of punishment.
- Condemnation of the condemners – offenders suggest that those who were victimised are hypocrites.
- Appeal to higher loyalties – offenders suggest that their behaviour was warranted because their immediate social group needed it to be carried out.

Other types of neutralisation have been identified since Sykes and Matza's original list. For example, Coleman (1994) proposed an additional neutralisation of 'everyone else is doing it'.

Some empirical research has attempted to determine which neutralisation techniques have been used by those involved in illegal file-sharing. Moore and McMullan (2009) found that most students did not use multiple neutralisations, although all showed support for at least one. The most common neutralisation techniques used were denial of injury, denial of victim and 'everyone else is doing it'. Moore and McMullan suggest that the anonymity of the internet may mean that they do not realise the harm that they are doing to the musician. Moore and McMullan also suggested that file sharers seemed to believe that musicians ultimately benefit from illegal file-sharing as it widens their fan base.

A similar study by Ingram and Hinduja (2008) found that denial of responsibility, denial of injury, denial of victim and appeal to higher loyalties predicted piracy participation (p. 334). Ingram and Hinduja suggest that the focus on group norms, rather than legal ones, might be a product of university settings. Conversely, Siponen *et al.* (2010) found that 'appeal to higher loyalties' and 'condemnation of the condemners' strongly predicted software piracy intentions. Morris and Higgins (2009) also found support for both neutralisation theory and social learning theory in explaining downloading of music, software and movies, but other studies (such as Hinduja, 2007) found only weak relationships between neutralisations and online software piracy.

The question then follows as to whether such use of neutralisation techniques during copyright infringement may be indicative of a lack of ethical standards, at least with regard to this particular offence. Yar (2010) describes several studies that found that illegal downloaders see the behaviour as acceptable, and Piquero suggests that people are either unable or unwilling to perceive piracy as an ethical problem. Gopal *et al.* (2004) found that ethical predispositions indirectly affect digital piracy, Garbharran and Thatcher (2011) found that moral disengagement is a significant factor in software piracy, while Yar (2007) indicates that downloaders generally do not try to hide their actions, and otherwise feel that they are law-abiding citizens. Bryce and Rutter (2005) found that while participants were aware of the illegal nature of sharing unauthorised copies of music files, such behaviours were considered widespread and normal, as well as being 'less wrong' than buying counterfeit CDs because of the lack of profits generated. Bryce and Rutter (2005) found similar results for illegal downloading of computer games. The variation in perceptions of how music can be illegally obtained was also highlighted by Wingrove *et al.* (2011), who found that students view illegal downloading and file-sharing as very different to shoplifting a CD. A slightly different view was found by Robertson *et al.* (2012), who also noted that downloaders were less concerned with the law, but that they were more likely to indicate that they would steal a CD if there was no risk of being caught. Findings such as these suggest that the illegal nature of digital piracy has little impact on the actions of offenders.

Bonner and O'Higgins (2010) similarly found that illegal downloaders of music 'choose to morally disengage from the non-ethical nature of the act in an attempt to avoid feeling guilty about illegal downloading and also to avoid any blame being attributed to them personally' (p. 1,341). Bonner and O'Higgins found that respondents felt that the act of illegal downloading is simply part of modern society, which could be considered to be a type of 'everyone else is doing it' neutralisation. While Jambon and Smetana's (2012) college students treated illegal music downloading as a complex moral issue, they rarely treated it as a conventional issue of law, despite displaying otherwise intact moral judgement abilities.

While the majority of studies have found that many users consider piracy to be ethically acceptable, many of these have used undergraduate students as participants. An exception to this, carried out by Bhal and Leekha (2008), examined the attitudes of Indian software professionals, many of whom considered software piracy to be unethical. Bhal and Leekha did find that for those who considered such piracy to be ethically acceptable, in many cases participants used neutralisation techniques.

Activity 8.2 Use of neutralisations
Which do you think are the most common neutralisations used by downloaders of illegal content online? Are these different to the neutralisations used by uploaders of the same content? Do you think that there are differences in the neutralisations used by people who share different types of content (e.g. music, films, television programmes, software, ebooks, etc.)?

Summary box 8.5 Neutralisations and ethical positions
- Neutralisations are techniques that offenders use to reduce the guilty feelings that offending creates, and are similar to cognitive distortions.
- Sykes and Matza (1957) proposed five different types of neutralisations – denial of responsibility; denial of injury; denial of victim; condemnation of condemners; and appeal to higher loyalties.
- Other researchers have proposed further types of neutralisations, including Coleman's (1994) 'everyone else is doing it'.
- Neutralisations seem to be widely used by those engaged in digital piracy, although studies vary in findings related to the most commonly cited neutralisations.
- Many studies have found that those engaged in digital piracy do not see it as an ethical or legal problem.

The theory of reasoned action, the theory of planned behaviour and optimism bias

Nandedkar and Midha (2012) examined music piracy in light of the 'theory of reasoned action' ('TRA') and 'optimism bias'. TRA was proposed by Fishbein and Ajzen (1975), and suggests that people make systematic use of information that is available to them at the time when making decisions about actions to take. Optimism bias refers to how an individual tends to believe that they are more likely to experience desirable events (such as having a long life, winning a lottery) and less likely to believe that they will experience negative events (such as divorce or serious illness) than an average person (Weinstein, 1980). Both the TRA and optimism bias have been explored and applied to many psychological and economic phenomena. Nandedkar and Midha found that optimism bias had an effect on attitudes towards piracy – people believed that they were less likely to experience the negative aspects of piracy-related behaviours, such as prosecution, poor quality products or lack of respect from significant others. Nandedkar and Midha therefore suggest that strict laws are insufficient when attempting to deter piracy, and that instead, people need to be made more aware of their susceptibility to optimism bias.

The TRA was later extended to the 'theory of planned behaviour' ('TPB'; Ajzen, 1988), which incorporates perceived behavioural control into the TRA, considering the person's beliefs about how likely it is that they have the resources, ability and opportunity to carry out the behaviour. The TPB has also been applied to digital piracy by some researchers. For example, Goode and Kartas (2012) considered how the TPB affected choice of video game consoles, and the ability to pirate console software was a significant factor for purchasers. Blake and Kyper (in press) also found that the TPB can help to explain intentions to share media files over peer-to-peer networks. The TPB has been found to be a more appropriate model for predicting piracy than other models (Yoon, 2012).

Knowing the psychological traits and techniques of those involved in illegal downloading may help in the development of solutions to this problem. The following section considers potential methods by which offenders might be penalised, along with how illegal downloading behaviours might be reduced.

Summary box 8.6 The theory of reasoned action, the theory of planned behaviour and optimism bias

- The theory of reasoned action, the theory of planned behaviour and optimism bias have all been applied to digital piracy.
- The theory of reasoned action (TRA) was proposed by Fishbein and Ajzen (1975), and suggests that people make systematic use of information that is available to them at the time when making decisions about which actions to take.
- Optimism bias was identified by Weinstein (1980) and refers to how an individual tends to believe that they are more likely to experience desirable events and less likely to believe that they will experience negative events than an average person.
- The theory of planned behaviour (TPB; Ajzen, 1988) incorporates perceived behavioural control into the TRA, considering the person's beliefs about how likely it is that they have the resources, ability and opportunity to carry out the behaviour.
- The TPB has been found to be particularly useful in explaining digital piracy.

Punishment and solutions

As with many types of crime, the ideal solution from the victims' perspective is if the piracy does not occur in the first place. Therefore this section will firstly examine potential methods of deterring new offenders from copyright infringement, as well as preventative methods, which attempt to make it difficult to commit the crimes. Other solutions, such as public information strategies and psychoeducational strategies, will also be considered.

Deterrence

Deterrence theory suggests that potential criminals will not engage in offending behaviours because of penalties that they may associate with them. Piquero (2005) considered such theories in relation to intellectual property crime. Penalties associated with crimes can vary in severity and certainty. In most societies, the harshest penalties are normally reserved for the most serious of crimes – if we perceive an offender has received either an especially light or an especially severe penalty based on the nature of their crimes, we tend to feel that a further injustice has been done. The certainty of the punishment is important – if an offender feels that they are unlikely to be apprehended or punished, then they are more likely to proceed with the crime. If they feel that they will be punished (even if the punishment is relatively lenient), then they are less likely to offend. Because of this, it could be considered that it is more important that all offenders are punished rather than a smaller number of offenders receiving harsher sentences.

Related to this are the concepts of general and specific deterrence. General deterrence relies on social learning theory – if a potential offender sees a criminal being punished severely, then they may be less likely to commit a crime themselves. Specific deterrence suggests that an individual should be punished after they commit a crime, with the hope that their personal experience will prevent them from committing further offences. Attempts have been made at using both general and specific deterrence for copyright infringement.

Some individuals have faced severe punishments for illegal file-sharing, as prosecutors hope that this will serve as a general deterrent, hopefully discouraging others from committing the same crimes (McQuade, 2006, pp. 144–5). One example of this occurred in 2007, when the Recording Industry Association of America (RIAA) took legal action against Jammie Thomas-Rasset. The RIAA accused Thomas-Rasset of pirating almost 2,000 music files, but they sought damages for only 24 of them (BBC News Online, 25 January 2010). She was initially found guilty and fined $200,000, but following a retrial in 2009 the fine was increased to $1.92 million (it was later reduced again to $54,000).

Several high-profile cases, similar to that of Thomas-Rasset, received a great deal of media attention. Nevertheless, one problem with general deterrence of this nature is that many illegal file-sharers may feel that they will not be punished, as to prosecute all who engage in such piracy would place too extensive a burden on the criminal justice system. Indeed, while LaRose et al. (2005) identified fear of punishment as a possible deterrent, they noted that regular downloaders were unlikely to stop. Also, many of those who download relatively small numbers of songs, movies or software files may feel that their offences are so petty as not to warrant prosecution, especially compared to those who download greater numbers of files, or who upload content (McQuade, 2006). To a certain extent, this may be true, and copyright holders have more recently turned their attention to the file-sharing services instead. As such, it appears that general deterrence will be relatively ineffective for most home users of illegally copied content. It is, however, possible that specific deterrence may be more effective.

Some jurisdictions are considering ways of employing specific deterrence by penalising all those involved in illegal file-sharing activities. This may involve cutting off or restricting the internet service of repeat offenders, normally following the issue of warning letters (see, for example, BBC News Online, 12 October 2010; BBC News Online, 26 June 2012), although this has met with considerable reluctance from some internet service providers (BBC News Online, 30 September 2010). Although this type of deterrence may seem easier and more practical to implement than attempting to prosecute all illegal downloaders, there remain some difficulties. For example, it may be difficult to enforce the punishment when an internet service is shared among several people or if it is possible that a computer has been hacked. Nevertheless, it is possible that if individuals perceive that they are more likely to be punished, they may abstain from the behaviour, as perceived prosecution risk has been found to impact intention to use pirated software (Liao *et al.*, 2010).

Another concept, learning theory, is related to deterrence. This is described in Chapter 1 and is different to social learning theory as it focuses on the impact of reward and punishment on behaviours, rather than how we learn from those around us. Piquero (2005) applied learning theory to intellectual property crime. The rewards of such crime are apparent – acquisition of a vast collection of music, software, movies and television programmes at little or no expense. It is interesting to note that LaRose *et al.* (2005) found that downloading behaviour was reduced by poor quality downloads – hence a less desirable reward. Since LaRose *et al.*'s study, internet connection speeds and overall quality of content have improved significantly, so this is possibly not as much of a factor as was previously the case. Several of the potential punishments relate to the consequences if the person is caught – such as the fines or reduced internet connections outlined above – and Wingrove *et al.* (2011) noted that concerns regarding punishment have a strong impact on self-reported downloading behaviour. Nevertheless, there can be other potential deterrents. For example, Wolfe *et al.* (2008) noted that fear of malware may influence people's intentions to engage in digital piracy – the risk of damaging their equipment may diminish the desirability of the content. Learning theory suggests that for as long as punishments seem unlikely or minor, and the rewards remain attractive, it is likely that offending will occur, especially when it is easy to commit the offence.

The perceived negative consequence need not be financial or material in nature, it may instead be emotional. Wang and McClung (2012) found that if college students felt that they would be likely to experience guilt after illegal downloading, then they were less likely to engage in the activity. They also noted that those students who perceived there to be greater social approval for the activity were more likely to download. It would seem that if people do not expect important others to approve of the action, or if they expect to feel guilty after the action, they may be less likely to engage in piracy.

Activity 8.3 Learning theory and deterrence

How can learning theory be applied to reduce digital piracy? In what ways could benefits of offending be reduced? How can perceived punishments be increased? What is the best way of communicating these changes in rewards and punishments to potential offenders?

Summary box 8.7 Deterrence

- Deterrence theory suggests that potential criminals will not engage in offending behaviours because of penalties that they may associate with it.
- Penalties associated with offending can vary in both severity and certainty.
- Certainty of punishment seems to be more important in deterrence than severity.
- Both 'general deterrence' and 'specific deterrence' have been used to reduce digital piracy.
- General deterrence relies on social learning theory – if a potential offender sees a criminal being punished severely, then they may be less likely to commit a crime themselves.
- Specific deterrence suggests that an individual should be punished after they commit a crime, with the hope that their personal experience will prevent them from committing further offences.
- General deterrence may be less effective for digital piracy, as most offenders see their crimes as too petty to warrant major legal responses.
- Learning theory focuses on the relative rewards and punishments of a behaviour. If an offender feels that the rewards outweigh the punishments, they are more likely to offend. For digital piracy, rewards refer to the content obtained. Punishments may refer to fines, risk of malware, or negative feelings such as guilt.

Preventative controls

In addition to deterrent controls (that attempt to dissuade users from attempting to commit an act), copyright infringement might also be avoided by using *preventative controls*, that make criminal activities harder or less rewarding (Piquero, 2005). Many preventative controls have been used to target piracy, to various extents of effectiveness. For example, digital media can be encrypted (Higgins, 2007), CDs can be developed that will not work in computers (Jewkes, 2010), or a user may be required to install monitoring software when installing a new application, which will report any instances of illegal copying to the development company (Stephens, 2008). Other possibilities include restrictions in the code of legally downloaded files that prevent excessive copying of the file, or writes identifying information about the purchaser into the file, so that if copies are illegally distributed at a later time, the source of the file can be identified (Stephens, 2008).

These technological controls may provide useful means of dissuading some offenders, but more motivated offenders can frequently find ways of circumventing such techniques. Nevertheless, they may help to reduce the problem, as the more difficult it is to engage in the activity, the more likely it is that individuals with impulsive natures will be discouraged from completing it (Higgins, 2007). It is, however, important to note that computer usage policies, put in place by universities, workplaces and other organisations, should not be seen as technological controls. Indeed, Cronan *et al.* (2006) found that university computer usage policies were ineffective at preventing misuse – many students had never even read the policy. Worryingly, those students who had read the policies had committed even more misuses than those who had not. It is possible that these students were aware that their actions were probably infringements, and they read the policy in order to determine what punishments were likely, or how the university managed such transgressions.

Other solutions

A further potential method of preventing copyright infringement involves the use of public information campaigns. These seem to primarily focus on young people, as the group most likely to be involved in illegal downloading (Wall and Yar, 2010). These campaigns aim to demonstrate to children and teenagers that illegal copying is a form of theft, and as such is similar to stealing a physical possession, but Wall and Yar indicate that these strategies may not work, and may be overcome by potential offenders through the use of neutralisations (p. 267). Similarly, D'Astous *et al.* (2005) found that many anti-piracy arguments, such as stressing the negative consequences for the artists, or the unethical nature of the offence, had no effect on user behaviours.

Higgins *et al.* (2006) suggest that the effects of social learning could be reduced by encouraging university students to build friendships with peers who do not engage in digital piracy, though they acknowledge that such strategies would have to be carefully implemented and evaluated. Malin and Fowers (2009) suggest that the reduced self-control associated with digital piracy might be another avenue for exploration in crime reduction methods.

Cockrill and Goode (2012) describe how not all of those engaged in DVD piracy are similar. They differentiated between four different types of individual – those involved in serious piracy ('devils'), opportunists ('chancers'), receivers ('receivers') and non-pirates ('angels'). They found that there were differences in key predictor variables between the four groups, and therefore suggest that different anti-piracy strategies should be employed for each group in order to improve effectiveness. In particular, Cockrill and Goode indicate that the film industry needs to improve user awareness of the damage that piracy can cause, and that the 'chancers' were those who were most likely to be successfully deterred by current strategies.

A final potential strategy emerged from research conducted by Higgins *et al.* (2008), which examined digital piracy by undergraduate students. Over the course of four weeks, both the rate of digital piracy, and the use of neutralisations, decreased. Higgins *et al.* (2008) suggest that as participants recorded their behaviours, they reflected more on the criminality of digital piracy, and reduced their deviant behaviours. As their deviant behaviours reduced, they no longer needed neutralisations to justify their actions. Therefore Higgins *et al.* (2008) suggest that piracy might be reduced by education along with an attempt to improve moral conscience.

Evaluations of prevention strategies are relatively rare, but an experimental study by Al-Rafee and Rouibah (2010) in the Middle East tested the effects of different interventions on piracy intentions. They found that informing students about laws relating to piracy had little effect, but that interventions that focused on religious teachings, or improving awareness of the harm that digital piracy can cause both contributed to a decline in piracy. These findings reinforce the studies described above that indicate that perceived legality of piracy seems to have little effect.

Summary box 8.8 Preventative controls and other solutions

- Preventative controls make criminal activities harder or less rewarding.
- They may include the use of technological means to make digital piracy more difficult to achieve, such as encryption.
- Technological preventative controls may dissuade some offenders, but others will find ways to circumvent such techniques.
- Computer usage policies have been found to be ineffective at preventing digital piracy.
- Public information campaigns have mostly been aimed at young people, although many anti-piracy arguments seem to have little effect.
- Arguments have been made that not all those engaged in digital piracy are similar, and so different intervention strategies should be considered for different groups (e.g. Cockrill and Goode, 2012).
- It is possible that raising potential perpetrators' awareness of the harm that digital piracy may cause could reduce likelihood to perpetrate such activities.

Conclusion

Self-control, social learning and neutralisations all seem to be important factors in explaining online piracy, but research in all three areas is still quite limited. More research has been conducted examining the applicability of the theory of planned behaviour, which seems to explain digital piracy well. A major problem with many of the attempts to deter or prevent online piracy is the lack of evaluation of their effectiveness (Piquero, 2005), which would be an interesting area of future research. In particular, it will be of interest to examine if the specific deterrence methods (such as withholding internet connections) might have an impact on the overall levels of these offences.

Essay questions

(1) Evaluate the relative effectiveness of specific and general deterrence in reducing digital piracy.
(2) Describe how self-control and social learning theory can contribute to online copyright infringement behaviours.
(3) Explain how neutralisations are used by those involved in digital piracy to justify their actions.

(4) Using the research to date, consider the theory that those involved in digital piracy are morally different to those who are not.

(5) Evaluate the usefulness of the theory of reasoned action and the theory of planned behaviour in developing an understanding of digital piracy.

Additional reading

Books and articles

Matthew David's (2010) book *Peer to Peer and the Music Industry: the Criminalisation of Sharing* (Sage Publications Ltd) provides a historical and criminological overview of music sharing.

The following journal articles consider various aspects of the psychological mechanisms thought to explain digital piracy.

Garbharran, A. and Thatcher, A. (2011). Modelling social cognitive theory to explain software piracy intention. In M. J. Smith and G. Salvendy (eds.), *Human Interface and the Management of Information: Interacting with Information: Symposium on Human Interface: HCI International Part 1*. Berlin, Germany: Springer-Verlag (pp. 301–10).

Jambon, M. M. and Smetana, J. G. (2012). College students' moral evaluations of illegal music downloading. *Journal of Applied Developmental Psychology*, **33**, 31–9.

Nandedkar, A. and Midha, V. (2012). It won't happen to me: an assessment of optimism bias in music piracy. *Computers in Human Behavior*, **28**, 41–8.

Wang, X. and McClung, S. R. (2012). The immorality of illegal downloading: the role of anticipated guilt and general emotions. *Computers in Human Behaviour*, **28**, 153–9.

Websites

The British Recorded Music Industry website considers online copyright infringement, commercial music piracy and file-sharing: www.bpi.co.uk/category/protecting-uk-music.aspx.

The Federation Against Copyright Theft (FACT) works to protect the UK film and broadcasting industry against copyright infringement: www.fact-uk.org.uk.

The United States Copyright Office website includes information about law and licensing: www.copyright.gov.

9 Cyberterrorism

Case studies

A city comes under terrorist attack. There are several explosions and people become confused and frightened. Suddenly there is a power blackout. Simultaneously the mobile phone networks stop functioning. Citizens are unable to find out what has happened and cannot contact the emergency services. There is additional loss of life as individuals cannot access medical aid in time. Hackers disrupting the power and communication systems have heightened the fear and confusion arising from a more traditional terror attack.

A young man is unhappy with how a foreign regime is governing his country. Searching online, he discovers that he is not alone. This increases his anger – the fact that there are others who feel the same suggests to him that he is correct to be upset. He finds that he can aid in the fight against this regime by donating funds, providing information or disseminating propaganda. If he wishes, he can even join a terrorist organisation and learn terror-related skills from online videos and websites. He finds that he can contact current members of the organisation via the website, and he feels that finally he has met other people who understand his perspective.

Chapter overview

The two cases above are fictional, and thankfully the world has not yet had to respond to a threat such as the first example. However, the second example is thought to be a common occurrence; the widespread availability of the internet has resulted in considerably easier access to terrorist organisations and information than was previously available. Despite considerable academic and media interest in cyberterrorism, there is relatively little empirical work in this area. There is much disagreement regarding the definition of cyberterrorism and the extent of the danger that it poses, and the online activities of terrorist organisations are inconsistently classified as 'cyberterrorism' or not by various authors. The complexity of these arguments is outlined in the section on definitions below. The chapter then goes on to describe the various online activities of terrorists, which include cyberterror attacks but also recruitment, networking, fundraising and gathering and dissemination of information. The distinction between hacktivism and cyberterrorism is also described here. The chapter then goes on to consider the process of radicalisation, the motivation for cyberterrorism and the psychology of cyberterrorists, with particular focus on determining whether terrorists have specific personality traits or psychological abnormalities. Finally, the effects on victims are discussed.

Definitions

There is some disagreement among writers in the area as to what should and should not be defined as 'cyberterrorism', with some authors suggesting that a solid definition of cyberterrorism is elusive (for example, Gordon and Ford, 2003). Many researchers and practitioners do not believe that operational issues and planning online should be classified as cyberterrorism, and some extend this belief to attacks such as website defacements or 'denial of service' attacks (where a website or other online presence is rendered non-functional because of a targeted attack). Such authors feel that the term 'cyberterrorism' should be reserved for activities that result in death, serious injury or severe disruption.

The complexity in defining cyberterrorism is confounded by problems defining traditional terrorism (Taylor, 2012, p. 208). For the purpose of this chapter, terrorism will be considered to be the use of violence or intimidation to evoke fear in a specific group, in order to achieve a desired goal, which is often political, ideological or religious in nature. Post (1984) distinguished between two main types of terrorist groups – anarchic-ideologue groups and nationalist-separatist groups. Anarchic-ideologue groups are usually smaller, attempting to overthrow a political or social regime, mainly for ideological reasons, and there may be alienation from the terrorist's family or immediate community. Nationalist-separatist groups are normally larger and do not generally involve estrangement from families or communities.

Activity 9.1 Defining terrorism
Consider the definition of terrorism above in light of previous terrorist attacks (with or without an online component). Identify the goal of the terrorist, the targeted group and the mechanism used by the terrorist(s) to evoke fear. Identify whether the terrorist group is anarchic-ideologue or nationalist-separatist in nature. Remember that terror attacks can be conducted by lone terrorists as well as groups.

Due to this disagreement in the perception of cyberterrorism by researchers, there is considerable discrepancy in the definitions that have been proposed to date. Some of these are listed in Table 9.1.

Aside from the specific definitions above, other authors have attempted to differentiate between different types of online terrorist activity. For example, Gordon and Ford (2003) describe 'pure cyberterrorism', where activities are carried out primarily online, as distinct from traditional terrorist activities that are carried out in online

Table 9.1 Definitions of cyberterrorism

Pollitt	'the premeditated, politically motivated attack against information, computer systems, computer programs, and data which result in violence against non-combatant targets by subnational groups or clandestine agents' (1997, as cited in Denning, 2001, p. 281).
Wilson	'the use of computers as weapons, or as targets, by politically motivated international, or sub-national groups, or clandestine agents who threaten or cause violence and fear in order to influence an audience, or cause a government to change its policies' (2005, p. CRS-7).
Denning	'The convergence of terrorism and cyberspace ... unlawful attacks and threats of attack against computers, networks and the information stored therein when done to intimidate or coerce a government or its people in furtherance of political or social objectives. Further, to qualify as cyberterrorism, an attack should result in violence against persons or property, or at least cause enough harm to generate fear. Attacks that lead to death or bodily injury, explosions, plane crashes, water contamination, or severe economic loss would be examples. Serious attacks against critical infrastructures could be acts of cyberterrorism, depending on their impact. Attacks that disrupt nonessential services or that are mainly a costly nuisance would not' (2007a). And also ... 'politically motivated attacks that cause serious harm, such as severe economic hardship or sustained loss of power or water, might also be characterised as cyberterrorism' (2001, p. 281).

environments, such as recruitment. A similar argument is made by Nelson *et al.* (1999), who suggest that online activities such as organisation and communication should not be classified as cyberterrorism, but rather 'cyberterror support' or 'terrorist use of the internet'.

Conway (2007) furthers this distinction, using a four-tiered system to classify online terrorist activity. These tiers are:

- use – using the internet to express ideas, which many internet users engage in legally;
- misuse – where the internet is used to disrupt websites or infrastructure, perhaps by hackers or hacktivists;
- offensive use – using the internet to cause damage or to steal;
- cyberterrorism – terrorists using the internet to carry out an attack which would result in violence or severe economic damage.

While it is important to remember the discrepancies in definitions used by authors, for the purpose of clarity this chapter will use the term 'cyberterrorism' to define those acts that could result in violence or severe economic harm (in line with the definitions proposed by Denning and Conway). The more inclusive term 'terrorist activity online' will also include activities such as fundraising, recruitment, organisation, dissemination and hacktivist activities by terrorist organisations. This chapter now considers several of the main types of terrorist activity online.

Summary box 9.1 Definitions

- There is considerable disagreement as to what does and does not constitute cyberterrorism.
- Some authors, such as Denning and Conway, have suggested that the term 'cyberterrorism' should be restricted to attacks which could result in violence or severe economic damage.
- Post (1984) distinguished between two main types of terrorist groups – anarchic-ideologue groups and nationalist-separatist groups.
- Conway (2007) argued for a four-tiered system to classify online terrorist activity, including 'use', 'misuse', 'offensive use' and 'cyberterrorism'.

Online activities of terrorists

Terrorists use the internet for a wide variety of activities. In some ways, terrorists use the internet for the same reasons as anyone else. For example, Conway (2002) reports that at least nine of the terrorists' airline tickets used on 11 September 2001 were booked online and emails were used to distribute operational details of the attack. Wilson (2007) indicates that terrorist organisations use websites for recruitment, fundraising and training, while Maghaireh (2008) describes how some websites propagating Islamic rhetoric and ideology have online schools teaching hacking techniques. Conway (2006) describes five main ways that terrorists use the internet – information provision, financing, networking, recruitment and information gathering. Weimann (2004) also suggested that psychological warfare, publicity and propaganda, planning and co-ordination and mobilisation are also engaged in by terrorists online. Although such uses are less likely to draw media attention than pure cyberterrorism, their importance should not be overlooked. Denning (2010) claims that 'despite the ordinariness of much of this use, the very practice of terrorism – the ways in which terrorists

Illustration 9.1 Cyberterrorism. Terrorists use the internet for a variety of activities, including information provision, financing, networking, recruitment and information gathering (Conway, 2006).

disseminate documents and propaganda, recruit and train new members, and inflict harm on their victims – is being fundamentally transformed and expanded because of the Net' (p. 194).

This section will consider several of the main activities of terrorists online. It will firstly examine cyberterror attacks, before examining how hacktivist style attacks might be used by cyberterrorists. Following this, other online terrorist activities will be considered, such as recruitment, networking, fundraising and the gathering and dissemination of information.

Cyberterror attacks

Denning (2010) suggests that due to the lack of physical and psychological effects resulting from online terrorist use so far, even denial of service attacks are generally not labelled as acts of cyberterrorism (p. 198). Stohl (2006) argues that terrorists are using the internet and other modern technologies to enhance ease of operations, but not as a form of attack. However, that is not to say that such an event will not occur in the future. There is evidence that some of these attacks could happen. In 2009, the US government admitted that the national power grid had been infiltrated by Chinese and Russian spies, leaving software behind that could shut the grid down (Shiels, 2009).

While many writers do not think that a cyberterror attack is imminent (see, for example, Conway, 2011), there are some who disagree. For example, Leman-Langlois (2008, pp. 2–3) states that:

A 'cyber Pearl Harbour' is looming, with attackers targeting essential infrastructures in attempts to cripple economies. They will co-ordinate attacks on . . . targets selected to produce cascading failures along our highly interconnected infrastructures.

Similarly, Whittaker (2004, p. 123) takes a somewhat pessimistic view of what is probably the worst case scenario:

At the throw of a few switches, a saboteur, sitting in relative comfort and with highly technical equipment, can shut down power grids, unravel telephone networks, bring chaos to road and rail transport and air traffic control, and break down the operation of pharmaceutical and food processing plants. A 'logic bomb' can be timed to detonate at a certain hour and there will be irreversible damage to software. Computer viruses, if carefully ordered, will completely shut down an entire computer system. A computer can browse through databanks thought to be confidential. Surveillance systems will be entered, examined, and, if necessary, destroyed. Death and destruction can be brought into being at a distance with nobody hostile there to watch.

Denning (2007b) suggests that likely targets for such attacks include water supplies, power supplies (including electricity, oil and gas), communications grids, banks, transportation, essential government services and emergency services. She suggests that there are varying indicators of terrorism, including:

- execution of cyber attacks;
- cyber weapons acquisition, development and training;
- statements about cyberattacks (including declarations of intent and discussions relating to the subject);

- formal education in information technology (particularly network and information security);
- general experience with cyberspace (such as the use of the internet for general communications and propaganda).

On this scale, Denning suggests that a failed attack against a power system is more indicative of a threat than a successful website defacement. She suggests that there is evidence for activity at the second most serious level – cyber weapons acquisition, development and training – and that some terrorist organisations train their members in hacking and engage in 'cyber reconnaissance' to gain information about infrastructure. Denning also indicates that some terrorist groups have employed external hackers to aid in gathering information, although it is also possible that terrorist organisations might recruit hackers directly.

Rollins and Wilson (2007) suggest that the tighter security put in place by the US might encourage terrorists to use other forms of attack, including cyberattacks. While so far these attacks have been mostly limited to email bombings and website defacements, Rollins and Wilson indicate that the US Federal Bureau of Investigation (FBI) predicts that future large conventional attacks might be amplified by cyberattacks. For example, cyberterrorists might disable the communication networks of a country while simultaneously detonating explosive devices – the disruption to communications might prevent emergency service calls, leading to a higher death toll. Wilson (2005) provides more detail on this scenario, indicating that there are three possible methods of attack:

- physical attacks – involving the use of conventional weapons directed against a specific computer facility or communication lines;
- electronic attacks – using electromagnetic energy (possibly an Electro-Magnetic Pulse, or EMP) to overload computer circuitry;
- computer network attacks – possibly using malware to infect computers and exploit software weaknesses.

There are several advantages for the terrorist organisation in employing virtual terror attacks, as outlined by Yar (2006). These include:

- allowing the terrorists to act remotely, thus reducing the impact of increased border controls and allowing the terrorist activity to occur within 'rogue states' that might protect the perpetrators;
- allowing small terrorist organisations with limited resources to function as more serious threats;
- using the anonymity provided by the internet as a method of reducing the likelihood of apprehension;
- using the security holes caused by lack of regulation of the internet.

It should of course be remembered that such threats do not only originate from cyberterrorists, but could also emerge from foreign governments or criminal gangs, and many countries, including the US, are putting in place greater security measures. For example, on 20 July 2012, a revised version of the Cybersecurity Act was introduced in the US Senate, seeking to make US infrastructure less vulnerable (BBC News Online, 2012).

Summary box 9.2 Cyberterror attacks

- To date, terrorists have mostly used the internet for purposes such as propaganda, recruitment, fundraising, information gathering and dissemination and networking.
- A cyberterror attack involving serious disruption, injury or loss of life has not yet occurred, and some researchers argue that it is unlikely to do so in the near future.
- Denning (2007b) suggests that likely targets for such attacks include water supplies, power supplies (including electricity, oil and gas), communications grids, banks, transportation, essential government services and emergency services.
- Denning (2007b) argues for a five-level categorisation of terror attacks, ranging from general experience of cyberspace to execution of a cyberterror attack.
- Terrorist organisations may hire external hackers, or recruit them to their organisation.
- Rollins and Wilson (2007) suggest that a cyberterror attack may be used to amplify a traditional terror attack.
- Wilson (2005) indicates that there are three possible methods of attack – physical attacks, electronic attacks or computer network attacks.
- There are several advantages for terrorist organisations using cyberterror attacks, particularly anonymity, acting from remote locations, use of security holes and allowing small organisations to function as more serious threats (Yar, 2006).

Hacktivism versus cyberterrorism

There have been several recent cases of hacktivism and hacktivist-style attacks. Campaigns by hacktivist groups have gathered considerable media attention. However, it must be remembered that hacktivists are a very different group to cyberterrorists – hacktivists are generally more interested in disrupting online activity, rather than causing destruction (Conway, 2007). The aim of hacktivist attacks is often to cause frustration and difficulty for administrators holding opposing views to the hacktivist and their group – they do not intend to cause terror as a cyberterrorist would. Because of the lack of fear evoked, Denning (2007b) argues that such activities should not be classified as cyberterrorism. However, that is not to say that terrorist activity online might not employ tactics more commonly associated with hacktivism, such as denial of service attacks.

Recruitment of new members

The widespread adoption of internet technologies allows potential recruits to become members of terrorist organisations in several ways (Conway, 2006). Information gathering is quicker and easier, and the wide variety of available formats, including video, audio and text files, makes content very accessible. For example, McDonald (2009) describes how propaganda videos for the Real IRA and Continuity IRA were easily available on video-sharing websites.

Potential recruits may also feel safer in searching for information and contacting terrorist groups due to the sense of anonymity online. New recruits could also have the option of assisting the terrorist organisation in a wider variety of ways – they may help the organisation through donations of money, software or expertise, rather than formally joining the group (Denning, 2010). Active recruitment online is also possible – the terrorist organisation may scan online chat or bulletin boards, searching for individuals who may be receptive to their cause.

The recruitment process varies from organisation to organisation. Denning (2010) indicates that different types of advice are offered by different websites and organisations. Some of these require the potential recruit to take an oath of loyalty to the organisation's leaders, while others indicate that all that is required is a wish to join. In some cases online recruitment is targeted to specific age groups – Denning (2010) describes how there is evidence to suggest that recruitment strategies for children include games, music videos and comic-book style readings.

Networking

Many terrorist organisations attempt to work as decentralised networks of cells, thus reducing the impact on the entire organisation should one cell be infiltrated or removed. Denning (2010) describes how the internet further enables this, possibly to the extent that cells may exist that would not be recognised by the terrorist leadership. Nevertheless, the members can still communicate rapidly, cheaply and effectively using online communication (Conway, 2006). Dean *et al.* (2012) describe how social networking sites, micro-blogging sites and video-sharing sites can all be used by terrorist groups for networking purposes, while Bowman-Grieve and Conway (2012) examine how online discussions support communication for both new and committed dissident Irish Republicans. Use of the internet can assist the terrorist organisation in reducing the need for a single headquarters, and encourages the dissemination of responsibilities to different centres. The reduced need for telephone or face-to-face contact also reduces risks for terrorists.

Summary box 9.3 Hacktivism, recruitment and networking
- Hacktivist attacks are high-profile, but should not be confused with cyberterrorism.
- Hacktivists focus on causing frustration and disruption for specific groups, while cyberterrorists attempt to cause destruction or terror.
- However, cyberterrorists may attempt to employ tactics more commonly associated with hacktivists, such as denial of service attacks.
- The accessibility of online propaganda and terrorist organisation presence enables individuals to join organisations easily.
- A variety of media are created by terrorist organisations, and distributed through social networking sites, video-sharing sites, bulletin boards and other online formats.
- These media are used for recruitment, propaganda and networking.

* Online communication allows terrorists to interact cheaply, rapidly and effectively, while also disseminating responsibilities away from a central headquarters.

Fundraising

Terrorist organisations can enjoy increased financial donations as a result of an internet presence (Conway, 2006), and these organisations may encourage such donations through direct payment options, either as pure donations, or through the sale of items which may or may not be directly related to the cause. Bowman-Grieve (2011) describes how terrorist groups might also request donations of items, and that an initial donation or purchase might 'be seen as indicative of a belief that the goals of the movement are legitimate and that their means of achieving these goals, even through the use of violence and terrorism, are acceptable. This may be a first step on the pathway toward involvement' (p. 78). However, terrorist organisations may also use online fraud to fund their activities, or may use a charity as a fundraising vehicle (Conway, 2006).

Gathering and dissemination of information

Information is an essential part of modern life – our decisions are formed by the information we gather, and we are continuously sharing information with the people around us. Terrorist organisations also gather and disseminate information. The vast quantities of information online can be extremely useful to terrorist organisations – providing knowledge of flight times and routes, floor plans of buildings, street maps of towns and villages, pedestrian-eye views of urban areas and information about upcoming events where large numbers of individuals will be in close proximity at a specific place and time. However, as well as gathering information, terrorist organisations may also disseminate information online, sometimes as a tool for psychological warfare (Conway, 2006). This information may be disseminated on many different online venues, including websites, social networking sites and commercial networks, and using a variety of multimedia and communication tools, such as video files, audio files, boards, blogs and chatrooms (Denning, 2010). Brown and Silke (2011) discuss how dissemination of propaganda through various media outlets, including the internet, is a core activity of modern terrorist organisations.

Terrorist organisations disseminate many kinds of information, including the issuing of threats, releasing videos of terrorist leaders and terrorist activities and spreading false information. This information can reach large numbers of people very quickly, very cheaply and very easily, circumventing established media routes and circulating the information without censorship (Denning, 2010).

Terrorist organisations also disseminate information in the form of training materials, including methods of creating explosive devices and establishing underground organisations (Conway, 2006). Of course, this information might be accessed by individuals other than potential terrorists, who may use these training materials for other purposes and causes. Some of the instructional materials online describe anti-quated technologies (sometimes as much as 100 years old), but other materials describe more modern techniques, including information on computers and the internet (Denning, 2010).

Activity 9.2 Terrorist use of the internet

Using the headings of 'recruitment', 'networking', 'fundraising' and 'gathering and dissemination of information', compare how terrorist organisations would have accomplished these tasks before the popularisation of the internet with how they can achieve them now. What effect do you think these changes may have on terrorist organisations?

Summary box 9.4 Fundraising and gathering/dissemination of information

- Terrorist organisations may use an online presence to raise funds through the sale of items or the direct donation of money or goods.
- Terrorist organisations can also gather information online, through publicly available information or hacking techniques.
- Information is also disseminated by terrorist organisations through the use of various online media.
- Information disseminated can include threats, videos of terrorist leaders, videos of terrorist activities, propaganda, training materials and spreading false information.
- Information disseminated online may bypass normal media, thus avoiding censorship.

Radicalisation

There seems to be a consensus that becoming a terrorist is a gradual process, involving several stages (Horgan and Taylor, 2001; Merari, 2007; Taylor, 2012). The process of being exposed to and sympathising with radical ideology is sometimes called 'radicalisation', defined by McCauley and Moskalenko (2008) as 'a dimension of increasing extremity of beliefs, feelings, and behaviours in support of intergroup conflict and violence' (p. 415). McCauley and Moskalenko (2008) distinguished between twelve mechanisms of radicalisation, and in the majority of these, radical-isation occurs in the context of a perceived threat to an identified in-group, such as the person's ethnic or religious group. It should be noted that holding radical views does not necessarily mean that these views will be expressed through violence (Taylor, 2012).

Attempts have been made to determine the demographic characteristics that are indicative of potential terrorists, with focus on variables such as specific religious beliefs, education, occupation, relative deprivation and low socioeconomic status. However, these tend not to be useful in predicting future terrorists, as many individuals will share the same background without engaging in terrorism (Sageman, 2004).

It is possible that a more useful method of predicting future terrorist activity involves examining a combination of factors, and it is possible that certain conditions must occur in the right combination for an individual to support or become involved in a terrorist organisation (Kruglanski and Fishman, 2006). These might include wanting to feel a sense of belonging, development of personal identity, social isolation and perception of injustice (Howitt, 2009).

One potential explanation of terrorist activity may include social learning theory (Victoroff, 2005), with the terrorist's moral imperatives being reconstructed by what they learn from others, rather than any specific characteristics of the individual. It is important to note that this social learning may previously have been restricted to face-to-face interactions, but it may now occur through the dissemination of literature, audio files and video files online. Nevertheless, this still does not sufficiently describe radicalisation, as many individuals are exposed to such avenues for learning, without becoming terrorists.

Terrorists who are recruited online possibly experience similar psychological processes to those recruited using traditional methods. For example, Sageman (2008) suggests that online forums allow the development of a type of social identity required by terrorists. Relationships can be built through forums, and the cognitions of recruits are developed. The interactivity in the forums is important, and considerably more persuasive than passive, non-interactive websites (Sageman, 2008).

Further difficulty exists in attempts to explain why an individual may become a leader in a terrorist organisation. Again, this may be due to a combination of personality attributes. Locicero and Sinclair (2008) suggest that terrorist leaders may demonstrate 'entrenched cognitive simplicity in one key ideological domain' (p. 227). This suggests that, in relation to one topic, they hold fast to one way of viewing the world, possibly making diplomacy more difficult to achieve. However, Locicero and Sinclair suggest that in other domains, the terrorist leader shows much greater complexity of cognitive function, allowing for enhanced planning and organisational skills. This combination of factors may result in a highly organised, but highly focused, terrorist leader.

Activity 9.3 'Lone wolf' terrorists

Not all terrorists join organisations – there have been many cases of 'lone wolf' terrorists. Research some of these cases (see, for example, David Copeland, Anders Behring Breivik, Timothy McVeigh and Theodore Kaczynski), identifying the characteristics of the terrorists, and determining why they engaged in terrorist attacks.

Summary box 9.5 Radicalisation

- Becoming a terrorist is a gradual process, involving several stages.
- The process of being exposed to and sympathising with radical ideology is sometimes called 'radicalisation'.
- Holding such radical views does not necessarily mean that a person is engaged in violence.
- Holding specific demographic traits is not a useful predictor of terrorist activity, as many others will hold those traits without choosing to engage in terrorism.
- It is possible that a combination of factors is required for a person to be radicalised, including feeling a need to belong and to develop personal identity, social isolation and perception of injustice.
- Social learning theory may explain some cases of terrorism, though not all (Victoroff, 2005).
- Terrorists recruited online may experience similar psychological processes to those recruited offline, and those recruited through interactive forums may develop a social identity associated with terrorism more strongly than those who only passively view non-interactive content.
- Terrorist leaders may experience extreme cognitive simplicity in an ideological domain, while demonstrating enhanced planning and organisational skills (Locicero and Sinclair, 2008).

Motives of terrorism and cyberterrorism

Motives of terrorism vary greatly – some terrorists and terrorist organisations are motivated by ideological reasons (such as prevention of animal cruelty, or anti-abortion groups), while others are motivated by ethnic or religious reasons (such as Al-Qaeda or Hamas). Whatever the ultimate goal of the terrorist organisation, Horgan (2005, pp. 1–2) indicates that:

very often, it seems that the goal of terrorism is simply to create widespread fear, arousal and uncertainty on a wider, more distant scale than that achieved by targeting the victim alone, thereby influencing the political process and how it might normally be expected to function.

Horgan suggests that most terrorist movements seek to overthrow or destabilise a target regime or influence, and that most are relatively small. He indicates that the goal of inducing terror is important – for example, the most important outcome for the terrorists of the attacks on 11 September 2001 was not the deaths of those killed in the attacks, but the 'humiliation of the American government and the subsequent psychological arousal for the greater populace' (Horgan, 2005, p. 2). It should therefore be asked: can a similar reaction be obtained through the use of information technology as a terrorist tool?

Both Veerasamy (2010) and Colarik and Janczewski (2008) suggest that online terrorist activity is best understood by examining the motives of traditional terrorist activity, particularly the generation of fear. Colarik and Janczewski (2008, p. xv) specifically refer to the 'spectacular factor', potentially resulting in negative publicity or direct losses. A third motive of an attack such as a denial of service might be to emphasise the vulnerability of an organisation, demonstrating weakness in the system. Hacking may also be used to steal information or make political statements about the entity being attacked.

Summary box 9.6 Motives of terrorism and cyberterrorism

- Terrorist organisations have different motives, but the goal of terrorist acts is to create fear and uncertainty among people other than the direct victim of an attack.
- Cyberterrorism is generally motivated by similar goals, but may also hope to demonstrate the vulnerability of an organisation, make political statements, steal information or bring about negative publicity or direct losses.

Psychology of cyberterrorists

There has been very little empirical research examining the psychology of terrorism, with most writings to date being theoretical or based on literature or anecdotal observations (Silke, 2008; Victoroff, 2005). Nevertheless, there has been an increase in terrorism-related research since the attacks on the US on 11 September 2001 (Silke, 2008).

There are several reasons why empirical research on the psychology of terrorists is rare:

- it can be difficult to find terrorists;
- even when terrorists are found, it can be difficult to find those willing to participate in a psychological study;
- studying incarcerated terrorists also holds some difficulty, as it is necessary to get approval from relevant authorities;
- travel expenses could be prohibitive;
- there may be difficulties in gaining approval from ethical boards;
- there could be a language barrier;
- there may be a risk of personal harm to the researcher, through directly contacting terrorists or because of travel to unstable regions.

Nevertheless, there has been some interesting research on the psychology of terrorism. Here, particular focus will be placed on the personality traits of terrorists and the potential for psychological deviance in terrorists. Finally, the possible similarities and differences between traditional and cyberterrorists will be considered.

Personality and profile

Potential demographic characteristics that might lead to radicalisation have already been discussed, but it has also been suggested that engagement in terrorist acts might be associated with some personality traits, such as having a sensation-seeking personality or subjective feelings of humiliation (see, for example, Victoroff, 2005; Zuckerman,

2002). However empirical evidence has failed to support the existence of specific personality traits in terrorists (Horgan, 2003a, 2008; Howitt, 2009; Silke, 2003; Victoroff, 2005; Wilson, 2010).

Nevertheless, it is possible that even if terrorists do not have unique personality traits, the study of personality may still be important. Kruglanski and Fishman (2006) distinguish between terrorism as a 'syndrome' (a 'psychologically meaningful construct with identifiable characteristics on individual and group levels of analysis', p. 193) and terrorism as a 'tool' (representing 'a strategic instrument that any party in a conflict with another may use', p. 193). If terrorism is a syndrome, then it is possible that distinctive personality traits, motivations and socialisation histories could be associated with terrorists, and that findings about one terrorist group could be generalised to other groups. If, however, terrorism is found to be a 'tool', then it provides little psychological insight into the terrorist or organisation – terrorism is just a means to an end, though it may still be of interest to determine why the individual chose terrorism as the means of achieving a goal, over other tools such as diplomacy or peaceful protest.

Kruglanski and Fishman indicate that there is little evidence to support the 'syndrome' theory of terrorism, and so the 'tool' view is probably more appropriate. This insight is important, as it suggests that the phenomenon can be studied in terms of means–end analysis – if potential terrorists have access to an alternative 'tool' of obtaining their goal, which is preferable to terrorist activity, then it is likely that they might choose that 'means' instead. It also suggests that if terrorism is not expected to be a successful means of obtaining the goal state, then it will not be utilised. Because of this, the 'tool' theory of terrorism is still very important from a psychological perspective, as elements of cognitive psychology, such as decision making and perception, can play an important role in understanding terrorist activity. Some research has determined that the gradual socialisation associated with terrorist groups is often accompanied by an increasing disillusionment with other means of achieving desired goals (Kellen, 1982; Taylor and Quayle, 1994).

Some of this examination of the cognitive psychology of terrorists has been done by Max Taylor and Ethel Quayle (1994), who suggest that terrorists may make fundamental attribution errors regarding their perceived oppressors, increasing their likelihood of becoming actively engaged. Similarly, Victoroff (2005) suggests that rational choice theory might help to explain the behaviour of terrorists, but again this does not explain why the vast majority of people who might have a desired objective do not engage in terrorism, even though it might help to achieve their goal. It may be that cognitive inflexibility or diminished executive functions might also play a part (Victoroff, 2005), and awareness of this might be helpful for negotiators.

Cognitive psychology should not be considered in isolation when discussing terrorist psychology – it is also useful to consider how social psychology can inform our understanding. Group dynamics are a very important aspect of terrorist organisations (Victoroff, 2005). The organisation provides support to the individual from others who have similar goals. They provide the terrorist with a well-defined role and a sense of purpose. The organisation also enables the terrorist to see behaviours that would otherwise go against social norms as acceptable. It is important that the group identity is not underestimated: as Post *et al.* (2003) describe, 'an overarching sense of the collective consumes the individual. This fusion with the group seems to provide the necessary justification for their actions, with an attendant loss of felt responsibility' (p. 176).

As with many other types of offenders, terrorism is probably determined by a combination of many factors, including developmental factors, biological factors, cognitive processes, cognitive capabilities, environmental influences, personality and group dynamics (Victoroff, 2005). Without further empirical research, it is unlikely that a full understanding of terrorist psychology can be developed. However, Victoroff (2005) suggests four traits which might characterise 'typical' terrorists:

- high affective opinion regarding an issue;
- having a personal stake that separates them from others holding the same opinion (such as a sense of personal oppression, a strong need for vengeance, or a drive to express aggression);
- low cognitive flexibility, with an elevated tendency towards attribution error;
- ability to suppress moral constraints against harming innocent people.

This is an interesting theory, but it requires considerable testing in order to ascertain validity.

Psychological abnormalities

It was once thought that terrorists were likely to hold psychopathic personality traits, but more recent research suggests that this is unlikely to be the case (Horgan, 2003b; Silke, 1998; Victoroff, 2005). Suggestions of any abnormal tendencies seem to be based mainly on anecdotal cases or secondary sources (Silke, 1998). Even suicide terrorists may not be clinically abnormal, although a multidisciplinary approach must be adopted to comprehend such attacks, involving historical, economic, political, psychological and anthropological factors (Post *et al.*, 2009). For example, a person may volunteer for a suicide attack following a lengthy process of disillusionment with an oppressing regime, during which they lost one or more loved ones. Victoroff (2005) concludes that terrorists do not usually exhibit any major psychiatric disorder or personality disorder, although some individuals with antisocial tendencies might use affiliations with terrorist groups to hide their aggressive tendencies.

Activity 9.4 Terrorist psychology

As demonstrated above, it is probably impossible to develop a list of terrorist attributes. However, as with most types of offenders, it is possible to list factors that may contribute to a tendency to choose terrorism over other methods in order to achieve a goal. List some of these factors under the following headings suggested by Post *et al.* (2009) – i.e. historical, economic, political, psychological and anthropological. Are there any other headings that might also be appropriate?

Comparison to offline terrorists

Understanding the psychology of terrorists in general is difficult, but it is even more problematic to consider the psychology of cyberterrorists. No in-depth psychological studies of this specific group have been completed to date, but some tentative hypotheses can be suggested.

It is possible that cyberterrorists might be very different to those who engage in traditional terrorist activities. Cyberattacks may allow non-violent individuals to support terrorist campaigns, thus expanding the organisation's potential for harm (Denning, 2010). A person may be attracted to cyberterrorism due to the relative lack of risk when compared to traditional methods of attack (Denning, 2001). As a result of these factors, a cyberterrorist may be a new type of individual in a terrorist organisation, attracting people who would not otherwise have become actively involved.

It is also possible that the possibilities of cyberterrorism may encourage the formation of new terrorist groups (Gordon and Ford, 2003). This could be due to the relatively small amount of finance required, and the fact that such a group could be quickly and easily organised. Gordon and Ford also suggest that the anonymity offered online could be advantageous for terrorist activities.

Summary box 9.7 The psychology of cyberterrorists

- There is relatively little empirical research on the psychology of terrorism, for several practical reasons.
- Empirical evidence has failed to support the existence of specific personality traits in terrorists.
- Kruglanski and Fishman (2006) distinguished between terrorism as a 'syndrome' and as a 'tool'.
  - a syndrome is a 'psychologically meaningful construct with identifiable characteristics on individual and group levels of analysis' (p. 193);
  - a 'tool' represents 'a strategic instrument that any party in a conflict with another may use' (p. 193);
  - there is little evidence for terrorism as a syndrome, but the concept of it as a tool is useful, especially in relation to cognitive factors such as decision making and perception.
- Group dynamics are another very important aspect of terrorist organisations.
- Terrorism is probably determined by a combination of many factors.
- While it was previously thought that terrorists would hold an abnormal psychological profile, this does not generally seem to be the case.
- Cyberterrorists may be very different to those who engage in traditional terrorist activities, due to the different nature of the attack (possibly non-violent and low-risk for the terrorist).
- Cyberterrorism may also encourage the formation of new terrorist groups.

Effects on victims

It is very difficult to predict what the effects of cyberterrorism might be on victims, due to the lack of a successful cyberterrorism attack to date (at least, according to the definition suggested by researchers such as Denning, 2007a). For traditional acts of terrorism, there can be considerable impact on those directly affected, with both DiMaggio and Galea (2006) and Gabriel *et al.* (2007) finding high rates of mental health problems following high-profile traditional attacks. Such problems can extend not only to those injured or present at the attacks, but also to those in the local area, or those who knew victims of the attacks. While post-traumatic stress disorder (PTSD) was prominent, other psychiatric disorders were also noted in those affected.

It is important to note that the threat, or perceived likelihood, of a cyberterrorist attack can also affect society. Stohl (2006) indicates that there has been a gap between the presumed threat of cyberterrorist attack and known online terrorist activities, but suggests that this may be partially caused by confusion between hacktivism and cyberterrorism and a failure to distinguish between cyberterrorist attacks and online terrorist activity. For this reason, it is important that media reporting relating to such activities is conducted responsibly, to prevent fear of cyberterrorism being unnecessarily raised in the general public (media reporting of criminal events has been shown to impact on public perceptions of crime; see, for example, O'Connell, 2002). More importantly, Brown and Silke (2011) describe how certain types of media reporting might escalate terrorist activity, and it is possible that the same might be true for cyberterrorism.

Summary box 9.8 Effects on victims
- As there has been no successful cyberterrorism attack to date, it is difficult to predict what the effects on victims might be.
- Those affected by traditional terrorist attacks can experience high rates of mental health problems, such as PTSD.
- But the perceived likelihood of a cyberterrorist attack can also affect society, raising fear levels.
- Media reporting of cyberterrorism and cyberterrorist risk should be carefully undertaken to avoid unnecessary fear.

Conclusion

The topic of terrorism, and cyberterrorism in particular, requires considerably more empirical research, but the practical difficulties with carrying out such work continue to impede large-scale studies. It should also be borne in mind that it seems unlikely that cyberterrorism will ever be as significant a risk as more traditional forms of attack, although a hybrid attack may cause considerable panic, disruption and/or loss of life.

It is also important that the role of the internet in terrorist activity generally not be underestimated – its facilitation of recruitment, information gathering and dissemination, networking and fundraising results in easier organisation of terrorist activity in general. As Wykes and Harcus (2010) state, the internet 'is the public space of the twenty-first century. Its global reach, chaotic structure, ease of access, anonymity and our increasing dependence on it for the information, education, entertainment and communication it offers makes it appear to be both a perfect tool for terrorists and site of terror activity, worldwide' (p. 216).

Essay questions

(1) 'Cyberterrorism' should only refer to attacks that are violent or cause economic disruption. Discuss.
(2) Are terrorists psychologically normal?
(3) Are there qualitative differences between traditional terrorists and cyberterrorists?
(4) Compare and contrast online and offline radicalisation techniques.
(5) Does media coverage of cyberterrorism create unwarranted fear?

Additional reading

Books and articles

Robert Uda's (2009) book *Cybercrime, Cyberterrorism and Cyberwarfare* examines cyberterrorism from policy, strategy and defence perspectives, but without a primary focus on psychological issues.

Jeff Victoroff and Arie Kruglanski's (2009) book *Psychology of Terrorism: Classic and Contemporary Insights* compiles many key papers examining key issues in the psychology of terrorism, such as radicalisation, motives and behaviour of terrorists.

Andrew Silke's (2011) book *The Psychology of Counter-Terrorism* considers several aspects of terrorism and psychology, along with dedicated chapters on the impact of media and the internet on terrorism.

Websites

The American Psychological Association provides an interesting article by Tori DeAngelis on understanding cyberterrorism: www.apa.org/monitor/2009/11/terrorism.aspx (2009).

The Federal Bureau of Investigation provides resources on terrorism and counterterrorism: www.fbi.gov/about-us/investigate/terrorism.

The United Nations provides resources on counter terrorism: www.un.org/terrorism.

The Economist includes a collection of articles on terrorism: www.economist.com/topics/terrorism.

10 Crime in virtual worlds

Case studies

Adam has been playing an online role-playing game for a number of months. He has been the subject of a number of bullying incidents where he has felt intimidated and targeted by other players. Adam is unsure if these are people he knows in the offline world or if they are strangers. He has been feeling depressed and isolated as a result of these incidents but is unsure what to do about it. Will anyone he tells about this take his concerns seriously or will they just tell him to stop playing 'computer games'?

Kate has spent several months playing the latest fantasy game online, progressing through the levels and building up her inventory. One day she logs in, to discover that her account has been hacked, and all her achievements have vanished. Wandering through the virtual world, she identifies the likely offender, who has suddenly accumulated vast new resources, probably by spending the in-world currency that Kate had saved. Kate wonders what she can do about the theft, and if she will ever get her inventory back.

Chapter overview

Relatively little academic literature has been published relating to crimes that occur in online virtual worlds (Wall and Williams, 2007). Several cases have come to light concerning specific crimes in these environments, including both property offences (such as theft) and crimes against the person (such as sexual assault). The term 'crime' is used in this chapter to describe these events; however they may not necessarily be illegal or criminal events, at least so far as the offline world would consider them to be. This chapter aims to describe these types of virtual crimes and determine if they could and should be considered criminal events. The effects of the crimes on the victims will also be considered, and the necessity for policing virtual worlds will be discussed. In addition, online communities need to consider how to deal with virtual offenders – if their offence has real-world consequences, should they be punished offline, or only in the virtual world?

Understanding virtual worlds

A virtual world, for the purposes of this chapter, refers to any computer-generated representation of three-dimensional space. This does not necessarily mean that the world includes graphics – early virtual worlds such as LambdaMOO were text-based, but the text used described a three-dimensional world. For example, upon entering LambdaMOO as a guest, you are greeted with the following description of your surroundings.

The closet is a dark, cramped space. It appears to be very crowded in here; you keep bumping into what feels like coats, boots, and other people (apparently sleeping). One useful thing that you've discovered in your bumbling about is a metal doorknob set at waist level into what might be a door.

Most modern virtual worlds provide computer-generated graphics in order for the user to more easily visualise their surroundings. Different virtual worlds have different functions. Some are socially based, such as 'Second Life' (www.secondlife.com, created by Linden Labs), where users are encouraged to interact with others and to develop their avatar and virtual property, but where there is no overall aim to the world (such as is often evident in structured video games). Second Life has become so popular that there have been several published accounts of virtual lives within the world (see, for example, Guest, 2007; Meadows, 2008). While Second Life targets adults, other social virtual worlds are aimed at children and adolescents, such as 'Habbo Hotel' (www.habbo.com) and Disney's 'Club Penguin' (www.clubpenguin.com).

Other virtual worlds are more goal-oriented, similar to traditional computer games. Probably the most famous of these is 'World of Warcraft' (or WoW, www.worldofwarcraft.com), a virtual world created by Blizzard Entertainment. World of Warcraft is a fantastical world, where users can choose to be human, or one of many forms of mythological beings, each with various skills and weaknesses. There are various levels of gameplay in WoW through which players progress, and new levels are added regularly to keep user interest high. Similarly, in 'The Legend of Mir' players can choose to be warriors, wizards or other mythical beings, and gameplay is again largely directed by the completion of quests. The now defunct 'Matrix Online' was a mission-oriented game based on the series of *Matrix* films, while 'EVE Online' (www.eveonline.com) is a science fiction-based virtual world. EVE Online is a particularly interesting world from the perspective of virtual crime, as it openly acknowledges the existence of criminal activities between players in the world (Verone, n.d.) and informs players that the games developer and publisher (CCP games) will not intervene in cases of virtual theft (EVElopedia, n.d.)

Many of these virtual worlds are also termed 'massively multiplayer online role-playing games' (MMORPGs), referring to the fact that there can be hundreds or thousands of people playing these games online at a given time, and that each player takes on a 'role' or a character. In some games, such as World of Warcraft and EVE Online, players can form teams and collaborations in order to achieve goals. These collaborations can be fairly permanent in nature (such as the 'guilds' in World of Warcraft), or may be temporary in order to obtain a specific goal, after which the users disband.

Activity 10.1 Identifying a virtual world

Make a list of all the virtual worlds you are familiar with. Consider the case of social networks; do they constitute a virtual world? If you do not consider

Facebook a virtual world in the same way that for example 'World of Warcraft' is; then is Farmville a virtual world? Make a list of all the instances of unacceptable behaviour that may occur in a virtual world and consider which of these you would consider a crime.

Summary box 10.1 Understanding virtual worlds

- Virtual worlds are computer-generated representations of three-dimensional space. They are commonly graphically rich but some early virtual worlds were text-based.
- Different virtual worlds serve different functions. Some are socially based and users are encouraged to interact with others and to develop their avatar and virtual property, but there is no specified goal. Other virtual worlds are more goal-oriented and similar to traditional computer games.
- Some virtual worlds are known as 'massively multiplayer online role-playing games' (MMORPGs). These environments can have hundreds or thousands of people playing online at a given time.
- In some MMORPGs players can form teams and collaborations in order to achieve goals.

Types of crime

In Chapter 2 a distinction was made between activities such as the theft of goods online, which is clearly a crime in the traditionally understood meaning of the term, and private law issues, such as disputes between buyers and sellers of online goods. In virtual worlds it is arguable as to the extent to which the term crime can be used, but there is no doubt that issues of antisocial behaviour or harassment arise, and the 'theft' of virtual goods can cause monetary as well and emotional loss. In this section the distinction is made between property crimes and crimes against the person in online virtual worlds.

Property crime refers to crimes such as larceny, burglary and theft, which normally do not involve violence or significant interaction between the offender and the victim. Crimes against the person, for the purposes of this chapter, involve any crime where there is significant interaction between the offender and victim, such as sexual assault, homicide and violence. Again, it should be noted that in this chapter these terms will be used where the event may be simply a simulation of an offline offence, without actually being a criminal event capable of prosecution in any offline court. As such while terms like 'offender' and 'criminal' will be used throughout, these are utilised in order to easily label the perpetrator of the virtual 'crime', rather than to indicate that they are offline offenders or have committed any actual infringements of the offline laws of any country. Indeed, as outlined in the case of EVE Online above, in some cases these actions may be considered part of normal gameplay, and while not actively encouraged, they may not be subject to specific penalty either.

Property crimes

There have been several instances of property crimes in online communities (BBC News Online, 2005, 2007; Hof, 2006). One case involved CopyBot – software which enabled users of Second Life to copy objects and creations of other users (Hof, 2006), instead of paying for them. As this case involved objects with specific monetary value in Linden dollars, which can be exchanged for US dollars, this is an example of a case which could be tried offline. A similar case occurred in Habbo Hotel in 2007, where Dutch teenagers allegedly stole €4,000 worth of virtual furniture by tricking other users into divulging their passwords (BBC News Online, 2007). In this case, at least one teenager was eventually arrested.

However, in some cases, offline authorities may not be able or willing to take action following a theft in a virtual world. One example of this occurred in 2005 when a Chinese 'The Legend of Mir' gamer, Zhu Caoyuan, sold a 'dragon sabre' which he had been loaned by Qiu Chengwei (BBC News Online, 2005). The sword had been earned through the investment of considerable time and effort playing the online game. Despite the sale value of the sword (approximately £460), the police claimed that it was not real property when Chengwei tried to make a complaint. Caoyuan offered to pay the money received from the sale to Chengwei, but despite this, Chengwei stabbed Caoyuan in the chest and killed him.

This case is interesting, both for the lack of action that the police took following the alleged crime, and the extreme reaction from Chengwei, despite the offer to repay the money. It demonstrates that the dragon sabre meant considerably more to Chengwei than its monetary value, and that he obviously experienced an extreme psychological reaction to the event.

Crimes against the person

I was new and on the receiving end of disturbing sexual behaviour. A male avatar teleported right in front of my character. He was so close that my avatar's body prevented me from seeing that he was nude. He stepped back, and then rammed my avatar so hard she was pushed back several steps. Before my character had come to a standstill he was coming at her again. After ramming her a second time he walked several steps past her and to the right, and then turned so that he was in profile. By stepping further away and turning he ensured that I, a [sic] offline, flesh and blood person, was able to see that he was naked and had rammed my avatar with an erect penis. Although simulated, it was a deliberate, calculated, and practiced act of violence. It happened in seconds. I felt the person behind the avatar thought he had raped or simulated rape on my character, and wanted me to know that's what he had done.

(Jay, 2007)

This event, described by a Second Life player on one of its mailing lists, was clearly disturbing for the human user behind the female avatar that was attacked. The victim goes on to express frustration at the inability to report her victimisation, as the attacker had used an unusually long name for their character, which she had not had time to note before the attacking avatar disappeared, and also because there was insufficient space in the complaints form of the online community to describe the details of the event. She later found her thoughts returning to the incident, even though she tried to forget it and remind herself that she had not been physically harmed. Hers is not the only case of online sexual assault.

Probably the most famous example is the case of Mr Bungle, as described by Julian Dibbell (1993), in which a series of sexual assaults occur in the online world Lambda-MOO. A character called Mr Bungle, described as 'a fat, oleaginous, Bisquick-faced clown', attacked several other players in the text-based online world using 'voodoo dolls', subprograms that attribute actions to other players' characters that they did not intend. Mr Bungle was actually controlled by several university students acting as one to direct the attacks (as clarified by Dibbell, 1998). Bungle's rampage continued until he was eventually stopped by a more senior player. The Bungle case is particularly interesting because of the reported after-effects on the victims. One, 'legba', reported severe distress in the aftermath of the attack. Several other players reported their anger at the events, to the extent that many called for Mr Bungle to be 'toaded' (banned from the virtual world, with the character deleted). Interestingly, Mr Bungle himself indicated that the assault 'was purely a sequence of events with no consequence on my RL (real-life) existence', and as such the virtual attack seems to have had considerably less impact on him than it did on his victims.

The calls to toad Mr Bungle led to debates among the community members, with some arguing that in the virtual world, rape had not been criminalised, and so it could not be considered punishable. It was also queried if the university students who had created the character of Mr Bungle could be punished offline, perhaps under laws concerning obscene phone calls, or by punishment from the university authorities, although this course of action did not seem to be popular among the players involved. While no final decision was made by the players, eventually a 'wizard' acted alone and toaded Mr Bungle independently. As such, those who played Mr Bungle were punished in the virtual world, where their 'crimes' took place, but not offline, where the effects were experienced by the victims. Eventually LambdaMOO developed a ballot system, where players could vote for the toading of a 'criminal' character, and if sufficient votes were received, then the wizards would complete the request. Interestingly, one of the players who controlled Mr Bungle eventually returned to Lambda-MOO with a new character, Dr Jest, who also behaved in an unacceptable fashion, although he did not engage in sexual assaults. In spite of this, the residents of LambdaMOO did not vote in sufficient numbers to toad Dr Jest. It appears that, at least in the minds of the residents of LambdaMOO, the character was the entity that needed to be punished, not the player who controlled that character.

More recently, in 2007, Belgian police commenced an investigation into an alleged rape in the online world Second Life (Lynn, 2007; Sipress, 2007). While publicly available details regarding that specific case are rare, to the extent that several online commentators queried whether the report was a hoax, it provoked widespread discussion of online rape. Some online reports about the incident demonstrate mixed views about the seriousness of online rape. While it is generally considered to be a negative event, it is difficult to determine the severity of the attack. No writer suggests that it is as serious as offline sexual assault, and some suggest that the victims should just try to forget about it, and move on, but others see worrying trends. Some note that it is illegal to engage sexually with a minor online, and therefore wonder if simulations of adult rape should be treated similarly (Lynn, 2007).

One crime in virtual worlds which is considered illegal in several offline jurisdictions is virtual age play. This can be covered under child pornography laws in some countries. The most famous example of this type of offence is the Wonderland area of Second Life, where 'child' avatars engaged in sexual behaviour with other avatars, both child and adult (Adams, 2010). Although all the players controlling the avatars may be over the legal age of consent, laws regulate the depiction of even simulated images of child sexual abuse. There are therefore queries as to which crimes in virtual worlds should be considered offline crimes, and which should not.

Summary box 10.2 Types of crime

- Crimes can be classified as crime against the person or as property crimes.
- Property crimes often involve theft of either online goods or result in the loss of offline goods.
- Crimes against the person can include bullying, assault or even online rape.

Incidence and motivation

As so little is known about virtual crimes, much analysis regarding these offences is speculative in nature, and requires empirical investigation. Whitson and Doyle (2008) outline several reasons that may explain why so little research has been done examining crime in virtual worlds. These include a perception that the worlds are seen as too trivial for study, the speed of technological change, the need for researchers to participate in the virtual worlds, difficulties in verifying participant data and difficulties in achieving ethical approval (pp. 89–90).

For instance, it is impossible to predict how much virtual crime exists, for several reasons. Firstly, it is likely that a significant number of victims of these offences do not report their victimisation, for a variety of reasons. This may be because they are unaware of their victimisation (perhaps an item was stolen from their inventory and they had not noticed its absence), or they may feel that it is unlikely that the authorities in the virtual world will do anything about the event (such as EVE Online's policy not to interfere in theft cases) or they may consider the event too trivial to report at all. Many may also feel that it is their own fault that they have been victimised, or that they will not be taken seriously if they report the incident (see the discussion on self-blame and victim-blaming below). So it is to be expected that there is a relatively high 'dark figure' of crimes in virtual worlds (that is, crimes which have occurred but do not appear in any official statistics).

The motives of the offenders are also largely unknown. For some virtual property offenders, it is doubtless to help them to progress in the game faster. This is most likely the case for most thefts in EVE Online. In the case of the Legend of Mir 3 dragon sabre, the motive seems to have been real-world financial gain, as Caoyuan sold the sword for an actual currency. The actions of Mr Bungle seem to have been a prank by a group of college students, which bears some resemblance to findings regarding offline gang rape. Scully and Marolla (1993) indicate that most gang rapists are in their late teens or early twenties when convicted, with part of the appeal of the rape involving the sense of 'male camaraderie engendered by participating collectively in a dangerous activity' (p. 39). The rape in Second Life described above appears to have been motivated by a desire for power, and so might be explained by Groth *et al.*'s (1977) taxonomy of rapists as either power-assurance or power-assertive. However, all this is speculation based on second- and third-hand accounts of online events, and it would be dangerous to rely on these conclusions. Similarly, there is currently too little information available regarding offenders in virtual worlds to allow conclusions to be drawn regarding the psychological profile or personality characteristics of these individuals. Until more empirical work is done to examine the motives and psychology of these individuals, it is impossible to provide any more conclusive answers to this question.

Summary box 10.3 Incidence and motivation

- A complete picture of the nature and extent of online crime in virtual worlds is difficult to achieve due to insufficient research, its not being taken seriously by some and lack of reporting.
- The motivations for online crime in virtual worlds are complex but include greed, ambition to accelerate progress through a game and a sense of empowerment or domination.

Effects on victims

Victimisation in online virtual worlds should not be considered as severe as if a similar offence occurred offline. There can be no doubt that a victim of an offline sexual assault is likely to experience post-victimisation symptoms that are far more severe than those of an online victim. On the other hand, it would be an error to believe that an online victimisation has no effect on the victim at all. In addition to this, it appears that crimes in virtual worlds appear to have a more severe impact on some victims than others. Yet the effects of this 'virtual victimisation' on the person, and the reasons why it is more severe for some than others, have not been considered in detail. It has been repeatedly demonstrated that victims of offline crimes can experience several negative consequences of their victimisation – including post-traumatic stress disorder (PTSD), self-blame and victim blaming by others (Hoyle and Zedner, 2007; Scarpa *et al.*, 2006). It could be argued that the more the person feels immersed online (the greater the sense of *presence* in the online environment), the more likely it is that the victim experiences similar after-effects to offline victims. If this is the case, then greater care needs to be taken in online virtual worlds to ensure the safety and psychological well-being of their users, particularly after a crime in an online virtual world occurs.

Victim blaming appears to be particularly common for crime in online virtual worlds, with many arguing that victims of crime in online virtual worlds could easily escape. In Second Life, it is possible to engage in rape fantasies, where another player has control over the 'victim's' avatar, but this is usually only possible with consent. It has been suggested that some individuals have been tricked into giving their consent, but even bearing this in mind, there has been widespread criticism by online commentators of anyone who allows an attack to take place, as it is alleged that it is always possible to 'teleport' away from any situation. Even if teleportation fails, it is always possible for the victim to exit the game, disconnect from the network connection or turn off their computer and thus end the offence. It is clear that victims of crime in online virtual worlds do seem to experience some extent of victim blaming by others – they are in ways being blamed for not escaping their attacker. Those victims who experience the greatest degree of presence – those who are most immersed in the game – are probably those who are least likely to think of closing the application to escape. It should also be considered that a victim may experience discomfort at being victimised, even if they do escape relatively quickly. As in offline crime, the initial stages of the attack may be confusing or upsetting enough to cause significant distress, even if the victim manages to escape quickly.

There is also some evidence of self-blaming by various victims of crime in online virtual worlds. Some victims refer to their relative naivety in the online world prior to victimisation (Jay, 2007), and indicate that if they had been more experienced they might have realised what was happening sooner. There are also suggestions that a victim who is inexperienced with the virtual world's user interface may inadvertently give control of their avatar to another user. Considerably more evidence needs to be completed on this topic before a definitive conclusion can be reached.

There is anecdotal evidence of limited symptoms of acute stress disorder (ASD) in some victims of crime in online virtual worlds, including accounts of intrusive memories, emotional numbing and upset from victims of virtual sexual assault (Lynn, 2007; Sipress, 2007). Some explanation of this is provided by Williams (2006) who highlights the effects of 'speech acts' in computer-mediated communication. He states that the 'possibility for the abusive illocutionary act to simultaneously convey action in speech means that it does more than represent violence; it is violence' (p. 101). Williams (2006) also indicates that 'it is important to understand that events within online settings are not wholly separate from those in the offline world' (p. 99), and he goes on to analyse the case of Mr Bungle with this in mind. Nevertheless, while it is impossible to make an accurate judgement without a full psychological evaluation, it seems very unlikely that these victims would receive a clinical diagnosis of either ASD or PTSD. This is because there is no mention of either flashbacks or heightened autonomic arousal (possibly due to the lack of real danger to the victim's life), nor does it appear that the symptoms lasted for very long (in most cases the symptoms appear to reduce or dissipate within a few hours or days). There are also several accounts of individuals who have experienced online victimisation but who do not see it as a serious assault and do not appear to experience any severe negative reaction. Those most at risk appear to be those who have previously experienced offline sexual assault, where the online attack has served to remind the victim of the previous attack. As such, while not a major risk, the possibility of developing ASD or PTSD is a factor that should be monitored in future victims of serious online assaults, especially those who have been previously victimised offline.

Finally, there is substantial anecdotal evidence of a need for retribution in victims of crime in online virtual worlds. The victims of Mr Bungle called for his toading, the Belgian victim of the rape in Second Life reported the incident to the police and Chengwei stabbed the alleged thief when he failed to achieve a satisfactory response from the police after the sale of the virtual sabre. This is possibly the strongest evidence that victims of crimes in virtual worlds experience similar psychological reactions to victims of offline offences, although again, empirical evidence is lacking to date. This also raises the issue of determining suitable punishments for perpetrators of crime in online virtual worlds, which will be considered in more detail later in this chapter.

Probably the single most important risk factor for determining how severe the victim's reaction will be is *presence* – how immersed the user feels they are in the environment. Kirwan (2009b) describes some of the literature that supports this. Jung (2008) found that presence can impact on members' intentions to participate in Second Life, and also emphasised the importance of vividness of the environment in increasing presence, a point also noted by Bente *et al.* (2008). Bente *et al.* (2008) also noted that the use of an avatar led to increased perceived intimacy, emotionally based trust and visual attention, particularly in the early phase of interaction, and so it seems that when controlling avatars users put themselves at greater emotional vulnerability. Pearce (2006) also notes that users of online virtual worlds demonstrate some significant dimensions of presence. Among these, she notes that some avatars' identities are partially constructed through a system of social feedback within the community, and so the online representation of the self is partially formed by how other avatars interact with it. It is conceivable, therefore, that a negative experience, such as an online victimisation, may influence the development of the user's online identity. Pearce also notes that after a period of time in an online community, users feel that they are entitled to citizenship, and to have their rights protected, especially if they play a part in creating the virtual world, as residents of Second Life are encouraged to do. This has very obvious repercussions for virtual victimisation – the cybercitizen has come to expect that they will be protected and cared for, because of their investment of time and energy into the online community.

It has previously been demonstrated that presence in virtual environments can induce specific emotional reactions in the user (Riva *et al.*, 2007), a phenomenon which is utilised by clinical psychologists when virtual environments are used during therapy for phobias, PTSD and other psychological difficulties (Josman *et al.*, 2006; Wiederhold and Wiederhold, 2005). Virtual environments have also been demonstrated to elicit behaviours indicative of fear of crime (Park *et al.*, 2008) and to heighten the realism of sexually threatening role plays designed to help college women resist sexual attacks (Jouriles *et al.*, 2009). Certain emotional states and personality traits can also increase the sense of presence in an immersive virtual world, including anxiety (Bouchard *et al.*, 2008). If the same applies to online virtual worlds, it could raise the question of whether the effects of an online crime, particularly a sexual or violent one, may be self-perpetuating.

It is likely that the more time spent in the online community, the more likely the victim will have a severe emotional reaction to the crime. If a person has invested heavily in their avatar, truly seeing it as an extension of themselves instead of just a computer-generated image, then their reaction could be understandably severe. This may be particularly so if others have witnessed the offence, as happened in the case of Mr Bungle – it may add a sense of shame and embarrassment, and a fear that their avatar will be permanently associated with the victimisation. On the other hand, it is likely that those who are merely experimenting in the online community, who feel less immersed in the virtual world and who have not built up an online life in that world, will emerge from an online victimisation relatively unscathed, though perhaps a little more cautious in the future. Much of the shame, self-blame and secondary victimisation could easily be removed by simply deleting the victimised avatar and replacing it with a new one. However, this course of action is not always ideal – the user would be unlikely to feel a sense of retribution, as they may not feel that their 'attacker' had been adequately punished. It should also be remembered that this reaction would likely be considerably more difficult and less desirable for the dedicated user of the virtual world, who would have to start again with new online acquaintances and social groups in order to have a truly fresh start.

> ### Activity 10.2 Representations of the self online
> Review the online representation (avatar, Facebook picture, etc.) of your classmates/colleagues. How many use a realistic representation of themselves, or an idealised image, or a fantasy or unreal representation. Do you think there is a relation to their use of online representation and their sense of presence online?

It should be considered that some personality traits such as locus of control and dissociation, which have been shown to increase the sense of presence in immersive virtual environments (Murray *et al.*, 2007), have also been linked with the development of PTSD after crimes and traumatic events (Hood and Carter, 2008; Marmar *et al.*, 2007). As such, further research into the relationship between these potentially intervening variables could provide further insight into the effects of victimisation of crime in virtual worlds. While considering personality variables, it is important to appreciate that interactions have been noted between certain personality traits and increased levels of PTSD. These include low self-esteem (Adams and Boscarino, 2006), neuroticism (Cox *et al.*, 2004; Fauerbach *et al.*, 2000; Lawrence and Fauerbach, 2003), low levels of extraversion (Fauerbach *et al.*, 2000), openness to experience (Kamphuis *et al.*, 2003) and agreeableness (Talbert *et al.*, 1993). However, it should be noted that some of these studies examined correlations rather than causality between the factors, and so remain inconclusive.

Summary box 10.4 Effects on victims

- Online crimes can cause post-victimisation symptoms.
- The greater a person's immersion in a virtual world the more severe post-victimisation symptoms can be.
- Victim blaming is common for online crimes as there is a perception that a victim can easily remove themselves from harm.
- Acute stress disorder has been observed in victims of online crime; this appears to be more common in those who have suffered an offline crime experience.

Victim aid

These reactions by the victims of crime in online virtual worlds suggest that it may be useful if some form of victim aid is put in place to assist them with the process of dealing with their difficulties. This aid could take a number of different forms, including help with reporting the offence, emotional, financial and legal assistance and the possible introduction of restorative justice.

Victims of offline offences normally have relatively straightforward procedures available to them for the reporting of criminal offences. Police helplines, patrols and stations are often the initial ports of call for a recent victim of offline crime. On the other hand, in online worlds, the reporting procedure may be less clear, and the user may need to invest time and energy to determine how to report their experience. Although many virtual worlds have procedures for reporting misconduct, these are not always found to be satisfactory by victims if they wish to report more serious offences (Jay, 2007). Similarly, reporting the occurrence to the administrators of the virtual world alone may not meet the victim's need for retribution, especially if they feel that they have experienced offline harm because of the crime in the online virtual world. In those cases, the victim may prefer to approach the offline authorities, as in the Belgian rape case and the theft of the dragon-sabre. To aid victims in this regard, many online worlds need to be clearer about their complaints procedures and the possible outcomes of these. They may also need to be clearer about the possible repercussions of reporting crime in online virtual worlds to offline authorities.

Victims of offline crimes receive varying degrees of emotional, financial and legal aid, depending on the offence that occurred. In some cases, this aid is provided through charitable organisations, such as Victim Support, sometimes through government organisations and also through informal supports such as family and friends. Financial aid is probably the least applicable to victims of crime in online virtual worlds, as although theft of property can occur, it is unlikely to result in severe poverty for the victim. Also, because items with a designated offline value are starting to be recognised by real-world authorities, there is some possibility of financial recompense. Legal aid, both in terms of the provision of a lawyer and in terms of help in understanding the court system, can also be provided to offline victims. The legal situation is somewhat less clear for victims of crime in online virtual worlds, particularly where the punishment is meted out in the virtual world, as in the Mr Bungle case. In that event, the victims and other users were required to effectively set up a legal system themselves. But from the cases that have been publicised to date, it appears that the greatest need for assistance that online victims have is for emotional support. In some cases victims have sought this from other members of the online community, although the evidence regarding victim-blaming in online virtual worlds suggests that such blaming may in fact result in increased upset for victims, instead of alleviating their distress.

One system that may help to alleviate any emotional anguish for the victim is restorative justice. This refers to processes involving mediation between the offender and the victim (Howitt, 2009). Rather than focusing on the criminal activity itself, it focuses on the harm caused by the crime, and more specifically, the victims of the crime. It often involves a mediated meeting between the victim and the offender, where both are allowed to express sentiments and explanations, and the offender is given the opportunity to apologise. The aims of restorative justice are a satisfied victim, an offender who feels that they have been fairly dealt with and reintegration of the community, rather than financial compensation or specific punishment. If the mediation does not meet the satisfaction of all involved, alternative punishments can then be considered. It would appear that the restorative justice approach is ideally suited for many crimes in online virtual worlds, as it allows the victim to feel that they have been heard, while allowing the community to remain cohesive. However, it should be noted that not all victims of offline crimes have felt satisfied by the process (Wemmers and Cyr, 2006), and so it is not suitable for all criminal events.

Summary box 10.5 Victim aid

- In online virtual worlds, reporting procedures for criminal activities may be unclear. Some have procedures for reporting misconduct but these are not always found to be satisfactory by victims.
- Online virtual worlds need to be clearer about their complaints procedures, and the possible outcomes of these. They may also need to be clearer about the possible repercussions of reporting crime in online virtual worlds to offline authorities.
- The greatest need for assistance that online victims have is often emotional support. In some cases victims have sought this from other members of the online community, but the evidence of victim-blaming for crimes in online virtual worlds may result in increased upset for victims.
- A restorative justice approach may be suited for crimes in online virtual worlds as it allows the victim to feel that they have been heard. Restorative justice focuses on the harm caused by the crime and, more specifically, the victims of the crime, and may involve a mediated meeting between the victim and the offender.

Policing, prevention and punishment

Police investigations and 'patrols' of online worlds are one possible approach to policing crimes in virtual worlds. On the other hand, many individuals would be displeased that taxes and police resources were being spent patrolling and investigating crime in virtual worlds while offline crimes often go unsolved. There is no doubt that online crimes with definite offline applications and risks should be under the remit of the appropriate police force. Yet in some cases the line is blurred – if a virtual attack is interpreted as an actual threat against the victim offline (where both the victim perceives it as a threat against their offline self, and the perpetrator intends it as an offline threat), it can be considered illegal in many jurisdictions.

As previously discussed, if an item is stolen in a virtual world, and the item can be judged to have an actual monetary value offline, then it may also be possible to prosecute the thief offline (Hof, 2006). However, the line between an offline crime and an event which is purely virtual (and hence not necessarily a 'crime' in the legal sense), is less coherent when the damages caused to the victim are emotional or psychological in nature, without any physical or monetary harm being caused. It is for these cases in particular that legal systems need to consider what the most appropriate course of action should be.

There are many ways in which this problem could be addressed. It is likely that each virtual world would need to be policed by separate law enforcement agencies, if only because different worlds have differing social norms and definitions of acceptable and unacceptable behaviours. For example, it would not be an acceptable solution if players in an online war game such as Battlefield began to sue each other for 'avatar-slaughter' when they lost, especially as the avatars respawn after a short time. Similarly, the piracy and theft which is considered normal in EVE Online should probably not be policed. Conversely, if the same virtual murder or theft occurred in an online world aimed at young children, such as Club Penguin, it would obviously be much less acceptable.

With this in mind, one solution might be that the creator of each virtual world is required to put in place a strict set of laws outlining what is and is not acceptable in the world, and to ensure that the virtual world is patrolled sufficiently well that all wrongdoings are observed and punished appropriately. This solution is probably particularly appropriate if the creators of the virtual world are profiting financially from its users. These actions would also condone a 'big brother' approach to life online, which could be strongly opposed by many cyber-citizens. It may be that the best alternative is to make cybersocieties mirrors of the offline world, where the police rely greatly on the citizens of the relevant society to report misconduct. As in real life, this approach may be open to abuse as one or more players could make unfounded allegations against another. In extreme cases, there may be a market for 'cyber-lawyers' who defend avatars against allegations by others or mount a case for cyber-prosecutions in virtual worlds. Finally, it needs to be considered what penalty should be imposed for committing a crime in a virtual world.

If a person carries out a crime in a virtual world, but their offence has real-world consequences for the victim or society (be they emotional, financial or physical), should the offender be punished offline, in the virtual world, or both? Probably the best solution would involve the restorative justice approach outlined above, but there may be cases where this technique is considered inadequate or fails to satisfy those involved.

It has been argued that virtual punishment is the appropriate recourse for crimes which occur in an online community (McKinnon, 1997). As was seen in the Mr Bungle case, banishment from an online community is often considered the most severe punishment possible in virtual worlds. This punishment is easily overcome, however, simply by creating a new avatar. Even if the offender's internet protocol (IP) address is blocked from using the virtual world, it is relatively easy to obtain a new IP address from which to access the world.

In theft cases where the item has a real-world value, it may be possible in some jurisdictions to enforce an offline punishment – perhaps a fine or a prison term. But to prosecute cases such as Mr Bungle offline would require that laws are rewritten, perhaps to include malicious infliction of emotional distress using computer-mediated communication (Brenner, 2001). It seems unlikely that these changes will be implemented unless victimisation in virtual worlds becomes a recurring complaint by users who feel that they have been persecuted in some way, to the extent that the criminal justice system finds it difficult to ignore.

Activity 10.3 Penalties for inappropriate actions

List all of the activities that you would consider to be inappropriate in a role-playing virtual world such as Second Life, and outline what penalty if any should be applied.

Summary box 10.6 Policing, prevention and punishment

- Online crimes with definite offline applications and risks should be under the remit of the appropriate police force.
- The distinction between an offline crime and an event which is purely virtual is less clear when the damages caused to the victim are emotional or psychological in nature, without any physical or monetary harm being caused.
- It is possible that each virtual world needs separate 'policing' as different worlds have differing social norms and definitions of acceptable and unacceptable behaviours.
- Creators of each virtual world should put in place a strict set of laws or social norms outlining what is and what is not acceptable, and ensure that the virtual world is patrolled sufficiently well that all wrongdoings are observed and punished appropriately.
- It may be that cybersocieties should mirror the offline world, where the police rely greatly on the citizens of the relevant society to report misconduct, and that virtual punishment is the appropriate recourse for crimes which occur in an online community.

Future trends and research

There is very little empirical evidence examining the topic of crime in virtual worlds. Research needs to be conducted in order to determine how widespread crime in online virtual worlds actually is, and to establish how severely most victims react to it. The factors which lead to more severe reactions should then be identified. If crime in online virtual worlds is determined to be a serious problem, with substantial effects on victims, then a greater focus needs to be placed on how online communities deal with this problem, and if legislation needs to be changed to reflect the psychological and emotional consequences of victimisation.

In terms of victim impact it would seem particularly important to examine what aspects of such an offence lead to psychological distress in victims, so that attempts can be made to reduce this distress for others. Presence seems to be a key variable that needs to be examined, and particularly the effect of the realism of the avatar and the virtual world in which the crime takes place. This is a particularly important consideration given the improvement in three-dimensional graphics of recent years.

These realistic avatars increase the sense of presence as they better reflect the appearance of the user. Research also indicates that the more realistic the behaviours of avatars, the greater the sense of presence experienced by the user (Garau *et al.*, 2003; Vinyagamoorthy *et al.*, 2004). Victims may consequently feel the effects of an assault more acutely than if they had chosen an avatar which did not resemble them physically. Second Life and other graphical online worlds are capable of generating very realistic representations of the user, and as such probably increase the victim's sense of presence. It is possible that by seeing the graphical representation of the self attacked, the effects of victimisation may be increased. This raises questions about the future of online virtual worlds – the more realistic they become, the more likely it is that the victim can be negatively affected. As technology progresses and virtual worlds and avatars become more realistic, it is important that the reactions of victims of offences in virtual worlds are carefully considered.

Law enforcement agencies and criminal justice systems are likely to need to develop strategies to deal with criminal events in virtual worlds. While there are some suggested strategies outlined above, these would need to be tested in the field in order to determine their true effectiveness – as, with many plans, those that seem feasible and suitable in theory may not be appropriate when put into practice.

Adams (2010) raises the question as to the impact of the likely emergence of haptic interfaces for virtual worlds. Haptic devices provide feedback to the user through tactile sensations, such as force or motion. Some haptic devices already exist for certain worlds, such as a gaming vest developed by the University of Pennsylvania which allows users to feel the physical effects of being shot in a game (Mancheno, 2010). If these devices become more common, and are used in a wider variety of worlds, then users may feel an online virtual assault as well as seeing it occur, which would possibly lead to a greater psychological reaction on the part of the victim.

Finally, some consideration is required of what may happen if users eventually control a single avatar which is used in several online virtual worlds. Should the same penalties be applied across all virtual worlds, or only the one in which the crime took place? This is a complex question to answer, especially given the varying nature of acceptable behaviours in different virtual worlds.

Conclusion

Up to this time, cybersocieties have in many cases been forced to make the rules up as they go, trying to deal with individual cases of crime in online virtual worlds as and when they arise, often without the action being criminalised in the community beforehand. In some cases this has been relatively successful, but in others victims of crimes in virtual worlds appear to experience quite serious emotional reactions to their victimisation, with limited acceptance of their reaction from others. As online virtual worlds become more realistic, the associated increased sense of presence may also lead to increased victim suffering. With increasing numbers of both children and adults joining multiple online communities, it is essential that this problem be addressed, so that adequate protection can be provided to the cybercitizen.

Essay questions

(1) What factors influence the feeling of presence in online virtual worlds?
(2) What are the potential psychological and economic side-effects of victimisation of crime in an online virtual world?
(3) Should online virtual worlds be policed by offline police forces?
(4) Is restorative justice a suitable method for dealing with crimes in virtual worlds?

Additional reading

Castronova surveys the growing popularity of virtual reality worlds in such online games as World of Warcraft and virtual social environments such as Second Life. He looks at how online virtual worlds have come to represent new social, political and economic environments that have captured the attention of millions of people:

Castronova, E. (2008). *Exodus to the Virtual World: How Online Fun Is Changing Reality*. New York: Palgrave Macmillan.

This paper highlights the emerging threats in cyberspace, with particular reference to financial crime in the virtual world, which have real life implications. It goes on to recommend ways in which the threat may be mitigated:

Keene, S. D. (2011). Emerging threats: financial crime in the virtual world. *Journal of Money Laundering Control*, **15**, 25–37. Retrieved from http://dx.doi.org/10.1108/13685201211194718.

Meadows addresses questions such as the nature of avatars, why there are nearly a billion of them, and who is using them. Can avatars be used to connect with people, or do they just isolate us? And as we become more like our avatars do they become more like us? He seeks to alter the way simple online profiles are seen and looks at the idea of avatars as part of daily life:

Meadows, M. S. (2008). *I, Avatar: the Culture and Consequences of Having a Second Life*. Berkeley, CA: New Riders.

This book brings together work from relevant disciplines to form a reference guide for practitioners, students and researchers interested in how we interact in computer-generated environments. It contains contributions from key people in this area and presents their findings in a way which is accessible to readers who are new to this field or who come from related areas:

Schroeder, R. (2002). *The Social Life of Avatars: Presence and Interaction in Shared Virtual Environments*. London: Springer

This article examines the boundaries between the real and the virtual worlds as they become blurred in the age of social networking and online fantasy games. It questions whether virtual activities should have consequences in the real world. It goes on to discuss whether the virtual/real divide is an excuse for state surveillance:

Simpson, B. (2011). What happens online stays online? Virtual punishment in the real world. *Information and Communications Technology Law*, **20**, 3–17. Retrieved from http://dx.doi.org/10.1080/13600834.2011.557494.

Young and Whitty describe how cyberspace is composed of a multitude of different spaces where users can represent themselves in many divergent ways. Moral questions arise such as why in a video game is it more acceptable to murder or maim than rape? This book provides a theoretical framework that helps us understand why such distinctions are typically made, and explores the psychological impact of violating offline taboos within cyberspace:

Young, G. and Whitty, M. (2012). *Transcending Taboos: a Moral and Psychological Examination of Cyberspace*. London and New York: Routledge.

Websites

Future Crimes provides resources on virtual world crimes: www.futurecrimes.com/resources/virtual-world-crime.

Drakontas and Drexel University have been awarded a grant by the US Department of Justice, Office of Justice Programs' Bureau of Justice Assistance to develop and deliver training courses to help law enforcement personnel identify, investigate and prevent crimes involving virtual worlds and online gaming communities. The Policy Brief about Crimes in Virtual Worlds and Online Gaming Worlds (March 2012) is at: http://drakontas.com/articles/Real%20Crimes%20in%20Virtual%20Worlds.pdf.

REFERENCES

Abbott, K. W. and Snidal, D. (2000). Hard and soft law in international governance. *International Organization*, **54**, 421–56.

Adams, A. A. (2010). Virtual sex with child avatars. In C. Wankel and S. Malleck (eds.) *Emerging Ethical Issues of Life in Virtual Worlds*. Charlotte, NC: Information Age Publishing (pp. 55–72).

Adams, R. E. and Boscarino, J. A. (2006). Predictors of PTSD and delayed PTSD after disaster: the impact of exposure and psychosocial resources. *Journal of Nervous and Mental Disease*, **194**, 485–93.

Ainsworth, P. B. (2001). *Offender Profiling and Crime Analysis*. Cullompton, UK: Willan Publishing.

Ajzen, I. (1988). *Attitudes, Personality and Behaviour*. Milton Keynes, UK: Open University Press.
(1991). The theory of planned behaviour. *Organisational Behaviour and Human Decision Processes*, **50**, 179–211.

Alexy, E. M., Burgess, A. W., Baker, T. and Smoyak, S. A. (2005). Perceptions of cyberstalking among college students. *Brief Treatment and Crisis Intervention*, 5, 279–89.

Alison, L. and Kebbell, M. R. (2006). Offender profiling: limits and potential. In M. R. Kebbell and G. M. Davies (eds.), *Practical Psychology for Forensic Investigations and Prosecutions*. Chichester, UK: John Wiley and Sons (pp. 152–63).

Alison, L. J., Smith, M. D., Eastoman, O. and Rainbow, L. (2003). Toulmin's philosophy of argument and its relevance to offender profiling. *Journal of Psychology, Crime and Law*, 9, 173–81.

Al-Rafee, S. and Rouibah, K. (2010). The fight against digital piracy: an experiment. *Telematics and Informatics*, **27**, 283–92.

American Psychiatric Association (2000). *Diagnostic and Statistical Manual of Mental Disorders: Fourth Edition, Text Revision*. Washington, DC: American Psychiatric Association.
(2011). *DSM-5: The Future of Psychiatric Diagnosis*. Retrieved from www.dsm5.org/Pages/Default.aspx.

Amir, M. (1971). *Patterns of Forcible Rape*. Chicago, IL: University of Chicago Press.

Anti-Phishing Working Group (APWG) (23 December 2011). *Phishing Activity Trends Report, 1st Half, 2011*. Retrieved from www.antiphishing.org/reports/apwg_trends_report_h1_2011.pdf.

Archer, N., Sproule, S., Yuan, Y., Guo, K. and Xiang, J. (2012). *Identity Theft and Fraud: Evaluating and Managing Risk*. University of Ottawa Press.

Armstrong, T. A. and Boutwell, B. B. (2012). Low resting heart rate and rational choice: integrating biological correlates of crime in criminological theories. *Journal of Criminal Justice*, **40**, 31–9.

Ashcroft, J. (May 2001). *Stalking and Domestic Violence: Report to Congress*. Retrieved from www.ncjrs.gov/pdffiles1/ojp/186157.pdf.

Babchishin, K. M., Hanson, R. K. and Hermann, C. A. (2011). The characteristics of online sex offenders: a meta-analysis. *Sex Abuse*, **23**, 92–123.

Bachmann, M. (2010). The risk propensity and rationality of computer hackers. *International Journal of Cyber Criminology*, **4** (1–2), 643–56.

Bandura, A. (1965). Influence of models' reinforcement contingencies on the acquisition of imitative behaviours. *Journal of Personality and Social Psychology*, **1**, 589–95.

Baron, S. W. (2003). Self-control, social consequences and criminal behaviour: street youth and the general theory of crime. *Journal of Research in Crime and Delinquency*, **40**, 403–25.

Bates, A. and Metcalf, C. (2007). A psychometric comparison of internet and non-internet sex offenders from a community treatment sample. *Journal of Sexual Aggression*, **13**, 11–20.

BBC News Online (31 March 2005). 'Game theft' led to fatal attack. Retrieved from www.news.bbc.co.uk/2/hi/technology/4397159.stm.

(14 November 2007). 'Virtual theft' leads to arrest. Retrieved from www.news.bbc.co.uk/2/hi/technology/7094764.stm.

(30 July 2008). Profile: Gary McKinnon. Retrieved from www.news.bbc.co.uk/2/hi/uk_news/7839338.stm.

(9 June 2009). Hacker 'too fragile' to extradite. Retrieved from www.news.bbc.co.uk/2/hi/uk_news/8090789.stm.

(28 July 2009). Hacker's 'moral crusade' over UFO. Retrieved from www.news.bbc.co.uk/go/pr/fr/-/2/hi/uk_news/8172842.stm.

(31 July 2009). Hacker loses extradition appeal. Retrieved from www.news.bbc.co.uk/go/pr/fr/-/2/hi/uk_news/8177561.stm.

(10 December 2009). Hacker to appeal over extradition. Retrieved from www.news.bbc.co.uk/2/hi/uk_news/8406643.stm.

(25 January 2010). $2 million file sharing fine slashed to $54,000. Retrieved from www.news.bbc.co.uk/2/hi/technology/8478305.stm.

(7 June 2010). Hacker explains why he reported 'Wikileaks source'. Retrieved from www.bbc.co.uk/news/10255887.

(24 September 2010). Stuxnet worm hits Iran nuclear plant staff computers. Retrieved from www.bbc.co.uk/news/world-middle-east-11414483.

(30 September 2010). Lawyers to continue piracy fight. Retrieved from www.bbc.co.uk/news/technology-11443861.

(12 October 2010). Irish court rules in favour of ISPs in piracy case. Retrieved from www.bbc.co.uk/news/technology-11521949.

(20 June 2011). Soca website taken down after LulzSec 'DDoS attack'. Retrieved from www.bbc.co.uk/news/technology-13848510.

(10 December 2011). 'More than 800 people' phone-hacked by News of World. Retrieved from www.bbc.co.uk/news/uk-16124553.

(26 December 2011). 'Anonymous' hackers hit US security firm Stratfor. Retrieved from www.bbc.co.uk/news/world-us-canada-16330396.

(26 June 2012). Internet piracy appeal fee challenged by Consumer Focus. Retrieved from www.bbc.com/news/technology-18594105.

(20 July 2012). Obama warns US on cyber-threats. Retrieved from www.bbc.com/news/technology-18928854.

Becker, J. U. and Clement, M. (2006). Dynamics of illegal participation in peer-to-peer networks: why do people illegally share media files? *Journal of Media Economics*, **19**, 7–32.

Benkler, Y. (2006). *The Wealth of Networks*. New Haven, CT, and London: Yale University Press.

Bennett, W. L. (2008). Changing citizenship in the digital age. In Bennett, W. L. (ed.) *Civic Life Online: Learning How Digital Media Can Engage Youth*. Cambridge, MA: The MIT Press (pp. 1–24).

Bente, G., Rüggenberg, S., Krämer, N. C. and Eschenburg, F. (2008). Avatar-mediated networking: increasing social presence and interpersonal trust in net-based collaborations. *Human Communication Research*, **34**, 287–318.

Beran, T. and Li, Q. (2005). Cyber-harassment: a study of a new method for an old behaviour. *Journal of Educational Computing Research*, **32**, 265–77.

Berlin, F. S. and Sawyer, D. (2012). Potential consequences of accessing child pornography over the internet and who is accessing it. *Sexual Addiction and Compulsivity: the Journal of Treatment and Prevention*, **19**, 30–40.

Bhal, K. T. and Leekha, N. D. (2008). Exploring cognitive moral logics using grounded theory: the case of software piracy. *Journal of Business Ethics*, **81**, 635–46.

Bhat, C. S. (2008). Cyber bullying: overview and strategies for school counsellors, guidance officers, and all school personnel. *Australian Journal of Guidance and Counselling*, **18** (1), 53–66.

Bissett, A. and Shipton, G. (1999). Some human dimensions of computer virus creation and infection. *International Journal of Human-Computer Studies*, **52**, 899–913.

Blackburn, R. (1993). *The Psychology of Criminal Conduct: Theory, Research and Practice*. Chichester, UK: John Wiley and Sons.

(1996). What is forensic psychology? *Legal and Criminological Psychology*, **1**, 3–16.

Blake, R. H. and Kyper, E. S. (in press). An investigation of the intention to share media files over peer-to-peer networks. *Behaviour and Information Technology*.

Blanchard, R. (2009). The DSM diagnostic criteria for paedophilia. *Archives of Sexual Behaviour*, **39**, 304–16.

Blundell, B., Sherry, M., Burke, A. and Sowerbutts, S. (2002). Child pornography and the internet: accessibility and policing. *Australian Police Journal*, **56** (1): 59–65.

Blumenthal, S., Gudjonsson, G. and Burns, J. (1999). Cognitive distortions and blame attribution in sex offenders against adults and children. *Child Abuse and Neglect*, **23**, 129–43.

Bocij, P. (2006). *The Dark Side of the Internet: Protecting Yourself and your Family from Online Criminals*. Westport, CT: Praeger Publishers.

Bonner, S. and O'Higgins, E. (2010). Music piracy: ethical perspectives. *Management Decision*, **48**, 1,341–54.

Bottoms, A. E. (2007). Place, space, crime, and disorder. In M. Maguire, R. Morgan and R. Reiner (eds.), *The Oxford Handbook of Criminology* (4th edn). Oxford University Press (pp. 528–74).

Bouchard, S., St-Jacques, J., Robillard, G. and Renaud, P. (2008). Anxiety increases the feeling of presence in virtual reality. *Presence Teleoperators and Virtual Environments*, August, 376–91.

Boulton, M., Lloyd, J., Down, J. and Marx, H. (2012). Predicting undergraduates' self-reported engagement in traditional and cyberbullying from attitudes. *Cyberpsychology, Behavior and Social Networking*, **15**, 141–7.

Bowman-Grieve, L. (2011). The internet and terrorism: pathways towards terrorism and counter-terrorism. In A. Silke (ed.), *The Psychology of Counter-Terrorism*. Milton Park, UK: Routledge (pp. 76–88).

Bowman-Grieve, L. and Conway, M. (2012). Exploring the form and function of dissident Irish Republican online discourses. *Media, War and Conflict*, **5**, 71–85.

Boyle, J. (1997). Foucault in cyberspace: surveillance, sovereignty, and hardwired censors. *University of Cincinnati Law Review*, **66**, 177–205.

Bremmer, L. A., Koehler, D. J., Liberman, V. and Tversky, A. (1996). Overconfidence in probability and frequency judgements: a critical examination. *Organisational Behaviour and Human Decision Processes*, **65**, 212–19.

Brenner, S. W. (2001). Is there such a thing as 'virtual crime'? *California Criminal Law Review*, Volume 4. Retrieved from www.boalt.org/bjcl/v4/v4brenner.pdf.

(2006). Defining cybercrime: a review of state and federal law. In R. D. Clifford (ed.), *Cybercrime: the Investigation, Prosecution and Defense of a Computer Related Crime* (2nd edn). Durham, NC: Carolina Academic Press (pp. 13–95).

British Psychological Society (2011). *Becoming a Forensic Psychologist*. Retrieved from www.bps.org. uk/careers-education-training/how-become-psychologist/types-psychologists/becoming-forensic-psychologist.

Britton, P. (1997). *The Jigsaw Man*. London: Corgi.

(2000). *Picking up the Pieces*. London: Corgi.

Broidy, L., Cauffman, E., Espelage, D. L., Mazerolle, P. and Piquero, A. (2003). Sex differences in empathy and its relation to juvenile offending. *Violence and Victims*, **18**, 503–16.

Brown, D. and Silke, A. (2011). The impact of the media on terrorism and counter-terrorism. In A. Silke (ed.), *The Psychology of Counter-Terrorism*. Milton Park, UK: Routledge (pp. 89–110).

Brown, J. M. and Campbell, E. A. (2010). Forensic psychology: a case of multiple identities. In J. M. Brown and E. A. Campbell (eds.). *The Cambridge Handbook of Forensic Psychology*. New York: Cambridge University Press (pp. 1–13).

Brown, K., Jackson, M. and Cassidy, W. (2006). Cyber-bullying: developing policy to direct responses that are equitable and effective in addressing this special form of bullying. *Canadian Journal of Educational Administration and Policy*, **57**. Retrieved from www.umanitoba.ca/publications/cjeap/articles/brown_jackson_cassidy.html.

Bryant, R. (2008). The challenge of digital crime. In R. Bryant (ed.), *Investigating Digital Crime*. Chichester, UK: John Wiley and Sons (pp. 1–26).

Bryant, R. and Marshall, A. (2008). Criminological and motivational perspectives. In R. Bryant (ed.), *Investigating Digital Crime*. Chichester, UK: John Wiley and Sons (pp. 231–48).

Bryce, J. (2010). Online sexual exploitation of children and young people. In Y. Jewkes and M. Yar (eds.), *Handbook of Internet Crime*. Cullompton, UK: Willan Publishing (pp. 320–42).

Bryce, J. and Rutter, J. (2005). *Fake Nation: a Study into an Everyday Crime*. Report for the Organized Crime Task Force – Northern Ireland Office. Retrieved from http://digiplay.info/files/FakeNation.pdf.

Burgess, A. W. and Hartman, C. (1987). Child abuse aspects of child pornography. *Psychiatric Annals*, **17** (4), 248–53.

Burgess-Proctor, A., Patchin, J. W. and Hinduja, S. (2009). Cyberbullying and online harassment: reconceptualizing the victimization of adolescent girls. In V. Garcia and J. Clifford (eds.), *Female Crime Victims: Reality Reconsidered*. Upper Saddle River, NJ: Prentice Hall (pp. 162–76).

Burke, A., Sowerbutts, S., Blundell, B. and Sherry, M. (2002). Child pornography and the internet: policing and treatment issues. *Psychiatry, Psychology and Law*, **9**, 79–84.

Burke, S. C., Wallen, M., Vail-Smith, K. and Knox, D. (2011). Using technology to control intimate partners: an exploratory study of college undergraduates. *Computers in Human Behavior*, **27**, 1,162–7.

Calcetas-Santos, O. (2001). Child pornography on the internet. In C. A. Arnaldo (ed.), *Child Abuse on the Internet*. Paris: UNESCO (pp. 57–60).

Calcutt, A. (1999). *White Noise: an A-Z of the Contradictions in Cyberculture*. London: Macmillan.

Campbell, J., Greenauer, N., Macaluso, K. and End, C. (2007). Unrealistic optimism in internet events. *Computers in Human Behaviour*, **23**, 1,273–84.

Cannataci, J. and Mifsud-Bonnici, J. (2007). Weaving the mesh: finding remedies in cyberspace. *International Review of Law, Computers and Technology*, **21**, 59–78.

Canter, D. (1995). *Criminal Shadows: Inside the Mind of the Serial Killer*. London: HarperCollins Publishers.

(2003). *Mapping Murder: Walking in Killers' Footsteps*. London: Virgin Books.

Canter, D. and Youngs, D. (2009). *Investigative Psychology: Offender Profiling and the Analysis of Criminal Action*. Chichester, UK: Wiley.

Carey, L. (29 July 2009). Can PTSD affect victims of identity theft? Psychologists say yes. *Associated Content*. Retrieved from www.associatedcontent.com/article/2002924/can_ptsd_affect_victims_of_identity.html.

Carney, M. and Rogers, M. (2004). The trojan made me do it: a first step in statistical based computer forensics event reconstruction. *International Journal of Digital Evidence*, **2** (4). Retrieved from http://cs.ua.edu/691Dixon/Forensics/trojan.pdf.

Carrier, B. and Spafford, E. (2003). Getting physical with digital forensics investigation. *International Journal of Digital Evidence*, **2** (2).
  (11–13, August 2004). An event based digital forensic investigation framework. Paper presented at Digital Forensic Research Workshop (DFRWS), Baltimore, Maryland. Retrieved from www.digital-evidence.org/papers/dfrws_event.pdf.

Carroll, E. and Romano, J. (2011). *Your Digital Afterlife*. Berkeley, CA: New Riders.

Casey, E. (2002). *Handbook of Computer Crime Investigation: Forensic Tools and Technology*. San Diego, CA: Academic Press.

Chesebro, J. W. and Bonsall, D. G. (1989). *Computer-mediated Communication: Human Relationships in a Computerised World*. Tuscaloosa, AL: The University of Alabama Press.

Chiesa, R., Ducci, S. and Ciappi, S. (2009). *Profiling Hackers: the Science of Criminal Profiling as Applied to the World of Hacking*. Boca Raton, FL: CRC Press.

Clarke, A. (2010). *Social Media: Political Uses and Implications for Representative Democracy*. Ottawa, Canada: Library of Parliament.

Clarke, R. V. and Felson, M. (1993). *Routine Activity and Rational Choice*. New Brunswick, NJ: Transaction Publishers.

Clough, J. (2010). *Principles of Cybercrime*. Cambridge University Press.

Cockrill, A. and Goode, M. M. H. (2012). DVD pirating intentions: angels, devils, chancers and receivers. *Journal of Consumer Behaviour*, **11**, 1–10.

Colarik, A. M. and Janczewski, L. J. (2008). Introduction to cyber warfare and cyber terrorism. In L. J. Janczewski and A. M. Colarik (eds.), *Cyber Warfare and Cyber Terrorism*. Hershey, PA: Information Science Reference (pp. xiii–xxx).

Coleman, J. (1994). *The Criminal Elite: the Sociology of White Collar Crime*. New York: St. Martin's Press.

Collins, J. M. (2006). *Investigating Identity Theft: a Guide for Businesses, Law Enforcement, and Victims*. Hoboken, NJ: John Wiley and Sons.

Computer Security Institute (2011). Fifteenth annual computer crime and security survey 2010/2011. Retrieved from http://gocsi.com/survey.

Conner, B. T., Stein, J. A. and Longshore, D. (2008). Examining self-control as a multidimensional predictor of crime and drug use in adolescents with criminal histories. *The Journal of Behavioral Health Services and Research*, **36**, 137–49.

Conway, M. (2002). Reality bytes: cyberterrorism and terrorist use of the internet. *First Monday*, **7**, 11.
  (2006). Terrorist 'use' of the internet and fighting back. *Information and Security: an International Journal*, **19**, 9–30.
  (2007). Cyberterrorism: hype and reality. In L. Armistead (ed.), *Information Warfare: Separating Hype from Reality*. Potomac Books, Inc. (pp. 73–93).
  (2011). Against cyberterrorism. *Communications of the ACM*, **54**, 26–8.

Cooney, R. and Lang, A. (2007). Taking uncertainty seriously: adaptive governance and international trade. *European Journal of International Law*, **18**, 523.

Couldry, N. (2007). Communicative entitlements and democracy: the future of the digital divide debate. In R. Mansell, C. Avgerou, D. Quah and R. Silverstone (eds.), *The Oxford Handbook of Information and Communication Technologies*. Oxford University Press (pp. 363–83).

Council of Europe (2001). *Convention on Cybercrime*. Retrieved from http://conventions.coe.int/Treaty/en/Treaties/Html/185.htm.

Cox, B. J., MacPherson, P. S. R., Enns, M. W. and McWilliams, L. A. (2004). Neuroticism and self-criticism associated with post-traumatic stress disorder in a nationally representative sample. *Behaviour Research and Therapy*, **42**, 105–44.

Cronan, T. P., Foltz, C. B. and Jones, T. W. (2006). Information systems misuse and computer crime: an analysis of demographic factors and awareness of university computer usage policies. *Communications of the ACM*, **49** (6), 84–90.

Cushing, K. (10 May 2001). Would you turn to the dark side? *Computer Weekly*, **34**.

D'Astous, A., Colbert, F. and Montpetit, D. (2005). Music piracy on the web – how effective are anti-piracy arguments? Evidence from the theory of planned behavior. *Journal of Consumer Policy*, **28**, 289–310.

Davey, G. (2008). *Psychopathology: Research, Assessment and Treatment in Clinical Psychology*. Chichester, UK: John Wiley and Sons.

David, M. (2010). *Peer to Peer and the Music Industry: the Criminalisation of Sharing*. London: Sage Publications.

Davies, G., Hollin, C. and Bull, R. (2008). *Forensic Psychology*. Chichester, UK: Wiley.

Davinson, N. and Sillence, E. (2010). It won't happen to me: promoting secure behaviour among internet users. *Computers in Human Behaviour*, **26**, 1,739–47.

Dean, G., Bell, P. and Newman, J. (2012). The dark side of social media: review of online terrorism. *Pakistan Journal of Criminology*, **3**, 103–22.

Dehue, F., Bolman, C. and Völlink, T. (2008). Cyberbullying: youngsters' experiences and parental perception. *Cyberpsychology and Behaviour*, **11**, 217–23.

De Masi, F. (2007). The paedophile and his inner world: theoretical and clinical considerations on the analysis of a patient. *The International Journal of Psychoanalysis*, **88**, 147–65.

DeMore, S. W., Fisher, J. D. and Baron, R. M. (1988). The equity-control model as a predictor of vandalism among college students. *Journal of Applied Social Psychology*, **18**, 80–91.

Dempsey, A. G., Sulkowski, M. L., Dempsey, J. and Storch, E. A. (2011). Has cyber technology produced a new group of peer aggressors? *Cyberpsychology, Behaviour and Social Networking*, **14**, 297–302.

Denning, D. E. (2001). Activism, hacktivism and cyberterrorism: the internet as a tool for influencing foreign policy. In J. Arquilla and D. F. Ronfeldt (eds.), *Networks and Netwars: the Future of Terror, Crime and Militancy, Issue 1382*. Santa Monica, CA: RAND (pp. 239–88).

(2007a). Cyberterrorism – testimony before the Special Oversight Panel on Terrorism Committee on Armed Services, US House of Representatives. In E. V. Linden (ed.), *Focus on Terrorism, Volume 9*. New York: Nova Science Publishers (pp. 71–6).

(2007b). A view of cyberterrorism five years later. In K. E. Himma (ed.), *Internet Security: Hacking, Counterhacking and Society*. Sudbury, MA: Jones and Bartlett Publishers (pp. 123–40).

(2010). Terror's web: how the internet is transforming terrorism. In Y. Jewkes and M. Yar (eds.), *Handbook of Internet Crime*. Cullompton, UK: Willan (pp. 194–213).

Dhamija, R., Tygar, J. D. and Hearst, M. (2006). *Why Phishing Works*. CHI 2006, 22–7 April. Montreal: CHI.

Dibbell, J. (1993). A rape in cyberspace. Retrieved from http://loki.stockton.edu/~kinsellt/stuff/dibbelrapeincyberspace.html.

(1998). A rape in cyberspace. Retrieved from www.juliandibbell.com/texts/bungle.html.

DiMaggio, C. and Galea, S. (2006). The behavioural consequences of terrorism: a meta-analysis. *Academy of Emergency Medicine*, **13**, 559–66.

Dimond, J. P., Fiesler, C. and Bruckman, A. S. (2011). Domestic violence and information communication technologies. *Interacting with Computers*, **23**, 413–21.

Dombrowski, S. C., LeMasney, J. W., Ahia, C. E. and Dickson, S. A. (2004). Protecting children from online sexual predators: technological, psychoeducational and legal considerations. *Professional Psychology: Research and Practice*, **35**, 65–73.

Donato, L. (2009). An introduction to how criminal profiling could be used as a support for computer hacking investigations. *Journal of Digital Forensic Practice*, **2**, 183–95.

Douglas, J. and Olshaker, M. (1995). *Mind Hunter: Inside the FBI's Elite Serial Crime Unit*. New York: Pocket Books.

(1999). *The Anatomy of Motive*. London: Simon and Schuster.

(2000). *The Cases that Haunt Us*. London: Pocket Books.

Douglas, J. E., Ressler, R., Burgess, A. and Hartman, C. (1986). Criminal profiling from crime scene analysis. *Behavioural Sciences and the Law*, **4**, 401–21.

Douglas, K. S. and Dutton, D. G. (2001). Assessing the link between stalking and domestic violence. *Aggression and Violent Behaviour*, **6**, 519–46.

Dunleavy, P., Margetts, H., Bastow, S. and Tinkler, J. (2005). New public management is dead – long live digital-era governance. *Journal of Public Administration Research and Theory*, **16**, 467–94.

(2006). *Digital-era Governance*. Oxford University Press.

Eckersley, R. (2007). Soft law, hard politics, and the Climate Change Treaty. In C. Reus-Smit (ed.), *The Politics of International Law*. Cambridge University Press (p. 80).

Edelson, E. (2003). The 419 scam: information warfare on the spam front and a proposal for local filtering. *Computers and Security*, **22**, 392–401.

Edgar-Nevill, D. (2008). Internet grooming and paedophile crimes. In R. Bryant (ed.), *Investigating Digital Crime*. Chichester, UK: Wiley (pp. 195–209).

Edgar-Nevill, D. and Stephens, P. (2008). Countering cybercrime. In R. Bryant (ed.), *Investigating Digital Crime*. Chichester, UK: Wiley (pp. 79–96).

Edwards, A. (2002). The moderator as an emerging democratic intermediary: the role of the moderator in internet discussions about public issues. *Information Polity*, 7, 3–20.

Einhorn, H. J. and Hogarth, R. M. (1978). Confidence in judgement: persistence of the illusion of validity. *Psychological Review*, **85**, 395–416.

Eke, A. W., Seto, M. C. and Williams, J. (2011). Examining the criminal history and future offending of child pornography offenders: an extended prospective follow-up study. *Law and Human Behaviour*, **35**, 466–78.

Elliott, I. A., Beech, A. R., Mandeville-Norden, R. and Hayes, E. (2009). Psychological profiles of internet sexual offenders: comparisons with contact sexual offenders. *Sexual Abuse: a Journal of Research and Treatment*, **21**, 76–92.

Elliott, M., Browne, K. and Kilcoyne, J. (1995). Child sexual abuse prevention: what offenders tell us. *Child Abuse and Neglect*, **19**, 579–94.

Endrass, J., Urbaniok, F., Hammermeister, L. C., Benz, C., Elbert, T., Laubacher, A. and Rossegger, A. (2009). The consumption of internet child pornography and violent and sex offending. *BMC Psychiatry*, **9**, 43.

Evangelista, B. (June 2011). Web users have better social lives, study finds. *San Francisco Chronicle*. Retrieved from www.sfgate.com/cgi-bin/article.cgi?f=/c/a/2011/06/18/BUC71JV2DD.DTL.

Evans, M. (2009). Gordon Brown and public management reform – a project in search of a 'big idea'. *Policy Studies*, **30**, 1.

EVElopedia (n.d.). Corporation management guide. Retrieved from http://wiki.eveonline.com/en/wiki/Corp_theft#Corp_Theft.

Eysenck, H. J. (1977). *Crime and Personality* (3rd edn). London: Routledge.

(1996). Personality theory and the problem of criminality. In J. Muncie, E. McLaughlin and M. Langan (eds.). *Criminological Perspectives: a Reader*. London: Sage Publications Ltd (pp. 81–98). Reprinted from McGurk, B., Thornton, D. and Williams, M. (eds.), *Applying Psychology to Imprisonment* (1987). London: HMSO (pp. 30–46).

Eysenck, S. B. G. and Eysenck, H. J. (1970). Crime and personality: an empirical study of the three-factor theory. *British Journal of Criminology*, **10**, 225–39.

(1977). Personality differences between prisoners and controls. *Psychological Reports*, **40**, 1,023–8.

Farrell, G. and Pease, K. (2006). Preventing repeat residential burglary victimisation. In B. Welsh and D. Farrington (eds.), *Preventing Crime: What Works for Children, Offenders, Victims and Places*. Dordrecht, The Netherlands: Springer (pp. 161–77).

Farrington, D. P. (1990). Age, period, cohort and offending. In D. M. Gottfredson and R. V. Clarke (eds.), *Policy and Theory in Criminal Justice: Contributions in Honour of Leslie T. Wilkins*. Aldershot: Avebury (pp. 51–75).

Farrington, D. P., Jolliffe, D., Loeber, R., Stouthamer-Loeber, M. and Kalb, L. M. (2001). The concentration of offenders in families, and family criminality in the prediction of boys' delinquency. *Journal of Adolescence*, **24**, 579–96.

Fauerbach, J. A., Lawrence, J. W., Schmidt, C. W., Munster, A. M. and Costa, P. T. (2000). Personality predictors of injury-related post-traumatic stress disorder. *Journal of Nervous and Mental Disease*, **188**, 510–17.

Fergusson, D. M., Horwood, L. J. and Nagin, D. S. (2000). Offending trajectories in a New Zealand birth cohort. *Criminology*, **38**, 525–52.

Festinger, L. (1957). *A Theory of Cognitive Dissonance*. Stanford, CA: Stanford University Press.

Finch, E. (2007). The problem of stolen identity and the internet. In Y. Jewkes (ed.), *Crime Online*. Cullompton, UK: Willan Publishing (pp. 29–43).

Finkelhor, D. (1984). *Child Sexual Abuse: New Theory and Research*. New York: Free Press.

(1986). *A Source Book on Child Sexual Abuse*. London: Sage.

Finn, J. (2004). A survey of online harassment at a university campus. *Journal of Interpersonal Violence*, **19**, 468–83.

Finn, J. and Atkinson, T. (2009). Promoting the safe and strategic use of technology for victims of intimate partner violence: evaluation of the technology safety project. *Journal of Family Violence*, **24**, 53–9.

Finn, J. and Banach, M. (2000). Victimisation online: the down side of seeking human services for women on the internet. *Cyberpsychology and Behavior*, **3**, 243–54.

Fishbein, M. and Ajzen, I. (1975). *Belief, Attitude, Intention and Behaviour: an Introduction to Theory and Research*. Boston, MA: Addison-Wesley.

Fötinger, C. S. and Ziegler, W. (2004). *Understanding a Hacker's Mind – a Psychological Insight into the Hijacking of Identities*. Danube University Krems, Austria: RSA Security.

Foucault, M. (1965). *Madness and Civilization: a History of Insanity in the Age of Reason*. New York: Pantheon.

(1975). *Discipline and Punishment*. London: Penguin.

(1978). *The History of Sexuality Volume 1: An Introduction*. New York: Pantheon.

Frei, A., Erenay, N., Dittmann, V. and Graf, M. (2005). Paedophilia on the internet – a study of 33 convicted offenders in the Canton of Lucerne. *Swiss Medical Weekly*, **135**, 488–94.

Furnell, S. (2010). Hackers, viruses and malicious software. In Y. Jewkes and M. Yar (eds.), *Handbook of Internet Crime*. Cullompton, UK: Willan Publishing (pp. 173–93).

Gabriel, R., Ferrando, L., Sainz Corton, E., Mingote, C., Garcia-Camba, E., Fernandez-Liria, A. G. and Galea, S. (2007). Psychopathological consequences after a terrorist attack: an epidemiological study among victims, police officers, and the general population. *European Psychiatry*, **22**, 339–46.

Garau, M., Slater, M., Vinayagamoorthy, V., Brogni, A., Steed, A. and Sasse, M. A. (2003). The impact of avatar realism and eye gaze control on the perceived quality of communication in a shared immersive virtual environment. Proceedings of the Special Interest Group on Computer–Human Interaction (SIG-CHI) of Association for Computing Machinery (ACM) on Human Factors in Computing Systems, 5–10 Apr., Fort Lauderdale, Florida, pp. 529–36.

Garbharran, A. and Thatcher, A. (2011). Modelling social cognitive theory to explain software piracy intention. In M. J. Smith and G. Salvendy (eds.), *Human Interface and the Management of Information: Interacting with Information: Symposium on Human Interface: HCI International Part 1*. Berlin, Germany: Springer-Verlag (pp. 301–10).

Gasson, M. N. (2010). Human enhancement: could you become infected with a computer virus? IEE International Symposium on Technology and Society, Wollongong, Australia, 7–9 June (pp. 61–8). Retrieved from www.personal.reading.ac.uk/~sis04mng/download/c.php?id=2.

Gleeson, S. (16 July 2008). Freed hacker could work for police. *The New Zealand Herald* (p. A3).

Goldsmith, J. L. (1998). Against cyberanarchy. *University of Chicago Law Review*, **65**, 1,199.

Goldstein, A. P. (1996). *The Psychology of Vandalism*. New York: Plenham Press.

Goode, S. and Kartas, A. (2012). Exploring software piracy as a factor of video game console adoption. *Behaviour and Information Technology*, **31**, 547–63.

Gopal, R., Sanders, G. L., Bhattacharjee, S., Agrawal, M. and Wagner, S. (2004). A behavioral model of digital music piracy. *Journal of Organizational Computing and Electronic Commerce*, **14**, 89–105.

Gordon, S. (1993). Inside the mind of the dark avenger. *Virus News International, January 1993*. Abridged version retrieved from www.research.ibm.com/antivirus/SciPapers/Gordon/Avenger.html.

(1994). The generic virus writer. Presented at the 4th International Virus Bulletin Conference, Jersey, 8–9 September. Retrieved from http://vx.netlux.org/lib/asg03.html.

(1996). The generic virus writer II. In Proceedings of the 6th International Virus Bulletin Conference, Brighton, UK, 19–20 September. Retrieved from http://vx.netlux.org/lib/static/vdat/epgenvr2.htm.

(2000). Virus writers: the end of the innocence? In Proceedings of the 10th International Virus Bulletin Conference, Orlando, FL, 28–29 September. Retrieved from www.research.ibm.com/antivirus/SciPapers/VB2000SG.htm.

Gordon, S. and Ford, R. (2003). Cyberterrorism? Retrieved from the Symantec Security Response White Papers website: www.symantec.com/avcenter/reference/cyberterrorism.pdf.

Gottfredson, M. R. and Hirschi, T. (1990). *A General Theory of Crime*. Stanford, CA: Stanford University Press.

Greenberg, A. (16 July 2007). The top countries for cybercrime: China overtakes US in hosting web pages that install malicious programs. *MSNBC*. Retrieved from www.msnbc.msn.com/id/19789995/ns/technology_and_science-security.

Griffin, D. and Tversky, A. (1992). The weighting of evidence and the determinants of confidence. *Cognitive Psychology*, **24**, 411–35.

Groth, A. N., Burgess, A. W. and Holmstrom, L. L. (1977). Rape, power, anger and sexuality. *American Journal of Psychiatry*, **134**, 1,239–48.

Grubb, A. and Harrower, J. (2008). Attribution of blame in cases of rape: an analysis of participant gender, type of rape and perceived similarity to the victim. *Aggression and Violent Behaviour*, **13**, 396–405.

Gudaitis, T. M. (1998). The missing link in information security: three-dimensional profiling. *Cyberpsychology and Behaviour*, **1**, 321–40.

Gudjonsson, G. H. and Haward, L. R. C. (1998). *Forensic Psychology: A Guide to Practice*. New York: Routledge.

Guest, T. (2007). *Second Lives: A Journey through Virtual Worlds*. London: Random House.

Gunkel, D. J. (2005). Editorial: introduction to hacking and hacktivism. *New Media and Society*, 7, 595–7.

Hadnagy, C. (2011). *Social Engineering: The Art of Human Hacking*. Indianapolis, IN: Wiley Publishing.

Haines, H. H. (1996). *Against Capital Punishment: the Anti-death Penalty Movement in America 1972–1994*. Oxford University Press.

Häkkänen-Nyholm, H. (2010). Stalking. In J. M. Brown and E. A. Campbell (eds.), *The Cambridge Handbook of Forensic Psychology*. Cambridge University Press (pp. 562–70).

Hall, G. C. and Hirschman, R. (1991). Towards a Theory of Sexual Aggression: a Quadripartite Model. *Journal of Consulting and Clinical Psychology*, 59, 662–9.

Halsey, M. and Young, A. (2002). The meanings of graffiti and municipal administration. *The Australian and New Zealand Journal of Criminology*, 35, 165–86.

Hastie, R. (1993). Introduction. In R. Hastie (ed.), *Inside the Juror: the Psychology of Juror Decision Making*. Cambridge University Press (3–41).

Hazler, R. J. (1996). *Breaking the Cycle of Violence: Interventions for Bullying and Victimization*. Bristol, PA: Accelerated Development.

Henderson, S. and Gilding, M. (2004). 'I've never clicked this much with anyone in my life': trust and hyperpersonal communication in online friendships. *New Media and Society*, 6, 487–506.

Higgins, G. E. (2007). Digital piracy: an examination of low self-control and motivation using short-term longitudinal data. *Cyberpsychology and Behavior*, 10, 523–9.

Higgins, G. E., Fell, B. D. and Wilson, A. L. (2006). Digital piracy: assessing the contributions of an integrated self-control theory and social learning theory. *Criminal Justice Studies: a Critical Journal of Crime, Law and Society*, 19, 3–22.

Higgins, G. E., Marcum, C. D., Freiburger, T. L. and Ricketts, M. L. (2012). Examining the role of peer influence and self-control on downloading behaviour. *Deviant Behaviour*, 33, 412–23.

Higgins, G. E., Wolfe, S. E. and Marcum, C. D. (2008). Music piracy and neutralization: a preliminary trajectory analysis from short-term longitudinal data. *International Journal of Cyber Criminology*, 2, 324–36.

Hill, C. W. (2007). Digital piracy: causes, consequences and strategic responses. *Asia Pacific Journal of Management*, 24, 9–25.

Hillberg, T., Hamilton-Giachritsis, C. and Dixon, L. (2011). Review of meta-analysis on the association between child sexual abuse and adult mental health difficulties: a systematic approach. *Trauma Violence and Abuse*, 12, 38–49.

Hinduja, S. (2007). Neutralization theory and online software piracy: an empirical analysis. *Ethics and Information Technology*, 9, 187–204.

Hinduja, S. and Patchin, J. W. (2008). Cyberbullying: an exploratory analysis of factors related to offending and victimisation. *Deviant Behaviour*, 29, 129–56.

(2009). *Bullying beyond the Schoolyard: Preventing and Responding to Cyberbullying*. Thousand Oaks, CA: Sage Publications (Corwin Press).

(2010a). Bullying, cyberbullying and suicide. *Archives of Suicide Research*, 14, 206–21.

(2010b). *Cyberbullying Fact Sheet: Identification, Prevention, and Response*. Cyberbullying Research Center. Retrieved from www.cyberbullying.us/ Cyberbullying_Identification_Prevention_Response_Fact_Sheet.pdf.

Hines, D. and Finkelhor, D. (2007). Statutory sex crime relationships between juveniles and adults: a review of social scientific research. *Aggression and Violent Behaviour*, 12, 300–14.

Hof, R. (2006). *Real Threat to Virtual Goods in Second Life*. Retrieved from www.businessweek.com/ the_thread/techbeat/archives/2006/11/real_threat_to.html.

Holt, T. J. and Graves, D. C. (2007). A qualitative analysis of advance fee fraud e-mail schemes. *International Journal of Cyber Criminology*, **1** (1). Retrieved from www.cybercrimejournal.com/thomas&danielleijcc.htm.

Holtfreter, K., Reisig, M. D., Piquero, N. L. and Piquero, A. R. (2010). Low self-control and fraud: offending, victimization and their overlap. *Criminal Justice and Behavior*, **37**, 188–203.

Home Office (2005). Fraud and technology crimes: findings from the 2002/03 British Crime Survey and 2003 Offending, Crime and Justice Survey (Home Office Online Report 34/05). Retrieved from www.homeoffice.gov.uk/rds/pdfs05/rdsolr3405.pdf.

Hood, C. (1983). *The Tools of Government*. Basingstoke, UK: Macmillan.

Hood, S. K. and Carter, M. M. (2008). A preliminary examination of trauma history, locus of control, and PTSD symptom severity in African American Women. *The Journal of Black Psychology*, **34**, 179–91.

Horgan, J. (2003a). The search for the terrorist personality. In A. Silke (ed.), *Terrorists, Victims and Society: Psychological Perspectives on Terrorism and its Consequences*. Chichester, UK: John Wiley and Sons.

(2003b). Leaving terrorism behind: an individual perspective. In A. Silke (ed.), *Terrorists, Victims and Society: Psychological Perspectives on Terrorism and its Consequences*. Chichester, UK: John Wiley and Sons.

(2005). *The Psychology of Terrorism*. Abingdon, UK: Routledge.

(2008). From profiles to *pathways* and roots to *routes*: perspectives from psychology on radicalization into terrorism. *The Annals of the American Academy of Political and Social Science*, **618**, 80–94.

Horgan, J. and Taylor, M. (2001). The making of a terrorist. *Jane's Intelligence Review*, **13**, 16–18.

Howitt, D. (2009). *Introduction to Forensic and Criminal Psychology* (3rd edn). Harlow, UK: Pearson Education.

Hoyle, C. and Zedner, L. (2007). Victims, victimization, and criminal justice. In M. Maguire, R. Morgan and R. Reiner (eds.), *The Oxford Handbook of Criminology* (4th edn). Oxford University Press (pp. 461–95).

Hsu, J. and Shiue, C. (2008). Consumers' willingness to pay for non-pirated software. *Journal of Business Ethics*, **81**, 715–32.

Huang, D., Rau, P. P. and Salvendy, G. (2010). Perception of information security. *Behaviour and Information Technology*, **29**, 221–32.

Humphreys, S. (2008). Ruling the virtual world – governance in massively multiplayer online games. *European Journal of Cultural Studies*, May, **11** (2), 149–71.

Hunter, A. (2009). High-tech rascality: Asperger's syndrome, hackers, geeks, and personality types in the ICT industry. *New Zealand Sociology*, **24**, 39–61.

Huss, M. T. (2009). *Forensic Psychology: Research, Clinical Practice, and Applications*. Chichester, UK: Wiley-Blackwell.

Ingram, J. and Hinduja, S. (2008). Neutralizing music piracy: an empirical examination. *Deviant Behaviour*, **29**, 334–66.

International Telecommunication Union (2011). *The World in 2011: ICT Facts and Figures*. Retrieved from www.itu.int/ITU-D/ict/facts/2011/material/ICTFactsFigures2011.pdf.

Jagatic, T., Johnson, N., Jakobsson, M. and Menczer, F. (2006). Social phishing. *Communications of the Association for Computing Machinery (ACM)*, **50** (10), 94–100.

Jahankhani, H. and Al-Nemrat, A. (2010). Examination of cyber-criminal behaviour. *International Journal of Information Science and Management, Special Issue*. Jan/Jun 2010. Retrieved from www.srlst.com/ijist/special%20issue/ijism-special-issue2010_files/Special-Issue201041.pdf.

Jaishkankar, K. (2008). Identity related crime in cyberspace: examining phishing and its impact. *International Journal of Cyber Criminology*, **2**, 10–15.

Jambon, M. M. and Smetana, J. G. (2012). College students' moral evaluations of illegal music downloading. *Journal of Applied Developmental Psychology*, **33**, 31–9.

Jamel, J. (2008). Crime and its causes. In G. Davies, C. Hollin and R. Bull (eds.), *Forensic Psychology*. Chichester, UK: John Wiley and Sons Ltd (pp. 3–28).

Jay, E. (2007). Rape in cyberspace. Retrieved from https://lists.secondlife.com/pipermail/educators/2007-May/009237.html.

Jewkes, Y. (2010). Public policing and internet crime. In Y. Jewkes and M. Yar (eds.), *Handbook of Internet Crime*. Cullompton, UK: Willan Publishing (pp. 525–45).

Jewkes, Y. and Yar, M. (2010). Introduction: the internet, cybercrime and the challenges of the twenty-first century. In Y. Jewkes and M. Yar (eds.), *Handbook of Internet Crime*. Cullompton, UK: Willan Publishing (pp. 1–15).

Johnson, D. and Post, D. (1996). Law and borders – the rise of law in cyberspace. *The Stanford Law Review*, **48**, 1,367–402.

Johnston, A. C. and Warkentin, M. (2010). Fear appeals and information security behaviours: an empirical study. *MIS Quarterly*, **34** (3), 549–66.

Jolliffe, D. and Farrington, D. P. (2004). Empathy and offending: a systematic review and meta-analysis. *Aggression and Violent Behaviour*, **9**, 441–76.

Jones, T. (2003). Child abuse or computer crime? The proactive approach. In A. MacVean and P. Spindler (eds.), *Policing Paedophiles on the Internet*. Bristol: John Grieve Centre for Policing and Community Safety, The New Police Bookshop.

Joseph, J. (2003). Cyberstalking: an international perspective. In Y. Jewkes (ed.), *Dot.cons: Crime, Deviance and Identity on the Internet*. Cullompton, UK: Willan Publishing (pp. 105–25).

Josman, N., Somer, E., Reisberg, A., Weiss, P. L., Garcia-Palacios, A. and Hoffman, H. (2006). Busworld: designing a virtual environment for post-traumatic stress disorder in Israel: a protocol. *CyberPsychology and Behavior*, **9**, 241–4.

Jouriles, E. N., McDonald, R., Kullowatz, A., Rosenfield, D., Gomez, G. S. and Cuevas, A. (2009). Can virtual reality increase the realism of role plays used to teach college women sexual coercion and rape-resistance skills? *Behaviour Therapy*, **40**, 337–45.

Jung, Y. (2008). Influence of sense of presence on intention to participate in a virtual community. *Proceedings of the 41st Hawaii International Conference on System Sciences*.

Kabay, M. E. (1998). *ICSA White Paper on Computer Crime Statistics*. Retrieved from www.icsa.net/html/library/whitepapers/crime.pdf.

Kahn, J. (April 2004). The homeless hacker v. the *New York Times*. *Wired*. Retrieved from www.wired.com/wired/archive/12.04/hacker_pr.html.

Kamphuis, J. H., Emmelkamp, P. M. G. and Bartak, A. (2003). Individual differences in post-traumatic stress following post-intimate stalking: stalking severity and psychosocial variables. *British Journal of Clinical Psychology*, **42**, 145–56.

Katsh, E. (2007). Online dispute resolution: some implications for the emergence of law in cyberspace. *International Review of Law, Computers and Technology*, **21**, 97–107.

Kellen, K. (1982). *On Terrorism and Terrorists: a Rand Note N-1942-RC*. Santa Monica, CA: Rand Corporation.

Kenny, M. C. and McEachern, A. G. (2000). Racial, ethnic and cultural factors of childhood sexual abuse: a selected review of the literature. *Clinical Psychology Review*, **20**, 905–22.

Kilger, M., Arkin, O. and Stutzman, J. (2004). Profiling. In The Honeynet Project (ed.), *Know Your Enemy: Learning about Security Threats* (2nd edn). Boston, MA: Addison-Wesley Professional (pp. 505–56). Retrieved from http://old.honeynet.org/book/Chp16.pdf.

Killias, M., Scheidegger, D. and Nordenson, P. (2009). Effects of increasing the certainty of punishment: a field experiment on public transportation. *European Journal of Criminology*, **6**, 387–400.

Kilpatrick, R. (1997). Joy-riding: an addictive behavior. In J. E. Hodge, M. McMurran and C. R. Hollin (eds.), *Addicted to Crime?* Chichester, UK: Wiley (pp. 165–90).

Kirwan, G. H. (June 2006). An identification of demographic and psychological characteristics of computer hackers using triangulation. PhD Thesis, Institute of Criminology, School of Law, College of Business and Law, University College Dublin.

(2009a). *Victim Facilitation and Blaming in Cybercrime Cases.* Proceedings of Cyberspace 2009. Brno, Czech Republic. 20–21 November.

(2009b). *Presence and the Victims of Crime in Online Virtual Worlds.* Proceedings of Presence 2009 – the 12th Annual International Workshop on Presence, International Society for Presence Research, 11–13 November, Los Angeles, California. Retrieved from http://astro.temple.edu/~tuc16417/papers/Kirwan.pdf PROCEEDINGS ISBN: 978-0-9792217-3-6.

Kline, P. (1987). Psychoanalysis and crime. In B. J. McGurk, D. M. Thornton and M. Williams (eds.), *Applying Psychology to Imprisonment: Theory and Practice.* London: HMSO.

Klinger, D. A. (2001). Suicidal intent in victim-precipitated homicide: insights from the study of 'suicide-by-cop'. *Homicide Studies, 5* (3), 206–26.

Knight, W. (18 August 2005). Computer characters mugged in virtual crime spree. *New Scientist.* Retrieved from www.newscientist.com/article/dn7865.

Kohlberg, L. (1969). State and sequence: the cognitive-developmental approach to socialization. In D. A. Goslin (ed.), *Handbook of Socialization Theory and Research.* Chicago, IL: Rand McNally.

Kowalski, R. M. and Limber, S. P. (2007). Electronic bullying among middle school students. *Journal of Adolescent Health, 41,* S22–30.

Kramer, S. and Bradfield, J. C. (2010). A general definition of malware. *Journal in Computer Virology, 6,* 105–14.

Krone, T. (2004). *A Typology of Online Child Pornography Offending. Trends and Issues in Crime and Criminal Justice, No. 279.* Canberra: Australian Institute of Criminology. Retrieved from www.aic.gov.au/publications/tandi2/tandi279.pdf.

Kruglanski, A. W. and Fishman, S. (2006). The psychology of terrorism: 'syndrome' versus 'tool' perspectives. *Terrorism and Political Violence, 18,* 193–215.

Lafrance, Y. (2004). Psychology: a previous security tool. Retrieved from www.sans.org/reading_room/whitepapers/engineering/psychology-precious-security-tool_1409.

Lam, A., Mitchell, J. and Seto, M. C. (2010). Lay perceptions of child pornography offenders. *Canadian Journal of Criminology and Criminal Justice, 52,* 173–201.

Langos, C. (2012). Cyberbullying: the challenge to define. *Cyberpsychology, Behavior and Social Networking, 15,* 285–9.

Lanning, K. (2001a). Child molesters and cyber paedophiles: a behavioural perspective. In R. Hazelwood and A. W. Burgess (eds.), *Practical Aspects of Rape Investigation: A Multidisciplinary Approach* (3rd edn). Boca Raton, FL: CRC Press (pp. 199–220).

(2001b). *Child Molesters: A Behavioral Analysis* (4th edn). Washington, DC: National Center for Missing and Exploited Children. Retrieved from www.ncmec.org/en_US/publications/NC70.pdf.

LaRose, R. and Kim, J. (2007). Share, steal or buy? A social cognitive perspective of music downloading. *Cyberpsychology and Behavior, 10,* 267–77.

LaRose, R., Lai, Y. J., Lange, R., Love, B. and Wu, Y. (2005). Sharing or piracy? An exploration of downloading behaviour. *Journal of Computer-Mediated Communication, 11,* 1–21.

LaRose, R., Rifon, N. J. and Enbody, R. (March 2008). Promoting personal responsibility for internet safety. *Communications of the ACM, 51* (3), 71–6.

Laulik, S., Allam, J. and Sheridan, L. (2007). An investigation into maladaptive personality functioning in Internet sex offenders. *Psychology, Crime and Law, 13,* 523–35.

Lawrence, J. W. and Fauerbach, J. A. (2003). Personality, coping, chronic stress, social support and PTSD symptoms among adult burn survivors: a path analysis. *Journal of Burn Care and Rehabilitation*, **24**, 63–72.

Lee, D., Larose, R. and Rifon, N. (2008). Keeping our network safe: a model of online protection behaviour. *Behaviour and Information Technology*, **27**, 445–54.

Lee, Y. and Larson, K. R. (2009). Threat or coping appraisal: determinants of SMB executives' decision to adopt anti-malware software. *European Journal of Information Systems*, **18**, 177–87.

Leman-Langlois, S. (2008). Introduction: technocrime. In S. Leman-Langlois (ed.), *Technocrime: Technology, Crime and Social Control*. Cullompton, UK: Willan.

Lenhart, A. (2007). Pew internet and American life project: cyberbullying and online teens. Retrieved from www.pewinternet.org/~/media//Files/Reports/2007/PIP%20Cyberbullying%20Memo.pdf. pdf.

Leonard, M. M. (2010). 'I did what I was directed to do but he didn't touch me': the impact of being a victim of internet offending. *Journal of Sexual Aggression*, **16**, 249–56.

Lessig, L. (2000). *Code and Other Laws of Cyberspace*. Princeton, NJ: Princeton University Press.

Levi, M. (2001). 'Between the risk and the reality falls the shadow': evidence and urban legends in computer fraud (with apologies to T. S. Eliot). In D. Wall (ed.), *Crime and the Internet*. London, New York: Routledge (pp. 44–58).

Levine, S. Z. (2008). Using intelligence to predict subsequent contacts with the criminal justice system for sex offences. *Personality and Individual Differences*, **44**, 453–63.

Levy, S. (1984). *Hackers: Heroes of the Computer Revolution*. London: Penguin Books.

Li, Q. (2007). New bottle but old wine: a research of cyberbullying in schools. *Computers in Human Behavior*, **23**, 1,777–91.

Liao, C., Lin, H. N. and Liu, Y. P. (2010). Predicting the use of pirated software: a contingency model integrating perceived risk with the theory of planned behavior. *Journal of Business Ethics*, **91**, 237–52.

Liebowitz, S. J. (2006). File sharing: creative destruction or just plain destruction? *The Journal of Law and Economics*, **49**, 1–28.

Lindsay, M. and Krysik, J. (2012). Online harassment among college students. *Information, Communication and Technology*, **15**, 703–19.

Lininger, R. and Vines, R. D. (2005). *Phishing: Cutting the Identity Theft Line*. Indianapolis, IN: Wiley Publishing Inc.

Livingstone, S. (2009). *Children and the Internet: Great Expectations, Challenging Realities*. Cambridge, UK: Polity.

Locicero, A. and Sinclair, S. J. (2008). Terrorism and terrorist leaders: insights from developmental and ecological psychology. *Studies in Conflict and Terrorism*, **31**, 227–50.

Lombroso, C. and Ferrero, W. (1895). *The Female Offender*. London: Fisher Unwin.

Lopez-Leon, M. and Rosner, R. (2010). Intellectual quotient of juveniles evaluated in a forensic psychiatry clinic after committing a violent crime. *Journal of Forensic Sciences*, **55**, 229–31.

Lyndon, A., Bonds-Raacke, J. and Cratty, A. D. (2011). College students' Facebook stalking of ex-partners. *Cyberpsychology, Behaviour and Social Networking*, **14**, 711–16.

Lynn, R. (2007). Virtual rape is traumatic, but is it a crime? Retrieved from www.wired.com/culture/lifestyle/commentary/sexdrive/2007/05/sexdrive_0504.

MacKinnon, R. C. (1997). Punishing the persona: correctional strategies for the virtual offender. In S. Jones (ed.), *Virtual Culture: Identity and Communication in Cybersociety*. London: Sage (pp. 206–35).

Macmillan Dictionary (n.d.). 'Cybercrime' definition. Retrieved from www.macmillandictionary.com/dictionary/british/cybercrime.

MacSíthigh, D. (2008). The mass age of internet law. *Information and Communication Technology Law*, **17**, 79–94.

Maghaireh, A. (2008). Shariah law and cyber-sectarian conflict: how can Islamic criminal law respond to cyber crime? *International Journal of Cyber-Criminology*, **2**, 337–45.

Maguire, M., Morgan, R. and Reiner, R. (2007). *The Oxford Handbook of Criminology* (4th edn.). Oxford University Press.

Maikovich, A. K., Koenen, K. C. and Jaffee, S. R. (2009). Posttraumatic stress symptoms and trajectories in child sexual abuse victims: an analysis of sex differences using the national survey of child and adolescent well-being. *Journal of Abnormal Child Psychology*, **37**, 727–37.

Malesky Jr, L. A. (2007). Predatory online behaviour: modus operandi of convicted sex offenders in identifying potential victims and contacting minors over the internet. *Journal of Child Sexual Abuse*, **16**, 23–32.

Malin, J. and Fowers, B. J. (2009). Adolescent self-control and music and movie piracy. *Computers in Human Behaviour*, **25**, 718–22.

Manchcno, C. (11 April 2010). With new vest, players feel the game. *The Daily Pennsylvanian*. Retrieved from www.dailypennsylvanian.com/article/new-vest-players-feel-game.

Maniglio, R. (2009). The impact of child sexual abuse on health: a systematic review of reviews. *Clinical Psychology Review*, **29**, 647–57.

Marmar, C. R., Metzler, T. J., Otte, C., McCaslin, S., Inslicht, S. and Haase, C. H. (2007). The peritraumatic dissociative experiences questionnaire: an international perspective. In J. P. Wilson and C. So-kum Tang (eds.), *Cross-cultural Assessment of Psychological Trauma and PTSD*. New York: Springer (pp. 197–217).

Marshall, A. and Stephens, P. (2008). Identity and identity theft. In R. Bryant (ed.), *Investigating Digital Crime*. Chichester, UK: John Wiley and Sons (pp. 179–93).

Martin, G., Richardson, A., Bergen, H., Roeger, L. and Allison, S. (2003). Family and individual characteristics of a community sample of adolescents who graffiti. Presented at the *Graffiti and Disorder Conference*, Brisbane, Australia, 18–19 August. Retrieved from www.nograffiti.com/martinstudy.pdf.

Maruna, S. and Mann, R. E. (2006). A fundamental attribution error? Rethinking cognitive distortions. *Legal and Criminological Psychology*, **11**, 155–77.

Massimi, M., Odom, W., Kirk, D. and Banks, R. (2010). HCI at the end of life: understanding death, dying and the digital. Proceedings of CHI (Computer Human Interaction) Conference on Human Factors in Computing Systems, Atlanta, GA, 10–15 Apr. (pp. 4,477–80).

Mazzarella, S. R. (2005). *Girl Wide Web: Girls, the Internet, and the Negotiation of Identity*. New York: Peter Lang.

McAfee–NCSA (2007). *McAfee-NCSA Online Safety Study – Newsworthy Analysis*, October 2007. Retrieved from http://download.mcafee.com/products/manuals/en-us/McAfeeNCSA_Analysis09-25-07.pdf.

McArthur, S. (2008). Global governance and the rise of NGOs. *Asian Journal of Public Affairs*, **2** (1), 54–67.

McCauley, C. and Moskalenko, S. (2008). Mechanisms of political radicalisation: pathways toward terrorism. *Terrorism and Political Violence*, **20**, 415–33.

McDonald, H. (2 August 2009). MP calls on YouTube to remove Real IRA propaganda videos: 'Cyber-terrorism' films of dissident republicans could be banned from site. *The Observer Supplement. The Guardian Newspaper*. Retrieved from www.guardian.co.uk/technology/2009/aug/02/youtube-ira-facebook-cyber-terrorism.

McFarlane, L. and Bocij, P. (2003). An exploration of predatory behaviour in cyberspace: towards a typology of cyber stalkers. *First Monday*, **8** (9). Retrieved from www.firstmonday.org/htbin/cgiwrap/bin/ojs/index.php/fm/article/view/1076/996.

McGhee, I., Bayzick, J., Kontostathis, A., Edwards, L., McBride, A. and Jakubowski, E. (2011). Learning to identify internet sexual predation. *International Journal of Electronic Commerce*, **15**, 103–22.

McGuire, J. (1997). 'Irrational' shoplifting and models of addiction. In J. E. Hodge, M. McMurran and C. R. Hollin (eds), *Addicted to Crime?* Chichester, UK: Wiley (pp. 207–31).

McKinnon, R. C. (1997). Punishing the persona: correctional strategies for the virtual offender. In S. Jones (ed.), *Virtual Culture: Identity and Communication in Cybersociety*. Thousand Oaks, CA: Sage (pp. 206–35).

McQuade, S. C. (III) (2006). *Understanding and Managing Cybercrime*. Boston, MA: Allyn and Bacon.

Meadows, M. S. (2008). *I, Avatar: the Culture and Consequences of Having a Second Life*. Berkeley, CA: New Riders.

Mears, D. P., Mancini, C., Gertz, M. and Bratton, J. (2008). Sex crimes, children and pornography: public views and public policy. *Crime and Delinquency*, **54**, 532–59.

Meier, M. H., Slutske, W. S., Arndt, S. and Cadoret, R. J. (2008). Impulsive and callous traits are more strongly associated with delinquent behavior in higher risk neighborhoods among boys and girls. *Journal of Abnormal Psychology*, **117**, 377–85.

Meinel, C. P. (1998). How hackers break in... and how they are caught. *Scientific American*, **279**, 98–105.

Melander, L. A. (2010). College students' perceptions of intimate partner cyber harassment. *Cyberpsychology, Behavior and Social Networking*, **13**, 263–8.

Meloy, J. R. (1998). The psychology of stalking. In J. R. Meloy (ed.), *The Psychology of Stalking: Clinical and Forensic Perspectives*. London: Academic Press (pp. 1–23).

(2000). Stalking (obsessional following). In J. R. Meloy (ed.). *Violence, Risk and Threat Assessment*. San Diego, CA: Specialised Training Services (pp. 167–91).

Menesini, E., Nocentini, A. and Calussi, P. (2011). The measurement of cyberbullying: dimensional structure and relative item severity and discrimination. *Cyberpsychology, Behavior and Social Networking*, **14**, 267–74.

Merari, A. (2007). Psychological aspects of suicide terrorism. In B. Bongar, L. M. Brown, L. E. Beutler, J. N. Brecenridge and P. B. Zimbardo (eds.), *Psychology of Terrorism*. New York: Oxford University Press (pp. 101–15).

Mesch, G. S. (2009). Parental mediation, online activities and cyberbullying. *Cyberpsychology and Behaviour*, **12**, 387–93.

Microsoft (10 February 2009). 29% of European teenagers are victims of online bullying. Retrieved from www.microsoft.com/emea/presscentre/pressreleases/OnlinebullyingPR_100209.mspx.

Middleton, D. (2004). Current treatment approaches. In M. Calder (ed.), *Child Sexual Abuse and the Internet: Tackling the New Frontier*. Lyme Regis, UK: Russell House Publishing (pp. 99–112).

(2008). From research to practice: the development of the internet sex offender treatment programme (i-SOTP). *Irish Probation Journal*, **5**, 49–64.

(2009). Internet sex offenders. In A. R. Beech, L. Craig and K. D. Browne (eds.), *Assessment and Treatment of Sex Offenders: a Handbook*. Chichester, UK: Wiley (pp. 199–215).

Middleton, D., Elliott, I. A., Mandeville-Norden, R. and Beech, A. R. (2006). An investigation into the applicability of the Ward and Siegert pathways model of child sexual abuse with internet offenders. *Psychology, Crime and Law*, **12**, 589–603.

Middleton, D., Mandeville-Norden, R. and Hayes, E. (2009). Does treatment work with internet sex offenders? Emerging findings from the internet sex offender treatment programme (i-SOTP). *Journal of Sexual Aggression*, **15**, 5–19.

Mintz, A. (2012). *Web of Deceit: Misinformation and Manipulation in the Age of Social Media*. Medford, NJ: Information Today.

Mishna, F., Cook, C., Saini, M., Wu, M. and MacFadden, R. (2011). Interventions to prevent and reduce cyber abuse of youth: a systematic review. *Research on Social Work Practice*, **21**, 5–14.

Mishra, A. and Mishra, D. (2008). Cyber stalking: a challenge for web security. In L. J. Janczewski and A. M. Colarik (eds.), *Cyber Warfare and Cyber Terrorism*. Hershey, PA: Information Science Reference (pp. 216–25).

Mitchell, K. J., Finkelhor, D., Jones, L. M. and Wolak, J. (2010). Use of social networking sites in online sex crimes against minors: an examination of national incidence and means of utilization. *Journal of Adolescent Health*, **47** (2), 183–90.

Mitchell, K. J., Finkelhor, D. and Wolak, J. (2007). Youth internet users at risk for the most serious online sexual solicitations. *American Journal of Preventative Medicine*, **32**, 532–7.

Mitchell, K. J., Wolak, J. and Finkelhor, D. (2005). Police posing as juveniles online to catch sex offenders: is it working? *Sexual Abuse: A Journal of Research and Treatment*, **17**, 241–67.

Mitnick, K. D. and Simon, W. L. (2002). *The Art of Deception: Controlling the Human Element of Security*. Indianapolis, IN: Wiley Publishing Inc.

(2005). *The Art of Intrusion: the Real Stories Behind the Exploits of Hackers, Intruders and Deceivers*. Indianapolis, IN: Wiley Publishing Inc.

Mizrach, S. (n.d.). Is there a hacker ethic for 90s hackers? Retrieved from www.fiu.edu/~mizrachs/hackethic.html.

Moore, R. and McMullan, E. C. (2009). Neutralizations and rationalizations of digital piracy: a qualitative analysis of university students. *International Journal of Cyber Criminology*, **3**, 441–51.

Moriarty, L. J. and Freiberger, K. (2008). Cyberstalking: utilising newspaper accounts to establish victimization patterns. *Victims and Offenders*, **3**, 131–41.

Morison, J. and Newman, D. (2001). On-line citizenship: consultation and participation in New Labour's Britain and beyond. *International Review of Law, Computers and Technology*, **15**, 171–94.

Morris, R. G. and Higgins, G. E. (2009). Neutralizing potential and self-reported digital piracy: a multi-theoretical exploration among college undergraduates. *Criminal Justice Review*, **34**, 173–95.

(2010). Criminological theory in the digital age: the case of social learning theory and digital piracy. *Journal of Criminal Justice*. Retrieved from http://dx.doi.org/10.1016/j.jcrimjus.2010.04.016.

Mullen, P. E., Pathé, M., Purcell, R. and Stuart, G. W. (1999). Study of stalkers. *American Journal of Psychiatry*, **156**, 1,244–9.

Muncie, J., McLaughlin, E. and Langan, M. (1996). *Criminological Perspectives: a Reader*. London: Sage Publications Ltd.

Murphy, C. (June 2004). Inside the mind of the hacker. *Accountancy Ireland*, **36**, 12.

Murray, C. D., Fox, J. and Pettifer, S. (2007). Absorption, dissociation, locus of control and presence in virtual reality. *Computers in Human Behavior*, **23**, 1,347–54.

Nandedkar, A. and Midha, V. (2012). It won't happen to me: an assessment of optimism bias in music piracy. *Computers in Human Behavior*, **28**, 41–8.

Nathanson, H. S. (1995). Strengthening the criminal jury: long overdue. *Criminal Law Quarterly*, **38**, 217–48.

National Fraud Authority (March 2012). Annual fraud indicator. Retrieved from www.homeoffice.gov.uk/publications/agencies-public-bodies/nfa/annual-fraud-indicator/annual-fraud-indicator-2012?view=Binary.

Nelson, B., Choi, R., Iacobucci, M., Mitchell, M. and Gagnon, G. (August 1999). *Cyberterror: Prospects and Implications*. Monterey, CA: Naval Postgraduate School, Center for the Study of Terrorism and Irregular Warfare.

New World Encyclopedia (n.d.). 'Cybercrime' definition. Retrieved from www.newworldencyclopedia.org/entry/Cyber_crime.

Ng, B. Y., Kankanhalli, A. and Xu, Y. C. (2009). Studying users' computer security behaviour: a health belief perspective. *Decision Support Systems*, **46**, 815–25.

Ng, B. Y. and Rahim, M. A. (2005). *A Socio-Behavioral Study of Home Computer Users' Intention to Practice Security*. The Ninth Pacific Asia Conference on Information Systems, 7–10 July, Bangkok, Thailand.

Nhan, J., Kinkade, P. and Burns, R. (2009). Finding a pot of gold at the end of an internet rainbow: further examination of fraudulent email solicitation. *International Journal of Cyber Criminology*, **3**, 452–75.

Nuñez, J. (2003). Outpatient treatment of the sexually compulsive hebophile. *Sexual Addiction and Compulsivity*, **10**, 23–51.

Nykodym, N., Taylor, R. and Vilela, J. (2005). Criminal profiling and insider cybercrime. *Computer Law and Security Report*, **21**, 408–14.

Oberholzer-Gee, F. and Strumpf, K. S. (2007). The effect of file sharing on record sales: an empirical analysis. *Journal of Political Economy*, **115**, 1–42.

O'Brien, M. D. and Webster, S. D. (2007). The construction and preliminary validation of the Internet Behaviours and Attitudes Questionnaire (IBAQ). *Sex Abuse*, **19**, 237–56.

O'Connell, M. (2002). The portrayal of crime in the media: does it matter? In P. O'Mahony (ed.), *Criminal Justice in Ireland*. Dublin: IPA (pp. 245–67).

O'Connell, R. (2003). *A Typology of Child Cyberexploitation and Online Grooming Practices*. Lancashire: Cyberspace Research Unit, University of Central Lancashire.

Ollmann, G. (2008). The evolution of commercial malware development kits and colour-by-numbers custom malware. *Computer Fraud and Security*, **9**, 4–7.

O'Sullivan, P. B. and Flanagin, A. J. (2003). Reconceptualising 'flaming' and other problematic messages. *New Media and Society*, **5**, 69–94.

Palmer, E. J. and Hollin, C. R. (1998). Comparison of patterns of moral development in young offenders and non-offenders. *Legal and Criminological Psychology*, **3**, 225–35.

Park, A. J., Calvert, T. W., Brantingham, P. L and Brantingham, P. J. (2008). The use of virtual and mixed reality environments for urban behavioural studies. *PsychNology Journal*, **6**, 119–30.

Parsons-Pollard, N. and Moriarty, L. J. (2009). Cyberstalking: utilising what we do know. *Victims and Offenders*, **4**, 435–41.

Patchin, J. W. and Hinduja, S. (2006). Bullies move beyond the schoolyard: a preliminary look at cyberbullying. *Youth Violence and Juvenile Justice*, **4**, 148–69.

   (2011). Traditional and nontraditional bullying among youth: a test of general strain theory. *Youth Society*, **43**, 727–51.

Payne, J. W. (1980). Information processing theory: some concepts and methods applied to decision research. In T. S. Wallsten (ed.), *Cognitive Processes in Choice and Decision Behaviour*. Hillsdale, NJ: Erlbaum.

PC Magazine Encyclopedia (n.d.). 'Cybercrime' definition. Retrieved from www.pcmag.com/encyclopedia_term/0,2542,t=cybercrime&i=40628,00.asp.

Pearce, C. (2006). Seeing and being seen: presence and play in online virtual worlds. In *Online, Offline and the Concept of Presence when Games and VR Collide*. Los Angeles, CA: USC Institute for Creative Technologies.

Peitz, M. and Waelbroeck, P. (2006). Why the music industry may gain from free downloading – the role of sampling. *International Journal of Industrial Organisation*, **24**, 907–13.

Perez, L. M., Jones, J., Englert, D. R. and Sachau, D. (2010). Secondary traumatic stress and burnout among law enforcement investigators exposed to disturbing media images. *Journal of Police and Criminal Psychology*, **25**, 113–24.

Philips, F. and Morrissey, G. (2004). Cyberstalking and cyberpredators: a threat to safe sexuality on the internet. *Convergence*, **10**, 66–79.

Piquero, A. R., Moffitt, T. E. and Wright, B. E. (2007). Self control and criminal career dimensions. *Journal of Contemporary Criminal Justice*, **23**, 72–89.

Piquero, N. L. (2005). Causes and prevention of intellectual property crime. *Trends in Organised Crime*, **8**, 40–61.

Pittaro, M. L. (2007). Cyber stalking: an analysis of online harassment and intimidation. *International Journal of Cyber Criminology*, **1**, 180–97.

(2011). Cyber stalking: typology, etiology, and victims. In K. Jaishankar (ed.), *Cyber Criminology: Exploring Internet Crimes and Criminal Behavior*. Boca Raton, FL: CRC Press (pp. 277–97).

Platt, C. (November 1994, Issue 2). Hackers: threat or menace? Wired, 82–8. Retrieved from www.wired.com/wired/archive/2.11/hack.cong.html.

Pollitt, M. M. (October 1997). Cyberterrorism: fact or fancy? Proceedings of the 20th National Information Systems Security Conference, pp. 285–9.

Post, D. (1996). Governing cyberspace. *The Wayne Law Review*, **43**, 155–71.

Post, J. M. (1984). Notes on a psychodynamic theory of terrorist behaviour. *Terrorism*, **7**, 241–56.

Post, J. M., Ali, F., Henderson, S. W., Shanfield, S., Victoroff, J. and Weine, S. (2009). The psychology of suicide terrorism. *Psychiatry: Interpersonal and Biological Processes*, **72**, 13–31.

Post, J. M., Sprinzak, E. and Denny, L. M. (2003). The terrorists in their own words: interviews with thirty-five incarcerated Middle Eastern terrorists. *Terrorism and Political Violence*, **15**, 171–84.

Power, A. (2010). The online public or cybercitizen. *SCRIPTed: a Journal of Law, Technology and Society*, **7** (1), 185–95. Retrieved from www.law.ed.ac.uk/ahrc/script-ed/vol7-1/power.asp.

Power, A. and Kirwan, G. (2011). Ethics and legal aspects of virtual worlds. In A. Dudley, J. Braman and G. Vincenti (eds.), *Investigating Cyber Law and Cyber Ethics: Issues, Impacts and Practices*. Hershey, PA: Information Science Reference (pp. 117–31).

Preuß, J., Furnell, S. M. and Papadaki, M. (2007). Considering the potential of criminal profiling to combat hacking. *Journal in Computer Virology*, **3**, 135–41.

Princeton University (n.d.). 'Cybercrime' definition. Retrieved from http://wordnetweb.princeton.edu/perl/webwn?s=cybercrime.

Privitera, C. and Campbell, M. A. (2009). Cyberbullying: the new face of workplace bullying? *CyberPsychology and Behavior*, **12**, 395–400.

Protalinski, E. (2012). Facebook has over 845 million users. *ZDNet*. Retrieved from www.zdnet.com/blog/Facebook/Facebook-has-over-845-million-users/8332.

Quayle, E. and Jones, T. (2011). Sexualised images of children on the internet. *Sexual Abuse: a Journal of Research and Treatment*, **23**, 7–21.

Quayle, E. and Taylor, M. (2002). Child pornography and the internet: perpetuating a cycle of abuse. *Deviant Behaviour: an Interdisciplinary Journal*, **23**, 365–95.

Quayle, E., Vaughan, M. and Taylor, M. (2006). Sex offenders, internet child abuse images and emotional avoidance: the importance of values. *Aggression and Violent Behavior*, **11**, 1–11.

Raine, A. (2008). From genes to brain to antisocial behaviour. *Current Directions in Psychological Science*, **17**, 323–8.

Rantala, R. R. (2008). Cybercrime against businesses 2005, NCJ 221943. *US Department of Justice, Bureau of Justice Statistics*. Retrieved from *http://bjs.ojp.usdoj.gov/content/pub/pdf/cb05.pdf*.

Raskauskas, J. and Stoltz, A. D. (2007). Involvement in traditional and electronic bullying among adolescents. *Developmental Psychology*, **43**, 564–75.

Rege, A. (2009). What's love got to do with it? Exploring online dating scams and identity fraud. *International Journal of Cyber Criminology*, **3**, 494–512.

Reijnen, L., Bulten, E. and Nijman, H. (2009). Demographic and personality characteristics of internet child pornography downloaders in comparison to other offenders. *Journal of Child Sexual Abuse*, **18**, 611–22.

Rennie, L. and Shore, M. (2007). An advanced model of hacking. *Security Journal*, **20**, 236–251.

Reyns, B. W. (2010). A situational crime prevention approach to cyberstalking victimization: preventive tactics for internet users and online place managers. *Crime Prevention and Community Safety*, **12**, 99–118.

Reyns, B. W. and Englebrecht, C. M. (2010). The stalking victim's decision to contact the police: a test of Gottfredson and Gottfredson's theory of criminal justice decision making. *Journal of Criminal Justice*, **38**, 998–1,005.

Reyns, B. W., Henson, B. and Fisher, B. S. (2011). Being pursued online: applying cyberlifestyle routine activities theory to cyberstalking victimization. *Criminal Justice and Behavior*, **38**, 1,149–69.

(2012). Stalking in the twilight zone: extent of cyberstalking victimization and offending among college students. *Deviant Behaviour*, **33**, 1–25.

Riegel, D. L. (2004). Effects on boy-attracted pedosexual males of viewing boy erotica. *Arch. Sex. Behav*, **33**, 321–3.

Riva, G., Mantovani, F., Capideville, C. S., Preziosa, A., Morganti, F., Villani, D., Gaggioli, A., Botella, C. and Alcaniz, M. (2007). Affective interactions using virtual reality: the link between presence and emotions. *Cyberpsychology and Behaviour*, **10**, 45–56.

Roberts, L. (2008). Jurisdictional and definitional concerns with computer-mediated interpersonal crimes: an analysis on cyber stalking. *International Journal of Cyber Criminology*, **2** (1). Retrieved from www.cybercrimejournal.com/lynnerobertsijccjan2008.pdf.

Robertson, K., McNeill, L., Green, J. and Roberts, C. (2012). Illegal downloading, ethical concern and illegal behaviour. *Journal of Business Ethics*, **108**, 215–27.

Robins, L. N., West, P. A. and Herjanic, B. L. (1975). Arrests and delinquency in two generations: a study of black urban families and their children. *Journal of Child Psychology and Psychiatry*, **16**, 125–40.

Rock, P. (2007). Sociological theories of crime. In M. Maguire, R. Morgan and R. Reiner (eds.), *The Oxford Handbook of Criminology* (4th edn). Oxford University Press (pp. 3–42).

Rocque, M., Welsh, B. C. and Raine, A. (2012). Biosocial criminology and modern crime prevention. *Journal of Criminal Justice*, **40**, 306–12.

Rogers, M. (2000). *A New Hacker Taxonomy*. Canada: University of Manitoba. Retrieved from http://homes.cerias.purdue.edu/~mkr/hacker.doc.

(2003). The role of criminal profiling in the computer forensic process. *Computers and Security*, **22**, 292–8.

Rogers, M. K., Siegfried, K. and Tidke, K. (2006). Self-reported computer criminal behaviour: a psychological analysis. *Digital Investigation*, **3S**, S116–20.

Rogers, M. K., Smoak, N. and Liu, J. (2006). Self-reported criminal computer behaviour: a big-5, moral choice and manipulative exploitive behaviour analysis. *Deviant Behaviour*, **27**, 1–24.

Rogers, R. W. (1975). A protection motivation theory of fear appeals and attitude change. *The Journal of Psychology*, **91**, 93–114.

(1983). Cognitive and physiological processes in fear appeals and attitude change: a revised theory of protection motivation. In J. Cacioppo and R. Petty (eds.), *Social Psychophysiology*. New York: Guildford Press (pp. 153–76).

Rollins, J. and Wilson, C. (2007). Terrorist capabilities for cyberattack: overview and policy issues. In E. V. Linden (ed.), *Focus on Terrorism, Vol. 9*. New York: Nova Science Publishers Inc. (pp. 43–63).

Rosenstock, I. M. (1966). Why people use health services. *Millbank Memorial Fund Quarterly*, **44**, 94–124.

Rusch, J. J. (21 June 2002). The social psychology of computer viruses and worms. Paper presented at INET 2002, Crystal City, Virginia. Retrieved from http://m4dch4t.effraie.org/vxdevl/papers/avers/g10-c.pdf.

Sageman, M. (2004). *Understanding Terror Networks*. Philadelphia, PA: University of Pennsylvania Press.

(2008). *Leaderless Jihad*. Philadelphia, PA: University of Pennsylvania Press.

Sanders-Reach, C. (6 May 2005). Beware pharming and other new hacker scams. *Law Technology News*. Retrieved from www.law.com/jsp/lawtechnologynews/PubArticleLTN.jsp?id=900005428456&slreturn=20130104095007.

Scarpa, A., Haden, S. C. and Hurley, J. (2006). Community violence victimization and symptoms of post-traumatic stress disorder. *Journal of Interpersonal Violence*, **21**, 446–69.

Schäfer, A. (2006). Resolving deadlock: why international organisations introduce soft law. *European Law Journal*, **12**, 194–208.

Schmucker, M. and Lösel, F. (2008). Does sexual offender treatment work? A systematic review of outcome evaluations. *Psicothema*, **20**, 10–19.

Schneider, J. P. (2000). Effects of cybersex addiction on the family: results of a survey. In A. Cooper (ed.), *Cybersex: the Dark Side of the Force*. New York: Brunner/Mazel.

Schneier, B. (November/December 2003). *IEEE Security and Privacy*, **1**, 6.

Scully, D. and Marolla, J. (1993). 'Riding the bull at Gilley's': convicted rapists describe the rewards of rape. In P. Bart and E. G. Moran (eds.), *Violence against Women: the Bloody Footprints*. Thousand Oaks, CA: Sage (pp. 26–46).

Senden, L. (2004). *Soft Law in European Community Law*. Portland, OR: Hart Publishing.

Sentencing Guidelines Council (2007). *Sexual Offences Act 2003: Definitive Guideline*. April 2007. Retrieved from http://sentencingcouncil.judiciary.gov.uk/docs/web_SexualOffencesAct_2003.pdf.

Seto, M. C. and Eke, A. W. (2005). The criminal histories and later offending of child pornography offenders. *Sexual Abuse: a Journal of Research and Treatment*, **17**, 201–10.

Shariff, S. (2005). Cyber-dilemmas in the new millennium: school obligations to provide student safety in a virtual school environment. *McGill Journal of Education*, **40** (3) 457–77.

Shariff, S. and Gouin, R. (2005). *Cyber-dilemmas: Gendered Hierarchies, Free Expression and Cyber-safety in Schools*. Paper presented at the Oxford Internet Institute (OII), Oxford University Conference on 8 September 2005. Retrieved from www.oii.ox.ac.uk/microsites/cybersafety/extensions/pdfs/papers/shaheen_shariff.pdf.

Sharp, T., Shreve-Neiger, A., Fremouw, W., Kane, J. and Hutton, S. (2004). Exploring the psychological and somatic impact of identity theft. *Journal of Forensic Science*, **49**, 131–6.

Sheldon, K. and Howitt, D. (2007). *Sex Offenders and the Internet*. Chichester, UK: Wiley.

Sheng, S., Holbrook, M., Kumaraguru, P., Cranor, L. and Downs, J. (2010). Who falls for phish? A demographic analysis of phishing susceptibility and effectiveness of interventions. Computer Human Interaction *(CHI)*, 10–15 April, Atlanta, Georgia.

Sheridan, L. P. and Davies, G. (2004). Stalking. In J. R. Adler (ed.), *Forensic Psychology: Concepts, Debates and Practice*. Cullompton, UK: Willan Publishing (pp. 197–215).

Sheridan, L. P. and Grant, T. (2007). Is cyberstalking different? *Psychology, Crime and Law*, **13**, 627–40.

Shernoff, D. J., Csikszentmihalyi, M., Schneider, B. and Shernoff, E. S. (2003). Student engagement in high school classrooms from the perspective of flow theory. *School Psychology Quarterly*, **18**, 158–76.

Shiels, M. (9 April 2009). Spies 'infiltrate US power grid'. *BBC News*. Retrieved from http://news.bbc.co.uk/2/hi/technology/7990997.stm.

Shirky, C. (2009). *Here Comes Everybody*. London: Penguin.

(2010). *Cognitive Surplus*. London: Penguin.

Siegfried, K. C., Lovely, R. W. and Rogers, M. K. (2008). Self-reported online child pornography behaviour: a psychological analysis. *International Journal of Cyber Criminology*, **2**, 286–97.

Silbert, M. (1989). The effects on juveniles of being used for pornography and prostitution. In D. Zillmann and J. Bryant (eds.), *Pornography: Research Advances and Policy Considerations*. Hillsdale, NJ: Lawrence Erlbaum.

Silke, A. (1998). Cheshire-cat logic: the recurring theme of terrorist abnormality in psychological research. *Psychology, Crime and Law*, **4**, 51–69.

(2003). Becoming a terrorist. In A. Silke (ed.), *Terrorists, Victims and Society: Psychological Perspectives on Terrorism and its Consequences*. Chichester, UK: John Wiley and Sons.

(2008). Research on terrorism: a review of the impact of 9/11 and the global war on terrorism. *Terrorism Informatics*, **18**, 27–50.

Sindico, F. (2006). Soft law and the elusive quest for sustainable global governance. *Leiden Journal of International Law*, **19**, 829–46.

Siponen, M., Vance, A. and Willison, R. (January 2010). New insights for an old problem: explaining software piracy through neutralisation theory. *Proceedings of the 43rd Hawaii International Conference on System Sciences, US*, 1–10.

Sipress, A. (2007). *Does Virtual Reality Need a Sheriff?* Retrieved from www.washingtonpost.com/wp-dyn/content/article/2007/06/01/AR2007060102671.html.

Slaughter, A. (2004). *A New World Order*. Princeton University Press.

Smith, F. and Bace, R. (2003). *A Guide to Forensic Testimony: the Art and Practice of Presenting Testimony as an Expert Technical Witness*. Boston: MA: Addison Wesley.

Smith, P., Mahdavi, J., Carvalho, M. and Tippet, N. (July 2006). An investigation into cyberbullying, its forms, awareness and impact, and the relationship between age and gender in cyberbullying. Retrieved from www.plymouthcurriculum.swgfl.org.uk/resources/ict/cyberbullying/Cyberbullying.pdf.

Smith, R. G. (2004). *Cyber Crime Sentencing. The Effectiveness of Criminal Justice Responses. Crime in Australia: International Connections*. Australian Institute of Criminology International Conference, Hilton on the Park, Melbourne, Australia, 29–30 November 2004.

(2007). Biometric solutions to identity-related cybercrime. In Y. Jewkes (ed.), *Crime Online*. Cullompton, UK: Willan Publishing (pp. 44–59).

(2010). Identity theft and fraud. In Y. Jewkes and M. Yar (eds.), *Handbook of Internet Crime*. Cullompton, UK: Willan Publishing (pp. 173–301).

Socarides, C. W. (2004). *The Mind of the Paedophile: Psychoanalytic Perspectives*. London: H. Karnac Ltd.

Spinello, R. (2000). Information integrity. In D. Langford (ed.), *Internet Ethics*. London: Macmillan Press (pp. 158–80).

Spiro, P. J. (1998). Review: non-state actors in global politics. *The American Journal of International Law,* **92**, 808–11.

Spitzberg, B. and Hoobler, G. (2002). Cyberstalking and the technologies of interpersonal terrorism. *New Media and Society*, **4**, 71–92.

Spitzner, L. (2003). *Honeypots: Tracking Hackers*. Boston, MA: Addison-Wesley Inc.

Steel, C. M. S. (2009). Child pornography in peer-to-peer networks. *Child Abuse and Neglect*, **33**, 560–8.

Steffgen, G., König, A., Pfetsch, J. and Melzer, A. (2011). Are cyberbullies less empathic? Adolescents' cyberbullying behaviour and empathic responsiveness. *Cyberpsychology, Behavior and Social Networking*, **14**, 643–8.

Stephens, P. (2008). IPR and technological protection measures. In R. Bryant (ed.), *Investigating Digital Crime*. Chichester, UK: Wiley (pp. 121–31).

Sterling, B. (1992). *The Hacker Crackdown: Law and Disorder on the Electronic Frontier*. New York: Penguin.

Stohl, M. (2006). Cyber terrorism: a clear and present danger, the sum of all fears, breaking point or patriot games? *Crime, Law and Social Change*, **46**, 223–38.

Strom, P. S. and Strom, R. D. (2005). When teens turn cyberbullies. *The Education Digest*, **71**, 35–41.

Sue, D., Sue, D. W. and Sue, S. (2005). *Essentials of Understanding Abnormal Behaviour*. Boston: Houghton Mifflin.

Sunstein, C. R. (2007). *Republic.com 2.0*. Princeton University Press.

Svenson, S. and Maule, A. (1993). *Time Pressure and Stress in Human Judgement and Decision Making*. New York: Plenum.

Swire, P. (2005). Elephants and mice revisited: law and choice of law on the Internet. *University of Pennsylvania Law Review*, **153**, 1,975–2,001.

Sykes, G. and Matza, D. (1957). Techniques of neutralization: a theory of delinquency. *American Sociological Review*, **22**, 664–70.

Symantec (n.d.). *What is Cybercrime?* Retrieved from www.symantec.com/norton/cybercrime/definition.jsp.

(2011a). *Symantec Intelligence Quarterly*: Apr.–Jun. 2011. Retrieved from www.symantec.com/content/en/us/enterprise/white_papers/b-symc_intelligence_qtrly_apr_to_jun_WP.en-us.pdf.

(2011b). *Symantec Internet Security Threat Report: Trends for 2010* (Vol. **16**, April). Retrieved from www.symantec.com/business/threatreport.

Talbert, F. S., Braswell, L. C., Albrecht, I. W., Hyer, L. A. and Boudewyns, P. A. (1993). NEO-PI profiles in PTSD as a function of trauma level. *Journal of Clinical Psychology*, **49**, 663–9.

Tam, L., Glassman, M. and Vandenwauver, M. (2009). The psychology of password management: a tradeoff between security and convenience. *Behaviour and Information Technology*, **29**, 233–44.

Tapscott, D. (2009). *Grown Up Digital*. New York: McGraw-Hill.

Tavani, H. T. (2011). *Ethics and Technology: Ethical Issues in an Age of Information and Communication Technology* (3rd edn). Hoboken, NJ: Wiley.

Taylor, M. (2012). Terrorism. In G. Davies and A. Beech (eds.), *Forensic Psychology: Crime, Justice, Law, Interventions* (2nd edn). Chichester, UK: BPS Blackwell (pp. 207–25).

Taylor, M. and Quayle, E. (1994). *Terrorist Lives*. London: Brassey's.

(2003). *Child Pornography: an Internet Crime*. Hove: Brunner-Routledge.

Taylor, M., Quayle, E. and Holland, G. (2001). Child pornography, the internet and offending, ISUMA. *The Canadian Journal of Policy Research*, **2**, 94–100.

Taylor, P. (1999). *Hackers*. London: Routledge.

Taylor, P. A. (2001). Hacktivism: in search of lost ethics? In D. S. Wall (ed.), *Crime and the Internet*. London: Routledge (pp. 59–73).

(2003). Maestros or misogynists? Gender and the social construction of hacking. In Y. Jewkes (ed.), *Dot.cons: Crime, Deviance and Identity on the Internet*. Cullompton, UK: Willan Publishing (pp. 126–46).

Thompson, C. (8 February 2004). The virus underground. *The New York Times Magazine* (pp. 30–3, 72, 79–81). Retrieved at www.nytimes.com/2004/02/08/magazine/08WORMS.html?pagewanted=all.

Thompson, R. (2005). Why spyware poses multiple threats to society. *Communications of the ACM*, **48**, 41–3.

Torres, A. N., Boccaccini, M. T. and Miller, H. A. (2006). Perceptions of the validity and utility of criminal profiling among forensic psychologists and psychiatrists. *Professional Psychology Research and Practice*, **37**, 51–8.

Toth, K. and King, B. H. (2008). Asperger's Syndrome: diagnosis and treatment. *American Journal of Psychiatry*, **165**, 958–63.

Trevethan, S. D. and Walker, L. J. (1989). Hypothetical versus real-life moral reasoning among psychopathic and delinquent youth. *Development and Psychopathology*, **1**, 91–103.

Turgeman-Goldschmidt, O. (2011). Identity construction among hackers. In K. Jaishankar (ed.), *Cyber Criminology: Exploring Internet Crimes and Criminal Behaviour* (pp. 31–51). Boca Raton, FL: CRC Press.

Turkle, S. (1984). *The Second Self: Computers and the Human Spirit*. New York: Simon and Schuster Inc.

Twyman, K., Saylor, C., Taylor, L. A. and Comeaux, C. (2009). Comparing children and adolescents engaged in cyberbullying to matched peers. *Cyberpsychology and Behaviour*, **12**, 1–5.

Tversky, A. and Kahneman, D. (1974). Judgement under uncertainty: heuristics and biases. *Science*, **211**, 453–8.

Tynes, B. M. (2007). Internet safety gone wild? Sacrificing the educational and psychosocial benefits of online social environments. *Journal of Adolescent Research*, **22**, 575–84.

UN News Service (2010). *Robust Demand for Mobile Phone Services will Continue, UN agency predicts*. Retrieved from www.un.org/apps/news/story.asp?NewsID=33770&Cr=Telecom&Cr1.

United Press International (9 April 2008). *Survey: Cyber-bullying Affects US Teens*. Retrieved from www.upi.com/NewsTrack/Health/2008/04/09/survey_cyberbullying_affects_us_teens/3823.

US Department of Homeland Security (2003). *National Strategy to Secure Cyberspace*. Retrieved from www.dhs.gov/files/publications/editorial_0329.shtm.

US Department of Justice (9 August 1999). Kevin Mitnick sentenced to nearly four years in prison; computer hacker ordered to pay restitution to victim companies whose systems were compromised. Retrieved from www.justice.gov/criminal/cybercrime/mitnick.htm.

Veerasamy, N. (2010). *Motivation for Cyberterrorism. 9th Annual Information Security South Africa (ISSA) – Towards New Security Paradigms*. Sandton Convention Centre, 2–4 August 2010 (p. 6).

Verone (n.d.). Piracy Guide. *EVElopedia*. Retrieved from http://wiki.eveonline.com/en/wiki/Piracy_guide.

Victoroff, J. (2005). The mind of the terrorist: a review and critique of psychological approaches. *Journal of Conflict Resolution*, **49**, 3–42.

Vinyagamoorthy, V., Brogni, A., Gillies, M., Slater, M. and Steed, A. (2004). An investigation of presence response across variations in visual realism. Proceedings of Presence 2004: The 7th Annual International Workshop on Presence, Valencia, Spain, 13–15 Oct.

Vishwanath, A., Herath, T., Chen, R., Wang, J. and Rao, H. R. (2011). Why do people get phished? Testing individual differences in phishing vulnerability within an integrated, information processing model. *Decision Support Systems*, **51** (3), 576–86.

Voiskounsky, A. E. and Smyslova, O. V. (2003). Flow-based model of computer hacker's motivation. *CyberPsychology and Behaviour*, **6**, 171–80.

Von Hirsch, A., Bottoms, A. E., Burney, E. and Wickstrom, P. O. (1999). *Criminal Deterrence and Sentence Severity*. Oxford: Hart.

Walker, C. (2001). The criminal courts online. In D. S. Wall (ed.), *Crime and the Internet*. London: Routledge (pp. 195–214).

Walklate, S. (2006). *Imagining the Victim of Crime*. UK: Open University Press.

Wall, D. S. (2007). *Cybercrime: the Transformation of Crime in the Information Age*. Cambridge, UK: Polity Press.

Wall, D. S. and Williams, M. (2007). Policing diversity in the digital age: maintaining order in virtual communities. *Criminology and Criminal Justice*, 7, 391–415.

Wall, D. S. and Yar, M. (2010). Intellectual property crime and the Internet: cyber-piracy and 'stealing' information intangibles. In Y. Jewkes and M. Yar (eds.), *Handbook of Internet Crime*. Cullompton, UK: Willan Publishing (pp. 255–72).

Wall, G. K., Pearce, E. and McGuire, J. (2011). Are internet offenders emotionally avoidant? *Psychology, Crime and Law*, 17, 381–401.

Walther, J. B. (1996). Computer-mediated communication: impersonal, interpersonal, and hyperpersonal interaction. *Communication Research*, 23, 3–43.

(2007). Selective self-presentation in computer-mediated communication: hyperpersonal dimensions of technology, language and cognition. *Computers in Human Behavior*, 23, 2,538–57.

Wang, W., Yuan, Y. and Archer, N. (2006). A contextual framework for combating identity theft. *IEEE Security and Privacy*, 4, 30–8.

Wang, X. and McClung, S. R. (2012). The immorality of illegal downloading: the role of anticipated guilt and general emotions. *Computers in Human Behaviour*, 28, 153–9.

Ward, T. (2001). Hall and Hirschman's quadripartite model of child sexual abuse: a critique. *Psychology, Crime and Law*, 7, 363–74.

Ward, T. and Durrant, R. (2011). Evolutionary behavioral science and crime: aetiological and intervention implications. *Legal and Criminological Psychology*, 16, 193–210.

Ward, T., Polaschek, D. and Beech, A. R. (2006). *Theories of Sexual Offending*. Chichester, UK: Wiley.

Ward, T. and Siegert, R. (2002). Toward a comprehensive theory of child sexual abuse: a theory of knitting perspective. *Psychology, Crime and Law*, 8, 319–51.

Warren, M. and Leitch, S. (2009). Hacker taggers: a new type of hackers. *Information Systems Frontiers*, 12 (4), 425–31.

Wash, R. (2010). Folk models of home computer security. Symposium on Usable Privacy and Security (SOUPS), Redmond, WA, 14–16 July. Retrieved from http://cups.cs.cmu.edu/soups/2010/proceedings/a11_Walsh.pdf.

Webb, L., Craissati, J. and Keen, S. (2007). Characteristics of internet child pornography offenders: a comparison with child molesters. *Sexual Abuse: a Journal of Research and Treatment*, 19, 449–65.

Weimann, G. (2004). www.*terror.net: How Modern Terrorism Uses the Internet*. Washington, DC: United States Institute of Peace. Retrieved from www.usip.org/pubs/specialreports/sr116.pdf, 5–11.

Weinstein, N. D. (1980). Unrealistic optimism about future life events. *Journal of Personality and Social Psychology*, 39, 806–20.

Welsh, B. C. and Farrington, D. P. (2004). Surveillance for crime prevention in public space: results and policy choices in Britain and America. *Criminology and Public Policy*, 3, 497–525.

(2006). *Preventing Crime: What Works for Children, Offenders, Victims and Places*. Dordrecht, The Netherlands: Springer.

Wemmers, J. A. and Cyr, K. (2006). Victims' perspectives on restorative justice: how much involvement are victims looking for? *International Review of Victimology*, 11, 259–74.

West, D. J. and Farrington, D. P. (1977). *The Delinquent Way of Life*. London: Heinemann.

Whitney, L. (26 March 2010). Symantec finds China top source of malware. *CNET Security*. Retrieved from http://news.cnet.com/8301-1009_3-20001234-83.html.

Whitson, J. and Doyle, A. (2008). Second life and governing deviance in virtual worlds. In S. Leman-Langlois (ed.), *Technocrime: Technology, Crime and Social Control*. Cullompton, UK: Willan (pp. 88–111).

Whittaker, D. J. (2004). *Terrorists and Terrorism in the Contemporary World*. London: Routledge.

Whitty, M. T. and Buchanan, T. (2012). The online romance scam: a serious cybercrime. *Cyberpsychology, Behaviour and Social Networking*, **15**, 181–3.

Wiederhold, B. K. and Wiederhold, M. D. (2005). *Virtual Reality Therapy for Anxiety Disorders: Advances in Evaluation and Treatment*. Washington, DC: American Psychological Association.

Willard, N. E. (2007). *Cyberbullying and Cyberthreats: Responding to the Challenge of Online Social Aggression, Threats, and Distress*. Champaign, IL: Research Press.

Williams, M. (2006). *Virtually Criminal: Crime, Deviance and Regulation Online*. Abingdon, Oxon, UK: Routledge.

Wilson, C. (2005). *Computer Attack and Cyberterrorism: Vulnerabilities and Policy Issues for Congress*. Washington, DC: Congressional Research Service: The Library of Congress. Retrieved from www.dtic.mil/cgi-bin/GetTRDoc?AD=ADA444799&Location=U2&doc=GetTRDoc.pdf.

(2007). *Botnets, Cybercrime and Cyberterrorism: Vulnerabilities and Policy Issues for Congress*. Washington, DC: Congressional Research Service: The Library of Congress. Retrieved from www.dtic.mil/cgi-bin/GetTRDoc?AD=ADA474929&Location=U2&doc=GetTRDoc.pdf.

Wilson, M. (2010). Terrorism research: current issues and debates. In J. M. Brown and E. A. Campbell (eds.), *The Cambridge Handbook of Forensic Psychology*. Cambridge University Press (pp. 571–8).

Wingrove, T., Korpas, A. L. and Weisz, V. (2011). Why were millions of people *not* obeying the law? Motivational influences on non-compliance with the law in the case of music piracy. *Psychology, Crime and Law*, **17**, 261–76.

Winterdyk, J. and Thompson, N. (2008). Student and non-student perceptions and awareness of identity theft. *Canadian Journal of Criminology and Criminal Justice*, **50**, 153–86.

Wolak, J., Finkelhor, D. and Mitchell, K. (2004). Internet-initiated sex crimes against minors: implications for prevention based on findings from a national study. *Journal of Adolescent Health*, **35**, 424–4.

(2005). *Child-pornography Possessors Arrested in Internet-related Crimes: Findings from the National Juvenile Online Victimization Study*. Alexandria, VA: National Center for Missing and Exploited Children.

(2008). Is talking online to unknown people always risky? Distinguishing online interaction styles in a national sample of youth internet users. *Cyberpsychology and Behaviour*, **11**, 340–3.

Wolak, J., Finkelhor, D., Mitchell, K. and Ybarra, M. (2008). Online 'predators' and their victims: myths, realities, and implications for prevention and treatment. *American Psychologist*, **63**, 111–28.

Wolak, J., Mitchell, K. and Finkelhor, D. (2006). *Online Victimization of Youth: Five Years Later. National Center for Missing and Exploited Children Bulletin – #07-06-025*. Retrieved from www.unh.edu/ccrc/pdf/CV138.pdf.

(2007). Does online harassment constitute bullying? An exploration of online harassment by known peers and online-only contacts. *Journal of Adolescent Health*, **41**, S51–8.

Wolfe, S. E., Higgins, G. E. and Marcum, C. D. (2008). Deterrence and digital piracy: a preliminary examination of the role of viruses. *Social Science Computer Review*, **26**, 317–33.

Woo, H. J. (2003). The hacker mentality: exploring the relationship between psychological variables and hacking activities. *Dissertation Abstracts International*, **64**, 2A, 325.

Woo, J. J., Kim, Y. and Dominick, J. (2004). Hackers: militants or merry pranksters? A content analysis of defaced web pages. *Media Psychology*, **6**, 63–82.

Working Group on Internet Governance (2005). *Report of the Working Group on Internet Governance*. Retrieved from www.wgig.org/docs/WGIGREPORT.doc,

Working to Halt Online Abuse (WHOA) (2012). Online harassment/cyberstalking statistics. Retrieved from www.haltabuse.org/resources/stats/index.shtml.

World Bank (1994). *Governance: the World Bank's Experience*, Washington, DC: World Bank.

World Summit on the Information Society (2010). Home. Retrieved from www.itu.int/wsis/index.html.

Wortley, R. and Smallbone, S. (2006). *Child Pornography on the Internet*. Retrieved from www.cops.usdoj.gov/files/ric/Publications/e04062000.pdf.

Wright, S. (2006). Government-run online discussion forums: moderation, censorship and the shadow of control. *British Journal of Politics and International Relations*, 8, 550–68.

Wrightsman, L. S. (2001). *Forensic Psychology*. Stamford, CT: Wadsworth.

Wykes, M. (2007). Constructing crime: stalking, celebrity, 'cyber' and media. In Y. Jewkes (ed.), *Crime Online*. Cullompton, UK: Willan Publishing (pp. 128–43).

Wykes, M. and Harcus, D. (2010). Cyber-terror: construction, criminalization and control. In Y. Jewkes and M. Yar (eds.), *Handbook of Internet Crime*. Cullompton, UK: Willan (pp. 214–29).

Yang, G. (2006). Activists beyond virtual borders: internet-mediated networks and informational politics in China. *Command Lines: the Emergence of Governance in Global Cyberspace, First Monday*. Retrieved from http://firstmonday.org/htbin/cgiwrap/bin/ojs/index.php/fm/article/view/1609/1524.

Yar, M. (2006). *Cybercrime and Society*. London: Sage.

(2007). Teenage kicks or virtual villainy? Internet piracy, moral entrepreneurship and the social construction of a crime problem. In Y. Jewkes (ed.), *Crime Online*. Cullompton, UK: Willan Publishing (pp. 95–108).

(2010). Public perceptions and public opinion about internet crime. In Y. Jewkes and M. Yar (eds.), *Handbook of Internet Crime*. Cullompton, UK: Willan (pp. 104–19).

Ybarra, M. L. and Mitchell, K. J. (2004). Online aggressor/targets, aggressors, and targets: a comparison of associated youth characteristics. *Journal of Child Psychology and Psychiatry and Allied Disciplines*, 45 (7), 1,308–16.

Yoon, C. (2012). Digital piracy intention: a comparison of theoretical models. *Behaviour and Information Technology*, 31, 565–76.

Young, R., Zhang, L. and Prybutok, V. R. (2007). Hacking into the minds of hackers. *Information Systems Management*, 24, 281–7.

Zentner, A. (2004). Measuring the effect of online music piracy on music sales. Retrieved from http://economics.uchicago.edu/download/musicindustryoct12.pdf.

Zona, M. A., Sharma, K. K. and Lane, J. (1993). A comparative study of erotomanic and obsessional subjects in a forensic sample. *Journal of Forensic Sciences*, 38, 894–903.

Zuckerman, M. (2002). Genetics of sensation seeking. In J. Benjamin, R. P. Ebstein and R. Belmaker (eds.), *Molecular Genetics and the Human Personality*. Washington, DC: American Psychiatric Publishing (pp. 193–210).

Zuckoff, M. (2006). The perfect mark: how a Massachusetts psychotherapist fell for a Nigerian e-mail scam. *The New Yorker*, 15 May, pp. 36–42.

INDEX

Printed in Great Britain
by Amazon

66612220R00160